AN INTELLECTUAL IN PUBLIC

An Intellectual in Public

Alan Wolfe

•

ANN ARBOR
The University of Michigan Press

2006   2005   2004   2003   4   3   2   1

A CIP catalog record for this book is available from the British Library.

Library of Congress Cataloging-in-Publication Data

Wolfe, Alan, 1942–
      An intellectual in public / Alan Wolfe.
         p.   cm.
      Includes bibliographical references.
      ISBN 0-472-09865-9 (Cloth : alk. paper)
      1. United States–Politics and government–1989-   2. United
States–Intellectual life.   3. United States–Social conditions–
1980-   4. Social problems–United States.   5. Political culture–
United States.   6. Right and left (Political science) I. Title.

   E885 .W645   2003
   305.5'52'0973–dc21   2003011963

The poem *The Old Dog Barks Backwards* copyright © 1972 by Ogden Nash, reprinted by permission of Curtis Brown, Ltd.

The essays originally appeared in the following publications.

Atlantic Monthly: "The Mystique of Betty Friedan," September 1999.

Books and Culture: "The Return of Evil," March/April 2003.

Chronicle of Higher Education: "Faith and Diversity in American Religion," February 28, 2002; "The Calling of the Public Intellectual," May 25, 2001.

Lingua Franca: "Higher Learning," March/April 1996.

New Republic: "Alien Nation," March 26, 2001; "Strangled by Roots," May 28, 2001; "Anti-American Studies," February 10, 2003; "The Hermeneutic Hole," January 31, 2000; "White Magic in America," February 23, 1998; "The Facts and the Feelings," September 29, 1997; "Margaret Mead Goes to Harlem," May 10, 1999; "The Jeremiah Racket," June 2, 1997; "Subject Matter Matters," December 11, 2000; "The Professor of Desire," November 24, 1997; "Up from Scientism," December 23, 1996; "Undialectical Materialism," October 23, 2000; "Buying Alone," March 17, 2003; "The Greening of Conservatism," June 12, 2000; "The Snake," October 1, 2001; "The Revolution That Never Was," June 1, 1999; "Idiot Time," July 8, 2002; "The Fame Game," January 7, 2002.

New Yorker: "Affirmative Action, Inc.," November 25, 1996.

New York Times Book Review: "Climbing the Mountain," January 18, 1998.

Poor Manfred, always in bad odor,
Muddled middle of the roader.
Veering Left towards visions bright,
Leftist jargon drives him Right
Until the Rightist hatchet men
Turn him to the Left again,
Searching for a category,
Spo-Radical and desul-Tory.

—Ogden Nash,
  The Old Dog Barks Backwards

Contents

Acknowledgments

MY ACKNOWLEDGMENTS ARE primarily to editors. My first and foremost—I hope the others forgive me—is to Leon Wieseltier, literary editor of the *New Republic*. Leon not only suggested many of the topics about which I have written, he also insisted, on more than one occasion, that I collect my essays in book form. This book literally would not have appeared without his encouragement.

I also want to express my debts to Karen Winkler and Ted Weidlein at the *Chronicle of Higher Education,* Alex Star, first at *Lingua Franca* and then at the *Boston Globe,* Barry Gewen and Caroline Rand Herron at the *New York Times Book Review,* Henry Finder at the *New Yorker,* and Jack Beaty, Cullen Murphy, and the late Michael Kelly at the *Atlantic Monthly.* They have all strengthened the sharpness of my writing. Tom DeNardo helped with the editing. Robert Calvert introduced me to the quote from Ogden Nash when introducing me to an audience at DePauw, and I thank him for it.

Phil Pochoda once edited a book I wrote when he was at Pantheon. Now the director of the University of Michigan Press, he has been extremely supportive of this effort. So have been the two political science editors with whom I have worked, Jeremy Shine and Jim Reische.

Introduction

I

T HERE HAVE ALWAYS BEEN public intellectuals, and there will
surely be more of them in the future, but in the years in which I
have been an intellectual in public–from the 1960s to the present–there
have not been many models to follow. During those years, the academic world engaged itself in forms of professionalism so strictly defined
that little room remained for those willing and able to reach large audiences with their views. Almost irrespective of field, academic departments rewarded those who published in scholarly journals, often in
ways guided either by recondite theories or advanced methodologies
accessible only to fellow specialists. At the same time, journalism
moved toward the immediate and sensational and away from the
reflective and considered. The result was a gap that few were anxious
to fill. Academics who viewed themselves as public intellectuals were
typically treated by their professional colleagues as dilettantes, while
journalists who took the longer view could easily find themselves out of
work in the here and now.

Naive to the point of oblivious, I never realized these things as I finished graduate school and began my academic career. I simply loved to
write, and so write I did, sending my stuff off to one publication or
another, not expecting much in the way of a breakthrough. (The first
article I ever submitted, in 1967, was to a now defunct magazine called
the *Reporter.* Its editor, Max Ascoli, rejected it, but with such encouraging words that I kept at it. Later I would become the Dean of the Graduate Faculty at the New School for Social Research, a position previ-

ously held by Max Ascoli.) Before long, editors did start to call me back; indeed, a few of them even began to call me before I called them. Perhaps they realized that if they were to fill the book review pages of their magazines–the pages that, if you are like me, you turn to before you begin to peruse the material dedicated to daily events–they had to find those academics who could write prose their readers could follow. So there I found myself, a bit too intellectual to appear in *Time* yet decidedly too generalist to write for the *American Political Science Review*. Fortunately, there were outlets like the *New Republic*, the *Atlantic Monthly*, the *Chronicle of Higher Education*, and others. I became a public intellectual without intending to do so; indeed, I did so without even knowing what a public intellectual was supposed to be.

While one would be foolish to predict an end anytime soon to the fascination academics have with theoretical jargon and methodological innovation, significant numbers of faculty now wonder if there is more to life than publication in peer-reviewed journals read only by peers, just as they are becoming increasingly convinced that the broad knowledge they need for teaching ought to be useful in what and how they publish. In the disciplines within which I work, political science and sociology, this unease with strictly professional writing is palpable; a revolt against rational choice theory, the dominant professional paradigm, took place in political science; sociologists are devoting their 2004 meeting to the question of the discipline's public responsibilities; and both fields have started new journals designed to be read by nonspecialists. At the same time, a small but important group of journalists is equally unhappy with the "gotcha" kind of sound bites that pass for political sophistication on cable news and wants to find ways of setting the daily controversies of politics into some larger understanding of America and why it functions as it does. This is, then, the appropriate time to offer some examples of what at least one intellectual does in public.

My examples inevitably, although not exclusively, involve review essays. Stimulated by books that address themselves to a common topic, the review essay seeks to explain and to offer criticism of those books but at the same time to raise questions about large and important topics. Those who write books–something I find myself doing when I am not reviewing them—generally do not like review essays, for they are likely to feel that their books are being used by the author of the essay for his or her own purposes. There is some justice to the charge, but books are written not only to be reviewed but to stimulate public conversation, a task for which the review essay can be the ideal vehicle.

Review essays by their very nature are topical, tied, as they are, to publishers' catalogs and the deadlines of magazine editors. There nonetheless exist good reasons to collect them into more permanent form. For one thing, little in the selection process that brings books into the public eye is all that random; in the late 1990s, for example, a rash of books appeared on the subject of race (see part III), while in the year or two after September 11, books dealing with the question of evil began to come out, even ones whose planning began long before that infamous date (see "The Return of Evil"). We sometimes think that books shape the zeitgeist, but it also true that the zeitgeist influences what gets published. The subjects with which *An Intellectual in Public* deals are ones that have preoccupied America in the last decade or so, and it is these subjects, and not just the books that addressed them, that continue to exercise a fascination over the American imagination.

I write review essays, moreover, because they are interesting and informative to write. With time as limited as it is, some people are so busy reading books that they never have time to write any, while for others the task of writing becomes so consuming that few hours are left for reading. As if by magic, writing review essays allows for both. It forces one to read, and to read carefully, all the while thinking about the writing that the reading is meant to inspire. I believe that the review essay format has allowed my writing to improve my reading and the other way around, an experience so gratifying that I hope, by publishing this book, to encourage others to take on the task.

II

BEING AN INTELLECTUAL IN public means discussing public things. The substantive essays of the volume begin in part I with reflections on the most public of the goods we value: membership in our society, or citizenship. The meaning of citizenship has become highly contested. On the right, apologists for capitalism talk about globalism as if nation-states, and the benefits they offer, have become obsolete, while many on the left are attracted to forms of identity politics that privilege the group over the nation. Can one believe in one's country without falling into blind loyalty? What does the nation mean in an era of globalization? I address these questions by examining what recent normative political theorists and historians have had to say on the subject, including a critical review of the way scholars of American studies have treated their subject matter.

Religion is both public, in the sense that faith helps shape the values that hold society together and give it a sense of purpose, and private, in the sense that it expresses an individual's personal relationship with the deity. The essays in part II deal with both aspects of faith, although they concentrate on its public manifestations. Here I address such issues as what social scientists and philosophers have taught us about evil, the relationship between fundamentalism and democracy, the influence of Mormon-inspired self-help manuals, and the relationship between religion and American higher education.

Race, too, has both a public side and a private one, involving on the one hand matters of etiquette and manners and on the other the diversity of such major public institutions as universities and the military. The essays included on this subject are devoted to racial realism, an effort to shift the dialogue about race in America away from what I call feelings in favor of an emphasis on facts (see "Higher Learning"). My position can be summarized in what I say about affirmative action in "Climbing the Mountain." It is a terrible idea in theory, I write, but a fairly effective one in practice. The more we focus on the facts rather than the feelings about race–the subject of another essay included in this book–the better off we will be.

Discussions about race, as the subject of affirmative action suggests, quickly turn into discussions about education, the subject of part IV. I am generally suspicious of books in which ideology takes command, as if the subject the book is discussing is of secondary importance to the preconceived framework the author brings to the subject; whenever I read a book that appears overly driven by ideology, I wonder why the writer bothered, since curiosity and surprise—one a pleasure that leads to writing, the other a joy to be experienced when the writing is done—are so often absent from the analysis. Education is, of all the subjects with which I am concerned, the one in which ideology has the least to offer—yet it is also one that seems to bring out the most ideological of writers. I discuss one such ideological combatant in this part but also show how another writer, although motivated by strong, if not passionate concerns, manages to transcend ideological labels.

The next sections of the book turn to matters more private in nature than public. Sex, the focus of part V, was also the main concern of one important twentieth-century thinker, Alfred Kinsey, and a major preoccupation of another, Betty Friedan. As influential as both of their major books were, they were also flawed. My discussion of these topics deals with the larger questions of individual responsibility touched on in the introduction: what happens when public figures whose ideas reach large audiences rely on distorted, or sometimes even false, information? To reinforce that point, I include with these essays another one that does not deal directly with sex—its subject is birth order—but which raises the question of how certain we can be about human behavior if we rely on seemingly scientific, but ultimately superficial, approaches to understanding it.

Consumption is another private act that has public consequences. Like the golden age of social criticism, the 1950s and 1960s, which featured attacks on the ways Americans buy and sell goods such as John Kenneth Galbraith's *The Affluent Society,* there has been an outpouring of recent scholarship on consumption. In part VI, I consider what we have learned since then and how we might find more appropriate ways to speak about the proper balance between the kind of personal happiness that consumption encourages and larger social responsibilities.

Despite my unease with heavily ideological writing, ideological polarization, as this book appears, is as strong as ever in the United States; we have a president firm in his conservative convictions, so firm, in fact, that in both domestic and foreign policy he seems to have sparked a revival of leftist opposition. Yet it remains the case that neither the right nor the left can speak for all of America. Ever hopeful that the state of elite opinion will someday catch up to the generally more consensual and moderate opinion of ordinary Americans, I discuss in part VII the utter irrelevance to contemporary America of a dense, jargon-laden volume called *Empire* as well as the light-to-the-point-of-parody best-seller written by Michael Moore. None of this makes me a conservative, however; I also include in this section of the book an essay seeking to demonstrate the extent to which conservatism, whatever its attraction to President Bush, has run out of serious ideas.

Interestingly enough, one of the things that public intellectuals write about these days is the status of public intellectuals. Books on the subject are starting to appear, and with those books has come a significant amount of commentary about whether the age of the public intellectual is over or whether, in this age of blogging and instant communication, it is beginning to enter a new era. *An Intellectual in Public* therefore concludes with two essays that engage the debate on public intellectuals, welcoming their continued presence in American life, even while warning of the seductions offered by fame on the one hand and the ever-present dangers of ideological conformity on the other.

PART I

Country

·

Alien Nation

I

O F ALL THE GOODS that people value, citizenship has been the most unfairly distributed. Moral philosophers propose various criteria for deciding who should obtain the best that life has to offer. The most just decisions, we are told, are those chosen behind a veil of ignorance, or taken when supply and demand are in equilibrium, or selected to reward the deserving. But citizenship routinely fails all such tests. It is usually conferred at birth, and under most circumstances it stays with you whether or not you lead a meritorious life. Except for the naturalized, and for them only the first generation, citizenship is due not to any decision you made, but to decisions made by your ancestors, up to and including your parents. If you are born in a society for which membership is in high demand, such as the United States, then you are unlikely to give up its associated benefits merely because a Rawlsian could prove to you that, were you to make a choice without knowing where you would end up, you would have opted for a fairer distributive scheme.

It is true that those who are not born American citizens are nonetheless born citizens of some other country. Yet this merely under-scores the arbitrariness involved, for not all citizenships are equal. In some cases, citizenship can be a burden, entailing excessive costs in taxation, loss of liberty, or adherence to stifling ethnic obligations. In the United States, citizenship is one of the world's greatest bargains, offering at relatively low cost the freedom to lead a life of one's own choice or the opportunity to keep the bulk of one's own fortune. Not only is the distribution of citizenship unjust, it is also irrational. No transaction that comes with such a cheap price should offer so many rewards. From an economic standpoint as well as a moral standpoint, there can be few more unattractive sights than apathetic Californians born on one side of the border turning their backs on hardworking Mexicans born on the other side.

Intergenerational differences multiply the inequities of citizenship. States grant citizenship, and states are formed through bloodshed: behind every citizen lies a graveyard. The dead of the Revolutionary War made the American state possible; the dead of the Civil War made the American state powerful. World War I was coterminous with women's suffrage. African Americans did not become full legal citizens until the aftermath of World War II. Thus are citizenship and violence inextricably linked. Once citizenship is created, however, subsequent generations treat it as a right, and usually as a rather casual one. Individuals who pay the highest price to make citizenship possible receive few of its benefits; and those for whom it has become banal receive the most. Having the luck to be born a century or two after your nation-state was created is among life's most precious, and most thoroughly arbitrary, advantages.

Modern nations have found only one way to eliminate some of the injustices of citizenship: immigration. It does not matter that immigration is sometimes motivated by fears of demographic decline, or a need for more workers, or a desire to increase the tax base to pay for future governmental benefits. When compared to arbitrary criteria based on blood–such as the one that gives people of German descent a greater claim to German citizenship, even if they live outside Germany, than people of Turkish descent who live inside Germany–the relatively open admissions policy that the United States has followed since 1965 is unusually fair. Legally, your chances of becoming an American citizen are by and large independent of the society from which you emigrated. When illegal immigration–which is repeatedly denounced and widely welcomed–is added to the picture, anyone who has the means and the desire has a decent shot at American citizenship, and an excellent chance of American citizenship for their children.

Immigration cannot eliminate all the unfairness of citizenship. Naturalized citizens pay a price not unlike the one paid by the generation that created citizenship through bloodshed. In Canada, the price can be explicitly monetary. In America, the price has usually been cultural: in return for relatively open borders, Americans have usually insisted on rapid and thorough assimilation. It is not just that one has to learn enough history to pass an exam—in itself not a bad idea, and one that ought to be applied to birthright citizens. It is that one inevitably leaves behind the culture of one's upbringing and loses control over the loyalties of one's own children.

Assimilation is a form of symbolic violence. Like the actual violence of war, assimilation is disruptive and heartless, the stuff of tragedy. Old ways of life are allowed to endure as sentimental memories, but as guides for conduct in the new world they are ruthlessly suppressed if they stand in the way of cultural integration. People with faint hearts who do not like hard choices ought not to consider immigration and assimilation.

Still, for all its associated pain and even violence, immigration underscores the value of citizenship, for the native-born and the immigrant alike. By risking life and limb to obtain this dispensation, immigrants remind the native-born why what they take for granted is priceless. And by granting citizenship to people from cultures radically different from their own, the native-born acknowledge that citizenship is too precious to be distributed solely on the basis of luck.

Conceptions of citizenship are changing as the more or less ethnically homogeneous welfare states of North America and Western Europe face ever higher levels of immigrants within their borders. And those borders have become increasingly tenuous as technologies of communication refuse to recognize their existence. Minority groups that once tried to live quietly now demand recognition, if not autonomy. Yet whatever the results of this period of ferment, the lesson is unlikely to be lost that citizenship is one of life's great gifts–unless, that is, one listens to a group of political theorists who, in defense of what they call multiculturalism, would redefine citizenship to the point where it would not be worth much of anything.

II

THESE POLITICAL THEORISTS BEGIN not with a question to be explored, but with a proposition to be defended. When it comes to citizenship, the basic proposition holds that states ought to respect the minority cultures within their borders. Depending on the theorist, different criteria of justice will be advanced, different minority groups will be considered, and different policies will be advocated. Still, in consonance with an academic discipline strongly influenced by the priorities of the 1960s, the presumption in nearly all of this literature is that an emphasis on patriotism, assimilation, and unity is unjust, and that a celebration of diversity is gloriously the opposite.

Will Kymlicka, a Canadian, is among the most prolific of these political theorists. Since Mill, if not earlier, liberals have worried that attempts to attach rights to groups–particularly ethnic, religious, or linguistic groups who stand for the particular against the universal– would restrict the rights of individuals to shape their lives as they choose. In his writings in recent years, Kymlicka has tried to show that such fears are misplaced. Liberals, he maintains, have long recognized that individuals are formed by their group attachments. Moreover, groups want recognition for the same reason that individuals want dignity. Cultural membership, Kymlicka wrote in 1989, "is important in pursuing our essential interests in leading a good life, and so consideration of that membership is an important part of having equal consideration for the interests of each member of the community."

In his book *Politics in the Vernacular: Nationalism, Multiculturalism, and Citizenship,* as in his previous work, Kymlicka distinguishes between the claims of indigenous people and the claims of immigrants, but he defends the appeals to diversity made by both. Indigenous people–Catalans, Quebecois, Puerto Ricans, Scots–constitute stateless nations. Since they lost out when the European state system came into existence, their desire to strengthen their national identity is at least as just as the desire of any existing state to strengthen its own. Kymlicka does not yet have a theory of how the claims of indigenous minorities ought to be judged, but he does believe that "the burden of proof surely rests on those who would deny national minorities the same powers of nation-building as those which the national majority take for granted."

Immigrants, having voluntarily chosen to move to a new society, have no such presupposition in favor of national identity. But, Kymlicka adds, this is not something they seek. He argues that nearly all the policies demanded by immigrants–from affirmative action to official recognition of religious holidays and customs to laws against hate crimes– "are intended precisely to make it easier for the members of immigrant groups to participate within the mainstream institutions of the existing society." Those who worry about balkanization–in an unfortunate choice of words, Kymlicka calls such distinguished worriers as Arthur Schlesinger Jr. and Robert Hughes "incomprehensibly paranoid"–are on the wrong track. It is the rejection of multiculturalist demands for justice that causes balkanization, not the acceptance of them.

By insisting upon a distinction between indigenous minorities and immigrant minorities, Kymlicka adds one more criterion of arbitrariness to the ways in which citizenship is distributed. National minorities have more extensive claims than immigrants, and their claims, in Kymlicka's scheme, supersede those of nonnational minorities. That is an odd conclusion. One could make a plausible case that immigrants, because they actively choose to become members of a new society, have a higher claim to justice than those who, born into a national minority, are more passive in their status. But such an argument would base justice on individuals and their actions, not on groups and their characteristics; and so Kymlicka will have none of it.

Kymlicka's distinction is founded on a desire for justice, but it accomplishes something altogether different. Consider the case of Quebec. It is not enough to let indigenous peoples keep their language among themselves, Kymlicka writes about the demands of the Quebecois for the official recognition of French, for "it is very difficult for languages to survive in modern industrialized societies unless they are used in public life." Since culture empowers individuals, the Quebecois can rightfully "use the same tools that the majority nation uses in its program of nation-building, i.e., standardized public education, official languages, including language requirements for citizenship and government employment." To meet the standard of what Kymlicka calls "ethnocultural justice," Quebec, an indigenous nation, must be allowed to fashion itself as a French society within the rest of Canada.

Since Quebec is a minority nation, it has the right, under Kymlicka's guidelines, to impose its way of life on those who live within its borders in a way that Canada, because it is a majority nation, cannot. To be sure, both are constrained by internal national minorities: Canada by the Quebecois, and the Quebecois by indigenous people. Yet each may pursue quite different policies with respect to immigrants. When Kymlicka writes of Canada in general, he speaks of the need for "services that are available in the immigrant's mother tongue" and asks that the host society provide "the same degree of respect and accommodation . . . that have been traditionally accorded to the majority group's identity." But those are not the kinds of provisions for which the Quebecois have shown much sympathy. The province follows a restrictive policy that gives priority to French-speaking immigrants. Those who do not speak French were once forbidden from advertising ethnic goods in the languages of the ethnic groups seeking to buy them, though now the use of ethnic languages is permitted so long as French is given pride of place. Anglophone Quebeckers can attend English-language schools, but immigrant Quebeckers, including those from the former colonies of the British empire, cannot attend them. If Kymlicka is correct to assert that only public languages can flourish, then non-French-speaking immigrants to Quebec are second-class citizens. Compared to Quebec, Pete Wilson and Ron Unz would have to be classified as soft on multiculturalism.

None of this ought to be surprising, for Quebec vehemently rejects the multiculturalist label. French culture, in the Quebecois view of these matters, is not one culture among many; it is one of the two founding cultures of Canada. For this reason, Quebec tries to assert its cultural hegemony over immigrants in much the same ways that English-speaking Canada once tried to assert its hegemony over Quebec. Assimilationists, who believe that justice is best served by making immigrants full members of their new societies as rapidly as possible, ought to appreciate Quebec's policies; but it is odd that Kymlicka, the defender of minority cultures, appreciates them as much as he does.

Kymlicka, a self-described liberal, proclaims that "illiberal policies may be required if national minorities are to successfully integrate immigrants." What he says may well be true, but he ought to emphasize, as he does not, the injustices that follow from his prescriptions. If you are a Muslim and can find your way to Toronto or Detroit, your chances of maintaining crucial aspects of your culture—which is essential to your rights, in Kymlicka's opinion—are stronger than if you happen to find your way to Montreal.

No wonder that Kymlicka has been criticized by other political theorists for stressing the differences between national minorities and immigrants. Joseph H. Carens, a Canadian who migrated from the United States in 1985, is such a critic. Kymlicka, he writes in *Culture, Citizenship, and Community: A Contextual Exploration of Justice as Evenhandedness,* "has fatally undermined the principled case for policies designed to take the cultural concerns of immigrants (and their descendants) into account." The problem, in Carens's view, is that Kymlicka remains too much of a liberal. His argument that immigrants have chosen to come to a new country, and in that way waived some of their cultural rights, smacks of social contract theory. His insistence that the culture of dominant nations and the culture of indigenous nations are equal owes too much to liberal notions of neutrality between competing conceptions of the good life. Just as liberals in the nineteenth century were often hostile to the claims of particular groups, Kymlicka's lingering liberalism, according to Carens, blinds him to the needs of immigrants to maintain their own culture in the host society.

If both immigrant minorities and indigenous minorities have the right to have their culture respected, Carens ought to be critical of the strong assimilationist policies of the Quebecois. But it seems to be characteristic of this type of political theory always to take the side of the underdogs, and from the perspective of an English-speaking Canadian the underdogs are by definition the Quebecois. And so Carens simply joins Kymlicka in double standards by shifting the discussion away from any discussion of principles of justice and toward an argument rooted in the empirical realities of the day. "What is surprising," he writes, "is how little adaptation Quebec expects of immigrants," for although Quebec does insist that they speak French, it is pluralistic with respect to all other aspects of culture. (Even if Carens is right about culture, Quebec's approach to language renders its immigration policy both more restrictive and less universal than that of the United States, a society usually held up in Canada as the very model of injustice.) And, Carens continues, bilingualism may seem in theory to be just, but if it were permitted in Quebec it "would lead to the erosion and eventual demise of French." Justice, it would seem, all depends on context: "A language policy that might be unjust in one set of circumstances might be morally permissible in another and even morally required in a third."

In *The Republic,* Thrasymachus tells Socrates that justice is little more than the interests of the stronger. Multiculturalists reverse the formula: justice is whatever works to the advantage of the weaker. The idea here seems to be that the consistent application of principle, when applied to groups unequal in their command over resources, will be unfair to "the potential claims of people who are vulnerable and powerless," as Carens puts it. Critics of multiculturalism dispute the argument; it is precisely those who are most powerless, they claim, who most benefit from policies that are applied universally. As Carens wrestles unsuccessfully with the situation of Quebec, an even more damning indictment of the idea of abandoning principle in favor of powerlessness appears: powerlessness is itself a relative category. The person from Quebec who is more vulnerable than a person from Toronto in predominantly English-speaking North America is more powerful than an English-speaking immigrant from Uganda in Montreal. Taking context into account, as Carens would have us do, would mean changing our standards of justice as frequently as we change our conversation partners. Kymlicka applies different standards of justice to different cultures, depending on whether they are majorities or minorities. Carens wants to make justice central to his concerns, but he urges that its stringency should vary according to circumstance. Bhikhu Parekh, a member of the House of Lords and the inspiration behind a widely discussed report on the future of multiethnic Britain, wants to move beyond justice altogether. Nearly all societies in Western Europe and North America are now multicultural, Parekh points out. These societies should pursue policies that enable minority cultures to flourish. For this, considerations of justice are necessary but not sufficient. Justice, Parekh writes in *Rethinking Multiculturalism: Cultural Diversity and Political Theory,* "is a cold and impersonal virtue. It prevents accumulation of resentment, frustration, and anger and generates a basic sense of satisfaction with the political community, but does not by itself foster an enthusiastic commitment to and sense of moral and emotional identification with it."

As we move beyond justice, we will also, in Parekh's view, have to move beyond citizenship. Citizenship is about "status and rights." But there is also something called belonging, which "is about being accepted and feeling welcome." Nearly all minorities, even those who become citizens in a legal sense, do not feel that they truly belong to a society such as Great Britain. True, "this feeling of being full citizens and yet outsiders is difficult to analyze and explain," but there are steps the majority can take in response: "Official and unofficial spokesmen of the wider society should publicly welcome the presence and contribution of different cultures, patronize their social and other events, and so forth, and help up their self-confidence."

Parekh does not believe that states such as Great Britain are obligated to accept all the cultural practices of immigrants. He would ban suttee, the Hindu custom in which a widow joins her dead husband on his funeral pyre, and he believes that female circumcision and polygamy are flawed. When prohibiting immigrant practices, however, the state should proceed cautiously. Restrictions on female circumcision "should be enforced with compassion and sensitivity," and the best way to limit polygamous attitudes is "by attacking the structure of patriarchal authority that generates and nurtures them." Moreover, such bans should only extend to the most extreme customs. Liberals may object to arranged marriages, but Parekh would permit them. "In the Asian view individuals are just an integral part of their family," he declares, "and their lives belong not just to them but also to their families. It therefore makes sense for parents to have a say in who their sons and daughters marry and how they lead their lives."

How would Parekh treat the efforts by Quebec to restrict the freedom of non-French-speaking immigrants to live as they please? Despite numerous discussions in his book about why Quebec requires autonomy from the rest of Canada, Parekh never once deals with the question of autonomy from Quebec. But he gives a hint. When cultures conflict, "dialogue between them is mutually beneficial . . . The dialogue is possible only if each culture accepts others as equal conversation partners." Differences that once led to war can now be solved through sensitivity training. (Parekh does not identify the language in which the momentous dialogue will take place; my guess is that, whatever the rule, it will turn out to be English, making the notion of equality in conversation impossible from the start.)

It ought to be clear that Parekh's passionate defense of minority cultures is accompanied by a passionless treatment of culture. Although he grounds his multiculturalism in the ideas of nineteenth-century romantics such as Herder, the emotional side of romanticism is foreign to Parekh's sensibility. Thus he is tone-deaf when it comes to explaining the conflict between Salman Rushdie and Islamic fundamentalists over *The Satanic Verses*. Muslims, he argues, were right to protest the novel, up to and including burning it, but it was "unjustified and unwise" for them to threaten violence. And Rushdie made the mistake of writing his novel in the wrong way. He showed "poor literary judgment" in those passages that Muslims found offensive, and "could easily have handled them in a manner that did not bear such a close historical resemblance to historical Islam."

There is something dangerous afoot when a writer of books seeks to justify book-burning: but once you deny people the right to choose their own marriage partners, restricting what they read is not all that surprising. An even greater danger, though, is letting culture loose in the hopes of controlling its effects. Both Rushdie and his Muslim opponents know, as Parekh evidently does not know, that culture kills.

A multicultural society must have many cultures. Although he fails to appreciate the zeal that culture can inspire, Parekh is nonetheless frightened by the thought of cultural dilution. At one point, he writes that immigrants should have the right to assimilate, if they so choose— but he doubts that they will so choose, for "total assimilation . . . requires biological assimilation, and many outsiders are unwilling to pay that price."

In at least one important way—it is probably the most important way—Parekh would prevent immigrants from paying that price. Depending on the ethnic group and the host society, the most common route out of ethnicity has been intermarriage. Parekh, whose concept of culture is as static as it is bloodless, fails to discuss it. Yet his defense of arranged marriage can be read as an indirect assault on intermarriage. After all, one of the reasons that parents insist on arranged marriages is precisely to prevent their children from marrying anyone outside the group.

Once a multicultural society comes into existence, it would be a multicultural society forever. Ever averse to conflict, Parekh believes that "the dialogically constituted multicultural society both retains the truth of liberalism and goes beyond it. It is committed to both liberalism and multiculturalism, privileges neither, and moderates the logic of one by the other." In his more candid moments, however, Parekh could hardly be more dismissive in his views about the individual rights that liberalism guarantees. "Free speech," he writes in a typical formulation, "is not the only great value, and needs to be balanced against such others as avoidance of needless hurt, social harmony, humane culture, protection of the weak, truthfulness in the public realm, and self-respect and dignity of individuals and groups."

Haunting the dreams of multiculturalists is the specter of nativism. As these political theorists understand the world, minorities are inevitably oppressed, and the oppressors are just as inevitably people of European descent who fear, and hence try to control (if not to eliminate), the cultures of people whom they do not understand. In the face of the extensive immigration that they have experienced in the past few decades, nativists in societies such as the United States and Great Britain would really prefer, or so the theorists seem to think, to send immigrants back to their homelands. But so, too, do multiculturalists such as Parekh—not literally, but symbolically. Instead of saying that immigrants would have been better off had they never left their countries of origin, Parekh would have them bring their countries of origin with them. In either case, immigrants would not have to deal with the complexities of living in a liberal democratic society, and residents of a liberal democratic society would not gain from immigrants the sense that the way they have always done things may not be the best way to do them.

By sealing off immigrants, even after they become citizens, in miniature replicas of the societies that they left, Parekh raises the question of why have immigration at all. Without the capacity to speak freely, to develop their capacities as individuals, and to plan their lives, immigrants might as well stay home (though if they did, they would most likely be poorer). And without exposure to, and integration with, the world's many cultures, natives might as well just close their borders. By moving beyond justice, Parekh leaves the situation in some ways worse than it was when citizenship was determined by place of birth. Your roots are your fate, and nothing you do, not even uprooting yourself, can change your destiny.

III

BRIAN BARRY HAS WRITTEN *Culture and Equality: An Egalitarian Critique of Multiculturalism* to destroy the ideas of Will Kymlicka, Joseph

Carens, Bhikhu Parekh, and some twenty or thirty other political philosophers, a large proportion of them from Canada, who think like they do. A liberal in the mode of Mill, Barry believes that it is the flourishing of individuals, and not the survival of their culture, that makes citizenship worth having. In the take-no-prisoners style of argumentation associated with Oxford philosophy, Barry argues that multiculturalism contributes nothing to the creation of a just society. Indeed, when multiculturalists do discover an injustice in the contemporary world, liberalism is by far the best philosophy for identifying and rectifying it.

Barry's most persuasive point is that multiculturalists start from a fantasy. Liberal citizenship, in their view, grew out of homogeneous societies that shared one vision of the good life–the liberal vision, with its emphasis on secular reason–and it is therefore irrelevant, if not harmful, to a multicultural world in which no one way of life ought to be privileged over any other. Quite the contrary, Barry reminds his readers. Liberalism emerged out of deeply divisive conflicts over the right way to live. It was precisely when European societies came to recognize that religious wars, if allowed to go on forever, would destroy everything worth saving that they imagined the notion of a state capable of appealing to all sides. And the liberal state did this, moreover, not by being neutral, but by being fair. Of course the liberal state takes sides, Barry contends. It takes sides in the sense that its very rationale assigns a higher priority to fairness than to unfairness. In pursuit of fairness, the impact of liberal procedures falls differently on different groups: insisting that religion be relegated to the private sphere, for example, discriminates against those who prefer to live in a society in which religion is present in the public sphere. All laws favor some and disfavor others. Laws against speeding "discriminate" against speeders and "privilege" those who obey the speed limit. Merely showing that a law burdens some more than others cannot, in itself, be taken as an indication that oppression exists.

When people from widely different cultural communities live together within the same borders, many laws passed without any attempt to discriminate will be viewed by some as burdensome. Every political theorist who has ever lived or worked in Great Britain seems to have been exercised by a law requiring hard hats for construction workers (or helmets for motorcyclists). Sikhs wear turbans. Should they be prohibited from doing so if they work in construction, as an astonishingly large number of Sikhs in Britain actually do, or if they drive mopeds? Barry's ruling is this: either a regulation is sensible, in which case it should be applied to all, or it is not sensible, in which case it should apply to none. Both approaches treat everyone equally. Problems arise only when we adopt a "rule and exception approach," one that seeks to retain a general regulation but to allow exceptions to avoid religious or racial discrimination.

Barry would not rule out all efforts at a "rule and exception" approach, but he would set the standard very high before adopting one. If Sikhs can prove that the need for hard hats is exaggerated, then the regulation should be suspended for all. If they claim that keeping the law discriminates against them because of their beliefs, then Barry questions whether their beliefs are quite as inflexible as they are often made out to be. Cultures change, after all, and within any religion or culture some are always more strict in their observance than others. And if Sikhs nonetheless prove that their beliefs are a requirement of their religion, then one can still question whether they need to ride motorcycles. The point is to narrow down the exceptions to as few as possible. When all is said and done, Barry would allow Sikhs already employed in construction the right to wear their turbans, since their livelihood is so clearly tied to that way of life, but not any newly arriving ones seeking jobs in the construction trade.

The case of the Sikhs illustrates how Barry treats citizenship in general. As early as the eighteenth century, liberal society abolished estates and castes in favor of a single status, the status of citizen; and Barry sees no particular reason to abandon the practice. Would this result in the denigration of group rights, as Kymlicka, Parekh, and others charge? It would, Barry replies, if groups were capable of having rights; but groups are not in this way capable. There is something called freedom of association–that people should have the right to join groups (and the right to leave them); and this gives groups a certain autonomy from rules that would curtail their membership. Yet so-called group rights are nothing more or less than individual rights: if an exception were allowed for Sikhs to wear their turbans on the job, it would still be individuals who benefited, not the group to which they belong. And applying the concept of group rights to cultural groups–by claiming, for example, that all cultures are deserving of respect–is illogical and dangerous. If there are no universal standards by which cultures can be judged, how can we judge them all to be deserving? And any insistence on the equal recognition of cultures forces upon a population that insists on making distinctions between them the views of undemocratic elites.

Barry's militantly liberal book is a refreshing alternative to the endless and repetitive books written by political theorists like Kymlicka, Carens, and Parekh, even if the reader (indeed, even if Barry) has to wonder sometimes whether ideas so ill-conceived really deserve such attention. But for all the clear air that Barry leaves behind, his treatment of what citizenship demands is thin and unsatisfactory. Citizenship, after all, is not an individual right in the way that free speech is an individual right. To be a citizen, you must be a member of a collectivity, usually a nation, that has sufficient authority to restrict some of your rights in the interest of strengthening others.

Liberals such as Barry are right to insist that citizenship implies one standard applicable equally to all within a state. But what do we do with the fact of different states? When states exist in various degrees of freedom and coercion, there will be no universal standards of citizenship that transcend all states, as there may be certain basic human rights. And if one responds by saying that in such a case all states should be held to the same standard, then there will be no distinctive states and therefore no specific citizenships worth anything to those who hold them.

Universalistic strains of liberalism find themselves uncomfortable with national citizenship precisely because it exists only when distinctions exist. Barry's commitment to universalistic thinking is so strong that he would seek justice not only for all human beings, but also for other animal species ("I can see no answer to the moral case for vegetarianism," he remarks). The result, however admirable from a moral point of view, is a bloodless conception of nationhood strikingly similar to Parekh's bloodless conception of culture.

Never do we get from Barry a sense of why the nation that guarantees citizenship may be worth dying for. Never does Barry evince any appreciation of the symbols of nationhood, and of the fact that to believe in those symbols sometimes means leaving analytical rationality behind in favor of sentimental attachment. In the preface of his book, at the point where an author often locates himself by place, Barry locates himself at "London-Merano-New York," as if to inform the reader that he is a man of the world and thus a citizen of no particular country. And Barry's prose really is placeless. Writing from way on high, he never seems to touch the ground of actually existing societies. And when he does discuss the ideas of those thinkers, such as Michael Walzer, who would develop standards of justice rooted in the traditions of real societies, he loses all patience. "Liberals," he writes, "are universalists . . . because everybody in the world is equally entitled to the protections afforded by liberal institutions, whether they actually enjoy them currently or not." To this categorical outburst one can only pose two questions: whose blood and sweat created those institutions? And do they not have a greater claim on them because of what they sacrificed to achieve them?

If leftists and liberals have difficulty understanding why a robust conception of citizenship requires a robust conception of the nation, can conservatives do better? Walter Berns does better, up to a point. His book *Making Patriots* is not written, he says, for academic specialists, but at least Berns understands, as so many political theorists do not, how demanding citizenship can be. "No one is born loving his country," he writes wisely; "such love is not natural, but has to be taught or acquired." It follows that "citizenship . . . cannot be taken for granted;

like patriotism, it has to be cultivated." (So, by the way, does culture, as the word implies. This, too, the multiculturalists fail to grasp.)

The process of making citizens is a process of toil, and it must overcome many obstacles. In America, those obstacles have come neither from immigrants nor from external enemies, but from America's own practices and values. As Berns puts the point: "In theory, this nation began with self-interested men, by nature private men, men naturally endowed not with duties or obligations but with certain unalienable rights . . . that each defines for himself, and, again in theory, government is instituted only 'to secure these rights.' So . . . why should self-interested men believe it in their interest to give up their lives for the idea or promise of their country?"

Unfortunately Berns does not offer much of an answer to the important question that he asks. An admirer of commerce, he sees little conflict between the needs of business and the demands of the state. He reminds us of Montesquieu's point that commerce softens morals, thereby permitting private self-interest to serve the public good. He appreciates Hamilton as the founder who most understood America's future as an industrial republic rather than an agrarian one. But neither Berns nor any other American patriot has figured out how to reconcile the love of freedom that is celebrated by American capitalism with the distaste for obligations that follows inexorably in the wake of laissez-faire. This is an especially glaring omission in a book that appears at the beginning of this hypercapitalist century. The challenge to national citizenship posed by multiculturalism pales before the creation of truly global corporations that put their faith in the bottom line before their love of country.

But it is not just self-interest that stands in the way of effective citizenship. If Christians are commanded to love their God before their country, then they do not always make the most reliable of citizens. Berns notes that the creators of American citizenship did not respond to the power of the church by confiscating its property and killing its priests, as did the revolutionaries in France–but neither did they establish an official religion to guide the affairs of state. Instead they built a secular state, a state that would be guided in its morality by religious belief but would separate the religious realm from the secular realm, and even ensure the domination of the former over the latter.

Berns makes the interesting point that at the time of the founding, most ordinary Americans did not understand, and would not have supported, the kind of state being created in their name. Madison and Jefferson held opinions on faith that were more "advanced" than those of, say, John Witherspoon, Madison's teacher at Princeton, who, as Berns puts it, "saw no conflict . . . between the principles set down in the Declaration of Independence and what he understood as orthodox Christianity." All of which suggests that citizenship, which sits uncomfortably with universalistic liberalism, also cannot easily be reconciled with populistic forms of democracy. Without leaders capable of looking beyond yesterday's majority opinion, Americans today might not have been so willing to offer citizenship to Catholics and Jews.

The greatest challenge to citizenship in America came, of course, from the slaveholding South. By insisting on clauses protecting slavery in the Constitution, the Southern states made it possible for Frederick Douglass to ask, in 1847, "What country have I?" His question was not answered until 1868, when, in adopting the Fourteenth Amendment, the United States finally established the principle of national citizenship. But it did not establish the reality of that principle until 1965, when the Voting Rights Act destroyed the last attempts by entrenched local interests to use the official machinery of government to deny citizens their rightful access to government. Berns is insufficiently appreciative of the obstacles to citizenship for black Americans put in place during Reconstruction. And while it is a terrible exaggeration to claim that the Florida vote in 2000 was a replay of Selma, the raw fact is that large numbers of Americans do not always get their votes counted and consider themselves less than full citizens as a result.

IV

WE USUALLY THINK OF rights as pre-political–found in nature or given by God. But citizenship is inherently political. When it exists, it has been created through the conscious actions of people. Natural rights, because they are inherent in us as human beings, are claims against the state. Citizenship rights, by contrast, have to be claimed in conjunction with the state. For realists such as James Madison, it was insufficient to rely on notions of republican virtue to ensure respect for the common good. Men who were not angels could become good citizens only with the help of institutions: the militia, the family, the schools, the churches, and (most importantly, at least as measured by the care that went into the writing of *The Federalist Papers*) a well-designed state.

One reason that citizenship is so problematic for contemporary political theorists is that almost nobody seems to like the state. Indeed, multiculturalists hate it. The state, writes Bhikhu Parekh, "is a deeply homogenizing institution" that "expects all its citizens to subscribe to an identical way of defining themselves and relating to each other and the state," and so we will have to discover "new modes of constituting the modern state and even perhaps altogether new types of political foundation."

Writers opposed to multiculturalism have a stronger sense of what citizenship requires; but they, too, are reluctant to get too cozy with the state. Liberals such as Brian Barry look beyond the nation-state to humanity as a whole. The resulting cosmopolitanism is as naive as it is hostile to the quite sensible idea of the love of one's country. And the only answer that Walter Berns provides to the dilemma of how a self-interested people can love their country is to cite a speech by Abraham Lincoln in 1864 urging Ohio troops to fight for the struggle to create free government—as if it takes a civil war, and not the ordinary actions of government, to make patriots. The age of nationalism is not far behind us, so it does not require too much imagination to recall the horrors carried out in the name of the nation-state. Citizenship, as we know from those horrors, cannot be an end in itself; it must serve substantive goals, and those goals, in turn, must respect fundamental human rights. For this reason, multiculturalists and liberals are right to put justice front and center in any discussion of citizenship, no matter how much their views of what justice requires differ. Yet to the degree that we seek justice through citizenship–and, in the absence of world government, there is no other way to seek it–we can do so only by accepting the legitimacy of the liberal state, upholding liberal principles when the state acts illiberally, and insisting on common political objectives when individuals or groups withdraw into self-interest or self-love.

Strangled by Roots

I

THROUGHOUT THE TWENTIETH CENTURY, Gary Gerstle observes in *American Crucible: Race and Nation in the Twentieth Century,* the United States has been influenced by "two powerful and contradictory ideals." The first ideal is civic nationalism: appalled by the preference for regionalism and limited government, it aimed to create a nation-state capable of ensuring equal treatment for all. The second ideal is racialized nationalism: in treating the country as reserved primarily for white men, it looked with disdain on minorities and women, insisted on the thorough assimilation of immigrants, and persecuted radicals who held dissenting views about the goals of the American state. Gerstle seeks to understand how we have wrestled with the profound tensions between these two ideals, and in the process he raises the important question of whether "a new American civic nation, strong but tolerant, is within reach."

During the New Deal, Roosevelt was accused of being a traitor to his class; but the real Rooseveltian traitor, as Gerstle tells the story, was not Franklin but Theodore. Unlike members of other patrician families in America, such as the one in possession of the presidency before and after Bill Clinton, Teddy Roosevelt saw no particular virtues in hereditary advantage. Quite the contrary. In his view, the Brahmin aristocracy was too refined, too preoccupied with social graces, to lead a dynamic society. Seeking volunteers for his charge up San Juan Hill, Roosevelt included Jews, Catholics, and Native Americans among his troops. Ignoring bureaucratic command structures and formal rules, he created "a frontier-type environment, where social distinctions and rank counted for little." War required men of courage, not men of connections.

When he became president, Roosevelt brought a meritocratic sensibility also to his domestic programs. He attacked the trusts for the same reason that he turned his back on aristocrats: too much of their wealth came from rigging the rules, and not from playing fairly by them. Unlike other Republicans (then or now), Roosevelt "acknowledged that grinding poverty was preventing workers, even those with full political and civil rights, from achieving economic security or the leisure necessary to cultivate civic virtue." Compared with others of his class, he appreciated the contributions of immigrants. "Jews, Injuns, Chinamen, Italians, Huns–the rubbish of the earth I hate–I've got some Winchesters and when the massacring begins, I can get my share of 'em, and what's more I will," Frederic Remington fulminated in a letter to Owen Wister. But Roosevelt, writes Gerstle, "understood how large a proportion of the working class comprised immigrants and their children. His New Nationalist program was meant to bring them into the nation, not just politically and culturally, but economically as well."

For all his bombast and his political miscalculations, Roosevelt welcomed the new society that was coming into being in the United States. But Gerstle does not wish to judge Roosevelt only in the context of his time. He wants also to invoke the standards of our time, and here he finds much wanting. Despite the fact that Roosevelt's ideas could be used to pursue ideas of equality between the sexes, Gerstle notes the "the deeply gendered nature of his nationalist thought." Appreciative of immigrants Roosevelt may have been, but he wanted them to Americanize, and therefore he feared radicals and anarchists. And Roosevelt's inclusiveness, which crossed the boundary of ethnicity, stopped at the boundary of race.

There were no African Americans among the Rough Riders, but there were four regular regiments involved in the taking of San Juan Hill that were black. Despite their valor in battle, Roosevelt never welcomed the racial mixing that took place during the Spanish-American

War in 1898. He also did little to win black support for his domestic agenda, going so far as to side with Southern whites at the expense of blacks at the Progressive party convention in 1912. Roosevelt, Gerstle concludes, stood for principles that "welcomed all law-abiding residents into the polity and disavowed distinctions based on race"–but at the same time he imagined "America as a land meant for Europeans in which blacks had either a subordinate place or no place at all." Ethnically inclusive but racially exclusive, Roosevelt's views represent, for Gerstle, "the true American dilemma" of "a nation divided against itself."

Those who followed Roosevelt were not so torn. He may have believed that civic ideals were forged in wartime, but World War I, in Gerstle's view, tilted the balance between America's two traditions in favor of the racial one. In the aftermath of the war, America's political leaders undertook what Gerstle calls "a disciplinary project breathtaking in its scope." The Palmer raids shut off dissent and enforced political conformity. A series of laws passed by Congress halted the flow of immigration. So pervasive did racism become that even liberals such as Fiorello LaGuardia and Representative Samuel Dickstein began to bait Asians and Mexicans in order to protect Jews and Italians.

Thus it came to pass that when civic ideals once again became dominant in the 1930s, during the presidency of Franklin Roosevelt, they were inevitably tainted by the racism of the 1920s. FDR, Gerstle writes, was under little pressure to adopt anti-immigrant views "because the disciplinary project had accomplished its aims, reducing the number of immigrants and increasing the pressures on those already here to Americanize." And however radical some of his legislative proposals, Roosevelt was something of a monarchist, capable of using language that made a place for Southern whites and Republican businessmen as well as union workers and displaced farmers. The Great Depression created a domestic situation not unlike the home front during wartime, which Roosevelt was quick to exploit. When real war finally came, everyone from communist to capitalist became a patriot, uniting together to defeat the enemy.

Franklin Roosevelt, unlike Theodore Roosevelt, avoided attributing individual abilities to group characteristics, but he was nevertheless incapable of containing the appeals of racist nationalism. Anxious to keep the white South in the Democratic fold, Roosevelt put civil rights for African Americans on the back burner. America may have fought World War II against fascism, but it relied on racist messages itself in its campaigns against Japan, and it tolerated racial segregation within its own armed forces.

Despite the cold war and McCarthyism, Gerstle believes that the Rooseveltian nation survived the 1950s. McCarthy himself bore unmistakable Teddy Rooseveltian traits, such as his "exaggerated and unruly masculinity" and his conviction that the WASP elite was effete. The signature legislation of the decade included the McCarran-Walter Act of 1952, passed over Harry Truman's veto, which made it easier for Asian immigrants to become citizens but also tightened controls on radicals. Between them, Gerstle believes, anticommunism and nativism constituted a warning "that minorities had better behave, that they should do everything possible to play by America's rules." And, generally speaking, minorities did behave. Jews made no conspicuous efforts to save Ethel and Julius Rosenberg, so palpable was their desire for acceptance into the American mainstream. By the end of the Eisenhower presidency, the tensions between America's two nationalist traditions were widening—"precursors," Gerstle writes, "of political and social upheaval."

Civic nationalism, in Gerstle's account, proved powerful enough to survive anticommunist crusades, in part because anticommunism was a part of its crusade; but it fell before the twin challenges of black nationalism and the Vietnam War. To be sure, Martin Luther King Jr. appealed to the tradition of civic nationalism, but with his death the momentum for racial equality passed into the hands of such nationalist groups as SNCC, CORE, the Black Panthers, and the Nation of Islam. These were not majority movements, as Gerstle concedes. (Indeed, he suggests that they may never have amounted to more than 50,000 people.) Still, they were "an articulate vanguard," and their influence was "immense." Not only did their "utter fearlessness" appeal to young blacks, but their way of protest was attractive also to other minorities and to some whites. Jews such as Meir Kahane, socially active Catholic priests, even the neoconservative Michael Novak found in black nationalism "a new imaginative landscape on which to build their own individual and group identities."

The Vietnam War furthered the collapse of the American state. Student protests disrupted campus after campus, forcing university administrators to call in the police. Soldiers themselves refused to fight. Veterans were anything but grateful for their experience. Blacks and whites fought together, and in so doing they seemed to strengthen civic nationalism, but at the same time racial integration destroyed "for all time Theodore Roosevelt's dream of war as the crucible for forging a superior white race." With the inability of the American military to impose its will on the world, Gerstle concludes, America had come full circle from the Spanish-American War. "The bonds of nationhood had weakened, and the Rooseveltian program of nation building that had created those bonds in the first place had been repudiated. A nationalist era that had begun in the early decades of the twentieth century had come to a stunning end."

II

IN THE CORRIDORS OF American academia, Gary Gerstle would have to be classified as a moderate. This is the age, after all, of "whiteness studies," according to which some groups that we usually regard as white—say, the Italians and the Irish—may be regarded historically as if they were black, because they once occupied the bottom of the social scale. In such an analysis, "whiteness" is not a biological characteristic, it is a socially constructed category that serves the powerful as an instrument for maintaining their power, and also as a way for whites to maintain their distance from nonwhites. In contrast to such scholars of whiteness, Gerstle writes that he does not see "race at the root of every expression of American nationalism"; and this is just one example of his distance from contemporary academic conventions. He is critical of the two Roosevelts, but he acknowledges the power of their appeals to civic ideals. He even calls the founding of the Progressive party "a crucial moment in the development of American liberalism" that would "help America become the greatest nation on the earth." These are not politically correct expressions. Moreover, Gerstle writes for the general reader, which is a rather controversial thing to do among academics at research universities. And he defies the postmodern protest against coherent narrative and reverts to the idea that history can be told through an all-encompassing story: his book is that rare academic thing, a text with a beginning and an end, and even a message sandwiched in between.

And yet these attractive features of *American Crucible* serve mainly as a melancholy reminder of how far leftward the scholarly study of American history has shifted. For Gerstle is finally no stranger to the assumptions of the academic left about the nature of the American experience. In his book they are merely more implicit than explicit. Indeed, they are the unexamined premises that permeate everything Gerstle writes, so that by the time he is done any difference between him and scholars of "whiteness"—or, for that matter, of "blackness"—is impossible to discern. His analysis, too, is finally a racialist analysis.

Gerstle's language is riddled with the terminologies of the moment. Thus Theodore Roosevelt's nationalism was not merely "gendered"; he also celebrated "hybridity," even while trying to "reinscribe" African American "subordination." There would be no problem with such language if something in the way of understanding were gained. But much is lost. To ungender himself, should Roosevelt have included women in his Cuban campaigns? The notion crosses Gerstle's mind, but we can be fairly sure that it never crossed Roosevelt's. Gender did not exist when Roosevelt lived, though sex did. Surely historians should be alive to the perils of anachronism.

By invoking the terms of today's fashions to account for yesterday's realities, Gerstle transforms ad hoc attitudes and improvised historical actions into hard, programmatic categories, and then he imposes those categories on people whom they never fit. In connection with J. Edgar Hoover, for example, he invokes the Foucauldian notion of a "disciplinary project." Hoover was a bureaucrat in search of more turf, and he found it by transforming the FBI into an agency that hunted criminals and communists. But to depict Hoover as a figure out of Foucault gives him more credit (and, in an odd way, less credit) than he deserves.

Then there is Gerstle's myopia. The Black Panthers receive considerable discussion in his book, while Christian conservatives receive close to none. Yet surely any account of the decline of the Rooseveltian nation ought to include those who put Christ before country, let alone gun-toting libertarians, neo-Confederates, and dyed-in-the-wool isolationists. Throughout *American Crucible,* but especially toward the end of the book, historical figures associated with the left assume a magnitude that is absurdly larger than life. The rantings of Molefi Kete Asante of Temple University are described as "seminal," an obscure radical priest named Geno Baroni enjoys two different treatments, and the literary scholar Janice Radway (see "Anti-American Studies," this vol.) is treated as an authority on American ethnicity. This, too, could be excused if Gerstle were writing a history of the American left's relationship to civic nationalism and racial nationalism. But while it sometimes appears that Gerstle is more interested in the left than in America, he is aware that Ronald Reagan did more to shape the country's destiny than Radway, which is why the paragraph after the paragraph about her finally turns to the subject of American conservatism, which is largely ignored throughout the book.

Like so many leftist professors, Gerstle is obsessed with race. I do not mean that he makes the failure of America to treat African Americans as full citizens central to his story. The American record on race is hardly one that inspires pride in the nation. Like Gerstle, I do not believe that the ideal of a civic nation has yet been achieved in the United States, and lingering racism is the reason for this failure. Yet Gerstle wishes to accomplish more than a historical treatment of American racism. He wishes to advance the idea of race as a central analytical category, accounting adequately for both blacks and whites and creating destinies for those who fit within its respective categories.

One race that appears with considerable frequency in Gerstle's book is the "Nordic" one. I confess to shuddering even at the use of such a word, but it does have a fairly precise technical meaning: it applies to the Nordic countries, of which there are five (Denmark, Finland, Iceland, Norway, and Sweden). If one wants to be a bit less technical, it could also include countries that in one way or another were introduced to variations of Nordic mythology, such as the Germany of Richard Wagner. But Gerstle's use of the term is far broader. Franklin Roosevelt's popularity, we are told, was racial in nature: "he became a kind of Nordic father whom everyone, Jews and Catholics included, wanted to claim as his or her own as a way of avowing a vicarious Nordic ancestry," as if Catholics, wherever they come from, cannot be Nordic, while anyone from Holland, where the Roosevelt clan originated, can be Nordic. Of course, this makes very little sense. Holland is primarily Protestant, but it has a significant Catholic population, and neighboring Belgium, the Flemish part of which is indistinguishable ethnically from Holland, is overwhelmingly Catholic.

And so it goes with each invocation of Gerstle's use of the term *Nordic.* Dorothea Lange's photograph *Migrant Mother,* taken in 1936, captures in a single image what it means to be poor. But Gerstle looks at the image of this unfortunate woman and sees her ethnicity. "She was the universal American," he writes. "She was a mother; she was also Nordic." I do not think of Humphrey Bogart as having any particular ethnicity at all, but Gerstle calls him a "capable Nordic." And, in perhaps the sloppiest use of the term, Gerstle manages to classify Finns—the one group to whom the term most directly applies—as ethnics hiding their true identity in the hopes of becoming Nordic types.

We might consider allowing Gerstle his terminology, if for no other purpose than to suggest that immigrants who were short and dark confronted more difficulties assimilating than those who were tall and blond. But Gerstle has as hard a time dealing with Italians as he does with Scandinavians. To be sure, there was one famous American in the former category, Joe DiMaggio, who married one famous American who may have belonged in the latter category, Norma Jean Mortenson. (Since we do not know the identity of Marilyn Monroe's father, we cannot know half of her ethnic makeup. Her birth name, changed at baptism to Baker, suggests Danish or Swedish ancestry, even though Gerstle, who must classify everyone he discusses, goes ahead and calls her "Anglo-Saxon.") DiMaggio, writes Gerstle, "was the model American ethnic: hardworking, respectful, and reserved, someone who played baseball brilliantly, but in a quiet, unprepossessing, even Anglo-Saxon, way." His success demonstrates that the child of southern European immigrants could become fully assimilated, even if there were conditions: "In public, the courteous and gentlemanly DiMaggio . . . . was never heard to utter a mean word or to issue a threat; nor was he ever seen in the company of disreputable, mob-related figures."

The problem with Gerstle's treatment of DiMaggio is not its descent into cliché. The problem is that it is incorrect. One need not subscribe to Richard Ben Cramer's recent screed against DiMaggio to recall that the man was known for hanging out at Toots Shor's, which was also frequented by a mobster or two. Moreover, DiMaggio was not the only Italian-American success story of the period. Had Gerstle chosen to discuss Frank Sinatra, a decision that would have given more texture to his story by offering events a bit less predictable in their interpretation, he would have had to come to the conclusion that very public identification with the Mob—and very public association with African Americans such as Sammy Davis Jr., not to mention the Rat Pack rowdiness that violated every canon of American respectability—was no obstacle to ethnic acceptance in postwar America. And Gerstle's description of DiMaggio is worse than incorrect; it is incoherent. If being a graceful ballplayer can turn someone into an Anglo-Saxon, then "race" hardly matters at all. Why, then, elevate race into the explanation for nearly everything that happens in America?

DiMaggio is not the only Italian American whose story Gerstle twists to his own purposes. Frank Capra was born in Sicily and arrived in the United States when he was six years old. He is most famous for the mushy idealism of films such as *Mr. Deeds Goes to Town* (1936) and *Mr. Smith Goes to Washington* (1939), starring, respectively, Gary Cooper (a "Yankee," in Gerstle's inevitable characterization) and Jimmy Stewart (who contributes to "the adulation of the Nordic" that runs through the film). Capra wrote about his heritage: he hated it, and he wanted to escape as far as possible from it.

But Gerstle cannot accept Capra's own words. Instead he tells the story of Capra's brother Ben, who had left Sicily before the rest of the family. Captured after he tried to jump ship, Ben Capra escaped to New Orleans and was taken in by a black family–"presumably," Gerstle remarks with abandon, "becoming a Negro," exactly as the scholars of whiteness studies suggest. "Was Capra himself distressed by his brother's descent to the level of the Negro?" asks Gerstle, thus shifting from something that "presumably" happened to something that actually did happen. "We cannot be sure," he answers, shifting back again, "but it certainly seems significant," he continues, shifting once more, "that Capra uses the story of his brother's racial descent as a framework within which to understand his own desperate quest for ascent." Out of such wild conjecture and dogmatic supposition do academic historians sustain their theories.

Gerstle has so much trouble with ethnic categories and racial categories because he has so much trouble with all his categories. Scholars of gayness have a category called "homophobic," and Gerstle, concentrating his attention on Joe McCarthy's thinly veiled attacks on effete bureaucrats, is quick to put him there. Never mind that McCarthy hired as his chief assistant Roy Cohn, a not terribly closeted homosexual, and watched with blithe disregard as Cohn and David Shine made quite public fools of themselves. In a similar manner, students of gender often make a distinction between the private woman and the public woman–the former, stuck in the home, falls victim to the feminine mystique, while the latter, out in the workplace, becomes a model of liberation. Not too many career women could be found in American popular culture before the 1960s, but one who fit the bill was Lois Lane, Clark Kent's colleague (and sort-of girlfriend) in what Gerstle describes as the "make-believe Nordic nation" of the Superman comics. But Gerstle is determined to prove the degree to which racial nationalism hinders women, even though women are not a race, and so he treats Lois Lane not as a model of liberation but as evidence of liberation's dangers. After all, her goal was to win Clark Kent's love and thereby to expose his secret. Give a historian a theory, even one as simple as positing a tension between two different ideals, and before you know it everything is bent out of shape to fit the one category or the other.

III

GERSTLE CONCLUDES BY ASKING whether the tradition of racial nationalism has so atrophied that America can finally build a strong society of civic inclusion. He notes that some American intellectuals—he lists Arthur Schlesinger Jr., Diane Ravitch, E. J. Dionne, and other names from the left, the right, and the center, including my own—believe that such a national redemption is possible. Gerstle is, on the whole, fair to us. Liberals who supported Bill Clinton's efforts to shift the Democratic party to the center, he writes generously, "aspire to what is best in the American inheritance—the creation of a society of equal opportunity in which no one suffers on account of race, religion, gender, or creed." In a similarly judicious tone, he points out correctly that John McCain, a civic nationalist from America's other party who much admires Theodore Roosevelt, shares none of Roosevelt's racial obsessions.

Yet despite this revival of civic ideals among American intellectuals, Gerstle is not convinced that our "disciplinary project" can succeed. He believes that America is destined for one of two possible futures: "either the resurgence of a strong, solidaristic, and exclusionary national identity of the sort that has existed in the past" or "a weaker identity, one that makes fewer claims on us, that allows us to cultivate strong ethnic, religious, regional, or transnational identities, but that is capable of generating only thin loyalty to nationalist ideals and limited ties of feeling and obligation to Americans outside our core identity groups."

Gerstle's first option, nightmarish as it may sound, is actually a left-wing historian's fantasy. Patrick Buchanan's program comes closest to meeting its terms, but he is an utter political failure. Even extremely conservative Republicans now fall over themselves trying to impress blacks and Hispanics of their sincerity. Militarism, America First patriotism, unquestioned adherence to Protestant morality: these are as foreign to America today as the Ku Klux Klan and the McCarran-Walter Act.

Like so many contemporary historians, Gerstle concentrates on the public language used by politicians to explain, and to justify, the world around them. When he turns to contemporary America, however, he never makes the obvious point that overt racism–not only Frederic Remington's ugly diatribe, but even Teddy Roosevelt's eugenic musings–simply cannot be found in official public discourse these days. This by no means suggests that racism has disappeared from the United States, but it strongly suggests that racial nationalism has disappeared. No credible public figure–literally none–seeks to bind white Americans closer together by means of rhetoric that sets them against blacks.

One would barely know this from Gerstle's book, but the United States is poised to take civic nationalism seriously for the first time in its history. To do so, it will have to overcome not the lingering racial nationalism of the past, but the fashionable racial multiculturalism of the present. Gerstle is remarkably soft on multiculturalism, even in its hardest versions. He treats Maulana Ron Karenga, the black nationalist who found his cause with the invention of Kwanzaa, as engaged merely in a search for "an authentic and proud past on which Afro-Americans might build a new future." Academic multiculturalists are in no sense separatists, in Gerstle's account. They are people seeking a "bold" program "to reestablish a sense of community on a basis of ethnicity, race, or gender." When Theodore Roosevelt obsesses about race, Gerstle condemns him; but when contemporary black nationalists do the same thing, he praises them. The fact is that ideas that once served to block America from becoming the civic nation that it ought to be are found these days on the left side of the political and intellectual spectrum rather than on the right side; but this irony passes Gerstle by.

Fortunately, hard multicultural ideas do not cut very deeply in America. We are increasingly a multicultural reality, and so "Nordic" ideals, or whatever else you want to call the worldviews of Euro-Americans, will blend together with the worldviews of people who come here from all over the world. And this soft multiculturalism is the friend of civic nationalism, not its enemy. We cannot know what will emerge in the absence of racial nationalism, but we have reason not only to hope but also to believe that out of the delegitimation of racism and racialism in America there will appear civic ideals different from anything that has come before, ideals capacious enough to gather all of America's groups around a creed fashioned by none of them.

Anti-American Studies

ORAGING NEAR THE HUT that he built with his own hands, cultivating beans whose properties provided him with opportunities for
speculation, gazing into the depths of the local pond, Henry David
Thoreau seems to epitomize a long-standing American worship of
nature. And so he was read by generations of students, whose teachers
assigned *Walden* as an illustration of the intensity with which America
was seized in the nineteenth century by a transcendental sensibility
protesting the intrusion into pastoral harmony of the forces of industri-
alization and urbanization. Understood this way, Thoreau looks back to
Jefferson and forward to John Ford. *Walden* was revered as a text of
regret, a lament for a world soon to pass out of existence.

Then Leo Marx came along in 1964 and published *The Machine in
the Garden*, which questioned this view of Thoreau and, in so doing,
challenged the way Americans had understood themselves. Marx's
Thoreau was anything but a pastoralist. He was sometimes ambivalent
about the mechanization that he saw around him and sometimes
downright enthusiastic. "When I hear the iron horse make the hills
echo with his snort like thunder," he proclaimed, "shaking the earth
with his feet, and breathing fire and smoke from his nostrils (what kind
of winged horse or fiery dragon they will put into the new Mythology I
don't know), it seems as if the earth had got a race now worthy to
inhabit it." Mechanization was not a false turn; it was our fate, an "Atro-
pos that never turns aside." Far from symbolizing a withdrawal from
the world, Thoreau's decision to leave Concord for the woods re-

engaged him with the busy clatter that he had seemingly abandoned. Out there in nature, civilization no longer seemed threatening. Documenting his expenses to the last half-cent and providing a full record of his purposeful energy, Thoreau discovered that the power unleashed by the machine is not that different from the power required to transform the wilderness into a productive garden.

For Marx, Thoreau's ambivalence toward nature was nothing less than a leitmotif in American consciousness. Tracing his theme from obscure colonial pamphleteers to twentieth-century classics such as Faulkner's "The Bear," Marx tried to show how American writers—and at least two American painters, George Innes and Charles Sheeler—grappled with the desire to remain pure and uncorrupted while still taking full advantage of what Henry Adams would call "The Dynamo." None of our great artists ever reconciled the contradiction, Marx concluded, because finally the question of what kind of nation we were to become could only be answered politically. Yet this does not mean that they were artistic failures. On the contrary, Marx's extensive analysis of works such as *Moby-Dick* and "Ethan Brand" provided a framework for understanding Ahab's obsession and Brand's self-immolation. The kiln into which Hawthorne's Brand throws himself, like the line used to rein in the white whale, represents what Marx calls "the attempt to know the nature of nature" as well as the inevitable loss of mystery that accompanies our alienation from Paradise.

The Machine in the Garden appeared during the golden age of an academic discipline called "American studies." Founded by polymaths such as Vernon K. Parrington, F. O. Matthiessen, Henry Nash Smith, and Perry Miller, who scrupulously followed Emerson's injunction to create an American scholarship, the field came to fruition with its second generation of practitioners. Books such as Leo Marx's, as well as John Hope Franklin's *From Slavery to Freedom* (1947), Marvin Meyers's *The Jacksonian Persuasion* (1957), Russel Blaine Nye's *The Cultural Life of the New Nation* (1960), Newton Arvin's *Longfellow: His Life and Work* (1963), Ray Allen Billington's *The Protestant Crusade* (1964), Daniel Boorstin's *The Americans* (1965), and Daniel Aaron's *Writers on the Left*

(1969), were widely read and discussed. (All of these writers save Meyers and Arvin would serve a term as president of the American Studies Association [ASA], which was founded in 1951.) Their work would be supplemented by numerous writers from allied academic disciplines, or from no academic discipline at all, who contributed to the ways Americans understood themselves during this period, including Richard Hofstadter, Henry Steele Commager, Alfred Kazin, Daniel Bell, David Riesman, and Seymour Martin Lipset. The 1950s and the 1960s were decades of turmoil–McCarthyism, the cold war, civil rights, the Port Huron Statement–but they were at the same time oddly stable decades in which American thinkers tried to make sense of the society that spawned them.

Looking back, one is struck by the absence of women among these writers. With that significant exception, however, the founders of American studies were a diverse group. Many were Jews whose explorations into American literature and history were a way of coming to terms with the decision taken by their parents and grandparents to move to the New World. One of them, Franklin, was African American, and another, Arvin, was gay and would suffer the indignity of a vice-squad raid on his Northampton home. Far from engaging in what C. Wright Mills would denounce as "the great American celebration," these intellectuals were often dissenters from the trends that they saw around them: Riesman and Marx were critics of nuclear brinkmanship, and others, even those who would become quite antagonistic to the New Left, could not abide Senator McCarthy and never made a sharp shift to the political right. The ambivalence that Leo Marx discovered in our national literature was shared by all these writers who interpreted our culture and contemplated our character: they appreciated America for its invention and energy while deploring the excesses that our way of life produced.

II

AMERICAN STUDIES STILL EXISTS as an academic discipline. If anything, it can be found in far more colleges and universities now than during the 1960s, it attracts significant numbers of graduate students, and its practitioners publish innumerable books and articles. Yet the third generation and the fourth generation of scholars in the field not only reject the writers who gave life to the discipline, they have also developed a hatred for America so visceral that it makes one wonder why they bother studying America at all.

According to Donald E. Pease and Robyn Wiegman in their collection of essays called *The Futures of American Studies,* previous efforts to understand the United States committed two unforgivable sins. One was "spatialization." Marx's generation of scholars claimed that there existed an entity called America, that is, an actual society with borders to which one either did or did not belong, and they further claimed that the land within these borders was somehow "exceptional" from other societies around the world. In so doing, writes Janice Radway of Duke University, "the early consensus in the field tended to elide the idea of America with the culture of the United States." The "imperial gestures" that these assumptions produce are obvious to her: "they unconsciously erased the fact that other nations, groups, and territories had already staked their own quite distinctive claim to the concept and name *American.*" Each of my three children discovered, usually around fourth grade, that Canada and the societies of Latin America have a legitimate claim to be called American; but Radway delivers the same point as a major idea. (Similarly, Amy Kaplan, the president-elect of the ASA for 2003–4, has a chapter in the Pease and Wiegman volume in which she "poses the question of how the ideology of separate spheres in antebellum America contributed to creating an American empire by imagining the nation as a home at a time when its geopolitical borders were expanding rapidly through violent confrontations with Indians, Mexicans, and European empires.")

The other sin of the earlier generation was "temporalization." Scholars in American studies divided up the history of their society into periods such that each constituted a progressive advancement over the other. In so doing, they left the impression that the United States no longer required radical reform, let alone revolution, since continued progress in the future was assured. Yet they also did the exact opposite simultaneously, imagining the history of their society as timeless. "In proposing that every moment of historical time constituted the occasion for the potential repetition of the sacred time of the nation's founding," as Pease and Wiegman put it, "the national mythos supplied the means of producing what Benedict Anderson has called the empty homogenous time of the imagined national community."

A body of scholarship produced in this way, in the view of Pease and Wiegman, is bound to be suspect. "American literature and American history tended to homogenize the popular memory that they also produced, and literature and history departments supplied the institutional sites wherein the field of American studies collaborated with the press, the university system, the publishing industry, and other aspects of the cultural apparatus that managed the symbolic field and policed the significance of such value-laden terms as *the nation* and *the people*." Poor Leo Marx. He may have thought of himself as a lover of literature, but it appears that he was really a cop, and a corrupt cop at that.

Pease and Wiegman are actually among the more temperate and jargon-free voices speaking on behalf of what John Carlos Rowe of the University of California, Irvine, calls (in a book of that name) *The New American Studies.* Consider the views of William V. Spanos, founding editor of a publication called *boundary 2.* It is one thing, he writes, to call attention to "America's tenacious historical privileging of the imperial metaphysic perspective as the agent of knowledge production, that perspective, synchronous with the founding of the idea and practices of Europe, which, in perceiving time from after or above its disseminations, enables the spatialization of being and subjugation or accommodation of the differences it disseminates to the identical, self-present, and plenary (global/planetary) whole." But things are worse even than that. For we must also consider "America's obsessive and systematic refinement and fulfillment of the panoptic logic of this Old World perspective in an indissolubly related relay of worldly imperial practices, the intrinsic goal of which is not simply the domination of global space but also of thinking itself." From this perspective, writers like Marx were not merely trying to police ideas, they were trying to run them out of town.

For these radical critics of American studies, nobody's revolutionary credentials are good enough. The revolt against the American studies of the immediate postwar period was led by people such as Paul Lauter, who teaches at Trinity College in Connecticut. An unrepentant Marxist, Lauter believes in the class struggle and wants to see professors of American studies join janitors, teaching assistants, and other exploited workers in their confrontations with academic administrators. Yet perhaps because he has a sense of humor—he knows that he sounds "like an opera libretto by Leonid Brezhnev," he writes at one point—Lauter comes in for substantial criticism from fellow members of his discipline. John Carlos Rowe finds that, for all his leftism, Lauter is "finally still nationalist," which means insufficiently committed to postcolonial criticism of the United States for its imperial pretensions.

Nor is Lauter truly committed to the task that American studies must adopt in this den of white privilege and capitalist exploitation. "Lauter's program for university reform consists only of a very general set of guidelines," writes Eric Cheyfitz of the University of Pennsylvania in disappointment. Lauter, along with other advocates of class struggle within the university such as Cary Nelson and Michael Bérubé, fails to realize that capitalism has already destroyed the idea of university. Dismissing these advocates of university-based class struggle as possessing "an ideological relationship in which the privileged class, as in the pastoral, dress up in the costumes of the dispossessed and perform a play we call 'multiculturalism,'" Cheyfitz would have American studies join with Frantz Fanon and "move cultural capital out of the closed circuit of the university" and into the hands of the poor and oppressed.

Even those academics who consider themselves indelibly stained by the original sin of the whiteness of their skin—a group I had once considered about as left-wing as it is possible to be (see "Strangled by Roots," this vol.)—are insufficiently radical for the new American studies. In the view of Noel Ignatiev, one of the founders of "whiteness studies," we have to recognize that "the United States is an Afro-American country," which means that "the adoption of a white identity is the most serious barrier to becoming fully American"; as Ignatiev once put it, "the most subversive act I can imagine is treason to the white race." But now Robyn Wiegman dismisses Ignatiev as just another practitioner of American exceptionalism: his mistake is that he "displaces the historical white subject as the national citizen-subject for a narrative of national origins cast now as black." So long as you believe in the existence of the United States, even if your belief envisions a society in which the descendants of slaves become masters of national identity, you are contributing to the creating of a "resignified nation," which is nearly as bad, it would seem, as the presignified nation that already exists.

Take this kind of thing far enough and before long you develop the mentality of the purge, the humorless, relentless quest to check the bona fides of everyone and in so doing to trust the bona fides of no one. William Spanos sums up this spirit by detecting counterrevolution not only in the scholars of Leo Marx's generation, but also among the New Leftists who followed them. The scholars of the new American studies may seem radical, he writes, but their work "remains vestigially inscribed by the ideology of American exceptionalism even as it criticizes it and tries to transcend its confining parameters." I have never known anyone to use the term *vestigially* in such a context who was not at heart a sectarian.

Oddly, though, Spanos has a point. Enthusiasts for the new American studies have clearly been influenced by the multiculturalism and the identity politics that have marked American society since the 1960s. When they sought a home in academia, as radical political movements always do, multicultural activists realized that all you had to do was add your ethnic and racial identity to the word *American* and you had created a new academic field. In this way, proponents of Asian American studies or Native American studies or any of the other myriad programs now found in higher education, including even "whiteness studies," by giving the term *American* equal billing with the name of the group seeking recognition, paid homage to their society, as well as to its capacity to assimilate many different kinds of experience. And this, in its way, is a tribute to America. It is the tribute that the America-hating Spanos eagerly sniffs out.

Still, once the intellectual energy passes to these "subaltern" movements, as all of these writers hope will happen soon, the question remains of what should happen to the original American studies out of which they grew. For Pease and Wiegman, American studies, owing to its neocolonial drive to obliterate all potentially competing ethnic and racial cultures, has little choice but to suppress the insurgencies led by women, gays, and people of color. "American studies became the Other against which cutting edge scholarship was to be defined," they write, "and national identity movements and anti-imperial discourses became the Other the field excluded to effect coherence." While the first half of the comment is true—nobody doubts that adherents to the new identity politics scorned the generations that preceded them—the second half of it is way off the mark. The academic discipline called American studies, at most colleges and universities in the United States, has enthusiastically welcomed identity politics into its ranks, to put it mildly.

In contrast to the era that spawned Leo Marx and his colleagues, the ASA now routinely elects women and members of racial minorities to its presidency. Of the fourteen presidents chosen since 1990, ten have been women, and of the four men, one is Latino and one Asian American. (The only two white males elected during this period were Paul Lauter and Michael Frisch.) To talk about the exclusion of minority voices and dissenting voices from the discipline, Pease and Wiegman must ignore the contents of their own book: the chapter by Janice Radway stems from her presidential address to the ASA, and in her musings she builds on the analysis of her predecessor, Mary Helen Washington.

Among those presidents, certainly, can be found individuals who love their country for its inventiveness and its diversity, and in turn love American studies for its innovative character. In her presidential address to the ASA in 1996, Patricia Nelson Limerick took great joy in the free-form nature of her discipline. "Thank heavens, then," she enthused, "for American studies: the place of refuge for those who cannot find a home in the more conventional neighborhood, the sanctuary of displaced hearts and minds, the place where no one is fully at ease. And here is the glory of the ASA: since no one feels fully at ease, no one has the right or the power to make anyone else feel less at ease. . . . The joy of American studies is precisely in its lack of firm limits and borders." But no such pride in anything associated with America is permitted among the contributors to the Pease and Wiegman volume. Russ Castronovo of the University of Miami accuses Limerick of offering "an entrenched narrative of national administration." Her crime, it seems, is to present a point of view that "hinges on a rhetoric of interpellation that accepts the nation as the ultimate collective arena for citizenship."

If we discard the idea of an American nation, as Castronovo and other contributors to this volume want us to do, there certainly cannot be any such thing as American studies. "In order to promote work that would further re-conceptualize the American as always relationally defined and therefore as intricately dependent on 'others' that are used both materially and conceptually to mark its boundaries," Radway asks, "would it make sense to think about renaming the association as an institution devoted to a different form of knowledge production, to alternative epistemologies, to the investigation of a different object?" This, it turns out, is not a simple question to answer, for once she starts finding imperialism in one place, Radway sees it everywhere. We in the United States, after all, expropriated the name *America* from the Latin Americans, but they, or at least their elites, were Europeans who aimed "to name geographically dispersed lands that they themselves had imperially expropriated for their own use from indigenous peoples who named the locales they occupied in their own, diverse, and distinct languages." Radway is dissatisfied with all proposed names for the field: even "inter-American studies," which suggests equality between all the components of what is now called the Americas, strikes her as insufficient because it leaves out Singapore and India. "What is to be done?" she asks, echoing you know who. The answer is: not all that much. Having twisted herself into corners from which she cannot escape, Radway concludes rather lamely that we might as well leave the term *American studies* in place and urge everyone to learn more languages.

Retaining the name *American studies* does not mean keeping the approach that long made it distinctive. If we keep it, we must tame it. For one thing, American studies can take a secondary role to those who study America's constituent groups. The field, writes John Carlos Rowe, cannot be allowed "to compete in adversarial ways with other disciplines and methods that complement our own work," and he provides a list of more than twenty such disciplines ranging from women's studies and folklore to Dutch and Korean. It also might be permissible to use the term, Rowe continues, if we modify it slightly by calling it *U.S. studies* or *North American studies*, so long as we include Canada in the latter. And we cannot allow American studies to find themes in our literature and culture that tell us who we are, as previous scholars had hoped; its more proper role, Radway instructs, is "to complicate and fracture the very idea of an American nation, culture, and subject."

The difficulty that these writers experience in naming their field stems from the difficulty they have in naming anything. There is a finality about naming; once a phenomenon has been named, it takes on a form that distinguishes it from other phenomena whose names are different. But this relatively simple act of finalization is alien to many of the practitioners of the new American studies. For all their political dogmatism, they are reluctant to be pinned down on whether terms such as *nation, culture, literature, citizenship,* and *gender* have specific meanings.

A particularly sad example of this refusal to put boundaries around concepts is provided by José Esteban Muñoz's essay in the Pease and Wiegman book—and the term in question is one that ought to be crucial to anyone who identifies with the political left. The term is *exploitation.* Muñoz is describing a gay bar in Jackson Heights, Queens called the Magic Touch. (How American studies moved from reading Hawthorne to venturing into gay Queens is another good story.) During the show, judges, chosen randomly, pick out the most attractive dancers, who have stripped down to their G-strings. Money, in the form of tips, is thrown around as mostly older men buy the sexual favors of mostly younger dancers. This kind of prostitution has the whiff of oppression, and Muñoz quotes an anthropologist friend of his to the effect that it is. But Muñoz himself will make no such firm declaration. "From another perspective," he writes, "we can see this as something else, another formation: this economy of hustler/john is an alternative economy where flesh, pleasure, and money meet under outlaw circumstances. This economy eschews the standardized routines in which hetero-normative late capitalism mandates networking relations of sex for money. This economy represents a selling of sex for money that does not conform to the corporate American sex trade on display for us via media advertising culture and older institutions like heterosexual marriage."

Not only does Muñoz resist naming prostitution for the exploitative relationship that it is, he also conflates it with heterosexual marriage, a conceit that allows him to normalize sex trade in a gay bar without perhaps realizing that, in so doing, he acknowledges that conventional marriage is still the gold standard against which all other kinds of sexual relationships must be compared.

Intention substitutes for conclusion when academics are reluctant to define anything definitively. The essays in Pease and Wiegman's book follow a convention widely used in the humanities these days. "I want to call attention" begins one of Radway's paragraphs dealing with the interaction between work in American studies and that found in many subaltern disciplines. "I want to suggest" starts the very next paragraph, claiming that the new work constitutes a fundamental challenge to the old. One after another of the contributors to the Pease and Wiegman volume adopt this way of making their argument; even Muñoz's claims about the normality of prostitution begin this way. This is scholarship as trial balloon: the writer who adopts this convention signals to the reader that what is about to follow is a highly contentious point that lacks sufficient documentation to be proved. To "call attention" and to "suggest" is not to establish or to demonstrate. Postmodernism influences the new American studies as much as identity politics, and postmodernism encourages a lazy, catch-as-catch-can approach to the study of whatever it touches, as if studying something means acknowledging that a real world does exist that can be studied– a lethal concession for postmodernism which destroys its controlling fantasy that reality is subordinate to its interpretations.

For this reason, only a few of the contributors to *The Futures of American Studies* actually engage specific texts. One who does is Nancy Bentley of the University of Pennsylvania. Like Muñoz, she does so to make the point that heterosexual marriage is not what it seems, but at least she discusses an actual historical situation–Mormonism–and the literature to which its practice of polygamy gave rise. Filled with the usual trappings of contemporary scholarship in the humanities–"Mormons were refused the status of white people," she writes of a religion that excluded African Americans from its priesthood–she nonetheless introduces her readers to Maria Ward's *The Mormon Wife* (1855) and Mary Hudson's *Esther the Gentile* (1880), popular novels that exposed the exploitation of women subject to plural marriage. To be sure, Bentley does not introduce them for that purpose; her aim is to suggest that if Mormon wives consented to plural marriage, then we ought to question the consent implicit in conventional marriage. Still, hers is one of the few chapters in the Pease and Wiegman volume in which the reader can learn something new.

"As American Studies reconceives its intellectual project as the study of the many different societies of the western hemisphere and of the influences of the different border zones that constitute this large region, such as the Pacific Rim and the African and European Atlantics, it will become a genuinely 'postnationalist' discipline whose comparativist methods will overlap and thus benefit from the work of other comparativists." So writes John Carlos Rowe. Once upon a time, American studies existed to rediscover a literature and a culture capable of rivaling Europe in the power of its artistic imagination. For the writers of Leo Marx's generation, this discovery liberated intellectuals from the Babbittry of those politicians and journalists who claimed that the greatness of America lay solely in its capacity to produce consumer goods. Now, we are told, the answer to the question of what makes America great is that nothing makes it great.

The reason that America is not great is that America, strictly speaking, does not exist. Revealing America as nonexistent is supposed to ease the task of those oppressed groups that are struggling to overcome its hegemony. It does not occur to these revolutionaries that the groups they hope will conquer America cannot do so if there is no America to conquer. Let the nation die, and all who aspire to its perfection die with it.

III

DEATH OF A NATION is in fact the title of David W. Noble's contribution to the future of American studies, and Noble is in many ways the most appropriate person to write it. Born in 1925 on a farm near Princeton, Noble experienced the fall of his family into poverty during the Great Depression, only to have his life turn around after he joined the army in 1943. After serving in Europe, he returned home to enter Princeton as an undergraduate and went on to Wisconsin for his doctorate, where his fellow graduate students included the future historians William Appleman Williams and John Higham. (Noble's first published article, which had originated as an undergraduate paper, was called "The *New Republic* and the Idea of Progress, 1914–1920," a subject that was suggested to him by the Princeton historian Eric Goldman.) A precocious scholar, he joined the faculty of the University of Minnesota in 1952 and has been teaching there ever since.

In his early years at Minnesota, Noble was a colleague of Henry Nash Smith and Leo Marx, men who, in his view, "discovered a nostalgic, even elegiac scholarship committed to preserving the memory of the period 1830–1850, when, for them, there had existed briefly an autonomous and natural, national culture." (In fact, *The Machine in the Garden* devoted considerable space to *The Great Gatsby,* a novel that appeared a long time after the Compromise of 1850.) Unlike them, Noble "could not write elegies for Emerson and his generation of male

Anglo-American artists and intellectuals." Marx's panoply of great writers created no timeless art, Nobel insists; their greatness, such as it was, lay only in the fact that they gave expression to what he repeatedly calls "bourgeois nationalism." Marx and Smith, searching for an America that does not exist, "did not try to evoke the ugliness, the corruption, the falsity of capitalism." Noble would have nothing to do with writers who "emphasized the beauty, the goodness, and the truth of the national landscape." America was not some virgin territory filled with innocence, he came to believe. It was an imagined community, an artifact, that came into existence only by destroying truly innocent people like the Native American tribes. "These doubts," Noble writes, "later caused me to distance myself from my colleagues in American studies at the University of Minnesota."

Noble did not distance himself from Minnesota's American studies program for long. More radical graduate students began to show up at the university, and, like Noble, they were unwilling "to worship at Emerson's tomb." Noble claims to have witnessed the "sadness" and the "pain" of Smith and Marx as students spurned them and their ideas, but he shows few regrets of his own, noting with cold dispassion that Smith "took a position elsewhere, where he would not have such an intense relationship with graduate students," and commenting with barely hidden academic snobbery that Marx "left to teach undergraduates at Amherst." Noble makes clear that Smith and Marx were simply out of touch with the newly emerging scholarship: they "did not want to think about what the relationship of American studies would be to the new world of 1946, when one could no longer imagine an isolated national culture."

Nobody could accuse Noble of being out of touch. He is a generation-skipper, not an uncommon phenomenon in academia. Although trained in the classic version of American studies that inspired so much of the "exceptionalist" literature, he broke with his contemporaries to join the new radicalism that was emerging in the field. His book blessedly lacks the heavy-handed jargon with which younger scholars have afflicted the field (although it shares with them their inane forms of leftist politics). And Noble can occasionally be interesting: he alone, of all these writers, seems to have a taste for music and acknowledges the existence of figures such as Edward MacDowell and Charles Ives, if only to accuse them of their dependency on a European musical tradition. (The gay composer Charles Tomlinson Griffes and the African American William Grant Still were just as dependent on European musical forms, identity politics or not, but Noble never mentions them.) Still, Noble adds little to what younger colleagues say in such anthologies as *The Futures of American Studies*. His book is noteworthy not for what it says—it is rambling and repetitive—but for what it reveals about a man ferociously eager to join the chorus of denunciation, even if those being denounced are people very much like himself.

Noble heaps scorn upon white male Protestants whenever he comes upon them. To his mind, the one thing that Emerson, Thoreau, Melville, Hawthorne, Whitman, Twain, Henry James, and Faulkner have in common is their ethnicity. (Terms such as *Protestant, Catholic,* and *Jewish* never refer to religious faith in his usage, only to national origins.) How odd it seems to Noble, therefore, that so many of the literary critics and the historians who called attention to their genius were Jewish. What gives? Well, white male Jews had at least two reasons for wanting to preserve and protect a Protestant literary canon. The more innocent explanation, says Noble, is that doing so would help them to overcome their disappointment with Marxism, although there is nothing particularly Jewish in that. The more sinister—if not downright ugly—explanation is that worshipping at the altar of Protestant creativity would enable Jewish scholars to "mask the revolutionary changes in national identity taking place in the 1940s."

That shift in identity, in Noble's view, was caused by the fact that America during that decade was changing from "Anglo-Protestant" to "pluralist." Jumping around from decade to decade, as he frequently does, Noble points out that "beginning in the 1950s, Congress began to lift restrictions on Chinese immigration. The Immigration Act of 1964 made it possible for people of color to become citizens, and the country began to experience large-scale immigration from Asia and Latin

America." But "many male Jews, the first group of unclear outsiders (after the southern male Anglo-Protestant New Critics) to become part of the academic establishment," wanted only to "obscure" the new pluralistic America coming into being. That is why so many of them "became the leaders of the consensus school of historical interpretation that was challenging the conflict school of the 1930s." Citing Lionel Trilling, Richard Hofstadter (who was half-Jewish on his father's side), Daniel Boorstin, Daniel Bell, and Louis Hartz, he writes that "these men wanted to believe that the tradition of nationalism in the United States did not share a commitment to racial exclusiveness with Nazi Germany." Noble's coterie of white male Jewish writers had a choice: they could join with the project of bourgeois nationalism and win acceptance by their social superiors, or they could reject it in favor of the insurgencies led by people of color. Their tragedy is that they opted for the former.

Everything about this explanation is wrong. The Immigration Act was passed in 1965, not in 1964. Before its passage, all kinds of people of color had become citizens, including African Americans and Asian Americans. The 1965 act did not target immigrants from any one place; it abolished national quotas, emphasized skills, and encouraged the reunification of families. But the most serious problem with Noble's speculation is not that he gets his facts wrong; it is that his thoroughly reductionist sociology of knowledge insults the motives of all those Jewish scholars of America who not only had perfectly good reasons to admire the United States, but who also welcomed the new pluralistic America that was coming into being.

Notice Noble's formulation of the comparison with Nazi Germany. He does not say that the United States in fact refrained from exterminating its non-Protestants, nor does he add that American lives were sacrificed to end the Nazi slaughter, both points reason enough for American Jews to love their country. All he says is that these Jewish scholars simply wanted to believe that America was better than Nazi Germany, as if it were an open question as to whether it was. At the same time, Noble's reading of what Jewish scholars of America had to say about pluralism in the 1940s and the 1950s is the exact opposite of the truth. The consensus that so-called consensus historians defended was not a vision of Protestant America, it was a vision of the melting pot. Jewish scholars such as Arnold Rose and Milton Gordon were in the forefront of defining, and defending, this new American pluralism. (Rose, as Noble well ought to know, also taught at Minnesota, worked on Gunnar Myrdal's *An American Dilemma*, shared the liberal anti-communism of his state's increasingly prominent politicians such as Hubert Humphrey, and, with his wife, published *America Divided: Minority Group Relations in the United States* in 1948.) Where Noble sees only the "power used by a dominant male Anglo-Protestant culture to protect its cultural virginity against the agency of all the groups in the United States who were imagined as outside the fraternity of citizens in the 1830s," the Jewish scholars attracted to the study of America saw a society and a literature too filled with paradox and promise to be so single-minded in its determination.

There was a kind of anti-Semitism around Princeton in the years when Noble grew up that worked assiduously to keep Jews out of day schools, country clubs, and the university itself. Noble would have nothing to do with it. He chose to work with Princeton's first Jewish professor, and a good part of the Protestant exclusivity that he rejects stems from its hostility toward Jews and Catholics. Still, Noble is clearly made uncomfortable by the Jewish love for America's Emersonian high culture. His detour into ethnic motivations for scholarship leaves a bad taste. How could these Jewish scholars not join him in his disgust with America? he is implicitly asking. Shouldn't they have known better? Shouldn't they have known what he, who shares "the racial heritage of North European Protestants," knows all too well, which is that the American dream is a nightmare of spoilage and exploitation?

Right-wing anti-Semites often attack Jews for failing to appreciate America. Is it all that different to single them out for loving it? Fortunately for Noble, Jews were not America's only minority group. In contrast to the exclusionary patriotism of the earlier generations of WASPs, Noble would "celebrate . . . the agency of those who were previously seen as un-American." The scholars who speak on behalf of women, African Americans, Native Americans, or Asian Americans—or so Noble believes—do not have the Jewish hang-up about America. (Many of the new Americanists whom he celebrates are in fact Jewish, but they are women and therefore acceptable to him.) Here, among the crowd that makes up the anthology assembled by Pease and Wiegman, Noble feels at home. With them he can finally shed himself of his white male identity. The dream of his lifetime is being realized. The nation that he cannot abide is expiring, and he has lived long enough to provide its epitaph.

IV

ALTHOUGH ONE WOULD NEVER know it from books like these, old-fashioned American studies is actually doing pretty well in America, even if it is underrepresented at the American Studies Association. (I think of Louis Menand, whose recently published collection of essays is called *American Studies,* Andrew Delbanco who writes about Melville and the Puritans, or the historian Lizabeth Cohen whose book on consumption is discussed in "Buying Alone" in this volume.) In theory, of course, it should not matter where good studies of America are done, so long as they are done. But in practice matters are not so simple. Critics of the old American studies are right about one thing: the field was created in the early years of the cold war, and American foreign policy-makers took an interest in what its practitioners had to say. That international aspect of American studies still exists; programs in Germany, Japan, India, Austria, Italy, and Great Britain are devoted to the study of the United States, and through its Fulbright Program and its Study of the U.S. Branch, the State Department sends American scholars abroad and brings foreign scholars to the United States.

For all their attacks on American imperialism, students of the new American studies are actually rather quiet about this side of their discipline, perhaps because of the opportunities for foreign travel it makes available to them. When they go abroad to denounce America to foreign students, these scholars practice a kind of imperialism in reverse, informing young idealists abroad that the America they tend to admire is actually a fiction, and a detestable place. The results can be rather comic. One of the contributors to the Pease and Wiegman book, Dana Heller of Old Dominion University, describes her efforts to offer a Marxist interpretation of *Death of a Salesman* to students at Moscow State University. Fortunately for American diplomacy, her students could not have cared less; they were much more impressed by an episode of *The Simpsons* that parodied one of Willy Loman's speeches.

This anecdote suggests that even if America-haters come to speak for America at colleges and universities around the world, students at those institutions will have enough sense to ignore them. But it also raises an interesting question of responsibility. Academics like to pride themselves on the notion that academic freedom means an absence of restraint in the topics that they choose to study and the methods with which they choose to study them. But all freedoms hinge on responsibilities, and people who choose to make the study of America central to their lives cannot avoid the fact that, spatialization or not, their country actually exists, and its actions are of consequence. Now, assuming responsibility hardly means engaging in a mindless celebration of America; the founders of the field never did that, and their books would now be worthless if they had been merely patriotic. Assuming responsibility means possessing both a curiosity about the society that they seek to understand and a capacity to convey both its possibilities and its pitfalls. Neither of those qualities is much in evidence among the bitter rejectionists who have filled the vacuum left by the retirement or the passing of Leo Marx's generation of scholars. It is a credit to our freedom that we have avoided turning American studies over to a propaganda arm of government and that we allow those who appreciate their society so little to speak in its name. If only they themselves could rise above their own propaganda, and muster just a smidgen of gratitude in return.

PART II

God

.

The Return of Evil

"T HE PROBLEM OF EVIL will be the fundamental question of postwar
intellectual life in Europe," wrote Hannah Arendt in 1945. She was
wrong. To be fair, her comment was not directed at the United States,
and it applied to intellectual life in general rather than to academic
trends in particular. Still, postwar thought in the West in the last half of
the twentieth century did not make evil central to its concerns. On the
contrary: philosophers retreated even more deeply into analytic preoc-
cupations with logic and language; social scientists reacted to the massive irrationalities of war and totalitarianism by treating all human
behavior as if it were ultrarational; both literary theorists and novelists
were attracted to forms of postmodernism that denied any fixed distinctions, including the one between good and evil; and the most influential theologians studiously avoided neo-Augustinian thinkers like
Reinhold Niebuhr. The one European thinker who comes closest to
Arendt in breadth of knowledge and passionate concern with the fate of
humanity—Jürgen Habermas—has devoted his work, not to exploring
the horrors of the modern world, but to the conditions under which
meaningful human communication is possible.

What was not true of the past fifty years, however, may turn out to
be true of the next fifty. Evil is getting increased attention. Presidents
Reagan and Bush used the term in their rhetoric, to significant public
acclaim. Popular culture addicts know all about Hannibal Lecter and
consume the plots of Stephen King. And the books under review here
are representative of a much larger number of recent titles, suggesting

that academic fields as diverse as philosophy, theology, and psychology are turning with increasing frequency to a subject they once ignored. It has taken a half century since the end of World War II for the study of evil to catch up with the thing itself–perhaps, given the traumas of the evils uncovered at war's end, not an unreasonable amount of time.

Now that evil is once again prominent on the intellectual and academic radar screen, the problems of understanding it have only just begun. A number of books on evil have appeared recently, and not only do they fail to agree on what evil is, they disagree on how it came into the world and whether it ever can be expected to leave. Consider them, as all of their authors save one would want them to be considered, provisional efforts to start an inquiry rather than foundational attempts to solve a problem.

II

THE EXCEPTION IS JAMES WALLER'S *Becoming Evil: How Ordinary People Commit Genocide and Mass Killing.* We need, he writes, a "unified" and a "new" theory about evil, and he plans to offer "an original interpretation," as well as a "model," that will make sense out of "extraordinary human evil." These are ambitious claims for so complex a phenomenon, and it should not come as a surprise that Waller fails to deliver on them. His book, the most immodest of the four under discussion in this essay, sheds the least new light on the problem. Waller, a social psychologist at Whitworth College in Washington State, begins by defining evil as "the deliberate harming of humans by other humans." This is, he writes, a behavioral definition that enables us to leave out people's motivations in order to judge them by their actions, an odd conclusion given that one must evaluate motivations to determine whether actions are deliberate. Mostly, though, Waller's definition suffers from its extreme broadness. Harm has been an unavoidable feature of social life since its origins. Without uprooting people from ways of life that limit their potential, and in the process imposing considerable harm upon them, there would be no progress in the world.

Sometimes such acts of displacement are clearly evil, as when agents of American expansion intentionally unleashed deadly viruses on Native American populations. But sometimes harm can have beneficial consequences, especially for later generations; ask the grandchildren of immigrants to America or Australia forced out of poverty-stricken Europe often against their will.

Rather than distinguishing between different kinds of harm and the consequences that follow from them, Waller jumps immediately to "extraordinary human evil," which, unlike evil in general, involves "the deliberate harm inflicted against a defenseless and helpless group targeted by a legitimating political, social, or religious authority." This definition also suffers from being too capacious. Under the spell of evil's seeming ubiquity, Waller intersperses throughout his text brief accounts of many of the major evils that have taken place in recent years, from Rwanda to Bosnia. But they serve mostly to underscore the point that, for example, violations of human rights in Latin America carried out by repressive dictators, as horrendous as they are, are not at the same level, morally speaking, as genocidal attempts to wipe out entire populations based on their religion or ethnicity. There is a reason for Waller's inclusiveness; he has a thesis to advance. "My central argument," he writes, "is that it is ordinary individuals, like you and me, who commit extraordinary evil." Furthermore, "being aware of our own capacity for extraordinary evil–and the dispositional, situational, and social influences that foster it–is the best safeguard we can have against future genocide."

To demonstrate his thesis, Waller argues that true evil such as that exhibited by the Nazis cannot be explained at least in part as a large-scale manifestation of psychopathology. Were many of the leading Nazis madmen? Did their actions reveal not only familiar human motives but also a strain of mental aberration such as we are inclined to impute to the perpetrators of certain horrible crimes–a Jeffrey Dahmer, for instance? Waller answers no, and the way he makes his case says volumes about his approach throughout the book.

It turns out that Rorschach tests were administered to some of the

Nazi war criminals at Nuremberg. Nearly everyone who studied the results of these tests disagreed about what they signified, including the two psychologists who administered them. In addition, only nineteen individuals underwent the test–a limited basis for sweeping generalizations. Indeed, the psychologists who were given the data in 1947 never published their conclusions. Perhaps they found the sample too small and the technique too crude.

But Waller charges that, confronted with evidence that the Nazis were normal, the psychologists would not go on record with their findings. When another research team comes to the conclusion Waller prefers, that Nazi leaders had no tinge of madness about them, Waller cites their work favorably, even if the bulk of the Rorschachs this group studied were not of Germans but of Danes who collaborated with the Nazis. "As much as we may wish it to be true," Waller concludes, "the Nazis cannot so easily be explained away as disturbed, highly abnormal individuals."

To appreciate how absurd this conclusion is, consider the following thought experiment. Wanting to find out who is abnormal and who is not, you design a projective test meant to measure mental health. But one of your colleagues comes up with a better idea. "Let's not be satisfied with a measure of madness," he exclaims, "let's observe the real thing." This colleague then proposes that we see which of our fellow citizens would be willing to round up all the Jews in the society, send them on trains to camps, and kill them with gas. "Anyone willing to go that far," he concludes triumphantly, "surely would be mad," but, we can picture him adding, "this would never happen in real life." Now we know, of course, that it did. Despite all the evidence that anyone could ever want demonstrating that the Nazis were psychopaths, Waller proposes that a test meant to measure something is a better indicator than the thing itself, a sad commentary on the way some psychologists view the world.

Seeking further support for his implausible thesis, Waller turns to Hannah Arendt's famous book *Eichmann in Jerusalem: A Report on the Banality of Evil.* But he gets nearly everything about Arendt wrong. He states that the controversy over her book centered on the notion of "the banality of evil"; actually, most critics focused on Arendt's suggestion that Jewish councils collaborated with the Nazis, an aspect of her book that Waller never mentions. Moreover, Arendt would be aghast at Waller's suggested thesis about extraordinary evil. The phrase "banality of evil" was meant to suggest that Eichmann was a cog in a machine without conspicuous evil motives of his own, but it never implied that the Nazi machine was just like any other machine. Indeed, in *The Origins of Totalitarianism,* Arendt talked about the "radical evil" that had emerged in the twentieth century, arguing that modern forms of totalitarianism were historically unique. Much ink has been spilled over whether "radical evil" is reconcilable with "the banality of evil"; there is no contradiction if one realizes that radically evil ends can be carried out through banal means.

Equally unsatisfactory is Waller's attempt to develop what he calls a "situational" explanation of evil. "People tend to do evil because of where they are," he writes, "not who they are." Yet Anton Schmidt, an ordinary German whose efforts to save Jews in Poland were cited at the Nuremberg trials, committed acts of goodness because of who he was–and to do so he had to overcome the situation in which he found himself. Despite repeated pronouncements that his model of evil is not meant to absolve individuals of the responsibility for their acts, Waller does just that.

All of this could be forgiven if Waller were correct that a recognition of our potential for extraordinary evil is a necessary first step to controlling future outbreaks of the phenomenon. But there is no reason for thinking he is. Forgive me, but I do not consider myself evil, nor would I apply that term to most people I know. (I have no doubt harmed people in the course of my life, sometimes deliberately, and people have done the same to me, but this does not make any of us evil.) Some concepts are useful only to the degree that they are rarely used, and evil is one of them. By restricting the term to exceptional acts committed by truly reprehensible people, we do not make the "other" responsible for our own failings, as Waller charges. Instead, recognizing that we cannot prevent extraordinary evil, we do the next best thing: we single out those who perpetrate it and condemn and punish them for the choices they made. We should "democratize" evil rather than engage in "demonizing" it, Waller suggests. I would rather leave the subject to poets than social psychologists; the former do a better job with devils than the latter.

Poets, however, are not specialists, and "most nonspecialists simply do not bring the training or experience necessary to fully mine the potential of what contemporary psychology can offer," Waller opines. This is his most immodest claim of all. Evil has a certain grandeur; it stands there in all its hugeness, challenging us to grasp its essence. Academic psychology, by contrast, is puny in its methods and conclusions, although, it would seem, not in its ambitions. Oblivious to the gap between his subject matter and his discipline, Waller proposes that "scholars in genocide studies" need to take his model "and test its applicability to a broader range of cases of perpetrator behavior than those I have included in this book." The thought sends a chill down my spine. To begin to grasp radical evil, the last thing we need is "genocide studies," as if the victims of systematic killings needed their own version of identity politics. And before we succumb to genocide inflation by finding ever more examples of deliberate harms against which we can test our theories, we need to spend considerably more time than Waller has trying to understand exactly what it is we seek to understand.

Waller concludes his book by telling his readers that they ought not to mind being compared to the worst monsters that ever lived. "The lesson does contain potential 'good news,'" he writes reassuringly. "The commission of extraordinary evil is no longer a mystery." Well, it remains one to me. I have read *Becoming Evil,* and I still do not understand why six million Jews were rounded up and sent to gas chambers.

III

PHILOSOPHERS SPEND CONSIDERABLE TIME trying to understand what something is; all the more reason to be grateful that some of them, like

Richard Bernstein and Susan Neiman, are turning to the question of evil. Both of these thinkers have been influenced by the Continental tradition in philosophy, which never ignored large moral and ethical questions to the degree that the analytical tradition did. Their books bring clarity and depth to the subject; I consider both of them essential reading for anyone who wants to start thinking about evil and what it means. Bernstein's *Radical Evil: A Philosophical Investigation,* as its title suggests, originates with Arendt and *The Origins of Totalitarianism.* In a letter to Gershom Scholem, Arendt wrote that despite what she claimed in *Origins,* evil could never be "radical." Bernstein argues that Arendt's comment is "misleading." To understand Arendt's point of view, we need to pay attention to what Arendt called "thought-trains," strands of ideas about a concept–to mix the metaphor–that need to be woven together to make an idea whole. However uncertain Arendt was of Eichmann's motives, according to Bernstein, she was consistent in her view that the concentration camps represented unprecedented evil. The camps, she wrote at one point, stand "outside of life and death," for what they accomplished was not death in the usual, physical, sense of the term, but "the murder of the moral person in man." Others have murdered and committed criminal acts. The Nazis were unique because they used every available aspect of modern technology to eliminate the idea of humanity itself.

This idea of "thought-trains" works for Bernstein because it describes not only Arendt's ideas but also Bernstein's approach to the ideas of any great philosopher. Unlike Arendt, Bernstein is not an original thinker; his books invariably are commentaries on the ideas of others. But what wonderful works of synthesis they can be, and in this book all of Bernstein's abilities as a teacher and clarifier are on display. Bernstein shows how Eichmann himself could cite Kant on duty, and do so with some fidelity to Kant's thought, even while missing the central point of Kant's "thought-train": "insofar as individuals have the capacity of spontaneous choice (*Wilkür*), they are accountable and responsible moral agents." Bernstein's chapter on Hegel muses over the question of whether there is anything to be gained by viewing good and evil as existing in dialectical tension with each other and concludes that not much is. Three other pre-Holocaust thinkers—Schelling, Nietzsche, and Freud—are treated in similar ways; Bernstein tries to extract from each crucial insights that help contemporary thinkers wrestle with the problem of radical evil.

The most interesting chapters in Bernstein's book are the three that deal with Jewish European philosophers who had to face the lessons of the Nazi era: Emmanuel Levinas, Hans Jonas, and Arendt. In many ways, Levinas had the most extreme reaction to the Holocaust. For Christians and Jews, theodicy has traditionally offered relief from the problem of evil; awful things can happen, but the God ultimately responsible for them can nonetheless be good. The true measure of radical evil in our time is that we live, as Levinas put it, at "the end of theodicy." Not only religious but also secular thought can turn inauthentic and dishonest if it succumbs too easily to the temptation to find some goodness in the face of genuine horror.

Does this mean that the only appropriate response is nihilism? Levinas, according to Bernstein, did not believe this to be the case: "The excess of evil, its malignancy that resists integration, solicits a transcendence that shines 'forth in the face of the other man; an alterity of the nonintegratable, of what cannot be assembled into a totality.'" Here Bernstein is less than clear, but that is no doubt because Levinas is as well. An epigrammatic thinker, Levinas never bridged the distance between his critique of the end of theodicy and his message of hope, and Bernstein, finally, cannot help him all that much.

The thought of Hans Jonas ought to receive more attention than it does. Like Levinas, Jonas rejected any theodicy that would too easily "explain away" the evil of the Holocaust. Jews even more than Christians should recognize the challenge to God represented by Auschwitz, for the Jew "sees in 'this' world the locus of divine creation, justice, and redemption." In 1984, Jonas discovered the diary of Etty Hillesum, who had been sent to the Auschwitz gas chamber in 1943. "And if God does not continue to help me," this young Jew wrote, "then I must help God." Jonas found these words overwhelming, for they fit with the preoccupation with responsibility that runs through his philosophical writings. We should not view the Holocaust as God's punishment for our sins, Jonas concluded, for God is not that powerful and we are not that sinful; attributing an evil like the Holocaust to God's displeasure with us conveniently lets us off the hook. "We human beings have inflicted this on the deity. . . . It remains on our account, and it is we who must again wash away the disgrace from our own disfigured faces, indeed from the very countenance of God."

Finding a way to distinguish God's responsibility from that of human beings also preoccupies Susan Neiman, the director of the Einstein Forum in Potsdam, Germany, in her book *Evil in Modern Thought: An Alternative History of Philosophy*. Neiman contrasts two events: the Lisbon earthquake of 1755 and the Nazi Holocaust. Those shaken by the former asked how God could have allowed such suffering. Those stunned by the latter asked how human beings could have done such horrible things to one another. Between these two reactions, Neiman argues, lies nothing less than "an alternative history of philosophy." Although Pierre Bayle wrote before the Lisbon earthquake–his *Dictionary* was published in 1697–Neiman finds his work relevant to her inquiry. She summarizes his argument in the form of three propositions: (1) evil exists; (2) God is benevolent; and (3) God is omnipotent. "Bend and maul them as you will," she writes, "they cannot be held in union. One of them has to go." For Bayle, if you drop the assumption of God's omnipotence, you have practiced heresy, but if you believe him to be omnipotent, you cannot explain why he put evil into the world. Recognizing Augustine as the thinker who provided the most serious effort to reconcile these propositions, Bayle refused to accept the answer that God gave us free will and retained the power to punish us for abusing it; donors as generous as Augustine presumed God to be do not dispense lethal gifts. For Neiman, Bayle embodies the belief that a reality such as evil is exactly what it seems; we are under no obligation to find the goodness that lies behind it because no such goodness exists.

There is a direct line, in her idiosyncratic history of philosophy, from Bayle to Voltaire, Hume, and the Marquis de Sade. For other thinkers of whom Leibniz is paradigmatic, by contrast, we are required to make evil intelligible because there is another reality behind it. Leibniz sought such intelligibility by turning to God: the term *theodicy* was his invention. But from Neiman's perspective, the key question is not whether God makes evil intelligible but whether *anything* does. Thus she views thinkers such as Rousseau, Kant, Hegel, and Marx as sharing the same tradition as Leibniz.

Neiman spends considerable time on Rousseau, endorsing Kant's view that Rousseau did for history and society what Newton did for the physical world. Sharing much of Augustine's views on free will, Rousseau changed only God's role; he "held the Fall, and any possible redemption from it, to be explicable in terms that are completely natural. Rousseau replaced theology with history, grace with educational psychology." For Rousseau, the Lisbon earthquake was a purely natural event that carried with it no implication of punishment for human sins. Rousseau, for Neiman, creates the modern approach to evil. On the one hand, he believes, with Leibniz, that one can make the inexplicable intelligible. On the other hand, however, it is not God who brings that intelligence to us but we who, by understanding history and sociology, fashion it for ourselves.

If Lisbon concentrated the modern mind on moral evil, Auschwitz raised the question of whether there was any morality at all. Its effect was so devastating because it undermined what could be called the post-Lisbon consensus. No longer could we agree that man-made evil differed from natural evil because the former, unlike the latter, contained an element of intentionality. Nazi leaders like Eichmann lacked any intentionality; this was Arendt's great insight. Another German, Hans Blumenberg, wrote that modernity began with theodicy. Does it end, Neiman asks (echoing Levinas), with "the realization that all such acts are forlorn?" She does not answer the question, as indeed Levinas did not either. But she does develop a readable and thought-provoking account of how that question came to be in our thoughts.

Neiman can reach too far in her interpretations; to say that "evil plays a major role" in the work of John Rawls is, at some level, true, but it also overlooks everything that is distinctive in Rawls in order to fit him into her story. Her categories also seem on occasion forced; Marx is lumped together with Leibniz because socialism would make the evil of capitalism intelligible, and thus would presumably count as a theodicy, yet it surely matters whether the agent of intelligibility is supernatural, natural, or artificial. At the same time, however, Neiman's audacity and occasionally morbid wit are a welcome addition to contemporary philosophy. If there is any hope after Auschwitz, we may find it in the fact that human minds will not stop trying to make some kind of meaning out of it.

IV

ALTHOUGH MANY OF THE THINKERS who tried to make sense out of the Holocaust were Jewish, they were influenced by Christian theology; Hans Jonas was a student of Rudolf Bultmann, and Hannah Arendt, as Charles T. Mathewes reminds us in *Evil and the Augustinian Tradition,* always worked in the shadow of Augustine. Mathewes's book features Arendt, along with Reinhold Niebuhr, as representing alternatives to what Mathewes calls "subjectivism," which he defines as "the belief that our existence in the world is determined first and foremost by our own (subjective) activities."

Niebuhr is often assumed to be a conservative, but, as Mathewes points out, this cannot be easily reconciled with his political activism, most of which was concentrated on left-wing causes. Moreover, because American conservatism is so tied to a Smithian love of the marketplace, it has never—with the exception of now somewhat forgotten figures such Whittaker Chambers or the Southern Agrarians—been able to develop the ironic, and often pessimistic, stance toward modernity than any good conservative mood should reflect. In Augustine's theology Niebuhr found an alternative to the prevailing American optimism of his day. Niebuhr's voice was tragic. Evil, the realist in him recognized, is "a fixed datum of historical science"; Niebuhr had little taste for the kind of naïveté that has often characterized religious leaders' involvement in politics. At the same time, our sins are not of such a depraved nature that any hope has to be ruled out of order. We can take responsibility for our acts, and Mathewes is especially good at describing this Niebuhrian sense of responsibility. "We have no intellectual resources for 'handling' evil," he writes, "if 'handling' it means *managing* it." Our thought is always torn open at its side, as it were, and bleeds from the knowledge that we sinners, we evildoers, are at fault and are yet the vehicles whereby God's salvation is made manifest.

Mathewes clearly prefers the way Niebuhr formulates the prospect for hope in the face of evil to Arendt's discussion of the same issue. Searching for an alternative to the totalitarianism of the twentieth century, Arendt did develop a rather romantic attraction to the Greek polis. Mathewes interprets this attraction as a preference for "a sort of 'heroic' agonal politics" and criticizes Arendt for idealizing "the anarchy of permanent revolution." Such a prospect, he writes, "cannot make sense of hope." But when he adds that Arendt's alternative is "equally banal" to the totalitarianism she so eloquently criticized, Mathewes inadvertently shows how easy it is for a scholar absorbed in texts to lose touch with reality. Such a comment treats the Holocaust as if were an intellectual game and not a real event with devastating consequences. Mathewes concludes that Arendt's treatment of these issues "is not very helpful for us in dealing with the evil we find around us, and *in* us, every day." He thus comes full circle back to where we began with James Waller, unable to recognize that some forms of evil are, so to speak, more evil than others.

This treatment of Arendt illustrates the most frustrating feature of Mathewes's otherwise illuminating book. Convinced that subjectivism is the problem, Mathewes finds it everywhere, even in thinkers like Niebuhr and Arendt whom he otherwise admires. His alternative is to return to Augustine, who "urges us to participate ever more fully in the world, and to understand that participation Christologically." Yet Niebuhr and Arendt witnessed unprecedented horrors on a scale made possible by modern technology. If their response is to conclude that real human beings like the Nazis were responsible for that evil, the resulting "subjectivism" seems justifiable compared to a historicism that would make no distinction between that evil and all the other forms that wickedness has taken over the centuries. Niebuhr and Arendt are interesting thinkers because they both know Augustine well *and* are aware of the need to account for specifically modern events. Their flirtation with "subjectivism" is to be admired, not criticized.

Mathewes's book, which originated as a doctoral dissertation, is, like Neiman's, ambitious and audacious. And like Neiman's, it demonstrates a bit too much razzle-dazzle, as it hops around from one thinker to another, engages in outrageous name-dropping, and leaves too many thoughts unfinished. *Evil and the Augustinian Tradition* can be taken as a sign that academic theology is returning to grand themes, including the existence of evil. And it can also be read as a note of caution, urging a bit more intellectual modesty than can be found in its pages.

V

THREE HUNDRED YEARS PASSED between Lisbon and Auschwitz, and if there is once again going to occur a historical event that will force thinkers to confront the reality of evil, one hopes that it will be at least another three hundred years before it takes place. (September 11, at least so far, does not qualify; while it was carried out by decidedly evil people, and while the number of lives lost was tragically high, this was an event that resonated with religious wars of the past rather than one that marked a hideous "breakthrough," some new way to wipe out an entire population.) Long after Arendt made her erroneous prediction about the effects of Auschwitz, the Holocaust has begun to stimulate brilliant thinking about evil, but one would trade all those thoughts for the lives that were so ruthlessly taken.

Still, that trade is not one we can make. We live with evil because evil has chosen to live with us. The best we can do is to be as ambitious as we can in trying to tackle one of the great mysteries surrounding us, without becoming so ambitious that we bring evil down to the level of ordinary existence. As Richard Bernstein concludes in an especially reflective summary of what we know and what we do not, evil is "an excess that resists total comprehension." Yet, he continues, "interrogating evil is an ongoing, open-ended process" which requires, not only a reaffirmation of the importance of personal responsibility, but a commitment to rethinking what responsibility means. Whether we are followers of Augustine or Kant, we are individuals with free will. Faced with the Holocaust, some people chose to do the right thing–even while far more chose evil.

The Hermeneutic Hole

I

W ORDS MUST MEAN SOMETHING. Words cannot mean any one thing. Those two propositions, clearly at odds with each other, yet in some sense true, place great difficulties upon our attempts to understand the world, especially when the world that we seek to understand is different from our own. If words cannot mean something concrete, and denote a reality that is taken by all in roughly the same way, then we cannot begin to act, let alone to possess such treasures as language, history, culture, science, or morality. But if words always mean exactly what their speaker intends them to mean, and always convey precisely that same meaning to all who hear them, then our actions will lack complexity, ambiguity, and richness.

Lest anyone doubt the transparency but also the treachery of language, consider the fateful words uttered by Gameel el-Batouty on October 31, 1999. "Tawakilt ala Allah!" el-Batouty exclaimed, as the Egypt Air flight on which he was a copilot began its descent into the sea: "I entrust myself to God!" If the words are taken literally, there can be little doubt that the person who uttered them deliberately crashed the plane. Confidence in the interpretation of the words provides closure for the inscrutability of the act. We can never know why a man with a wife and two children would take his own life, and also the lives of two hundred and sixteen people. Still, if we can at least establish through his words that his intent was to crash the plane, then we will have removed from our fearful consciousness one more of the world's terrors.

But do el-Batouty's words mean what they appear to mean? Just about every anthropologist in America would say that they do not. For one thing, the words were uttered in Arabic, and unless one is fluent in that language, one has to rely on the meaning of other words, translators' words, and it does not take an anthropologist to know that something is always lost in translation. Even if the translation problems are put aside, the meaning of words often lies in the context in which they were said. Not only does context establish whether irony or humor were intended—and when they are intended, words mean exactly the opposite of what they appear to mean—but some words have no meaning unless context is taken into account. To modify an example used by the sociologist Harold Garfinkel, if I were to say "pick me up at five," you could not know whether I wanted to be lifted off the ground or be taken out on a date, let alone whether I had in mind early morning or late afternoon, unless you knew the surrounding sentences of my utterance.

Once knowledge of el-Batouty's words became public, a veritable seminar in cultural anthropology became inevitable. The prayer was an everyday expression, we were told, a little like an American saying "Jesus Christ" when startled. Just because a person invokes Christ's name under such circumstances does not mean that he is a Christian, or a religious believer. In a similar way, el-Batouty might have uttered those words upon realizing that the plane was out of control and he could do little to stop it. You cannot understand what el-Batouty said, many commentators added, unless you understand the culture of which he is a part. His words may look like those of a person intent on suicide, but "there is such a taboo on suicide in Islam, it is completely prohibited in Islam, that we find it inconceivable that somebody would invoke the name of God and then commit some act that is totally opposed to the faith," Ibrahim Hooper of the Council on American-Islamic Relations told ABC News, evidently hoping to persuade us that those Islamic militants who take their lives as the price of taking others are not really Islamic. For those attracted to this way of thinking, the fact that the U.S. National Transportation Safety Board concluded that "human action" might have caused the plane's crash was taken as further proof of "Orientalism," of Western efforts to define the reality of non-Western people for them. In any event, the news was filled with "man in the street" interviews from Cairo denouncing America for its presumption, as if it were a crime against humanity to insist that we can ascertain responsibility from the understanding of language.

The economic, political, diplomatic, and emotional stakes involved in the meaning of el-Batouty's words are enormous. Lawsuits involving fantastic sums of money will hinge on whether it can be established that he deliberately crashed the plane. Lives lost can never be returned, but relatives and friends of the victims can hardly be blamed for wanting some explanation of why their loved ones are gone. Already the United States finds itself caught between those American officials who want to treat this case as a crime and those State Department officers who remind us of the importance of Egypt as a strategic ally. Yet the whole tormented matter may be moot. Despite all the reasons why we may want to ascertain the meaning of el-Batouty's words, we may never be able to do so. Unless further evidence comes forward, we will have to live with the ambiguity and the opacity of language, with the frustration of desperately needing words to possess meaning yet being utterly powerless to get them to mean anything definitive.

II

VINCENT CRAPANZANO's *Serving the Word: Literalism in America from the Pulpit to the Bench* was written before the crash of Egypt Air 990. Unlike many works by anthropologists, it deals with Americans, not with exotic others living far from our shores. Understanding one of its two subjects–fundamentalist religious believers–required something like fieldwork, as anthropologists understand the term; but understanding its other subject–judges and legal theorists who believe that the meaning of law is determined by the intent of those who wrote it– required no fieldwork at all. Despite these deviations from the anthropological script, Crapanzano's book is prescient, for it takes as its central theme the question of what words can, and cannot, do. But it is a flawed and frustrating book, one that quickly leaves behind the objective of understanding people who believe in the literal truth of words in favor of criticizing them for their presumed epistemological naïveté.

Crapanzano begins with a rather startling claim. "Literalism in the United States," he writes, "is far more widespread than most realize or are even prepared to accept." We know that there are a large number of Christians who assert that the Bible means exactly what it says, and we know that one can find judges who try to resolve today's disputes by seeking answers in the intentions of the Constitutional writers of the eighteenth century. But there are also psychologists who instruct us to take as gospel truth the recollections of presumed victims of sexual abuse, even when their recollections were long delayed and emerged only after seemingly suggestive questioning. And there are those who believe that the truth of what it means to be black or female or gay can only be known to those who are black or female or gay. We can even include among the literalists those who are certain that our behavior is determined by our genes, as if DNA were also a pellucid language whose original meaning can never be questioned.

If Crapanzano is correct, and I believe he is, then literalism cannot be associated with any particular ideology, even though conservatives would seem to have more at stake in relying on the authority of original documents than liberals or radicals. Had Crapanzano followed up his own original intent, he might have explained why so many different kinds of people, holding so many different kinds of beliefs, are nonetheless persuaded that words can really mean what they seem to say. But, for reasons that he never adequately explains, he chose not to write that kind of book.

Instead, with the exception of a few pages in his conclusion, he focuses only on Christians and conservatives, all the while making clear his own leftist sensibilities. I cannot imagine a more damaging decision. Without the inclusion of literalists who share Crapanzano's own politics, every element of surprise—the anthropologist's "aha!" at discovering something not known—is taken out of this book, and it comes to feel rigged. Crapanzano tells us that his intent was to write a "critical ethnography." There is no doubt that his book is critical. It is certainly not an ethnography, at least not a responsible one.

When he deals with fundamentalists, Crapanzano's methods do not include an attempt to reproduce their way of life for readers who know little of the rituals and the practices of these unfamiliar people. It is the words that fundamentalists speak that engage him, not the behavior in which they engage. Crapanzano divides his chapters around theological concerns, not matters of religious practice. He reproduces long declarations made to him by fundamentalist religious believers, mostly from southern California, as well as significant passages from their writings. He will frequently interrupt a monologue to challenge a point and will then report on the response—if there is one. His method is designed to get these people to express their theory of interpretation so that Crapanzano can counterpose his own.

As it turns out, many of Crapanzano's subjects are as wordy and as argumentative as he is. Offered a platform, they leap onto it without hesitation. One of the points upon which they insist, not surprisingly, is the unquestioned authority of the Bible. "The best teacher," said Martin Luther (as quoted by Bernard Ramm, a fundamentalist author cited by Crapanzano), "is the one who does not bring his meaning into Scripture but gets his meaning from the Scripture." For Crapanzano, this is an absurd argument, for there is no one Scripture to which we can turn to seek meaning. Should we look at the King James Version? School ourselves in Greek, Hebrew, and Aramaic? Search for the long-lost original manuscripts? And even if we could find the one true original source, we could not escape from the hermeneutic circle. For if we ground the truth of Scripture in the words of Scripture, then what is the grounding for those latter words? Try as they might, Crapanzano concludes, fundamentalists cannot avoid prejudiced accounts of the word of God, because all accounts of God's word are prejudiced.

Since the Bible's words are literally true, fundamentalists believe, our only hope for salvation lies in judging our everyday actions against its Commandments. Crapanzano correctly points out that fundamentalist Protestants in America are not, in Max Weber's terms, otherworldly. They work, they make careers, they consume, and they take vacations like everyone else in our society. What makes them different is that, when faced with problems of adjustment or unhappiness, they do not turn to friends and relatives, nor to psychologists, for assistance. They turn to God's Word.

"Fundamentalists," Crapanzano writes, "tend to read Scripture as though it were an instruction manual, verse by verse, passage by passage, story by story, always in a very narrow manner, with little regard for context." All of us can be guided by texts; we read great literature, and great theorists such as Freud, not only for aesthetic pleasure, but also to change the way we act in the world. But such readings are metaphorical: *Anna Karenina* is not a marriage manual, it is a tour of the heart. Distrustful of metaphor, fundamentalists read texts differently from the rest of us. They trust the Word more than they do experience; for some of them, writes Crapanzano, the Word "changes the way they experience and even perceive the world." This strategy of reading accounts for their confidence and their sense of fellowship; but Crapanzano adds that it is also a thin theory of reading, one that prevents its practitioners from experiencing the depth and the nuance offered by great works of the human imagination.

Fundamentalists, finally, have a theory of history, and it too, Crapanzano argues, is epistemologically flawed. In particular, there are two aspects of their philosophy of history that other approaches generally lack: an end and a beginning. They read the Bible as prophetic, as prefiguring when we can expect history to end. And they also know, as evolutionary biologists do not, exactly when history began. Neither encourages an open-ended sense of history. For fundamentalists, history is rather like a giant jigsaw puzzle; one reads a Biblical prophecy, looks for an event that seems to confirm it, and then goes back and reinterprets the prophecy. Everything stays within the text. When Crapanzano asked some of his respondents about history outside the Bible, he realized that for them there was no history outside the Bible. Modernity, writes Crapanzano, citing the German philosopher Reinhart Koselleck, is associated with the notion that history can be periodized. By that criterion, fundamentalists are premodern because, for them, history does not take place in chronological time.

The fatal flaw of modern anthropology has been its inability to achieve distance from those it studies. After one goes through all the trouble of picking a people about whom we know little, learning their often unwritten language, spending a year or two in their company, and finding out more about their society than one knows of one's own, it is easy to go native and write an apology for one's subject. Crapanzano has the opposite flaw. He provides no full account of his research methods: we do not know how long he spent among fundamentalists, how he identified his subjects, what steps he took to ensure their representativeness, or any other details of what usually goes into an ethnography.

It is nonetheless clear that he went into the field to fight, not to understand. Crapanzano finds his subjects to be intellectual lightweights. They were "open, cooperative, and even interested in my research," but he is not especially interested in them. At various times he mentions their "arrogant self-certainty," "decentered egocentricity," "ventriloqual assumption of authority," and "militancy for arguments for the sake of argument." Although he never tells us much about their lives, except that they are not otherworldly, Crapanzano insists that "their lives appeared emotionally flattened, seamlessly removed from all worldly complexities, so politely God-filled that they seemed to disappear." Also, they were sexist: "Fundamentalism is very much a male discourse." Fundamentalists exist in his book as foils for Crapanzano's own sense of superiority. Look at these yokels outside of Manhattan: not only do they drink weak coffee, they don't even recognize the contradictions of their hermeneutic stance.

Something is seriously wrong with social science when the anthropologist feels the need to deploy every item of postmodern artillery in his arsenal to fire at people who are doing little more than believing in God as they see fit. Myself, I have no love of fundamentalists; my own

taste in Christians runs toward Catholics (who remain, for Crapanzano's subjects, too easily seduced by metaphor). But why beat up on
them so? We should try to understand them or we should leave them
alone. Crapanzano does neither. "Theirs is an assertive discourse: one
does not debate them," he writes. The same can be said for postmodern
anthropology, at least as Crapanzano practices it. Never engaging his
subjects, never rendering their humanity to us, never putting them into
any meaningful context, he stands there asserting counterclaims to
their claims, no doubt appearing as foolish to them as they appear to
him.

III

ONCE THE READER KNOWS what Crapanzano has to say about fundamentalists, it is pretty clear what he is going to say about Robert Bork,
Antonin Scalia, and other believers in the jurisprudence of original
intent. There are differences, of course, between biblical literalists and
legal literalists. The Bible, according to fundamentalists, does not allow
for amendment, while the Constitution does. And constitutional faith,
however much it may look like religion, is not really religion, since its
founding text was written by people, by relatively modern people, not
by God.

And yet, according to Crapanzano, the theory of original intent suffers from the same epistemological flaws as the theory of biblical
inerrancy. A constitution cannot authorize itself as the final authority.
Those who write words at one point in time cannot police their meaning at a later point in time. Are we to be guided by the actual words of
those who wrote the Constitution or by what they intended their words
to mean? Since the jurisprudence of original intent fails to pass the tests
of interpretation established by Roland Barthes, Crapanzano assumes
that those who insist upon its validity are unworthy of serious intellectual engagement.

Even more than with fundamentalists, Crapanzano lets polemics
fly against the constitutional originalists. Bork, though he is called an

intellectual, is "in fact an anti-intellectual–an ideologue." He is also described as "a promiscuous originalist," and while Crapanzano would not apply that term to Scalia, he does remark upon the latter's "inordinate intensity" and his "epistemological naivete." Some of Bork's former colleagues gently told Crapanzano that the books that he wrote in the aftermath of his failed nomination to the Supreme Court were the works of a wounded man and ought best be ignored, but Crapanzano insists that "they must be taken into account" without ever telling us why. He wonders if Scalia, who took a position in a child abuse case with which Crapanzano disagrees, can even understand the trauma associated with child abuse. (Presumably we should take the child's testimony on this matter as the literal truth.) It is Crapanzano's scorched-earth method all over again.

Crapanzano's criticism of originalism is even more heavy-handed than his criticism of fundamentalism. Consider the case of Scalia's Tanner Lectures, delivered at Princeton in 1995 and later published as *A Matter of Interpretation*. Scalia took up *Church of Holy Trinity v. United States* (1892). In that case, the Supreme Court considered a statute outlawing any attempt "to assist or encourage the immigration of any alien" into the United States by offering that person a job before he came here. The Church of the Holy Trinity in New York City had hired an Englishman to become its rector. The Court ruled that the original law clearly never meant to exclude such a deserving person. Scalia took the view that this was a terrible decision. The statute may have been poorly written and ill-thought-out, but "the decision was wrong because it failed to follow the text. The text is the law, and it is the text that must be followed." Criticizing Scalia's literalism in this case is easy stuff, especially for anyone trained in literary theory. Yet it also misses the point. In his lecture, Scalia was very careful to make a distinction between words in general and legal words in particular. "Men may intend what they will," he said, "but it is only the laws they enact which bind us." When words are meant to regulate our conduct, to distinguish between what is permissible and what must be punished, we have to take special care with them. On this, Scalia insisted. It is not an especially controversial view; many liberals would agree with it. Scalia cited Oliver Wendell Holmes saying much the same thing, and in his response to Scalia's lecture Laurence Tribe, Scalia's ideological foil, indicates his complete agreement with the judge on this point.

If legal texts are special kinds of texts, we have to assume that their authors meant what they said by them; for if we do not, then there is no need for legislatures at all. In his discussion of *Holy Trinity*, Scalia pointed out the number of times that this case was cited by lawyers asking for judicial intervention. For him, this decision opened the door to what has been called "the imperial judiciary," the effort by courts to substitute their judgment for the judgments of those actually elected by the people to make laws for them. Agree or disagree with him, Scalia's statement that the law is a particular kind of text that must be followed was made in its own context, a context that Crapanzano–presumably the antiliteralist on this matter–ignores.

Since legal words are special kinds of words, moreover, we can agree to the fiction that, for purposes of governing us, they have an unvarying meaning, even if we know that they cannot have an unvarying meaning. We bracket our doubts about them because the alternative is chaos. Anyone who dwells on the indeterminacy of legal words, therefore, has a duty to say something about how this bracketing ought to occur. This matter comes up twice in Crapanzano's book, and twice he ducks the issue. Instead he simply offers reassurances that arguments such as his own are not "skeptical to the point of nihilism," when, without any effort to show that the meaning of words is as necessary as they are dubious, his arguments seem to be exactly that.

Crapanzano wants it both ways. He attacks literalism with full-bodied postmodern vigor, only to insist that he really is not a postmodernist. The result is something like this: "I do not mean to say that we are living in the extreme world that many postmodernists describe. Rather, we are living in a world in which the challenge of whatever the postmodernists mean by 'postmodernism' produces a frequently reactionary response–one that idealizes the past, fetishizes the original, and indulges in nostalgia for that which was never experienced and probably never existed." If this is not postmodernism, it is certainly anti-anti-postmodernism. Which is to say, literalism may have its problems, but so does antiliteralism. Once one is liberated from the task of fixing the meaning of words, one is free to write anything one wants. This is precisely the sort of looseness about language that turns people like Scalia into originalists.

"One prerequisite for democracy," Crapanzano writes in his conclusion, "is an openness to the position of the other." If so, then Crapanzano is no democrat. He ends his book with a reflection on the reaction of his students to his account of a recent visit to Germany. The dutiful professor tells them that in Europe, people have high wages, take long vacations, have generous unemployment insurance and good medical care benefits. (He does not tell them about Germany's extremely high unemployment rate, nor does he point out that young people who have not been in the labor market do not get the generous unemployment insurance.) Students in the class, if they are interested at all, respond by blaming themselves for the conditions of their lives, even though Crapanzano was using the example to stress the role that political and economic structures play in determining our life chances. And so, instead of listening to the insistence of his students that personal responsibility is a virtue worth appreciating, he finds himself terrified by what he calls their "passivism." They were not religious like the fundamentalists that he studied, but, like them, "there was something lonely and grim about their vision of the world."

Vincent Crapanzano's self-righteous sense of his own superiority—and his conviction that others exist only to be criticized or pitied—makes one long for the naive, didactic, sloppy, and inaccurate anthropology of Margaret Mead. One reads anthropology, after all, to be reminded of the possibility of wonder that exists in the human world. Indeed, humanism is written into anthropology's very name. But this book, far grimmer than anything said by its author's subjects, closes its readers off from experience in ways that are eerily similar to the literalists with whom it is so self-righteously concerned.

White Magic in America

I

As JOSEPH SMITH RELATED the story fifteen years later, he had been saying his evening prayers on September 21, 1823, when a flash of light revealed the presence of God's messenger. Smith was informed that in the fields around his house in Palmyra, New York, he would find a book, written in gold plates, which would tell of the struggle on the American continent between the prophet Nephi, who had left Jerusalem for America in 600 B.C., and his brothers Laman and Lemuel, who, for their sinful behavior, had been cursed by God with red skin. For four consecutive years, Smith visited the spot where he found the plates, until he was permitted to take them home. Later Smith would translate the Book of Mormon to a small group of followers—six followers, to be precise, who, on April 6, 1830, established what they called The Church of Christ.

New religions of consequence are founded once every thousand years or so. Smith's would become, in this century, one of the fastest-growing and most economically dynamic religions in America. Still, Mormonism has always been the odd man out in America's Christian universe. "Smith's theology promised a radical departure from traditional Protestant Christianity," writes John L. Brooke in *The Refiner's Fire*, his superb study of Mormon cosmology. For one thing, the new religion offered a reinterpretation of the story of Creation. It was not that God came into being and then created man. Quite the contrary. "Man was also in the beginning with God," as The Doctrine and Covenant of the Church of Jesus Christ of Latter-day Saints puts it, and

88

so man can aspire to divine status once again. Entry into the celestial kingdom was one of the most important promises that Smith offered his followers.

Heaven and hell were also revised by the new church. In fact, there was to be no hell at all—only three levels of heaven, depending on one's saintliness. The celestial realm was reserved for the Mormon priesthood, the followers of Adam the firstborn, who were worthy of divine exaltation. Below them in the terrestrial kingdom were those devout non-Mormons whose faith was sincere but who, as gentiles, could never experience the "fulness" of the Father. The lowest level, the telestial, was reserved for everyone else, even including, in Smith's words, "liars, and sorcerers, and adulterers, and whoremongers." But this level, too, remained a heavenly one. Indeed, as Brooke points out, with the exception of a few "sons of perdition," "all mankind would find a place in one of the Mormon heavens." This was a cosmology of universal salvation. No one, from a Mormon perspective, need ever face the prospect of eternal damnation.

To put it mildly, Mormonism challenged traditional Christian notions of original sin. If latter-day descendants of Adam can aspire to divinity, then perhaps Adam never sinned at all. His decision to eat from the Tree of Knowledge, Mormons believe, was made voluntarily, just as those of the true Mormon faith come to their beliefs through the exercise of their own free will. God forgives Adam, who is eventually baptized and becomes His son. In 1852, Brigham Young would proclaim that Adam himself was a God. Atonement is not as important in the Mormon faith as forgiveness.

Gone were gloomy doctrines of predestination. And gone was the stern Protestantism that judged man as so constantly falling short of perfection that only through God's dispensation could he hope for even a glimmer of forgiveness. And gone was the Catholic conception of saintliness as an otherworldly quality reserved only for the very special few. In Mormonism, observes Brooke, "exaltation to godhead in the celestial kingdom would be fundamentally based on merit, rooted in a firm advocacy of moral free will." The Mormon God was, as we now say, nonjudgmental. You need not have been of high status to become one with God. Nor was it important that you led a life free of wrongdoing. It was enough that you chose, with powers under your own control, to obey Mormon law. Taken to its logical conclusion, Mormonism finds the source of divinity not in God at all, but within human beings themselves.

II

STEPHEN R. COVEY TAUGHT business management and organizational behavior for twenty years at Brigham Young University before becoming the most revered management guru in America. His book, *The Seven Habits of Highly Effective People,* which appeared in 1989, has sold over ten million copies, and it has been translated into twenty-eight languages. His subsequent books—*Principle-Centered Leadership* (1991) and *First Things First* (1994), written with A. Roger Merrill and Rebecca R. Merrill—never enjoyed such astronomical sales, but they did appear regularly on lists of business best-sellers. Along with the inspirationalists Tony Robbins and Marianne Williamson, Covey met with President Clinton over Thanksgiving in 1994, after which Clinton informed a conference on work that productivity in America would increase dramatically if people would read Stephen Covey. In *The Witch Doctors,* a study of management gurus, John Micklethwait and Adrian Wooldridge attribute the success of Covey's books partly to the fact that they "actually have some relevance to mainstream management theory."

Covey resigned his teaching job at Brigham Young in 1985 to found the Covey Leadership Center, later called the Franklin Covey Company, in Salt Lake City, Utah. His firm, which offers "effectiveness advice," includes among its clients 82 of the Fortune 100 and more than two-thirds of the Fortune 500, as well as thousands of smaller companies. Its seminars have proven wildly attractive to organizations of many purposes. Covey works particularly well with school districts, Indian tribes, and prisons.

You do not have to travel to Utah to engage the services of the Franklin Covey Company. The company organizes "Seven Habits" workshops in over 300 cities in North America and 40 countries worldwide. For $15,000, it will provide one of its senior staff as a speaker for corporate events. Its audio- and videotapes are widely available. Covey's "Seven Habits" organizers, which have proved popular as daily planners, are available in handheld and software formats. All the company's books and magazines can be purchased through its Web page, as can such accessories as "Seven Habits" page-finders. Rarely if ever in the history of publishing has one book spawned so many profitable by-products.

Covey's books are catechisms. They are devoted to elaborating "principles," which he defines in *Seven Habits* as "natural laws that are woven into the fabric of every civilized society throughout history and comprise the roots of every family and institution that has endured and prospered." These natural laws are "just as real, just as unchanging and unarguably there as laws such as gravity." They are, for Covey, self-evidently true. They can be transformed into habits so that we obey them automatically. And they are spiritually fungible, empowering us to act effectively whatever the situation we face. Through his books, seminars, and workshops, Covey does not tell us what to do; he tells us instead how to reach inside ourselves, find the right universal principle, and apply it, even when tempted to do otherwise by self-interest, the desire to be popular, or shortsightedness.

Seven such principles exist in the world, no more and no less. They are: (1) be proactive; (2) begin with the end in mind; (3) put first things first; (4) think "win-win"; (5) seek first to understand, then to be understood; (6) synergize; (7) sharpen the saw, by which Covey means engage in frequent self-renewal. Highly effective people begin within their immediate "circle of concern," those aspects of their lives in which they have significant emotional investments. As they learn to be "proactive," people win little victories in their private lives, and these victories gradually expand their circle of concern. As individuals master the first three habits, they lose dependency and gain independence,

becoming responsible for the decisions that they make. But autonomy
is only half the way to true effectiveness. We must also learn to transform our private victories into public ones, which we can only do by
moving beyond the first three habits to the next three. Interdependence,
not independence, must be our objective. Through synergy and win-
win approaches, we avoid gloating and ego-tripping. We take pride in
what our organizations do for all their members, not just in our personal achievements. And finally we realize that the process of applying
these universal habits to our lives never stops, for the seventh habit
calls upon us to commit and recommit ourselves to increasingly higher
planes of effectiveness.

To move people along toward interdependence, Covey advises the
importance of mission statements and time management. Every individual should have his own mission statement, focusing on what he
wants to be and do. All successful organizations require mission statements, too. These should not be the products of top-down decision
making. Everyone in the organization has to be involved. Covey's company provides examples of successful mission statements; and it offers
a worksheet, compatible with Microsoft Schedule+, to help people and
organizations develop their own.

Mission statements are for long-term organizing; they are designed
to help people and firms realize their goals (Habit 2). Yet it is also
important that people learn how best to use their time in the short run.
Many of us allow urgent activities such as deadlines and interruptions
to determine our priorities for us. We need to become Quadrant II people, capable of distinguishing tasks that are important but not urgent
from those that are urgent but unimportant, and those that are neither
urgent nor important. This is what Covey means by putting first things
first (Habit 3), and it can be facilitated with the help of the weekly planners available from the Covey organization. These planners are not just
for remembering appointments. They also enable highly effective people to list their weekly priorities for each week of the year. Then we can
see how much time we actually spend doing those tasks that contribute
to furthering our mission statements. Should we remain in need of

guidance, Covey (along with A. Roger Merrill and Rebecca R. Merrill) recently issued *First Things First: Every Day,* a pocket-size book of "daily reflections." This is the edification for June 6: "Quadrant II does not act on us; we must act on it. This is the Quadrant of personal leadership." "Can you begin to see the difference," Covey asks, "between organizing your week as a principle-centered Quadrant II manager and planning your days as an individual centered on something else? Can you begin to sense the tremendous difference the Quadrant II focus would make in your current level of effectiveness?"

Now there is a new book, *The Seven Habits of Highly Effective Families.* "Applying the Seven Habits material to the family is an absolute natural," Covey writes. "It fits. In fact, it's where it was really learned." Obviously, principles deemed to be universal must be applicable to all realms of life; if they work in prisons and personnel, they must also work on parents and partners. As his wife informs readers in her foreword to the new book, Covey has fathered nine children—an accomplishment that surely requires effective time management. There are far more families in America than there are firms, though not very many of them are as large as Covey's. For that reason alone, there is a certain inevitability to the appearance of Covey's new book. Here truly is the prospect of universality. Just about everyone has been raised in a family, and just about everyone can find a fault or two with the family that raised them. The family is as common across cultures as it is central to our own discontents. It is certainly at the center of some of our most difficult political debates.

Covey advises family members to internalize proactivity (Habit 1) by developing an Emotional Bank Account. When you speak disrespectfully, or break a promise, or criticize someone, or refuse to apologize, or act insincerely, you make withdrawals from your account; and if you do this persistently enough, you will eventually have nothing left. To make deposits, you have to win the trust of those with whom you share your family. There are many ways to do this: by listening to what you say, by keeping your promises, by apologizing when you said or did the wrong thing. But one thing builds up the account more rapidly than anything else: "to get out of a judging mind-set, to stop trying to manipulate or give love conditionally." When you give up trying to control everyone around you, you learn that "one of the most empowering and exciting aspects of the Emotional Bank Account idea is that we can proactively choose to turn every family problem into an opportunity for a deposit."

Beginning with the end in mind (Habit 2) requires, as the reader has come to expect, a family mission statement. "Just as the United States Constitution has survived for more than two hundred sometimes turbulent years, your family constitution can be the foundational document that will unify and hold your family together for decades–even generations–to come." The mission statement for the Covey family took eight months to develop, and now, we are told, it applies across four generations. Simply writing the statement, Covey maintains, can be a bonding experience. He cites the story of a man who, in his own words, "was deep into the Seven Habits material and thought it would be great if we could write an extended family mission statement." So he asked his entire extended family to come together during vacation time, irrespective of whether they lived in Virginia, Ohio, or Utah. Each was asked to come with a prepared draft. "We made copies of everyone's mission statement drafts and distributed them," this man's testimony continues. "As each person read his or her draft, we marked our favorite lines." Eventually a family motto emerged from the exercise, which was printed on T-shirts for all members of the family to wear. The benefits were real and immediate. When the motel selected for the vacation turned out to be a disaster, everyone communicated openly, and crisis was avoided. Members of the far-flung family decided to move closer to Mom and Dad. They even decided to run a business together. Writing a mission statement has "begun a new era in our family," the man concludes.

"Outside of making and honoring the basic marriage covenant," Covey writes in his chapter on putting first things first (Habit 3), "I have come to feel that probably no single structure will help you prioritize your family more than a specific time set aside every week just for the family. You could call it 'family time.'" Such spots of time are great opportunities for teaching the Seven Habits, since "family time is a wonderful time for problem solving." Out of the family hour, in fact, can grow a weekly schedule for everyone in the family, so that everyone will know his or her proper roles and goals. (In addition to family calendars, customers/disciples can purchase roles and goals worksheets from Franklin Covey; and teenagers can look forward to the publication of *The Seven Habits of Highly Effective Teens,* written by Covey's son.) But no one should get the idea that Habit 3 is all work. "One of the most important ingredients of any family time is fun. This is what unites and bonds family members. This is what creates joy and pleasure in being together."

"All people are very, very tender and sensitive," Covey writes in a discussion of win-win (Habit 4) and seeking first to understand (Habit 5). "Is empathy always appropriate?" he asks. "The answer is 'yes.' Without exception, empathy is always appropriate." Family pain, as we know from Deborah Tannen and John Gray, is usually the product of miscommunication. Such pain can be avoided by following principles of empathic listening. If we evaluate, advise, probe, or interpret, we generally do so from our own point of view. Instead we should reflect back on what others tell us, mirroring, summarizing, and reflecting their words so that they know we are really listening. In a win-lose situation, such as a basketball game, one plus one equals less than one. In a compromise situation, where each party gives a bit to accommodate the ego of the other, one plus one equals one and a half. A genuine transaction between two people creates a situation in which one plus one equals two. But those who practice the Seven Habits attain a situation of synergy (Habit 6), in which one plus one equals at least three. Once a family gets to that point, its traditions and daily practices will continually sharpen the saw (Habit 7). This will be a highly effective family.

III

UNABLE TO MAKE MUCH GROW in the hostile soil of Vermont, Joseph Smith's family moved west to New York State in search of better farmland. There the soil was still flinty; but if it could not produce abundant crops, it did produce something else: Indian relics. Smith and many of his contemporaries became avid money-diggers, constantly turning up the ground in search of rare stones and an occasional gold coin. Around such activities there developed a cult of magic, as if the uncovered stones, when read in the context of animal sacrifice and ritualistic incantation, could tell people whose fates were so harsh what they could expect in life. Smith's biographer Fawn M. Brodie is clearly hostile to her subject (and relies on a generally discredited psychoanalytic framework), but she is right to argue that the origins of Mormonism can be found in Smith's hatred of soil-grubbing. His "discovery" of the *Book of Mormon* gave him the opportunity to elevate folk magic into a religion—and, in the age of a new awakening, into power, too.

The area of New York State whose religious fervor gave it the name "The Burned-over District" was also obsessed with counterfeiting. Money was in great demand in a cash-short economy. If it could not be had in the usual ways, unusual ways of providing it would be found. One of the great strengths of John Brooke's account of Mormon cosmology is that it locates the roots of Mormon thinking in European intellectual history. Still, even Brooke stresses the magical side of this new religion. He uncovers, for example, a relationship between divining (or money-digging), alchemy (or magical methods of turning ordinary minerals into gold), and counterfeiting: "All three were species of the miraculous, situated on points along a gradient from sincere spirituality to pure fraud, a gradient of hermetic purity and danger." Out of such conditions there developed a particular American version of the "confidence man," someone who could combine esoteric knowledge, technological secrets, and religious charisma in ways that would win the trust of desperate people, encouraging them to part with things of value to themselves.

For Brooke, Mormonism inherited a long tradition of hermeticism that produced such religious practices as numerology, astrology, exorcism, millenarianism, and new dispensationism. But Brooke is careful to distinguish between the optimistic hermeticism of the Renaissance and the more dualistic and pessimistic accounts of man's fall. It was the former that influenced Joseph Smith, not the latter. Instead of Satanism and its fascination with black magic, Mormonism grew out of a culture of "white magic." Practitioners of white magic claimed that they–the cunning folk–could intervene with God. In Brooke's words, they "offered their supernatural services to solve mundane personal problems, claiming to heal the sick, to divine the future, to cast spells, to control the weather, to find lost property and ancient treasure hoards, and to protect against the devil and his minions, the sorcerers or black witches." White magic, while clearly containing elements of folklore and superstition, was, as Brooke points out, also a step on the road to modernity: "Hermetic thought would provide the key to the secrets of the cosmos. It was at its core an optimistic, expansive philosophy, celebrating the potential divinity and power of humanity."

White magic took special root in that new Jerusalem called the United States. This, after all, was the place of modernity's triumph, in which dark versions of the Apocalypse were never going to find a permanent home. Joseph Smith's new sect was in no way "revivalist." Suspicious of enthusiasm, Smith draped his theology in pseudoscience. He asked his adherents to read a book. He relied on witnesses and legal documentation to buttress his claims about his discovery. Mormonism, especially when compared with more emotional religions, had its share of intellectual appeal. "The importance of this appeal," Brodie notes, "cannot be overestimated, for it drew into the Mormon ranks many able men who had turned in disgust from the excesses of the local cults." Through its projects, especially the building and the rebuilding of its temples, Mormonism was an engineer's religion, a doctrine for the pragmatic, no-nonsense kind of person who practiced a kind of white magic on the material world, demanding that it yield its secrets for the cause of human betterment.

Joseph Smith claimed the title of prophet, but he was not prophetic in the Old Testament sense of the term. This was not a man invoking with passionate eloquence a world that had been lost, or judging the people of his day unjust and insufficiently sincere in their professions of faith. Smith practiced reverse charisma. Rather than holding up to his followers a vision and demanding that they follow it, he divined what his followers wanted and offered it to them. There would always be an element of what Brooke calls "interactive performance or theatre" in the relationship between Smith and his audience. Semi-modern in its content, Mormonism was also semi-modern in its delivery. Its founder anticipated the consumer preference survey more than he anticipated the Scopes trial.

To the degree that non-Mormons know anything about Mormon history, what they know is the church's early encouragement of polygamy. Plural marriage has its biblical and hermetic origins, but it is also possible to see in the sexual practices of the Mormon elders an anticipation of modernity. A qualified modernity, to be sure: as the Mormons practiced it, polygamy reflected strongly articulated notions of male superiority. It was also a hierarchical system designed to reinforce the privileges of the Mormon elite. Still, there is a certain perverse logic to plural marriage. Like many a modern man, Joseph Smith was unwilling to rein in his libido. Yet Mormons were fearful of anarchy, and they preached obedience to priestly (and highly uncivil) law. What better way to link male sexual libertarianism with respect for order than by legalizing practices which, outside of Mormon circles, were considered adulterous? In their effort to reconcile hedonistic impulses with productivity and discipline, the Mormons not only discovered what Daniel Bell would later call the cultural contradictions of capitalism, they also found a way to bridge them.

IV

THERE IS NO EASY ANSWER to the question of why Stephen Covey's books have been such a commercial success. It cannot be the prose; Covey writes in a flip-chart manner, as if he barely pauses between the oral presentation to a seminar and the printed page. Nor can it be the logic: a book of practical advice that warns against advice-giving is incoherent. Nor can originality play much of a role. *The Seven Habits of*

Highly Effective Families repeats just about everything that one finds in Covey's earlier books, and in a remarkably uninteresting way. No, Covey's books are popular in spite of themselves.

One reason for Covey's success surely lies in the fact that, in contrast to old-fashioned management gurus such as Peter Drucker, today's purveyors of managerial wisdom aspire not to the profane but to the sacred. In contemporary America, management consultants have become moral leaders. It is not gaps in production they seek to fill, but gaps in the spirit. The theory of management is now more and more the theory of the management of the soul. No religious notion—no matter how New Age, mystical, or exotic—is alien to them. And now Covey joins them, adding to the mix one of the world's truly remarkable religious traditions: Mormonism.

Micklethwait and Wooldridge write that "Covey's own Mormonism has been lifelong and unflinching," before adding that "he bridles at the thought that his ideas are particularly American, let alone Mormon." Nowhere in his books does Covey talk about his specific religious beliefs; his discussions of God are offered in broadly ecumenical language. Covey's beliefs, moreover, are his own business. Reducing his thoughts to his Mormonism would be as wrong as reducing my thoughts to my (lapsed) Judaism. Still, we need not take what he told Micklethwait and Wooldridge as the final word on the subject. For Mormons have not always been honest about their ideas. Smith urged his followers to deny the existence of plural marriage even while encouraging them to practice it. Even today, despite official renunciation of the idea, unofficial plural marriages flourish as the legal authorities in Utah, imbued with the same spirit of moral relativism and unconcern with "victimless crime" that characterizes the rest of the country, look the other way.

One would hardly expect a man aiming for massive audiences in the gentile culture, and proclaiming laws that are deemed to be universal, to acknowledge openly the influence of a religious movement not fully trusted by most Americans. Yet the influences are incontrovertibly there. I do not mean to suggest that the Seven Habits books are written cabalistically, translating Mormon doctrine into language acceptable to the gentiles and recognizable to the initiated. It is more that the ways in which Joseph Smith promoted his ideas and the ways in which Stephen Covey promotes his ideas are quite similar. Both are practitioners of a form of white magic. Indeed, Covey has brought the art of white magic to the writing and the publication of books.

Magicians of the more traditional sort aim to create an air of illusion, to convince their audience that something has just taken place which could not possibly have taken place. White magic has another purpose: its goal is to persuade people that things which are perfectly obvious, even completely known to them, can nonetheless be revealed to them. The Seven Habits, Covey's wife writes in her preface to his new book, are ones that "you already know in your heart to be true. That is why they seem so familiar. You've seen them in action. They've worked in your own life. You've even used them yourself—often." White magic redefines how we think about mystery. Its secrets are this-worldly, not otherworldly. Indeed, its secrets are not even secrets. Satan needs secrets because his struggle with God is win-lose: whatever serves evil cannot serve good. But Covey's teaching exists in a win-win world. I am going to tell you what you need to know to be effective, he promises, but I am also going to tell everyone else as well, as publicly and as visibly as my entrepreneurial efforts allow me, even those who may be your antagonists. Not to worry, however. If we all know what we have all known all along, we will all be better off.

Spiritual reflection—which Covey once defined as "a Quadrant II activity"—is very much a part of the Seven Habits system. "In our own family," he writes, "we have found great strength in worshiping together." Nothing is more resonant with American culture than invocations of religion. Yet few things are more alien to most Americans than people who come across as religious fanatics. Americans want to be religious without having to suffer through the denial, the sacrifice, and the hard-boards endurance that religious asceticism demands. Joseph Smith offered them a way to do so. A religion without a conception of sin is, for all its earnestness, nondemanding. Spirit need never stand in the way of success. Joseph Smith was not in the business of building a movement of men of sorrow.

Covey shares this sense of weightless spirituality. Religion cannot possibly offer a true and narrow path toward righteousness, for in a culture of nonjudgmentalism nothing can be righteous. Thirty years ago a law professor named Charles Reich wrote a best-seller called *The Greening of America* in which he argued that a new consciousness–Consciousness Three, he called it–was emerging in America, promoted by the young in rebellion against corporate culture. What Reich never realized was that corporate culture was itself undergoing an entry into the new consciousness. You do not get ahead in today's corporate environment by sternly judging the moral character of others. The law of corporate moral life is that everything is forgivable. For who knows which of today's sins will turn out to be tomorrow's growth markets? Stephen Covey is simply the Charles Reich of the management class. "When you understand, you don't judge," he writes, citing, of all people, Solomon, one of the great judges in the history of any religion.

One of the things that Joseph Smith clearly understood was that a nonjudgmental religion, when linked to a hierarchical and authoritarian structure, would result in a religion incapable of judging its supreme leader. Covey's habits build upon the same idea. For all his talk about communication, empathy, and sensitivity, Covey displays throughout his books a deeply authoritarian outlook on the world. He begins his analysis of family life by relying on the metaphor of a flight plan. To get to your destination, he reminds his readers, you need to know where you are going. I have yet to fly on an airplane that asks for broad participation from its passengers in matters of navigation and safety. Similarly, in Covey's world, someone is always calling for a family meeting, asking for mission statements to be written, setting goals, defining roles, or determining which plans should have priority. It does not take much insight to guess the gender of that very significant person. And this is the case with Covey's family as well. "We've all felt a sense of unity and contribution over the years as the family supported me in my work–and later some of our children's work–in the Covey

Leadership Center (now Franklin Covey)," he writes. There can be no doubt about who the pilot is in this family.

Nonjudgmentalism is usually associated with tolerance. By refusing to condemn the behavior of others as wrong, sinful, or immoral, we recognize and we accept a wide variety of human practices. But this is not an adequate analysis. It is essential to see that nonjudgmentalism is not at all like tolerance. To tolerate something, you first have to judge it. Toleration consists in being willing to allow something to exist even if you judge it to be wrong–which is why Mill, in *On Liberty*, argued for the right of Mormons to practice plural marriage even while asserting his moral repulsion at the practice. When people refuse to pass judgment, they manifest, if anything, an intolerant outlook on their world, for they are essentially saying that they do not have sufficient respect for anyone whose behavior or worldview differs from theirs to criticize it.

This may explain why Coveyism, like the doctrine of Joseph Smith, has such a low threshold for dissent. Covey's true attitude toward toleration comes out best in the many examples that he provides of people who have successfully used the Seven Habits system. None of this testimony sounds like the way real people talk. "I remember the first time my dad shared with us a principle of life," one of them says. "At that point we decided to put our faith in principles instead of in all the popular advice we were receiving," adds another. "When we learned about Habit 5, we decided that this might be the key to greater peace in our home," says a third.

All of Covey's stories have the same plot: People. Trouble. Habits. Happiness. There is never an unsuccessful application of a habit. No one questions the system and wins. Covey wants to share with us the experiences of real people. What he shows instead is the power of cult-speak. I hope Covey made these stories up. (Names and important details are not provided.) For if he is being truthful, then the implications are far worse. Following The Seven Habits, it would seem, produces obedient automatons.

Obedience to law is itself an important aspect of Mormon theology. But the law to which one has to conform is not the man-made law fashioned out of democratic conflict, revisable by appeal to moral principles of liberty and equality, and capable of being changed when proven shortsighted or ill-advised. Joseph Smith, the advocate of patently illegal plural marriage, viewed civil law with contempt, as if society were a vast conspiracy organized to prevent true believers from finding God as they saw fit. Covey shares this sense of hostility to organized society. He invokes the Constitution as changeless law, failing to note serious debates among eighteenth-century political theorists about whether later generations could properly be bound by laws they played no role in making. Like many spiritualists, he distrusts official religious institutions such as churches. He views children who have lost their way as "seduced by the culture," not appreciating the fact that "the culture" has been shaped by diverse and valuable influences, including Judeo-Christian morality, the ideals of democracy, and the canons of great literature. And he occasionally drops his didactic tone for an incendiary one. "We can no longer depend on society or most of its institutions," he writes, sounding like the Unabomber. "We must develop a new flight plan. We must rise above the turbulence and chart a true north path."

The laws to which our obedience must be pledged are not the laws of the land, they are the Seven Habits of Effective Everything. Covey illustrates his way of thinking when he misunderstands a story about translation. On a trip to Jakarta, he notices that his remarks are being translated into Indonesian simultaneously as he talks. For Covey, "those translators . . . had to be listening to what I was saying at the moment as well as restating what I had just said," rendering their work an example of what he calls "empathic listening." This is self-aggrandizing nonsense. Anyone who does translation of this sort knows that the one thing not involved is empathy. Search for understanding as you try to translate rapidly, and you will fall behind. Simultaneous translation requires a way of listening to words without actually hearing them. And that is very much the way Covey thinks about obedience.

Without habits, society would fall apart. Some things need to be internalized: looking out for cars as you cross the street, treating other people with respect. But thinking ought never to be habitual. For the essential characteristic of a habit is its unreflectiveness. And Covey wants his habits, too, to be reflexes. He does not want his instructions to be considered intellectually; he wants them to be absorbed unconsciously. When the message of a law or a habit comes into your brain, you are expected to translate it immediately into the action it demands. It is not your job to think about the message, to place it in a context, to interpret it, to find shades of ambiguity in its expression. The more simultaneous you are in transforming advice into a command requiring your assent, the more effective you are. This is not wisdom, it is indoctrination. In Covey's system, you gain control over your life by giving up control over your destiny.

V

THE FANTASTIC ECONOMIC SUCCESS of Mormons in late-twentieth-century America—combined with the fact that our leading management guru is a member of the Mormon faith—demands that we revisit Max Weber. The most important affinity between Protestantism and capitalism, he believed, was precisely the theological tenet which Mormons reject: the possibility of grace. Protestants, especially the more puritanical sects, placed "premiums upon 'proving' oneself before God in the sense of attaining salvation," and in that way contributed to "a certain methodical, rational way of life which—given certain conditions—paved the way for the 'spirit' of capitalism," as Weber explained.

Coveyism suggests that Weber was not wrong. If anything, it is not only capitalism that owes a debt to Protestant ideas about salvation. The black magic of Faust, romanticism, the Bildungsroman, scientific exploration: all seem somehow related, as Weber stressed, to a theology that divided the world dualistically into forces of light and forces of darkness, and made the passage from one to the other a matter of self-sacrifice, discipline, and a sense of a calling. Mormonism, lacking a conception of grace, is unlikely to produce world-class literature. Its universities, suspicious of academic freedom, will hardly be hotbeds of artistic creativity. Its scientists, lacking the vocation for science, will be attracted to shortcuts such as cold fusion. And, most importantly for understanding Stephen Covey, its capitalism will not be the entrepreneurial, exploratory, dynamic capitalism about which Weber wrote, but a postmodern kind of capitalism organized for no particular purpose other than self-reproduction.

If, for Weber, religion was a spur to the development of capitalism, for Covey religion is capitalism. Nowhere does this become clearer than in Covey's startling and ugly metaphor of the Emotional Bank Account. Love, hate, rage, wonder, ecstasy, sympathy: they are to be regarded not as the all-too-human emotions that protect us from the rationality of the market, but as commodities to be stored for use when the price finally becomes right. For this reason, all is surely not well in Coveyville. For a family that expresses its love through mission statements is very much a family without feeling. It can have no character of its own. Its sole and only purpose is to survive in a world of similarly self-protective enclaves. It is merely a firm united by blood.

Stephen Covey's books must be read as a description of a capitalism that has no place to go. His ideal reader is not the person who creates wealth, it is the middle-level bureaucrat working in a large-scale organization trying to get through the day. Into this world of purposeless activity, Covey introduces structure. For people powerless to influence the destiny of the organizations for which they work, he offers the illusion of efficacy. In a world in which competition is sublimated into furious struggles over seating arrangements around tables, as if any change from yesterday to today must be divined for meaning, he tells his readers that win-lose is over. Mormonism's great contribution to the work of Stephen Covey has been to provide the unwritten and perhaps unconscious assumptions for a secular version of what life means in organizations in which most people spend most of the time spinning their wheels. And now, we are told, the family has become another one of those organizations.

Bourgeois ideology rarely treated success in capitalism as a precondition for success in other realms of life. Hard-nosed and realistic when it came to the world of business, the bourgeoisie turned romantic and sentimental when it came to the world of the family. Feminists of a certain sort have criticized this division into separate spheres, as if, for women to achieve equality, the rules of the professions and the practices of the family have to be the same; and they have just been joined by Stephen Covey, whose self-announced objective is to further, not loving families, not self-respecting families, not nourishing families, not decent families, not autonomous families, but effective families. This amounts to a managerialist redefinition of the family. By treating the family as just another form of organization, no different in any significant way from the firm, Covey conveys, in his breezily chilling manner, the sense of an Iron Cage far more impregnable than anything that the more tragic and pessimistic Weber could have imagined.

For this reason, Covey's intervention into America's debate over family values is not what one might expect. "Over the past thirty years the situation for families has changed powerfully and dramatically," he writes near the beginning of his book, citing increasing rates of illegitimacy, divorce, teenage suicide, and the usual indicators of cultural decline. This is the boilerplate of contemporary politics in America. But if the conservative response to family decline is to urge individuals to recommit themselves to traditional family values, then Covey is no conservative. One finds almost no discussion in this book of the factors that have caused the family to weaken. There is no criticism of women for entering the workplace. Covey never tells parents to discipline their children; indeed, he demands that parents listen to their children "without any moral evaluation or judgment." Nobody is blamed for the increase in divorce. Nobody is asked to suppress his or her desires for immediate gratification for the sake of long-term family stability.

And none of this should be surprising. Mormons are not exactly in the best position to take the lead in urging a restoration of conventional family structures. Indeed, radical feminists, postmodernists, and critical-race theorists—for whom the same conventional family ideology is taken to be oppressive to gays or people of color—recognize in the polygamous history of Mormonism a potential ally in their efforts to undermine the moral legitimacy of the nuclear family. To be sure, writers of this persuasion are not enamored of the ways in which plural marriage oppressed women; but at least one of them, Peggy Cooper Davis in her recent book *Neglected Stories,* would reopen *Reynolds v. United States,* the Supreme Court decision that upheld a congressional law outlawing plural marriage in the states and territories.

Covey himself does not advance an argument on behalf of plural marriage. He expresses nothing but undying love for his wife and children. Yet if we listen to the way Covey talks about the family, it becomes clear that he holds an extreme version of moral relativism from which it is impossible to support and to justify one kind of family over any other. We do not, from Covey's point of view, need a moral sense. We can live without strong institutions. We need not rely on culture. The Judeo-Christian tradition—a judgmental way of approaching the world if ever there was one—would lead us in the wrong direction. We do not need law. All we need is the doctrine of the Seven Habits. "With this framework you can diagnose or figure out just about anything that happens in any conceivable family situation."

Yet there is a significant difference between Stephen Covey and the radical postmodernists. Covey reaches millions of Americans. And so there is something wrong when conservatives attack feminism for weakening the family and ignore (when they do not actually praise) the work of a best-selling writer as morally anarchistic as Stephen Covey. If the American family is in trouble, it may be because too many Americans have already followed Covey's nonjudgmental advice. "Whatever your situation," he writes, "it is vitally important that you do not compare your family to any other family." What could sound more reasonable? And what could be more misguided? The fact is that families work when the individuals who comprise them struggle through conflict, and judge themselves by judging others, and negotiate compromises, and challenge each other's stubbornness, and insist on the dignity of disagreement, and find unexpected and imperfect resolutions. You do not make a successful family by following principles alleged to be universal for no other reason than that someone claims them to be universal.

Moreover, a family is not a business, or a corporation, or a bureaucracy. You do not make a successful family by consulting books, tapes, guides, and a Web page to know what to do next. You make a successful family by taking the resources offered to you by culture, church, history, society, tradition, even government—all those things for which Covey has nothing but suspicion—and shaping them to your needs.

For many non-Mormons, Joseph Smith has never lost his shady reputation. Time has not mellowed the sense that he was a confidence man whose theological ideas, had it not been for the brilliant organizational abilities of his disciples, might have disappeared into a footnote in the history of American religion. But there is little doubt that Smith understood one thing. Take insecure people, offer them an answer to their problems, clothe your advice in language that seems intelligent but is mostly gibberish, proclaim the world rotten yet demand changes that require little or no transformation in how people actually live—and, who knows, maybe you will be called a prophet.

Faith and Diversity in
American Religion

I

ONE WOULD BE HARD pressed to find a private college or university in the United States that cannot trace its founding to a religious denomination. One would be equally hard pressed, at least as far as America's elite universities are concerned, to find one that would identify faith as central to its current approaches to teaching, research, and student life. No aspect of life is considered so important to Americans outside higher education, yet deemed so unimportant by the majority of those inside, as religion.

The relative indifference to religion in higher education may be changing, however, as a wide variety of social and intellectual trends converge. Parents concerned about excessive drinking and promiscuous sex look more favorably upon religious colleges that they once might have dismissed as academically inferior. A widespread fascination with spirituality in the general culture has increased awareness of, and interest in, religious studies courses on campuses. Social scientists have begun to realize that it is impossible to understand American politics, race relations, volunteerism, and law without a fuller appreciation of religion's role in shaping social institutions. Already under way before September 11, such impulses will only be strengthened in the wake of events that thrust to the fore of just about everyone's mind questions of religious freedom and religious diversity.

Not surprisingly, therefore, scholarly attention to the role religion plays—in our colleges and universities, our local communities, and our society at large—is growing. In itself, that represents a shift of academic interest, especially in the social sciences, since religion—which received considerable attention in the writings of the nineteenth- and early-twentieth-century founders of the social science disciplines— went out of fashion in the years after World War II.

Perhaps concerned that the study of a human activity pregnant with values would corrupt the objective of value-free inquiry, postwar social scientists were more likely to examine the economy or the political system of Western societies than they were its faith commitments. Whatever studies were produced throughout the 1970s and 1980s, moreover, tended, in the name of objectivity, to rely on quantitative methods, which included analysis of survey data and demographic transformations.

As academics have come to appreciate the role religion plays in the lives of real people—including their own students—more of the scholarship they produce takes on a qualitative character. Many recent books want to know what faith means to the faithful. Are religious people different from secular people? Do their beliefs influence the choices they make, not only with respect to such public activities as voting, but in how they lead their lives? Are we experiencing a new religious awakening? How has the arrival of so many non-Judeo-Christian immigrants, who themselves tend to be very religious, affected American religion?

II

RELIGION ON CAMPUS, written by Conrad Cherry, Betty A. DeBerg, and Amanda Porterfield, deals with the way America's young people approach religion, as well as with the ways that America's colleges and universities respond to them. Because its subject matter involves the young, who will determine America's approach to religion in the future, and because it also involves institutions of higher education, which have had such a long and ambiguous relationship with religion, it offers a good introduction to American understanding of faith.

Religion on Campus is primarily an ethnographic report, describing the religious situation at four institutions whose identity the authors choose to keep secret: a public research university, a historically black university, a Roman Catholic university, and a Protestant-affiliated four-year college. The president of South University, the name the authors give to the historically black institution, informed Conrad Cherry that she would not think of attending worship services on the campus. That is not because she is an atheist; on the contrary, she is a practicing Episcopalian. It is the enthusiasm in the born-again religion that predominates on her campus that disturbs her. "Imagine, services that last one-and-a-half hours," she exclaimed. "And I don't want to stand up when my name is called. I will not file down to the front to drop in my offering. I don't like the swaying and shouting and amening." Perhaps the university chaplain had her in mind when he told the authors of *Religion on Campus* that the problem with some religious believers is that "they fear emotion." "I don't yell and rant and rave," he continued, "but I'm not afraid to let my emotions show."

As Cherry correctly points out, there is a serious conflict within African American religion between many older denominations, which emphasize the importance of specific doctrinal traditions and their texts, and Pentecostally inspired charismatic practices, which lean toward spirited forms of worship and postdenominational identities. But that is true not just of the black church.

At West University, the public research institution the authors describe, a freshman attended meetings of the mainline Protestant Campus Ministry Center and two evangelical groups, Campus Crusade and InterVarsity. Asked about his reactions, he described the former as too conservative for his taste. When religion is usually discussed in America, it is the evangelical churches that are identified with conservative Christians and the mainline churches with liberals. But this student can be forgiven for getting the distinction backward. As far as he is concerned, the hymns and liturgical predictability of the mainline Protestants seem downright reactionary when compared with the contemporary Christian rock of the evangelicals. "I know CMC believes in Jesus," he told Betty DeBerg, "but I can't understand their relationship with him." For this student, as for many American religious believers, faith involves a personal relationship with the Lord; it does not involve sitting passively as others preach.

North College, an institution affiliated with the Evangelical Lutheran Church in America, requires that all freshmen take a class called "Bible in Culture and Community," as well as one other course in Christian theology, sometime during their college careers. That commitment to make religion an essential part of the curriculum harks back to an era when colleges, concerned about the formation of student character, mandated courses in religion and moral philosophy. Yet the actual courses at North College are as contemporary in their subject matter as they are in their assignments. One section of the Bible course features novels by James Baldwin and Chaim Potok. Written projects include three personal essays in which the students talk about their own religious experiences in relationship to the texts. No didactic lectures from the podium characterize these classes; students are divided into small groups to discuss the reading assignments among themselves, as the professors walk around to each group to answer questions or join the discussion. Indeed, the informality and intimacy of the class resemble very much the ways in which American religious practices, in general, have moved toward forms of small-group worship and personal witnessing–even, if not especially, in huge megachurches whose popularity has as much to do with the small groups they sponsor as with their overall size.

The Roman Catholic university described in *Religion on Campus* also imposes requirements–in its case, courses in theology and philosophy. (Those can be filled through a yearlong course that explores the connections between classic texts and a Jesuit-inspired commitment to social service.) Porterfield, who wrote the chapter on this institution, frequently heard complaints from devout Catholics that East University had lost its religious identity. Nonetheless, she found herself impressed with the persistence of Catholic ritual and Catholic social teachings in the lives of most students. Expecting Jesuit culture to be "militaristic and sternly patriarchal," she discovered, instead, that it was inclusive and caring. And because it was, Catholic identity, however important it was to the leadership of the institution, was not pursued in a way that would make non-Catholics feel unwelcome. East University could hardly be identical to the other institutions discussed in this book, given its different history and religious nature. But, like them, it has become inclusive and tolerant.

None of the institutions examined in *Religion on Campus* asserts one official religious truth to the exclusion of all other faiths. Religion, instead, tends to be understood as a broad and capacious phenomenon. When the student-body president at South University was asked if students there were very religious, he replied, "No, but most of them are very spiritual." Insofar as the distinction between religion and spirituality at least partly revolves around an openness to eclectic religious experience, a playing-down of denominations, and an inclination toward passionate, personal religious experience, the students on all the four campuses studied in *Religion on Campus* can be said to be leaning toward spirituality.

III

INDEED, ACCORDING TO ROBERT C. FULLER, a professor of religious studies at Bradley University, Americans have long made that distinction between religion, which they usually view as bureaucratic and formal, and spirituality, which is transcendent and individual—a quest for a personal understanding of faith that Fuller says dates as far back as colonial times. Fuller says in *Spiritual, but Not Religious: Understanding Unchurched America* that many of America's "unchurched" have avoided denominational membership and Sunday worship not because they are atheists, but because their religious beliefs do not take traditionally organized forms. In the book, in part a historical account of the unchurched in America and in part a meditation on their significance, Fuller estimates that roughly 20 percent of Americans today hold such views. If true, that would make the "spiritually inclined" one of America's largest religious faiths. Fuller argues that unchurched religion has been so common that it has "gradually established its own tradition." Whether those who call themselves spiritual but not religious know it or not, they are part of a movement.

Fuller argues that, instead of criticizing them for an eclectic and seemingly superficial approach to faith, as those who believe that religion and church membership are the same thing often do, we should recognize them as serious people trying to find their own spiritual ways. Refreshingly, Fuller comes to the defense of Sheila Larson, the woman interviewed with not-very-hidden disapproval by Robert N. Bellah and his colleagues in the 1985 book *Habits of the Heart,* who proclaimed a belief in "Sheilaism"—a faith that puts the individual and her needs ahead of obligations to God or to other people. The fact that Larson did not join an established church, in Fuller's view, "is hardly a sign of religious immaturity." Perhaps her determination to find a faith that worked for her had more to teach scholars of religion than Bellah and his colleagues recognized: that regular churchgoers may attend more out of habit than out of conviction, and that many who do not attend church are still searching for conviction.

Looking at *Religion on Campus* and Fuller's *Spiritual, but Not Religious* together suggests that one reason Americans so often describe themselves as spiritual rather than religious is that they have increasingly been introduced to religions outside the Judeo-Christian tradition, many of which emphasize the more spiritual aspects of faith. And American institutions of higher education, for their part, have responded to that expanded ecumenical sensibility. The theology department at the Roman Catholic university described in *Religion on Campus,* for example, would never think of confining its mission to Catholic apologetics. East University includes courses on Buddhism taught by a practicing Buddhist, who made clear to Porterfield that he does not approach his subject from the point of view of scholarly detachment, but instead from active engagement. In fact, students at all the institutions studied by the authors of *Religion on Campus* are introduced to religions other than the ones they had grown up with. At the historically black university, which was founded after the Civil War by

Presbyterians, for example, the chapel on campus sponsored a talk by an African American who grew up in the Muslim faith and who told students that it is an ecumenical and practical religion strongly linked to Christianity and Judaism.

IV

DIANA L. ECK DELVES deeper still into the influence of traditions from around the world on how Americans understand their faith. *A New Religious America: How a "Christian Country" Has Now Become the World's Most Religiously Diverse Nation* deals with the changes in American religious life brought about by the arrival in this country of religious believers from all over the world since the reform of America's immigration laws in 1965. Originally a specialist in the religious life of the Indian subcontinent, Eck, who teaches at the Harvard Divinity School, first broadened her focus to include Indians who came to America in search of new opportunities, then to include all of America's recent immigrants and their religions. Her enthusiasm for her subject has led her to write in this book about Chinese and Japanese Buddhists (and their American coreligionists), Muslims, and the often-lesser-known religions from the Indian subcontinent, including the beliefs of Hindus and Sikhs.

Eck occasionally lapses into cheerleading; her chapter on Muslims, in particular, stresses the degree to which they "are increasingly engaged participants in the American pluralist experiment," giving scant attention along the way to those adherents to Islam who continue to believe that America is the Great Satan and who, even while living here, reject this country and its values. Still, Eck's book, rich in description and its appreciation of diversity, will stand as the definitive account of American religious pluralism for some time to come.

Tending to see no wrong among immigrants and their beliefs, Eck nonetheless does see something wrong in the way Americans respond to them. Indeed, one of her contentions is that not all Americans welcome and appreciate this new diversity. She cites, for example, harassment of Muslims in Michigan and Indians in New Jersey, as well as the persistent stereotypes that Americans hold about recent arrivals to their shores.

But are we really, as she believes we are, "afraid of ourselves"? Do we really not want to acknowledge the diversity that Eck chronicles? To be sure, some foreign-looking Americans were harassed and attacked in the aftermath of September 11. Yet, compared with any other episode in America's religious history, this one, seemingly pitting Muslims against non-Muslims, was met by both the president of the United States and by ordinary citizens with serious commitments to diversity and pluralism. If we consider those responses in the light of *Religion on Campus,* we ought to come away impressed by how much America has changed since the days when anyone of a faith other than the majority's was considered a pagan.

The young are likely to set the future course of religion in America. If the institutions studied in *Religion on Campus* are any guide, students reveal the general sense of religious tolerance that Eck finds missing in American life: None of the campuses can be described as "triumphalist" in their assertions of Christian supremacy. North College offers one example. Although affiliated with a specific denomination, North attracts students like Mary Delillo (the students' names are fictitious, as well), whose father is Roman Catholic and whose mother is Chinese Buddhist, and Kevin Solomon, who believes that students ought to consider activities like "going abroad and discovering that not every one is a Lutheran, and engaging in Buddhist meditation." It is inconceivable to imagine these North students, or any of the other students at the other institutions described in *Religion on Campus,* engaging in hate crimes against people whose faith is not Christian.

American religion, in short, has undergone some remarkable changes since the arrival of the Puritans. Those are the subject of Amanda Porterfield's *The Transformation of American Religion: The Story of a Late-Twentieth-Century Awakening.* Porterfield presents a passionate defense of her own discipline. Against those who find the field of religious studies in disarray, if for no other reason than its tendency to treat all religions as equally worthy of respect, Porterfield celebrates her discipline because it "has served as a vehicle for open and informed discussion of the varieties of religious belief and practice." Porterfield compares religious studies to "a corridor in a hotel through which exemplars of different religious persuasions pass through on their way to and from their respective rooms."

It is clear from her treatment that the academic study of religion in America mirrors the ways in which American religion is actually practiced; in both arenas, we are no longer a society in which Protestantism is assumed to be the unofficial faith, forcing people who believe in something else to consider themselves members of a barely tolerated minority.

Alas, Porterfield's book will never be the definitive historical account of how America came to be the way it currently is. Rambling and disjointed, it examines such topics as Catholic spirituality (much of this discussion borrowed from her chapter in *Religion on Campus*), the decline of Protestant hegemony, the impact of the Vietnam War and gender consciousness on religion—without tying them together.

Porterfield's most interesting idea is that the spiritualists and proponents of religious diversity found in late-twentieth-century America are actually heirs to the Puritan tradition because, like Jonathan Edwards, the great eighteenth-century Calvinist, they identify "spiritual life with recognition of the beauty of being." Unfortunately, such an emphasis on continuity does more than just undermine the very title of her book—and the findings of all the other books discussed here. It also misunderstands and strips away from Puritanism just about every one of its core beliefs, including the inherent sinfulness of man, the superiority of Protestantism over all its rivals, and the dedication to stern moral judgmentalism. Anyone wanting an overall assessment of the changing nature of American religion, therefore, will have to look beyond Porterfield's book.

Other questions about the way Americans today understand religious faith go beyond these four books, as well. While all detect an increasing interest in spiritual and religious matters, in America and on its campuses, none of them, save Fuller's, sufficiently addresses whether the loose denominational character and weak theological underpinnings of contemporary religion should be condemned or celebrated. (As a defender of the unchurched, Fuller holds an unabashedly positive view of the decreasing salience of organized religion.) But one of the priests interviewed by Porterfield at East University told her that students there, like the ones at the Catholic university in which I teach (who knows? perhaps they are one and the same), are "dim, fourth-carbon copies of religious people. Certain things remind them of religion—crosses and statues. But theology is in desperate straits here. It would die without Buddhism and other religions to discuss."

Are we better off when religion is as broad, but also as thin, as the kinds of faith one finds on American college campuses today? As if grateful to find any religion at all, the authors of *Religion on Campus* tend to be, if not celebratory, at least upbeat in their assessment of the generally nondoctrinal forms of religious faith one finds on campus. I share their appreciation of how religion on campus has changed, for it does not take much excursion into history to recall days of Christian dogmatism, anti-Semitism, hostility toward science, and lack of respect for nonbelievers. Certainly America's institutions of higher learning—and conceivably America's religious denominations as well—are better off in that respect.

Still, the priest from East University has a point. Religious students are very much like nonreligious students in their efforts to personalize knowledge, to avoid difficult and controversial positions that might cause anger in others, and to insist that, if we just try hard enough, everyone can get along with everyone else. Each of the books here, in its own way, documents the absence of a sense of the tragic in the way Americans practice their faith. Religion has returned to America, not as an alternative to the value relativism and personal seeking associated with the often quite secular 1960s, but as the logical extension of the cultural revolution first glimpsed at that time.

Higher Learning

I

INTELLECTUAL FASHIONS BEING WHAT they are, the next major issue facing American higher education may well be the revival of religious faith. If politicians can discover values, perhaps even academics will.

There certainly exist sufficient grounds for thinking they should. Universities, shaped by faculty priorities, are hands-down the most secular institutions in American society. And at those institutions, disputatious professors, who quarrel about everything else, are all too quick to agree that religious education is a contradiction in terms. Meanwhile, students who had come to college familiar with at least one great literary work cannot now be expected to know the major biblical narratives—let alone the history and dogma of their own creeds. Across the spectrum, the college years are a time for questioning faith, not reaffirming it.

When everything modern is under attack, it can hardly be surprising that the secular university, modernity's most representative accomplishment, is also found wanting. The case for reintroducing religion into the American university crops up across the map. Relying on the arguments of University of Utah law professor Michael McConnell, the U.S. Supreme Court recently ruled that the University of Virginia could not deny funds to a student group that published a Christian newspaper. (In November 2002, the U.S. Senate approved President Bush's nomination of McConnell to the Tenth Circuit Court of Appeals.) In the January and February 1996 issues of *First Things*, a "monthly journal of religion and public life," distinguished scholars ranging from Gertrude Himmelfarb and Father Richard John Neuhaus to Stanley Fish criticize the liberal compromises that define the secular university. And recent books by George Marsden, Mark R. Schwehn, and Warren A. Nord together present a well-stated case for injecting more religious feeling and more religious content into the modern academy.

These arguments deserve a wide hearing. Although secular academics—with visions of the Scopes trial dancing through their heads—may think of the deeply devout as wanting nothing more than the reimposition of dogma, most of these writers present their ideas the way all academics should: through argumentation, appeals to history, and familiarity with the latest ideas in philosophy. Their accounts are among the most stimulating analyses of higher education one can find, far more profitable to ponder than the by now repetitive broadsides for or against identity politics or multiculturalism. And they lead in some unexpected directions. One of the ironies of the emerging debate over faith and knowledge is that outsiders necessarily become liberal and pluralistic in defense of religious values, while insiders all too often appear closed-minded and intolerant in defense of secular ones. But it is precisely the values of openness and tolerance to which advocates for religious inclusion appeal that ultimately undermine the case they so passionately make.

II

IF THERE IS A MOVEMENT to reintroduce faith into American intellectual life, George Marsden is its leader. Marsden taught for twenty years at a religious institution, Calvin College, in Grand Rapids, Michigan, before moving to Duke University and eventually to Notre Dame. His 1980 book, *Fundamentalism and American Culture* (Oxford), established him as one of the major historians of American religion. Although Marsden made his Christian devotion clear in an afterword, his book, perhaps reflecting the times, was hardly confessional or polemical. Not so his later work and career. In a 1993 address to the

American Academy of Religion, Marsden denounced the bias against religion inherent in the American academy. "I have seen cases in the field of religion," he wrote in the *Wall Street Journal* at the same time, "in which applicants for teaching positions or for graduate schools have been dismissed out of hand because they revealed that religious motives would shape their scholarship." Marsden says that he wrote *The Soul of the American University: From Protestant Establishment to Established Non-Belief* to prove that "it is perfectly possible to have strong evaluative interests in a subject and yet treat it fairly and with a degree of detachment."

In that he succeeds: His historical narrative can be read with profit both by those who welcome and by those who fear a greater role for religion in higher education. With typical fairness and detachment, he writes that "there were undesirable features of the American Protestant establishment which led to equally flawed features of American dis-establishment."

Early American universities, as Marsden relates, were explicitly sectarian and religious. Harvard and William and Mary followed Oxford and Cambridge in excluding dissenting sects. As a result, Pres-byterian, Baptist, Congregationalist, and Dutch Reformed clergy took the lead in creating their own respective schools—Princeton, Brown, Rutgers, and Dartmouth among them. But if universities spoke to the faithful, they were also public institutions: Harvard College, for exam-ple, was created by the civil government of Massachusetts. The Bay colony's Calvinists saw no conflict between civil and church authority. But in a society in which there was no Church but many churches, it was only a matter of time before the sectarian and the secular impulses of the university came into conflict.

When they did, the religious character of the American university survived, says Marsden, only by accommodating itself to civil author-ity. Well into the nineteenth century, American colleges and universi-ties remained committed to their religious mission. Eighty percent of the presidents of denominationally related colleges were members of the clergy in 1840, as were two-thirds of the presidents of state colleges.

As late as 1879, G. Stanley Hall, the founder of Clark University in Worcester, Massachusetts, surveyed the teaching of moral philosophy in American colleges and concluded that "the grounds of moral obligation are commonly deduced from Revelation."

Yet despite these signs of religious flowering, university expansion also had worldly aims: building the nation, reinforcing common values, abolishing slavery, preparing the ground for industrial expansion. To meet those objectives, Marsden points out, dogma and sectarianism had to give way–and more or less promptly, they did. Religious commitments began to take the form of a generalized Protestantism not devoted to the propagation of any specific interpretation. "A university cannot be built upon a sect," Harvard's Charles Eliot proclaimed in 1876 (at the founding of Johns Hopkins), words that resonated with other university builders such as Andrew Dickson White of Cornell. There need not be any conflict between religion on the one hand and science and humanism on the other, these men believed–as long as religion was cast in very broad terms.

Low-church universities were even quicker to accommodate themselves to secular forces. The University of Chicago may have sprung from John D. Rockefeller's Baptist faith, but the driving forces that made it a major player in American academia were its ties to industry, its openness to pragmatic thought, and its commitments to science and medicine. The career of one of its most illustrious faculty members, John Dewey, captures the transformation of the American university in the early decades of the twentieth century. Dewey was hired, at least in part, because–as a letter of recommendation written on his behalf put it–he was "a man of religious nature, a church member, and believes in working with the church." In later years, however, Dewey came to define religion so broadly that it became indistinguishable from what is now called secular humanism. "The simple fact was that once a college expanded its vision to become a university and to serve a broad middle-class constituency," Marsden writes, "the days were numbered when any substantive denominational tradition could survive." That was surely why Methodist schools–Duke, Vanderbilt,

Emory, Boston University, Northwestern, Southern Methodist, Syra-cuse–all followed the same secularizing path from sectarian origins to regional and national stature.

Even Catholic universities prove Marsden's point, though in a con-trary sort of way. A long suspicion of Catholic education in the United States lasted well into the 1950s, when Paul Blanshard published an infamous book called *American Freedom and Catholic Power* (1949). In that and a subsequent book, Blanshard painted a lurid picture of a Catholic cabal against American democracy, especially against the schools, one no different in form (and one perhaps even more danger-ous) than the communist conspiracy. So hostile was the atmosphere to Catholics in higher education that, as Marsden relates, when William Buckley published his *God and Man at Yale* in 1951, McGeorge Bundy essentially accused him of ingratitude in not recognizing how generous Yale was in accepting Catholics.

With hindsight we now know that this picture is incomplete. In *Contending With Modernity: Catholic Higher Education in the Twenti-eth Century,* Philip Gleason points out that Washington, D.C.'s Catholic University of America (CUA), founded in 1889, was at first led by "Americanists," men who believed that Catholics "should accept what was good in modern civilization, integrate it with traditional teaching, and employ it as a resource in the church's evangelical mission of sal-vation." Between 1920 and 1930, ideas rooted in Aristotle and Aquinas revitalized conservative Catholic thought and influenced Protestant thinkers such as the University of Chicago's Robert Maynard Hutchins and the "New Humanists" Paul Elmer More and Irving Babbitt. Consid-ering their distance from Europe, and the suspicions of many immi-grants toward higher education, Catholic institutions struggled against huge odds to establish themselves as seriously committed to education.

Yet for at least forty years the odds won. Pius X's encyclical *Pas-cendi Dominici Gregis* (1907) effectively brought Americanism, and the reforms of CUA, to an end. *Studiorum Ducem* (1923), issued by Pius XI, pointed out that the teachings of Aquinas have "given us a complete refutation of the erroneous views of the Modernists." To the Church, philosophy was a method for finding the answers that it already knew. Hostile to modern thought, the Church was unwilling to allow American Catholic institutions of higher learning to join the "mainstream." No wonder that a 1934 survey of the American Council on Education found only five fields at Catholic University qualified to offer graduate work, one at Notre Dame, and none in any of the Jesuit institutions in America.

"Catholics," Marsden writes, "emerged from this era with one thing Protestants did not: universities with substantial religious identities." But they paid a very high price. Marsden notes that the 1927 *Who's Who in America* listed twice as many Unitarians as Catholics, even though there were three hundred times more Catholics in America than Unitarians.

After Vatican II, of course, things did begin to change. By the 1960s, Catholic educators had agreed to reforms such as allowing laity to serve on governing boards, and Catholic universities had established themselves as major centers of research and liberal arts education. But the history told by Marsden and by Gleason underscores the dilemma that religious universities have always faced: give religion priority of place, and a certain alienation from success in an increasingly secular and meritocratic culture followed; adjust to America's mobility and economic dynamism, and the old-time religion would have to go.

That dilemma remains to this day the defining reality in the conflict between college and church, whatever the denomination. Some institutions—primarily fundamentalist or Catholic—choose, with full appreciation of the consequences, to retain their commitments to a particular faith. A few others, such as Brandeis, Boston College, and Notre Dame, while retaining a religious identity, have followed the path of once denominational Protestant universities in establishing themselves as inclusive institutions. Most of the rest have long lost any sense of religious purpose and have become, at least according to conservative critics, the spawning grounds of militant atheism. The founding bylaws of Duke, promulgated in 1924, stated that the aims of the university were "to assert a faith in the eternal union of knowledge and religion set forth in the teachings and character of Jesus Christ, the Son of God." A mission statement for the same university adopted in 1988 spoke of promoting free inquiry, supporting diversity, educating students, fostering the exchange of ideas, and enriching the lives of people in the region. Therein lies the story of how the forces of secularization won their victory over the forces of faith.

III

CAUGHT BETWEEN ITS RELIGIOUS origins and its accommodation to modernity, the American system of higher education developed what Marsden calls "a righteous consensus, Whig style." That consensus, fashioned in the latter half of the nineteenth century, is still firmly in place today. Compulsory chapel has long been abolished; religious concerns are largely ignored in the classroom; and when professors do teach about matters of faith, they tend to do so in widely inclusive, nonevaluative ways. While there are no doubt many professors who are believers, they tend to keep their religion to themselves amid the university's secular and liberal culture. Meanwhile, parents who find this system contrary to their values can send their children to private religious universities, where efforts are still undertaken to teach from within particular religious traditions.

Is this a good compromise? For critics like Mark Schwehn, Warren Nord, and Marsden, the answer is emphatically no. It is their contention that the academy contradicts its own values when it insists on strict secularism. Modern universities say they are committed to academic freedom, but they discourage believers from following their truth wherever it leads. They organize themselves into disciplines such as biology and economics which, in assuming that they have final answers to questions about nature or society, shut themselves off from important arguments made by religiously inspired critics about human origins or the limits of self-interest. They teach moral philosophy but have little understanding of moral character. And they have convinced themselves that they can teach about religion without teaching religion, a mistake that could be corrected by reintroducing theology back into departments of religious studies.

The central argument of Mark Schwehn's *Exiles from Eden: Religion and the Academic Vocation in America* is that religious virtues can act as a corrective to a dominant, and misguidedly hubristic, view of the professor's vocation. Believing that their mission is to create knowledge, academics ignore at least two other historically important purposes of learning: shaping character and transmitting ideas and skills. How could the situation be different? For one thing, there is much to be said for humility. Both students and faculty make their mark by pointing out how Kant ignored this or Tolstoy neglected that. "Such quick, easy, and dismissive appraisals preclude the possibility of learning from these writers," Schwehn points out, asking us instead to be a little humbler in the way we approach greatness. Nor is faith inappropriate for an academic; to understand we first have to believe–if not in God, then at least in something. In the end, it is not mastery we ought to seek but understanding, which in turn "follows quite naturally from the affections of awe, wonder, and gratitude that constitute piety."

From this perspective, Schwehn offers a program for the reform of higher education. He would put less emphasis on pure scholarship and recognize many forms of academic writing, including more popular writing, as legitimate criteria for membership in the academic community. Teaching would not only count more, but would be expanded to develop the moral character of one's students. Even collegiality would be redefined to include love and friendship, the kind of pleasure in one another's company that the joint quest for learning best brings out. A university more open to the spirit would not pose false dichotomies between research and teaching but would ask "Why inquire?" or "What is the point or the worth of this inquiry?"

Where *Exiles from Eden* focuses on the profession of teaching, Warren Nord's *Religion and American Education: Rethinking a National Dilemma* concentrates on the curriculum itself. Nord, who is director of the Program in the Humanities and Human Values at the University of North Carolina, argues that "all students should receive a liberal education that takes seriously a variety of ways of making sense of the world, religious ways included, if they are to be informed, reasonable, and responsible individuals." Our schools and universities, he believes, have become "tone deaf" to religion because we assume more of a conflict between religion and secular authority than the actual course of church and state in our history warrants. After all, religious thinkers themselves, especially Protestants, helped create the secular world.

To advance his argument, Nord takes his readers through some of the most contentious battles in our culture wars. Reviewing the leading textbooks most high school subjects used in North Carolina, he finds that they contain "a coherent worldview, a loosely structured set of philosophical commitments," which considers religion "irrelevant to understanding the world." Taking his point one step farther, he insists that these texts, when combined with the actual curriculum in most schools, promote indoctrination, not education. Even when the subject of religion is introduced, the effort is so cursory—"a few facts here and a snippet of insight there"—that the nature of religious experience is never conveyed. When a phenomenon so central to human experience is so thoroughly ignored, the tenets of liberal education are violated, for a liberal education requires not only critical thinking but "initiating students into the communities of memory which tentatively define them."

At the very least, Nord would require all high school and college students to take at least one course in religion. He asks: "How can anyone believe that a college-bound student should take twelve years of mathematics and no religion rather than eleven years of mathematics and one year of religion?" Moreover, once we begin to teach religion, we should teach it in a serious way: "We routinely require students to practice science and music, to experience them, but in public education we do not allow students to participate in the practice of religion." We ought to approach religion the way we do history or the study of other cultures, by trying "to understand them from the inside, and engage them in the effort to discover more sensitive and reasonable ways of thinking and living for all involved." Although Nord speaks in a reasonable tone of voice, his proposals amount to a fundamental restructuring of the compromise under which American universities have operated for some time. As he puts it, we have chosen modernity over faith when what we should do instead is to restore the tension between them.

Reading Marsden, Schwehn, and Nord leaves one with the impression that thoughtful, respected scholars who wish for a more religious university believe themselves to be marginalized in contemporary academic culture. Their voices have none of the religious right's stridency. Yet when all is said and done, their arguments are unpersuasive, and their remedies unrealistic. In a fashion that surely none of them intended, their books serve as a reminder of why the compromises that the contemporary university has reached on these issues are probably the best means we have of reconciling the contradictory demands of faith and knowledge.

IV

IN RECOUNTING HOW HE came to write *Exiles from Eden,* Mark Schwehn begins by describing a 1982 meeting of the Chicago Group on the History of the Social Sciences, an informal colloquium of some of the leading academics in the Chicago area. One of the many stimulating products that came out of that group was Peter Novick's 1988 book *That Noble Dream: The "Objectivity Question" and the American Historical Profession.* Novick's work, which argued that the eternal quest of historians for untainted knowledge can never be realized, supports the contention of all these writers that religious ways of knowing are as deserving of respect as any other ways of knowing.

Yet the most comprehensive historian among these three, George Marsden, demonstrates why, despite Novick's argument, historical facts still matter when we discuss current controversies. Marsden, after all, does have a story to tell, and it is not one that necessarily supports his own case for religious inclusion. Under what Marsden calls Harvard's "Unitarian old-boy network," the college increasingly became an intellectual backwater until it finally rejected religious tests for appointment. When American academics in the mid–nineteenth century were learning from German professionalism, Columbia turned down distinguished scientist Oliver Wolcott Gibbs for a faculty appointment because he belonged to the wrong church. Before philosophy, psychology, and sociology could become proper academic subjects, they had to be liberated from theology. Yale's anti-Semitism, which, like Columbia's, lasted until the middle of the present century, was not only morally wrong, but kept the university mediocre in many fields, especially the social sciences. Although Marsden refrains from commenting on his own historical narrative, the burden of proof for his argument has to be somewhere in all this. A persuasive case on behalf of greater religious inclusion now would first have to show why the unhappy conflicts between faith and knowledge that have been so much a part of our history would not occur all over again.

That may be why, when it comes to advocacy, Marsden skips over the rich historical material he has presented and bases his case on other grounds entirely. Using a somewhat obscure term, but one popular among political and religious conservatives, he argues that the claims of "pure naturalism" are unsubstantiated and unfalsifiable. Not only are objective facts hard to find in history, he is suggesting, they are hard to find anywhere. And consequently, Marsden concludes, "there seems no intellectually valid reason to exclude religiously based perspectives that have strong academic credentials." This is thin ice indeed. Marsden's attempt to rest his polemical case on dubious propositions associated with the postmodern critique of science weakens what is otherwise an outstanding narrative.

As a believer, after all, Marsden cannot really be a postmodernist. He rejects the claim that all truths reflect conventions for reaching the truth, since the truth of God's existence would in no way be altered if a community of interpreters concluded otherwise. But, like Schwehn and Nord, he adopts many assumptions of the postmodernists.

Fashioning their own identity politics, all these critics become advocates for diversity, multiculturalism, and the thesis that power colors knowledge. Marsden praises feminists for incorporating personal details of their lives into their books and endorses Stanley Fish's view that "questions of free speech on campus can be reduced to issues of political power." Religiously-oriented schools, he writes, "have been outsiders to the dominant academic culture." And now that diversity is the watchword of academic life, this is unacceptable. "Institutions that claim to serve the whole public and to be internally diverse," as Marsden put it in the *Wall Street Journal,* "should be challenged to apply the principle of diversity by openly allowing responsible religious perspectives in the classroom."

Claims of victimization are tiresome enough, even when advanced by real victims. There is something truly ill-fitting when they are advanced by white male Christians. For there is a significant difference between arguments for racial and gender inclusion and similar arguments made on behalf of people of faith: The latter have already been tried. "A biology textbook that tells the story of evolution without bringing religious points of view into the discussion is taking sides," Nord claims. But surely it matters that works by women or African Americans were excluded out of ignorance, while the present decision to exclude creation science from biology courses is informed by experience.

Nord's comment about biology textbooks raises another parallel between advocates of multiculturalism and enthusiasts for religious inclusion: their conviction that the liberal belief in neutral standpoints is a chimera. The claim that there is a contradiction between faith and knowledge is itself a faith, they believe; as Gertrude Himmelfarb writes in her contribution to *First Things,* the university is not so much secular as secularist, "propagating secularism as a creed, a creed that is not neutral as among religions but is hostile to all religions, indeed to religion itself." The beauty of this line of argument is that it enables advocates of religion to claim to be the genuine liberals in all this; we are the true believers in tolerance, they are saying, for it is only we who speak on behalf of including everyone. But the downside in this way of thinking is that, in claiming to be more liberal than the liberals, they open themselves to the charge of neglecting their own faith. In *First Things*, Stanley Fish argues that Marsden's newfound liberalism undermines "what Marsden should want: not the inclusion of religious discourse in a debate no one is allowed to win, but the triumph of religious discourse and the silencing of its atheistic opponents."

Fish is onto something here, but it is not necessarily his point that religious believers ought to be wary of liberalism because liberalism invariably dismisses religious belief. What is far more problematic for religious believers who use the language of tolerance and inclusion is that such liberal virtues are more demanding than many believers are prepared to accept. Tolerance and inclusion are two-way streets. One cannot stand outside a liberal institution and ask for admission without being prepared to extend to others the tolerance that one demands for oneself. If you believe, as Father Richard John Neuhaus does, that "a Christian university has as its premise the knowledge that all truth is one and all ways to truth are one because the Author and the End of truth is One," you will probably be uncomfortable in a secular university, and the university will probably be uncomfortable with you.

What, then, is a believer to do? If he remains true to his faith, he will put that faith first, as Neuhaus does when he endorses religious tests for appointments (in private religious institutions): "Discrimination is necessary in hiring and promotion—not necessarily discrimination on the basis of religious belief but discrimination on the basis of belief in the great good of being a Christian university." But if he wants to be accepted in the secular world, he will, in praising the tolerance which is that world's first virtue, have to open himself to questions that will sit uncomfortably with his faith. This is why some theologians argue that critical theology can be welcomed into the university, but not dogmatic or conservative theology—or why Jewish scholars frequently point out that *theology* itself is a Christian term. Such compromises are insufficient for Warren Nord, who writes, "I see no problem with an evangelical Christian or an orthodox Jew or a traditional Muslim teaching theology in a public university so long as they do not do it dogmatically, they are not subject to the control of religious authorities, and they are professionally competent." I would not see any problem either, but I would question whether such individuals, if we could find them, could be true to their religious beliefs.

In short, there is no escaping the historical dilemma faced by earlier advocates of a religious university. Marsden, Schwehn, and Nord, unlike Neuhaus, are reluctant to be too explicit here; they prefer to soften the hard edges of sectarian doctrine, offering inclusive language that sits uneasily with deeply held beliefs. Hence Nord does not come right out and say that creation science ought to be taught in the university; he instead makes the weaker claim that it is a viewpoint that ought to be recognized. Nor does Schwehn argue for the end of academic careerism, merely for softening it by emphasizing Christian virtues. By qualifying their position to make it more acceptable to contemporary academic norms, these writers also make it far more unrealistic in a world of religious belief. They have either defined a difficult problem out of existence or ignored the dilemmas that would follow if their qualifications proved to be irrelevant.

V

OF ALL ASPECTS OF the human condition, religion is the one that has had the hardest time with compromise. Schwehn reminds his readers of the tragic side of faith, the age-old resort to violence to silence those whose faith is different. But, he continues, while religious strife has been ubiquitous, so has secular strife; if anything, godless totalitarianism has killed more people in this century than all the religious wars of previous centuries. Yet surely this is an argument neither for politics nor for religion but for reason and accommodation in both. And although politics and religion both can lead to tragedy, civil authority has been far more often used to quell religious conflict than religious belief has been found to quiet civil war. Reason and compromise in politics we call democracy. Reason and compromise in faith we call civil religion, or pluralism, a giant step toward secularization. Draw the line between church and state anywhere, and some religious believers will find it in the wrong place. So long as the university is committed to knowledge, some of the faithful will always be excluded.

But they can create institutions of higher learning designed to reinforce their own beliefs. Nothing in American law or tradition prevents the devout from attending their own universities: That is the genius of the distinction we make between public and private institutions. Mark Schwehn voluntarily (and, he says, happily) chose to teach at Lutheran Valparaiso University (where he had been an undergraduate), and many parents are delighted to send their children to denominational schools. The First Amendment requires only that the state neither encourage nor discourage such efforts. This compromise is unsatisfactory for those, like Neuhaus and Himmelfarb, who believe that their church has a responsibility for the "public" soul, not just for the "private" beliefs of its adherents. And it is not an arrangement that resolves such thorny issues as whether it ought to be legal for the government to subsidize private religious education with vouchers. But no compromise can ever be perfect, and given the fact that religious conflict has led so often to bloodshed, the American compromise, which has worked so well for almost a century, is not yet obsolete. Although all these writers make eloquent statements about why they are unhappy with it, none of them comes up with a compelling case for abandoning it.

It is because our public/private compromise does work that Marsden and Neuhaus are right on one major point. In the name of pluralism and academic freedom, they argue, we insist that all institutions, even religious-oriented ones, be alike. Marsden criticizes efforts by the Middle States Association of Colleges and Schools to strip Westminster Theological Seminary of its accreditation because the institution required that its board members be clergy (in a faith that refused ordination to women). Such efforts to turn every educational institution into a carbon copy of every other one are the secular equivalent of fundamentalism. Why bother to have a distinction between public and private if we allow the public to micromanage the private? American pluralism is strong enough to survive institutions that insist not only on doing things their own way, but on paying their own way as well. That is why Marsden and Neuhaus are correct in pointing out that efforts to apply secular notions of academic freedom to private religious institutions deprive those institutions of a distinctive voice. If the distinction between public and private requires institutions in the former sector to be secular, it cannot prevent those in the latter sector from being religious.

VI

ALMOST ANYONE WHO TEACHES in the contemporary university can understand why religiously oriented critics add an important voice to the debate over higher education. Suburban prosperity does funny things to college students. Often unable to grasp the tragic sense of life, blasé to the point of indifference about the miracles of nature, art, and culture, taking for granted what required centuries of deprivation and struggle to create—American students are in desperate need of something, anything, that will offer experiences of transcendence, paradox, and wonder. As a nonbeliever, I crave religious students. At least they have something in their backgrounds to which I can appeal that was not the subject of last night's prime-time programming. Teaching classes on abortion or AIDS to students who simply cannot understand that there really are people who think about such issues in other than utilitarian ways is incredibly frustrating.

I hope, then, we can agree that students ought to develop an appreciation of and respect for religion. The question is how. Efforts to reintroduce faith into public universities—and into large private research universities—are not the way to go. In part this is because students resist anything that others do in their name and in part it is because advocates of Christian identity politics, like advocates of other identity politics, are speaking to their own needs as well as to those of the objects of their attention. But there is an even more compelling reason why disestablishment is ultimately in everyone's interest, even the interests of the faithful. Recent debates over hate speech and sensitivity training should have taught us that the university ought not to be in the business of healing the afflicted or comforting the aggrieved; we have other institutions for that. In a similar way, if the debate over the inclusion of religion in the university teaches us anything, it is that faith is vital, religion ubiquitous, and belief admirable. But we have families, churches, circles of friends, and private religious institutions to serve those needs; the inclusive university should be for something else. If it remains committed to its core mission of advancing and transmitting knowledge, some students will emerge secular, others religious, and still others indifferent to the whole business. All of us, secular and religious alike, have to take our chances with that, certain only that the university is not the place for certainties.

PART III

Race

•

Climbing the Mountain

I

To RECOUNT THE LIFE and times of Martin Luther King Jr. is to tell the story of how, more than fifty years after the century began, America finally became a modern society. It did so literally kicking and screaming, when not clubbing and killing. Our century's destiny has been to ensure that the ideal of civic equality announced to the world in 1776 would become a reality. Just to help make that come about, King had to overcome the determined resistance of terrorists without conscience, politicians without backbone, rivals without foresight, and an FBI director so malicious that he would stop at nothing to destroy a man who believed in justice.

Taylor Branch has been working on Martin Luther King Jr.'s biography for more years than King was active in the movement for civil rights. *Parting the Waters: America in the King Years, 1954–63*, the first volume in what is now planned as a trilogy, was published in 1988 and won the Pulitzer Prize for history. *At Canaan's Edge*, the final volume, will appear sometime in the future. For the time being, readers fascinated by the story of King and his country can follow events through 1965 in *Pillar of Fire: America in the King Years, 1963–65*. And what events they were. Branch's second volume begins and ends with violence: demonstrations in St. Augustine, Florida, and Selma, Alabama. In between, John F. Kennedy was assassinated, the United States became deeply involved in Vietnam, Malcolm X broke with the Nation of Islam and paid for it with his life, and President Lyndon B. Johnson

signed the Civil Rights Act of 1964 and began furious lobbying for the
even more important Voting Rights Act of 1965.

As he did in *Parting the Waters,* Branch brings to these events both
a passion for their detail and a recognition of their larger historical significance. By giving King such epic treatment, Branch implies that he
was an epic hero. Was he? The great merit of Branch's stunning accomplishment is to prove definitively that he was.

II

LIKE ODYSSEUS, KING HAD to break with comforts of home to undergo
distant, threatening, and often barely comprehensible adventures
beyond. As Branch tells the story in the trilogy's opening volume, King
was born in 1929 into a world unfamiliar to most white Americans: the
black elite of the pre–World War II South. Black Baptist preachers in
the former Confederate states, typified by King's father, were usually
Republican in their politics and entrepreneurial in their ministries. The
younger King fought against his father's insularity all his life. He left the
South for the predominantly white Crozer Theological Seminary in
Chester, Pennsylvania, and then Boston University. When called to the
ministry, King rejected the option of eventually becoming his father's
successor at Ebenezer Baptist Church in Atlanta in favor of Dexter Baptist Church in Montgomery, Alabama. Unlike Odysseus, King showed
no great desire to return home. Indeed, one measure of his accomplishment was that there was no longer a home to which he could
return. By leading the campaign to abolish segregation, King not only
destroyed the privileges Southern whites enjoyed through racism, he
also toppled the complacent black isolationism in which his father had
flourished.

All his life, King would be plagued by lesser black rivals who
resented his success. One of the more fascinating stories told in
Branch's first volume involved the power struggle between King and
the Reverend J. H. Jackson of Olivet Baptist Church in Chicago, an
acquaintance of King Sr. who, as president of the National Baptist Con-

vention, was the most powerful African American of his time. As effective as he may have been as a charismatic leader, King was no match for the wily Jackson, who not only defeated King's challenge to his leadership within the National Baptist Convention but, as Branch reports in this volume, spent $50,000 after King's death to have the entrance of his Chicago church moved around the corner so that it would no longer be on the newly named Martin Luther King Drive.

An underlying theme of *Pillar of Fire* is King's move to the national stage, which intensified the bitterness of his potential rivals. Branch tells us that Adam Clayton Powell's response to the killing of four children in a Birmingham, Alabama, church–surely the most despicable event of the civil rights era–was to predict publicly that a civil rights bill would never pass Congress (and then to offer King a job in his church in New York). At a later point Powell asked the House of Representatives to "forget about Mississippi for a while" in order to concentrate on the tribulations of Adam Clayton Powell. Every time King was criticized as too militant for the conservative black elite, he would also be criticized as too timid for the bloody taste of Malcolm X, for whom the Mau Mau warrior–"He's not humble. He's not nonviolent. But he's free"–served as an appropriate model of black protest. Even King's closest advisers allowed their petty jealousies to stand in the way of his leadership. When King was in Oslo to receive the Nobel Peace Prize, Ralph Abernathy, his designated successor, insisted on riding in the same car, objecting, to the embarrassment of all, to the careful plans of the Norwegian protocol chief. "Ralph's estrangement was much more worrisome to Martin than anything he thought J. Edgar Hoover might do," Andrew Young told Branch.

Had King actually known what Hoover was doing, he might have been more worried on that front. In August 1963, the FBI, in an internal memo, designated King "the most dangerous Negro of the future in this nation," and it began a campaign to tap his telephone and plant bugs in his hotel rooms as he traveled. The systematic character of the FBI vendetta astonishes to this day. After the bureau learned of assassination threats against a number of prominent Americans, each was notified—except King. The FBI persuaded Marquette University not to award an honorary degree to King. Under FBI prodding, Francis Cardinal Spellman of New York telephoned Pope Paul VI's secretary of state in a vain effort to prevent a papal audience for King.

"I am amazed that the Pope gave an audience to such a degenerate," Hoover wrote after the meeting. Through his bugs, Hoover had picked up evidence of marital infidelity on King's part. "This will destroy the burrhead," Hoover gloated. Doing its best to bring this prophecy about, the FBI sent some of its damaging material to King along with an anonymous suggestion that he do the honorable thing and take his own life. King, of course, did himself no favors by making himself so vulnerable. "When a man travels like you and I do," he once said to James Farmer, "there are bound to be women," hardly a sufficient excuse for his actions. Still, Branch, in one of the few times he loses his dispassionate tone in favor of sarcasm, is right to remark that when the FBI was called upon to investigate such things as bombings, it viewed those tasks "as an irritating distraction from the serious business of intercepting King's sex life."

III

DURING KING'S LIFE, BLACK Americans completed their passage from the Republican to the Democratic party; 96 percent of the black vote went to Lyndon Johnson in 1964. Yet the persistence of quasi-feudal political arrangements in the South gave disproportionate influence to racist politicians bent on obstructing King's goals. John F. Kennedy, ever fearful of the power of Southern oligarchs, appointed outright segregationists to the federal bench and shied away from any strong commitment to civil rights. Johnson's support for the passage of civil rights legislation dominates the second volume of Branch's trilogy in the way that Kennedy's political cowardice dominates the first. Still, King could never count on the backing of Democratic party politicians. Branch reports Governor Carl Sanders of Georgia as saying, "It looks like we're turning the Democratic party over to the nigras," when the Mississippi Freedom Democratic party demanded recognition at the 1964 Democratic convention in Atlantic City. Nor were Northern politicians welcoming of King. So new was the idea of massive black suffrage in American politics during the 1960s that King took care to campaign among blacks for Johnson in a way that would not arouse suspicion or resentment among whites.

Of all the obstacles to King's leadership, none was as paralyzing as the terror unleashed by racists in the South. As befits the time period he covers, Branch devotes considerable attention to the violence that took the lives of Lemuel Penn, James Chaney, Mickey Schwerner, Andrew Goodman, Vernon Dahmer, and others who were in the wrong place at their rightful time. Segregation did not kill; people did. And just as we were made witness to the inhumanity of Mississippi's Parchman penitentiary in *Parting the Waters,* so in *Pillar of Fire* we learn through Branch's meticulous attention to detail who these murderers were, how they planned their deeds, and how they too often escaped the consequences of their acts. Terrorism relied for its effectiveness on the racism of genteel society. Senator George Smathers of Florida told President Johnson that King must have organized most of the violence against himself, because "he loves the headlines." Caught near a violent mob in Neshoba County, Mississippi, Branch recounts, Claude Sitton, a reporter for the *New York Times,* ducked into a furniture store that he knew to be owned by the uncle of Turner Catledge, the managing editor of his newspaper. "I wouldn't lift one damn finger to help you," Catledge's uncle told him. Even after King won the Nobel Peace Prize, powerful white Atlantans tried unsuccessfully to stop a dinner in his honor. The South really was another country. To enter its precincts in search of goals as conservative as the right to vote or to drink a cup of coffee in a restaurant, individuals had to entertain the possibility that they would never come out alive. As horrible as slavery was, slaveholders could at least claim that the Constitution gave them sanction. That was no longer possible after passage of the Fourteenth Amendment. In this one way was segregation worse than slavery, for its practitioners not only showed enormous disrespect for human life but in the process corrupted the supreme law of the land.

Against all these forces, Martin Luther King Jr. managed to build upon America's religious and moral foundations to uphold the dignity of the individual. "Mississippi has treated the Negro as if he is a thing instead of a person," King declared, echoing Immanuel Kant. On another occasion, he said of civil rights demonstrators: "The patter of their feet as they walked through Jim Crow barriers in the great stride toward freedom is the thunder of the marching men of Joshua. And the world rocks beneath their tread. My people, my people, listen, listen, the battle is in our hands." In the aftermath of the Birmingham bombing, King spoke not of retribution but of redemption: "We must not lose faith in our white brothers. Somehow we must believe that the most misguided among them can learn to respect the dignity and worth of all human personality." Words like these are rarely heard in American politics these days, because so few have the moral stature to utter them.

But King's accomplishments moved well beyond words. Without him, the United States might not have got the legislation that enabled it to become the democracy it had always proclaimed itself to be. After King, we argue how his dream can best be fulfilled. We forget how significant it is that we no longer argue about whether it should be fulfilled. Taylor Branch's treatment of King's life raises no new issues of historical reinterpretation. It uncovers no new documentary evidence. It tells no story that has not been told before. But it does something more important; it reminds us that there once arose in our midst a man who, as Odysseus's son, Telemachus, said of his father, "more than all other men, was born for pain." America was lifted up because King would not lay his burden down. King's tragic sensibility was the direct opposite of today's feel-good therapeutics. "If freedom is to be a reality," he told the 1964 annual convention of the United Synagogues of America, "the Negro must be willing to suffer and to sacrifice and to work for it." For all the tribulations his enemies confronted him with, it is not those who foolishly and vainly stood in his way whom we remember, but Martin Luther King Jr., our century's epic hero.

The Facts and the Feelings

I

A S IF WRITTEN TO COLLIDE with each other, two huge books have appeared that advance radically different interpretations of the state of race in America. David Shipler, the author of a book on Arabs and Jews and a book on Russia, has returned to the United States after years as a foreign correspondent. In *A Country of Strangers: Blacks and Whites in America,* he engages in "an act of discovery . . . a personal quest" to explain how "a white person who had grown up in privilege" reacts to a country "where racist thoughts and images are quieter, subtler, insidious." Stephan Thernstrom and Abigail Thernstrom—the one a Harvard historian and renowned student of ethnicity, the other a fellow at the Manhattan Institute—conclude in *America in Black and White: One Nation, Indivisible* that America has experienced dramatic improvement in its racial agony since Gunnar Myrdal's *An American Dilemma* (1944).

These accounts not only differ in their conclusions, they differ also in how they reach them. Shipler's method is subjectivity: he allows those with whom he speaks, including his own children, to speak through him to the rest of America. Empathic and emotional, Shipler writes as a revivalist preacher, asking white people to look into their souls and to change their ways. The Thernstroms believe that it is not people's feelings that are important, but, as Marxists used to say, objective conditions. They are no Marxists, but they are certainly objectivists, and they write as social scientists, assembling data, weighing evidence, testing ideas. Shipler sometimes turns to numbers, and the

Thernstroms occasionally get passionate; but you would be hard pressed to find two books that go about the same task in such dramatically different ways.

For this reason, the appearance of these books is a fine occasion for a reckoning. Contrasting Shipler and the Thernstroms yields answers to the question of how much progress America has made on the racial front, answers that have important political implications; but it also yields answers to the question of how we make judgments about the extent of such progress. The question of method should never be neglected. President Clinton asked Americans to have a national dialogue on race. Before people can talk to each other, however, they must have some way of verifying the truth of what they are saying. If people will not agree on method, they will not agree on substance.

II

HERE IS A STORY about method. As Shipler describes it, Roger Wilkins, a journalist and historian who teaches at George Mason University, bumps into Senator John Danforth in the lobby of the Senate office building. "Hello, Senator," he says to him, "I'm Roger Wilkins." The senator, used to this kind of greeting, takes his hand and responds: "Hello, Roger." Wilkins is offended. Whites, he believes, too often belittle blacks; and calling a distinguished-looking professional such as himself by his first name is a sure sign of racism. But Danforth is a politician, Shipler responds. He would call anyone, white or black, by his first name. Not so, responds Wilkins.

After this incident, Shipler encounters the senator. "Hello, Senator Danforth," he says, holding out his hand. "I'm David Shipler." "Hello, David," responds Danforth. The obvious conclusion is that Danforth has been offered a test of racism and, to his credit, has flunked it. But Wilkins is unconvinced. Since whites once held blacks in conditions of second-class citizenship, he tells Shipler, Danforth should have known better. The only way that Danforth could prove his lack of racism would be to call him Mr. Wilkins. Shipler never says what he thinks of

Wilkins's reasoning. But he trusts Wilkins as "insightful," and he tells the reader that he relied on him as an expert in "the nuances of black-white miscommunication."

Shipler is a journalist, but here he aspires to be a microsociologist of race relations. He focuses on the everyday interactions, the casual conversations, the daily rituals of contact between blacks and whites in America. The underlying theme of his book is that whites, having witnessed the passing of macroracism in the form of legal segregation, believe that racial justice has been all but achieved, whereas blacks, witnessing microracism everywhere around them, believe the opposite. This difference in perception permeates everything: language, deportment, manners, memory, sex, morality, cognition, style. Whites, rarely thinking about racism, walk around self-confident, open, innocent—and oblivious to the myriad ways they offend black sensitivities. Blacks, thinking about racism all the time, become defensive and suspicious, withdrawing into racial exclusion or proclaiming racial pride.

Now, America desperately needs a microsociology of race relations. One can only wonder what Erving Goffman, if he were still alive, would make of the daily interactions between blacks and whites in our inflamed and hypersensitive racial environment. But the very mention of Goffman's name reminds us how few have the skills to penetrate the secrets of the games that people play with each other, especially about race. David Shipler does not possess those skills. Indeed, he commits two mistakes that distort his sentimental tour through these minefields.

Shipler's first mistake is that he approaches his interviews knowing what he wants people to say. Consider Nancy Deuchler, who is the black manager of a B. Dalton's bookstore in Chicago. Every now and then a white person will approach her and ask to speak to the manager. When she responds that they are speaking to the manager, they are often taken aback. But only for an instant: "Then they would just get over that and deal with me," she tells Shipler. "I have no problems, I've never had problems." Here is a case that undermines Shipler's thesis that for black Americans racial insult is omnipresent. But he will not be dissuaded. "Still," he manages to conclude, "she mentioned it." As if a person being interviewed for a book about race is going to bring up the subject of mountain biking! And off he goes to tell the stories of other African Americans whose experiences with whites are less positive. Goffman taught microsociology to search for the unexpected, for the jarring incident that forces the conclusion that reality is always more complicated than we are prepared to admit. Shipler is so persuaded that he understands reality that he cannot hear those who are telling him that he is wrong.

Shipler's second mistake is to overempathize with his subjects. He simply cannot look his friend in the face and say, "You know, Roger, you were completely wrong about Danforth." It is not Shipler's task, as he understands it, to point out the error of others' ways, especially if they are black. The empathic scribe records, he does not criticize. True, Shipler exposes the factual inaccuracies of some of the more extreme versions of Afrocentrism, such as Portland's Baseline Essays, but he also implores white Americans to understand why it is so important for black Americans to claim ancient Egypt as their own. No such empathy is shown for Afrocentrism's critics. They are engaged in "a backlash of defensive outrage," people who "sneer at any Afrocentric 'facts' that violate what they think they know" and as a result express "contempt" for leading Afrocentric thinkers such as Molefi Kete Asante.

The best ethnographers bend over backward to avoid excessive identification with their subjects. They know that understanding requires distance. Shipler holds instead to what the professors call a "standpoint epistemology": how you understand the world is directly tied to your place in the world. Wittingly or not, Shipler is a party to the fashionable assault on objectivity. When it comes to race, certainly, there is never, in Shipler's view, one truth about a specific situation; there are at least two truths, and perhaps more. Since only blacks can know the truth of black pain, ethnographic distance is impossible. Whites and blacks perceive different truths, and so whites must give blacks the benefit of the epistemological doubt.

From Shipler's perspective, there is one place that we are particularly forbidden to enter in our flawed attempts to establish truth, and that is history. For blacks and whites think about the past in different ways. White Americans have "short memories," but "black America . . . feels the reverberations of slavery, yearns for roots, searches for pride, and reaches back to grasp at ancient uncertainties." Shipler talked to an African American student at Colgate who, on his dean's advice, takes two sets of notes in his courses. One is based on the "white lies" told by his teachers—Socrates was Greek, Columbus discovered America—which he duly recounts to pass the tests he had to pass. The other, Afrocentric in texture, is designed "to keep your own sanity." "You got to lie, you can't tell the truth," a University of Nebraska student told Shipler. "He reminded me," he comments, "of the freethinking Soviet students I had known, who had learned one set of facts around the kitchen table but knew what they were required to say in school." But those Soviet students were right: they were being fed lies. Shipler's African American students are wrong. Had Socrates not been Greek, as Mary Lefkowitz has pointed out, surely a xenophobic Athenian would have mentioned it. And it is not only the fanciful adherents of Afrocentrism who are misled by false historical accounts. One of Shipler's respondents waxes nostalgic for the segregated schools of the South. "Since white schools didn't hire blacks with Ph.D.'s, a lot of them were teaching in predominantly black schools," this sociologist told him. "Yes, it was segregated," a vice principal in Chicago reflects. "Yes, the books were probably five years old, but they were wonderful books— Carter G. Woodson and that kind of thing," he says, referring to one of the leaders of the revival of interest in black history.

Actually, as the Thernstroms point out, Jim Crow schools were "dreadful." They deliberately tried to keep black students ignorant of the world. When Myrdal toured the South in the late 1930s, one-third of the teachers in Southern black schools lacked even a high school degree. Horace Mann Bond administered the Stanford Achievement Test to black public school teachers in Alabama in 1931 and found their scores below the national norm for ninth graders. Nor were these schools examples of black pride in miniature: Myrdal visited one in which not a single black student had heard of the National Association for the Advancement of Colored People or W. E. B. Du Bois, though one student did recognize Booker T. Washington as "a big white man." Shipler's vice principal dates his experience in the segregated South to 1952, and it may have been the case that at that time, determined to head off the Supreme Court, white legislators had set about improving black schools in the South. But none of this is considered by Shipler. He seems to think that if his black respondents believed things were better under Jim Crow, then better they must have been.

In his effort to posit divergent racial styles of recall, Shipler appears to suggest that for black Americans facts do not matter. Not all of his respondents agree. Levi Nwachuka, a Nigerian historian at Pennsylvania's Lincoln University, was appalled that not a single one of his students could identify an African country on a blank map of Africa. Maybe, he gently suggested to Shipler, his students would be better off with more facts and fewer myths? To which Shipler contrasts the view of Haki Madhubuti, a poet and publisher in Chicago: "I can claim anything in Africa I want." Shipler himself is not the best of historians; he predates Boston's busing controversy by eight years, for example. Perhaps that explains why he seems so indifferent to the tragedy of students so cruelly stripped of the capacity of learning how the world around them came to be.

History, for Shipler, has a primarily therapeutic function. It allows blacks to believe in things that give them pride, even in things that never happened. It gives whites an opportunity for redemption. Visiting Somerset Place, a North Carolina plantation once run by the slaveholding Collins family, Shipler encounters John Graham, a Duke University administrator who is a descendant of the Collins clan. Graham is actively involved in reconstructing the plantation and regularly attends the gatherings organized there by descendants of the slaves. He expected resentment from them, but he found that "people were really very easily engaged. . . . There really was an opportunity for dialogue and a relationship." Of course, Graham himself never owned slaves. Still, he tells Shipler, "I suspect that if I had lived in those times and been in their shoes, I would have been a slave-owner too." Shipler is attracted to Graham because he wrestles with his responsibility for racism, "something few whites do." Yet what can responsibility mean in this context? Graham cannot undo what his ancestors did, and the descendants of the victims cannot forgive him, since there is nothing to forgive. No doubt Graham is a very sincere man, but there is actually little "wrestling" going on here; each side plays its assigned role in the drama of race relations, drawing the appropriate therapeutic conclusions from history without ever confronting the reality of the history that they are discussing.

For Shipler, racial justice will not occur in America until the entire country has experienced one massive sensitivity training session. Whites "rarely know how their behavior is perceived, how their comments are taken, how their actions may be subtly shaped by latent biases." Blacks have no monopoly on the truth, Shipler concludes, but "they can teach white Americans how to examine themselves, how to interpret their own attitudes, how to gain self-knowledge." The trouble is that "there is much that is deeply buried, and unless we work at digging it up for inspection, we remain strangers to ourselves as well as to each other." We can learn to talk to one another, but we have to learn to cry on one another's shoulders first.

III

Stephan Thernstrom and Abigail Thernstrom see very little to cry over in contemporary America's race relations. Like Shipler, they turn somewhat didactically to history for lessons. But whereas the tender-minded Shipler knows all he needs to know about the present and looks to the past for catharsis, the tough-minded Thernstroms insist that the more we learn about the past, the better we will be able to make judgments about the present. If things have gotten worse, then radical steps may be necessary to further racial justice. If they have gotten better, then it is time to rethink the way we consider race.

The Thernstroms maintain that things have gotten better. They comb census data, public opinion polls, and the research of other social scientists to come up with tidbits such as these: in the 1980s the rate of suburbanization for blacks was four times what it was for whites; 40 percent of African Americans consider themselves middle class; some whites express a dislike for blacks, but in far lower proportions than Bulgarians express for Turks, East Germans for Poles, or Russians for Azerbaijanis; schools attended by minority students generally receive more public funding than schools that are not; the income gap between Jews and Gentiles is nearly twice that between whites and blacks; a greater proportion of whites convicted of murder are handed the death sentence compared with blacks; blacks have not been admitted to the University of Mississippi in proportion to their percentage of the state's population, but their graduation rate is roughly equal to that of whites.

Behind such numbers, they argue, lie profound changes in America's racial fabric. In politics, the number of black officeholders increased from 1,469 in 1970 to 8,406 in 1995. Black mayors have been elected in Dayton, Cincinnati, Grand Rapids, Pontiac, Boulder, Roanoke, Little Rock, Hartford, and Dallas, among other cities. Once invisible in Southern legislatures, 312 black Americans served in them by 1993. On the national level, "the Democratic party would have lost every presidential election from 1968 to the present if only whites had been allowed to vote." Racist campaigns have all but disappeared in America "because they cost votes."

The same kind of progress can be seen in the growth of the black middle class. Economic achievement is linked to schooling. In 1960, the percentage of whites who attended college (17.4 percent) was more than twice that of blacks (7.2 percent). By 1995, a gap still existed (49.0 percent for whites, 37.5 percent for blacks), but it had significantly narrowed. And with it, so has the income gap. Black males now earn 67 percent of what white males earn, up from 41 percent in 1940; and the figures for black females are even higher. If we compare the median income of intact black families with intact white families, blacks make 87 percent of what whites make. Now, 31.9 percent of blacks in America live in the suburbs, compared to 15 percent in 1950. Forty-two percent of all black households in America own their own home, still below the 69 percent of whites, but more than twice the proportion reported by Myrdal in 1944.

The Thernstroms spend considerable energy demolishing the prediction of the Kerner Commission in 1968 that racism would create two nations in America, separate and unequal. The Kerner Commission never anticipated immigration, which brought new life to America's inner cities. It was unable to imagine that white flight from the cities would someday be equaled by black flight. The dire warnings of the Kerner Commission begin to approximate reality only in some cities, especially formerly industrial ones in the Midwest such as Detroit. The great bulk of urban growth in America since 1968, however, took place in cities such as San Jose and Phoenix, where the black population was, and still is, relatively small. Some residential segregation persists, moreover, because blacks want it that way. In sum, "by every possible measure . . . the residential separation of blacks and whites in the United States has diminished substantially over the past three decades."

Is the Thernstroms' positive interpretation of these trends justified? It is not, after all, as if they come to the subject without opinions; they are both known as right-of-center participants in the debates about race. They do not hide their political views in their book, and they acknowledge support from the same kind of conservative funding sources that supported Charles Murray and Dinesh D'Souza. Yet nothing in the Thernstroms' work resembles the work of Murray or D'Souza. The Thernstroms criticize the conservative "see no evil" view as well as the left's "going nowhere picture of black America and white racial attitudes." They rarely rely on rhetoric or polemic to make points, preferring arguments about data. If they cannot draw a conclusion, they do not draw one: when they discuss why black SAT scores have declined since 1988, they admit to being "stumped." And when there is bad news to report, findings that run against the grain of their positive story, they generally report it. They note, for example, that in spite of the narrowing of the income gap between blacks and whites, there remains a huge gap in the accumulation of wealth. They record the depressing news that whites think that 32 percent of the American population is black. And they are fully aware that black poverty—a state in which 29 percent of African Americans find themselves, triple the rate among whites—remains "the single most depressing fact about the state of black America today."

Still, the Thernstroms sometimes read the data as they would prefer to read them. Take that "depressing" news about black poverty. They contend that it is not racism that explains why black poverty persists; rather, "it is family structure that largely divides the haves from the have-nots in the black community." In 1959, 61 percent of children in intact families were poor compared to 13 percent in 1995. Today very few Americans who hold full-time jobs—white or black, male or female—live below the poverty level. Black poverty is therefore primarily due to an increase in the number of single mothers. Since 1987, the Thernstroms point out, fertility and marriage have been negatively correlated among blacks; that is to say, the birth rate among married black women was lower than the birth rate for unmarried black women, "the first time that has happened for any ethnic group." This is truly an astonishing trend, and the Thernstroms are right to confer such significance upon it. And yet I see no reason to conclude that racial discrimination no longer plays a significant role in perpetuating higher poverty rates among blacks than whites.

Those who believe that discrimination is still a powerful force in American life often cite "audit studies" in which equally matched black and white job applicants will present themselves to unsuspecting vendors or employers. Three such studies are reviewed by the Thernstroms. A Denver study in 1991 showed no substantial differences between black and white testers; a Chicago study in 1990 indicated that whites were preferred over blacks twice as often as blacks were preferred over whites; and a Washington, D.C., study in 1990 found that whites were chosen over blacks in 20 percent of the cases while blacks were preferred over whites in 5 percent, a fourfold preference for the one group over the other.

One conclusion to be drawn is that Chicago seems the typical case, with Washington atypical because discrimination there was so high and Denver atypical because it was so low. Yet the Thernstroms dismiss the Chicago results as based on too small a sample, and they criticize the Washington results for concentrating on private employers when the public sector is so large in the capital. Now, it is always possible to find fault with studies such as these. That is how social scientists make their living. Yet who can deny that some racial discrimination in employment still exists? Indeed, the Thernstroms are careful to say as much. Since they find any such discrimination abhorrent, one wonders why the Thernstroms are so reluctant to display a little more empathy toward those who are refused jobs through no fault of their own.

Another potential indication of the persistence of discrimination by race involves housing. "The residential separation of the races is one of the most conspicuous features of the typical American metropolis today," the Thernstroms correctly point out. But how much of that separation is caused by discrimination? Not much, they answer. They discuss a study that showed that black buyers and renters were shown 25 percent fewer available properties than whites and that roughly one out of ten black testers were steered to primarily black neighborhoods. "These figures do not seem high enough to support the claim that patterns of exclusion are the norm rather than the exception." But the question is not whether discrimination is the norm. The question is whether discrimination at the margins can have substantial effects on the persistence of residential segregation.

For the Thernstroms, it cannot. Demand, in their view, is sovereign; bias resides in customer preferences, not in manipulations of supply. "The 'steering' metaphor is misleading in its implication that real estate agents are in the driver's seat, and that they take their clients to destinations they would not have chosen on their own," they conclude. "The agents are more like taxi-drivers; they turn the wheel, control the gas pedal and the brakes, but the customer decides where the vehicle is headed." Yet housing is not governed by the universal logic of supply and demand but by local customs. In Atlanta and Washington, D.C., the

Thernstroms may be right: black suburbanites prefer to live in black suburbs. But what if there are no black suburbs?

In Boston, black middle-class families fleeing the city have little choice but to find housing in suburbs predominantly occupied by whites. Highly publicized incidents—such as the one in which police stopped a member of the Boston Celtics in his own suburb for no other reason than his race—have created a veritable folk culture around which suburbs welcome blacks and which do not. Should a relatively large number of potential black residents choose not to look for housing in those perceived as hostile—and then should there be a 10 percent rate of racial steering imposed on those who do—the result would easily turn into a nearly all-white suburb. "Biases in the real estate market certainly exist, but they appear minor compared to the biases of real estate customers themselves," the Thernstroms write. I see nothing in their data that warrants such a sweeping conclusion.

There are occasions in which the Thernstroms' distaste for affirmative action affects their interpretation of data. "On many accounts," they write, "the socioeconomic gains made by African Americans in the affirmative action era have been less impressive than those that occurred before preferential policies." Yet their own data show dramatic increases in the percentage of black doctors, lawyers, and engineers between 1970 and 1990. This suggests that it is not the pace of middle-class growth that matters, but the shift to more professional middle-class jobs. Acknowledging this, the Thernstroms write that such a result "undoubtedly does reflect the fact that the nation's professional schools changed their admissions standards for black applicants." But instead of concluding that a policy they clearly do not like nonetheless had at least one positive result, they ask whether such gains are really worth the costs of affirmative action. Besides, "black practitioners of these professions make up a small fraction of the total black middle class today." This backtracking sounds disturbingly like Roger Wilkins in reverse: if the results of the test are unacceptable, change the test.

America in Black and White is neither a work of scholarship written from no particular point of view nor a personal essay that asserts a point of view without evidence. It is a bit of both: an intervention into a public debate that asks that the criteria for resolving the debate be factual. The book's great strength, revealed most clearly in its historical sections, is its insistence that some of our most contentious questions have answers. Its most conspicuous weakness, most prominent in its treatment of contemporary debates over federal contracts or voting rights that rely less on data collection, is that it sometimes finds those answers too predictably.

IV

IS IT POSSIBLE TO SAY anything conclusive about racial progress in America? If the empathic approach of David Shipler is too subjective and anecdotal to be trusted, the data-driven approach of the Thernstroms is neither value-free nor unambiguous. Still, this is not one of those subjects for which evenhandedness is the best policy. Both of these books have flaws, but it would be wrong to conclude that neither has an advantage over the other.

Where race is concerned, it is time for facts to win out over rhetoric. One could discount by 25 percent every development that the Thernstroms discuss and still come away astonished at how radically America has changed in so short a time. Any American fifty years old has witnessed America move from a society in which most whites would never have the opportunity to interact with black people on equal terms to a society in which David Shipler's black respondents complain of not being able to discuss Malcolm X in a class at the Air Force Academy, of finding King Kong racist, of meeting whites curious about their braids, of worrying about losing their street jargon if they attend suburban high schools, and of being refused service in a Princeton eating club. The notion that we live in the same old racist America–"as segregated now as it was in 1954," as President Franklyn Jennifer of Howard University said in 1992–is absurd.

As if it were not enough in one lifetime to have abolished legal segregation, America has also made dramatic progress in matters closer to the heart. Shipler relates the occasional rudeness experienced by interracial couples; but the Thernstroms point out a dramatic increase in interracial marriage from 0.7 percent of all new marriages by African Americans in 1963 to 12.1 percent in 1993. Shipler asks white Americans to recognize the lurking racism in the way they think about crime; but the Thernstroms discuss data showing that blacks are more fearful of crime than whites. Shipler tells tales of isolation and separation; but the Thernstroms report data showing huge increases in black and white social contact–churches, friendships, neighborhoods–since the 1960s. Taken together, the data assembled by the Thernstroms paint a picture of progress on enough fronts that the methodological questions can once and for all be resolved: race relations have improved dramatically in America, and those who believe otherwise are wrong.

Of course, people may agree that great progress has been made toward racial equality and still disagree about how much remains or about what ought to be done. Shipler, and those who think like him, continue to adhere to what can be called "black exceptionalism." This way of thinking suggests that all groups in America have to obey the same rules, except blacks. To those who feel that African Americans need special legislative districts or separate admissions committees for professional schools, Shipler adds the idea that blacks are also exceptional in their feelings. I find this notion of an apartheid of the mind repellent. It reverberates with discredited theories that how we think or feel is inextricably linked to the genes that we happen to have. And it does something that a liberal polity ought never to do: it probes too deeply into feelings. Shipler declares that "this is the ideal: to search your attitudes, identify your stereotypes, and correct for them as you go about your daily duties." His language reminds me of China's thought police, and leaves my blood running cold.

Black exceptionalism, as the Thernstroms' history makes clear, grew out of demands for "black power" that came to dominate the civil rights movement after the riots of the 1960s. In retrospect, the problematic term in that demand is not *black,* it is *power.* Our society can tolerate expressions of black pride just as it tolerates expressions of Jewish pride or Italian pride. But it also requires that our politics be held together by something more than power. No group in our society–no matter how small, no matter how victimized–can ever be permitted to believe that it can have a slice of power to itself, beyond the scrutiny and the checks of others. That applies as much to the power of sympathy as it does to political power. Black exceptionalism in politics corrupts democracy. A black exceptionalism of the emotions is not a recipe for understanding. It is a license for psychological blackmail.

Or so one of Shipler's examples demonstrates. In the most pathetic moment in his book, he describes one of those workshop exercises so favored by diversity trainers these days. Each person in the room was asked to walk about and choose the person most different from himself. Shipler and a young black woman found each other. How many of you, the facilitator asked the entire group, have considered not having children because of racism? Not only did Shipler's partner stand, but so did a dozen or so other women, mostly black and Latino. "Since my children are my fondest joy," Shipler writes, "I cannot imagine many sadnesses more profound than this." Give me a break. Either the women who stood were indulging in an emotional theatricality that cost them nothing or they were sincere. If the former, then they may fool the Shiplers of the world, but they are unlikely to persuade anyone with even a modicum of common sense. If the latter, then they have a problem that not even the complete elimination of white racism will help them solve.

When President Clinton called for a national conversation on race, my first reaction was indifference: commissions rarely do any good, but they rarely do any harm. Having read Shipler, I am now convinced that a national conversation on race can be downright harmful. For Shipler shows why the current craving for dialogue is actually just another form of black exceptionalism. Any good conversation presupposes equality among the speakers; each has something to say and is expected to say it. But the "dialogue" that Shipler urges goes only one way: the self-designated victims are given the right to lecture all and sundry, in any way they want, on any topic they choose, based on the supposition that contrary opinions do not constitute legitimate disagreement but examples of the very kinds of racism the conversation was called into being to stop. This is talk to end all talk, a conversation designed to shut people up and shut people in.

What Shipler thinks of as heartfelt dialogue and profound conversation strikes me as demeaning to all sides. His examples paint a picture of black America represented not by those who have struggled against persistent discrimination to make it, but by those who, in insisting that black success is impossible in racist America, send out a message of numbing resignation. And his white America is symbolized not by those who have taken dramatic strides to move beyond the racism of their parents' generation, but by those so ashamed of themselves that they take pleasure in confessing to sins they never committed. When black self-pity meets white self-hatred, we are better off not speaking.

The Thernstroms, one presumes, are not big on talk. They offer the implicit message that, while intellectuals complain about our lack of racial equality, ordinary people of both races are simply making it happen. They do not conclude that we have reached a state of genuine racial equality or that we no longer need the Civil Rights Act. They do suggest that we should start treating African Americans as an ethnic group trying to make its breakthrough in pluralist America and stop treating them as a racial group confronting persistent discrimination.

I am more cautious than the Thernstroms. I would not go as far in claiming that color-blind public policies and continued economic growth will produce the further progress in racial equality that our society requires. Yet I think that they are right to insist that what has most characterized discussions of race in the United States is a "lack of analytic rigor," and that this has permitted a remarkable amount of demagoguery to pass as serious thinking. For this reason, their tough-minded book serves the cause of racial justice. It shows that the issue is not whether black exceptionalism should end. The issue is when.

Margaret Mead Goes to Harlem

THE FIRST POINT THAT Katherine Newman sets out to establish in
No Shame in My Game: The Working Poor in the Inner City is that
there really are working poor in the inner city. Newman believes that
most Americans are so hostile to those who live at the bottom of the
economic pyramid that they fail to recognize how many of them work,
and work hard. An anthropologist by training, she went to Harlem not
to study drug addicts and squeegee men, but to record the lives of ordinary people trying to form families, to hold down jobs, and to make
ends meet.

Newman calls these people "the invisible poor." This echoing of
Michael Harrington is meant to remind us that before poverty became
"racialized"–that is, before we automatically assumed that poor people
were black and lived in the inner city–we used to be more sympathetic
to those left behind by capitalism's progress. If we come to realize how
hardworking poor people in Harlem really are, she believes, we will be
less likely to view them as residents of some other world to which we
have no obligation.

Newman organized her research around working at a chain of
hamburger outlets very much resembling McDonald's. If you have not
spent much time in Harlem, she tells her readers, you probably do not
understand the kinds of people who flip hamburgers for the company
she calls Burger Barn. In the suburbs, where workers are scarce,
teenagers take such jobs to gain extra income for their wardrobes. In
demand, they earn somewhat more than the minimum wage. Their

jobs are transitional, ending when the kids go off to college or find "real" work doing something else.

In Harlem, however, many African American and Latino young people growing up in the area will be lured by street life. But some will not be lured. Determined to set out on their own, they search for work, hoping to land a job in the public sector, but lacking the necessary contacts and skills, especially at a time when such jobs are disappearing. Contacts are necessary even to find work at Burger Barn; Newman cannot emphasize enough the role that informal networks play in labor markets. For those with access to such networks, McJobs pay the minimum wage and offer few opportunities for advancement. What they provide is an opportunity to establish an employment record. That is why such jobs are not be scorned; working at a hamburger franchise is, in its own way, a certificate of respectability.

As they work, so do they live. Most of us, Newman argues, have a distorted view of what family life is like among the inner-city poor. Convinced that young black females have large numbers of illegitimate children, and that young black males flee their financial and emotional responsibilities, we fail to appreciate how difficult it is to support a family on low pay without health insurance. People who live on very little income may not have conventional families, but they still have families. Immigrants live together in large extended families, pooling their incomes, whether from welfare or work, to make ends meet. Young unwed mothers love their babies just like everyone else. And many men in Harlem "help to support the households they live in and often provide regular infusions of cash, food, and time to the mothers of their children with whom they do not live."

If working gives structure to family life, it also undergirds education. Focused on middle-class kids, we tend to think that working takes time and energy away from schooling. But not in the inner city. People who work at Burger Barn are often high school dropouts. Lest the reader think that dead-end jobs match their lack of skills, Newman emphasizes the maturity and the discipline needed to work under pressure. Given responsibility for the first time in their lives—and suddenly realizing what will happen to them in the future if they do not shape up—they return to school or obtain a GED degree, finding themselves in possession of the discipline and the study habits they once lacked.

Do any of these workers actually make it out of the ghetto? Newman, whose previous book was on downward mobility, is not about to turn into an enthusiast for the upward variety. Emphasizing her own brush with low-wage labor when her parents fell on hard times, she notes the degree to which she benefited from middle-class values and the availability of financial aid to attend college. Yet Burger Barn workers do not have the advantages now that she did then. They try, heaven knows, to work their way up, but all too often they find themselves stuck in the same place. Confronting employers' racial stereotypes, cutbacks in municipal services, and the burdens of their own pasts, a few of them are able to enter management training programs, but most churn about in jobs meant for teenagers, not for adults with family responsibilities.

Newman deserves praise for bringing to life the working poor of Harlem. Prescient in her choice of subject matter, she understood, even before welfare reform made it the law of the land, that work, not government support, was going to shape the debate over obligations to the poor. Her research focuses, moreover, on people with whom every sympathetic middle-class reader ought to identify. Who can doubt that, in turning its back on the ne'er-do-wells of the underclass, America has also turned its back on people deserving of all the support an affluent society can give them? Reasonable people can disagree about how much equality there ought to be, but no one but the cruelest can think a society just if it allows some people to reap unearned stock options worth millions while others struggle, through no fault of their own, with conditions of life beneath the threshold of decency. There was a time, before academics studied pornographers and tattoo artists, when social scientists held up the plight of the working poor as emblematic of society's capacity for solidarity. Newman belongs in that great tradition.

And her accomplishments do not stop there. Newman's kind of urban anthropology is, to put it mildly, not the easiest kind of research to conduct. Finding and winning the confidence of the people whom she studied required dogged persistence. To carry out her project, Newman employed a veritable army of graduate students unwilling to settle for superficial impressions; when Newman describes the complexities of what many of us might characterize as dead-end jobs, she does so by reporting on the efforts of her students to actually perform these jobs under real-life conditions. Newman, in short, is the very opposite of the bloodless social scientist poring over numbers in an effort to establish significant correlations.

The problem is that the impressive scholarship that shines through Newman's book is attended by an utterly conventional political sensibility. Rarely have I read a book so marked by deep curiosity about how the world works but connected to so many platitudes about how the world ought to work. Newman is not content to let her empirical work speak for itself. She peppers her book with minieditorials chastising middle-class readers for their unenlightened views about the poor. There is a shame in Newman's game, a deeply regrettable shame. She is so persuaded of the need to fit everything she observes into her unexamined presuppositions that she is incapable of telling the real story that is found on every page of her book. It is the story that our country needs; for if, as Newman insists, it is a story that challenges conservative prejudices, it challenges even more—and in every way—the usual answers offered by the left to the perplexities of poverty in America.

II

CONSIDER, FOR A START, the hero of Newman's book: capitalism, and more specifically the policies of a company that, at least in Newman's account, is more committed to eradicating urban poverty than any Upper West Side liberal. It turns out that Burger Barn did not come into Harlem to exploit customers and workers. Acutely alive to its location, the company has a deliberate policy of overlooking early brushes with the law among potential employees. From Newman's descriptions of the hassles of living in poverty without medical insurance or adequate child care–frequent emergency room visits which can last most of a day, crippling asthma and diabetes–one gets the sense of an employer willing to give its workers considerable latitude in bending their work schedules to accommodate their hectic lives.

Newman paints a picture of franchise owners as deeply engaged in the civic life of Harlem, working closely with kids on a one-to-one basis, owing not only to their own idealism but also to the requirements of their company. Despite Newman's pessimism about the life chances of these workers, Burger Barn has instituted extensive programs to train minority workers to become franchise owners. (Harlem residents in the program are trained in a comfortable hotel on Long Island.) We even learn at one point that, for all of Newman's talk about contracting opportunities, "the inner city is actually an expanding market for Burger Barn," which means that "demand for management is steady."

I confess to being stunned by what I learned from this book about the enlightened corporate policies of this chain of hamburger restaurants. I am enough of an old-fashioned social democrat to have believed that only extensive government programs can do anything to reverse the conditions of life in the inner city; but Newman's book, more than any tract from the Heritage Foundation, has persuaded me otherwise.

Consider the National Youth Apprenticeship Program. Sixty years ago, such a name would have conjured up images of a New Deal agency. But this is a program run by private companies such as Walgreen's, Hyatt, and McDonald's. Working in some of the toughest inner-city schools in the country, NYAP separates promising students out from the rest of the school population and works with them, and their teachers, to improve their school performance–with often dramatic results. In return for taking on a more demanding academic program, students are offered summer jobs, managerial-track work at the age of eighteen, and help with community college costs. Newman rightly praises this program. What she does not discuss is how middle-class America can be so hostile to the poor if such quintessential institutions of middle-class America are doing so much good.

There is another hero in Newman's tale, and it is work. One would have to comb out-of-print management manuals to find encomia to work as enthusiastic as those of Newman's inner-city residents. After confessing a certain embarrassment at wearing the franchise's uniform, one of her respondents says: "I'm proud that I'm working. You know my daughter's father . . . used to grab pigs and clean pigs all day. But he was respected for his job . . . Anybody who could work any kind of job should be respected. Because they was getting that money honestly. They don't have to go out there and get it illegal." Middle-class morality, Newman convincingly demonstrates, does not stop with the middle class. If these inner-city poor voted, and if they voted based on their attitudes toward work, they would almost certainly vote Republican.

And they cling to these attitudes in the face of withering criticism from the nonworking poor. Serving hamburgers to people with whom they once dropped out of school, broke into buildings, or shared drugs, these young workers need to steel themselves against the "dissing" of those who are convinced that working, like doing well in school, is one more way of acting white. The tormentors, moreover, torment for a reason; all it takes is one angry outburst from the person punching orders into the cash register and one is back on the street, the dissing having accomplished its objective of guaranteeing a kind of primitive equality. Reading Newman's account of such people fills the reader with admiration for their moral courage.

But alas, moral courage is a term not permitted in Newman's political ideology. Deathly afraid that praising some for their moral backbone will be taken as a judgment that others–including the dissers–lack it, Newman attributes the bravery of her respondents not to their individual character, but to the workplace culture in which they find themselves. As she recounts stories of individual bravery, she emphasizes the role that friends and managers play in shoring up the fragile egos of young people dealing with the treachery of ghetto life; but all the networks in the world cannot help you if you lack character.

One would think that Newman, struck by these remarkable people, would want to know at least a little bit about how they developed their fortitude. Yet these are speculations that she will not permit herself. Instead she writes Solidarity Forever prose about how true dignity requires "a common bond within the organization and across the nation of fellow workers." Her determination to attribute as much as she can to social structures, and therefore as little as she can to the moral strengths and the moral weaknesses of individuals, is so relentless that at one point she blames the noise and the daily chaos surrounding one Harlem resident's apartment on "the concentration of troubled people whom the city has deposited on her doorstep."

No story can have only heroes. For Newman, no villain is more insidious than middle-class stereotyping of the poor. There is not a chapter in her book in which she does not pause to comment on how "misleading" are our views on poverty, how we "dismiss" ghetto kids for wanting only gold chains and sneakers, how "public perceptions" about McJobs are incorrect, how "moralistic exhortations" about sex out of marriage are naive, how African Americans are subject to a "powerful discourse of condemnation" as they face insuperable odds, or how our assumptions "blind us" to the values people learn from sources other than the family. "We inhabit an unforgiving culture that is blind to the many reasons why some people cross that employment barrier and others are left behind," Newman concludes. And our reasons are entirely selfish: "These days, our puritanical attitudes owe some of their force to the resentment the employed bear toward the taxes they must pay to support those who cannot earn on their own."

It is a truism of modern anthropology that Samoa is overflowing with lessons for Scarsdale. And so, in Newman's view, is Harlem. Newman ventures frequently into Margaret Mead–like lecturing, informing us that extended immigrant families have more "social capital" than conventional suburban families, that many middle-class jobs are just as rote as Burger Barn jobs, that stay-at-home moms outside the city play the same role of sustaining social and civic life as welfare moms inside the city, and–in language far closer to political rhetoric than to social science–that "in the inner city, the last place most Americans would look for expressions of the work ethic, the drive to join the labor force is stronger than it is in Westchester."

This way of thinking is wrong on two counts. For one thing, it gets middle-class America wrong. It would be difficult to find too many unforgiving Puritans left in middle-class America; and in fact Americans support taxing themselves if they think that the money will reach its intended target. And more seriously, Newman gets underclass America wrong. "Through sheer, baseless repetition, and through nonrepresentative case studies of a few Afro-American housing projects by urban anthropologists," writes Orlando Patterson in *Rituals of Blood*, "it has become an accepted belief that large networks of support and natural neighborhood communities are out there waiting to be developed and built on." But no one in America is lonelier than the poverty-stricken of the inner city, isolated from the world around them. "There are no 'hoods' out there," Patterson continues, "which is precisely why murderous gangs, like opportunistic social cancers, rush in to fill the vacuum."

For Newman, as for so much of contemporary anthropology, this conviction that the other is different from us only to the degree that the other is superior to us is linked to the notion that whatever villains may exist, they are not to be found among the noble victims with whom the anthropologist so strongly identifies. Yet Newman's book is filled with data that suggest that, no matter how much we admire these people and want them to succeed, they are sometimes their own worst enemies. Consider the portrayal of men in *No Shame in My Game*. It almost never crosses the minds of the men studied by Newman that, having impregnated their girlfriends, they should marry them and do their best to support their children. So pervasive is this behavior that even Newman admits that "there are men in Harlem who have turned their backs on their mothers, wives, girlfriends, and children."

Yet there are other men in this story as well. There are men such as Jamal, Newman's "favorite" among her respondents. Weighing 220 pounds, son of a crack-addicted mother, hot-tempered, Jamal gives off the impression of exactly the kind of young black male worth crossing the street to avoid. When Jamal is introduced, however, we are told of the "doting love he has for his young wife" Kathy and his dedication to working hard to support her and their infant daughter Tammy. Beware of your stereotypes, Newman warns her readers, for people like Jamal are "honorable examples" of men trying to do the right thing.

Now surely Newman is correct that the stereotype of the irresponsible black male does not apply to all men in Harlem. One expects, therefore, that she will offer the reader some numbers. How many of those she studied are selfish egotists and how many are like Jamal? But here we stumble upon one area in which Newman's political commitments so overwhelm her social scientific responsibilities that her research, and not just her sensibilities, can be faulted. For not only are no such comparisons provided, but it turns out that Jamal is no exception at all.

For one thing, Jamal and Kathy are not married. Newman describes their relationship elsewhere as a "common law" marriage, but not even that term is correct. In most American states, common-law marriages must contain "holding out," some indication, such as the woman taking the man's last name or filing joint income-tax returns, that the partners consider themselves married; cohabitation by itself does not constitute a common-law marriage. Their baby does not live with them because Jamal, in a fit of anger, harmed Tammy, leading to her removal by Social Services. Jamal's story is a fascinating one, and one wants to know more. What did he actually do to the child? Given that drug addicts are notorious liars, exactly how "occasional" are the hits of cocaine that he admits he still takes? Why have Jamal and Kathy been unable to "meet the court's conditions for the return of Tammy"? Indeed, what were those conditions? Why is it that when Jamal and Kathy hold a birthday party for Tammy, no one comes except for Newman's research assistant? And why does Tammy's foster mother decide not to bring the child to the party?

If Jamal is to be held up as an indicator of how hard some people toil to create appropriate family values, one craves answers to all these questions, but Newman evidently did not think that she should apply her anthropological skills to address questions that may have made her uncomfortable. When the reader learns at the end of the book that Jamal, Kathy, and Tammy have literally disappeared–Newman is unable to find a trace of them anywhere, including both at Burger Barn and at Social Services–one only hopes that tragedies even more gruesome than those described have not taken place.

Does any of this matter? Newman's book proves that it does. For a surprising number of the Burger Barn workers whom Newman studied actually did succeed. She describes one of them, Latoya, as hopelessly longing for a dream job that she can never realistically attain, one that would limit her working hours so that she can spend time with her children. But Latoya is one of the genuine success stories of the book. She is admitted to a training program. Although she has had three children, she did manage to get the father of one of them, who has a well-paying job, to assume financial responsibility for their child. Ultimately, Latoya not only becomes the second assistant manager of one outlet, she is, as the book closes, promised a general manager's position.

The fact that this young woman achieves something fairly close to her dream flies in the face of Newman's insistence that the fates of Harlem's residents are in the hands of large-scale structural forces over which they have precious little control. Grit, determination, and character evidently matter a lot.

III

WHEN CONGRESS PASSED, AND President Clinton signed, the Personal Responsibility and Work Opportunity Reconciliation Act of 1996, America's approach to the question of federal assistance to the poor underwent a sea change. The nation as a political entity no longer committed itself to help for the poor, as that responsibility was assigned to the states; and people who received public assistance were told in no uncertain terms that they would eventually have to work to support themselves, no matter how small their children or how impoverished their skills. Welfare reform was one of the most radical pieces of legislation enacted in this century. "The real consequences of this reform will not be known for some time," Newman writes of the 1996 law, before proceeding to tell us exactly what those consequences will be: "But it does not take a rocket scientist–or even a trained economist–to know that pushing thousands of low-skilled women with little recent job experience into a labor market that already has a surplus of would-be workers will worsen conditions for everyone." Newman belongs to that school of leftist social criticism that holds that everything is deteriorating all the time.

In Newman's picture of reality, conditions for African Americans have been "worsening" since the mid-1970s, when in fact the size of the black middle class has expanded dramatically. "Immigrants face particularly difficult conditions today," she writes, and public sector jobs are constantly being lost, even though America is more open to immigration than any other rich country in the world, and private-sector jobs are constantly being created. If you subscribe to this gloomy picture of the American situation, then welfare reform's consequences can only be bad, for legislators who insist that people ought to take care of themselves are, in Newman's view, unable to overcome their stereotypes about the poor, and so they are determined to stigmatize those whose worlds are incomprehensible to them.

How odd, then, that Newman reaches conclusions so similar to those of the conservative supporters of welfare reform. Determined to persuade her readers that the working poor of Harlem are responsible, Newman demonstrates why welfare as we knew it was so irresponsible. Here are Juan and Kyesha, both of whom work at Burger Barn. Kyesha is introduced as the very model of an underclass female: hanging out in the projects with pregnant girls already on welfare, doing badly in school. She meets Juan, has a child with him, and they break up. With everything in place for another addition to the welfare rolls, this couple becomes the honorable example that Jamal and Kathy did not become.

"It is important to recognize," Newman writes, "that although Kyesha and Juan have had a child out of wedlock, it was their first and last, not their third." So sexual restraint matters after all. And Juan supports his baby financially, so male responsibility matters as well. How did this couple, amidst all the social disorganization of the ghetto, manage to do the right thing? "Employment brought these two young people together, generated a sense of responsibility that keeps them involved in the care of their child, provided the wherewithal for them to act as reasonably responsible parents, and gave them something else to focus on besides serial pregnancies."

The capacity of work to impose self-restraint carries over beyond matters of sexuality. Kimberly wanted to do better in school, and her boss, another of these Burger Barn do-gooders, promised her lots of breaks in which she could finish her homework. Still, in order to work and to go to school simultaneously, Kimberly was forced to give up track and cheerleading. Newman calls these "real losses," yet there is little doubt that young people like her will benefit more from the job than from the extracurricular activities. "While working may not be the ideal choice for them," Newman writes in typically begrudging fashion, "it is probably the best choice under real-world circumstances, one that provides structure, sources of discipline, caring adults who watch over them, and a better shot at the future than is available to their non-working friends, many of whom are destined to drop out altogether."

Work, in short, acts as something of a wonder drug for which dependency on the state was the disease. This, at least, is one way to read what Newman's actual research demonstrates. For all its leftist asides, *No Shame in My Game* is in some ways a thoroughly conservative book. When a book written from the left praises employers for expanding opportunities and laments military cutbacks for constricting them, it is clear how far from the 1960s we have traveled. And from the 1980s, too. The world described by Newman is one in which black Burger Barn managers will not hire unkempt black teenagers, and Spanish-speaking immigrants, to the resentment of many blacks, grab up as many of the available jobs in Harlem as they can get their hands on. This is not the stuff of the Rainbow Coalition.

It may be true, of course, that conservatives were right all along, and that we should thank Newman for pointing this out. But I do not think that this is the proper conclusion. If Newman's book shows how many success stories there are in Harlem, it also shows, often powerfully, that there are people in Harlem who really do need public assistance. The pressures on the people described by Newman are enormous, and they can bring the reader close to tears.

As her book makes perfectly clear, not everyone can respond to them all. If a twenty-year-old finds herself unable to work, to raise a child or two, to continue in school, and to take care of a drug-addicted mother, can we really conclude that she is undeserving if she falls apart and loses her job? Newman would say no, and so would I. It is welfare, not affirmative action, that should have been mended rather than ended. Newman and I also agree that we went too far in abolishing the federal guarantee on public assistance and in imposing time limits on the states. She is certain that we will rue the day that we instituted those reforms. I have less purchase on the future, but I worry that she will be proved right.

But if the worst case comes to pass, how much will be due to conservative hostility to the poor and how much to the failure of the left to recognize that while we cannot all succeed, we all must try? Conservatives treat the poor as Marx once described the Lumpenproletariat, as a sack of potatoes in which one is indistinguishable from another. Yet so, all too often, does Newman. In response to the right's picture of welfare cheats, she offers a picture of suffering nobility. But the really important point is that poverty, welfare, and work are about individuals, some of whom act in ways that deserve our help and some of whom do not.

Newman's respondents know this, even if Newman does not. "Some people act stupid," says Helena, the daughter of Dominican immigrants, talking about the right way to go to a job interview. "Don't wear an earring in your nose. That looks disgusting ... You have to look neat, not all bummed out." Newman's insistence that those who impose morality tests on the poor are ignorant and misguided not only violates common sense, it undercuts the dignity of the people whom she has so movingly brought to our attention.

Affirmative Action, Inc.

I

WHEN THE 1996 POLITICAL campaign began, race was going to be the theme, and affirmative action the policy, around which a new conservative coalition would solidify its majority. By the campaign's end, theme and policy had gone out with barely a whimper. Despite the Supreme Court's decision last year that race could not be the predominant factor in drawing congressional districts, two black Democrats from Georgia won reelection in redrawn districts, including Representative Cynthia McKinney, who had predicted "the ultimate bleaching of the U.S. Congress" as a result of the Court's decision. (McKinney eventually lost her seat to another African American in 2002.) California voters approved a ballot initiative requiring state institutions to renounce what the initiative's major backer, Ward Connerly, called p's and q's—preferences and quotas—and yet the wedge issue of affirmative action failed to divide the country at large. This was the election in which politicians from both parties went eyeball to eyeball with racial polarization and blinked. Americans are too moderate, and women (who are among the primary beneficiaries of such programs) too numerous, to make opposition to affirmative action a path to power.

The great debate that bypassed the electorate did take place among intellectuals, policy wonks, and social scientists, many of whom rushed their thoughts into print during the year. Their books make one thing clear: it's impossible to discuss affirmative action in the nineties without a theory about what happened in the sixties. Affirmative action, depending on which side is speaking, is either a culmination or a con-

tradiction of the civil rights movement and the legal upheavals inaugu-
rated by the landmark Civil Rights Act of 1964.

Opponents of the act back then relied mainly on two tenets of the
conservative faith. They invoked the doctrine of states' rights to argue
that federal power should not overrule local customs, even when such
customs treated black Americans as second-class citizens. And they
held that the act, in prohibiting racial discrimination in public accom-
modations and in employment, was an unwarranted intervention of
government power in private transactions between individuals. (Pass
this law, conservatives warned, and poor old Mrs. Murphy would have
federal bureaucrats telling her which customers she would have to
accept in her boarding house.) In the end, 130 members of the House
voted against the act. So did 27 senators, including such luminaries of
American politics as Sam Ervin, of North Carolina, William Fulbright,
of Arkansas, and Barry Goldwater, of Arizona.

Listen to the opponents of affirmative action now–thirty years after
the police dogs and fire hoses–and you would think that the civil rights
movement had included even the most stalwart rightwingers. In *The
New Color Line: How Quotas and Privileges Destroy Democracy,* Paul
Craig Roberts, an assistant treasury secretary under Ronald Reagan, and
Lawrence Stratton, a fellow at the Institute for Political Economy, criticize aspects of the Civil Rights Act but praise the civil rights movement
as "popular" and "democratic." "The civil rights movement captured the
moral high ground in American politics," Terry Eastland, a former
spokesman for the Reagan Justice Department, writes in *Ending Affirmative Action: The Case for Colorblind Justice.* He also calls the passage
of the Civil Rights Act of 1964 "the most dramatic movement"–indeed,
"the triumph"–of our nation's long march toward color blindness.

What to make of this new Republican fealty to civil rights? Terry
Eastland's former job, after all, involved defending Reagan's Justice
Department, which retreated to pre-1964 days by supporting a tax
exemption for segregated private schools. (So poisonous was the
atmosphere that even Clarence Thomas, then the chairman of the
Equal Employment Opportunity Commission, publicly complained

that the Justice Department had "set a negative rather than a positive agenda on civil rights.") But surely the sensible strategy for liberals is to welcome late converts to the ranks. Countries, like people, grow up in funny ways; if it takes the right wing to establish a consensus on principles that are traditionally identified with the left, so be it. In focusing on the obvious ways in which the affirmative action debate divides us, we've failed to recognize the less obvious ways in which it unites us.

II

THE SUPPORT OF BUSINESS for affirmative action is one of the better-kept secrets of the debate. Even before the Civil Rights Act was passed, President John F. Kennedy was urging businessmen to make the hiring of Negroes a priority, and many were eager to comply. The Reagan revolution finally left affirmative action intact, in no small part because business liked things fine the way they were. When, early in Reagan's second term, attorney general Edwin Meese tried to mobilize the Cabinet to end racial preferences in government contracting, he was stopped in his tracks by labor secretary Bill Brock. Being far more closely in touch with business sentiment than Meese, Brock knew that private employers, accustomed to counting everything, had no serious problems with counting by race. And in 1996, to the surprise of conservatives, a phalanx of corporate executives lined up to oppose the California Civil Rights Initiative. In this context, the embittered badinage of some Texaco executives–which has prompted headlines and threats of a boycott–sounds very much like the ugly sniping of history's losers.

In *Backfire: A Reporter's Look at Affirmative Action*, Bob Zelnick, a former ABC television correspondent, expresses dismay at the endorsement that affirmative action has received from the National Association of Manufacturers, the Equal Employment Advisory Council (which includes most of the Fortune 500 companies), and the chairmen of Procter & Gamble and Merck. American capitalists rarely act the way Milton Friedman or Karl Marx would have them do. If you want to see political correctness run rampant, forget the universities and visit the human resources–formerly called personnel–departments of the big corporations. Behind closed doors, some corporate executives are no doubt as racist as those at Texaco seem to be, but not as many doors are closed. It's difficult these days to tell where Gilded Age ends and New Age begins: business support for affirmative action fits well into corporate cultures suffused with "empowerment," "holism," "wellness," and "win-win."

Conservative opponents of affirmative action, hoping that the capitalists they so deeply admire have not turned into mushy-headed idealists, emphasize the special circumstances that have pushed business into the arms of affirmative action. Most obvious is the effort to preempt expensive lawsuits by plaintiffs alleging discrimination. But there is also the desire to appeal to diverse markets, respond to political pressure, and even, in the case of very large companies, impose costs on smaller companies to gain a competitive edge. Still, if more African Americans and women are hired by private companies, it hardly matters whether the reasons are self-interested or altruistic. When people discuss affirmative action, they talk in the language of principle, invoking the need for color blindness (if they're against it) or the need for active measures to overcome racism and resistance (if they're for it). When companies practice affirmative action, they do so out of pragmatism, trying to meet particular corporate objectives. A lot of progress could be made in the debate if we all paid less attention to principle and more attention to prudence.

III

PRACTICAL, PRUDENTIAL TYPES DON'T write books and articles, and so their voices have been lost in the debate. But, if they did, surely they would say that the point of diversifying isn't to end racism in one fell swoop but simply to avoid conflict–to keep peace in the house. That's not necessarily a bad thing. The reason businessmen seek out opportunities for growth isn't that they believe in creating jobs; they want to make money. Maybe the same thing applies to diversity: you do not have to believe in the ideal of a rainbow coalition in order to create one. Just as smart political bosses have wanted candidates of every significant ethnic group on their ticket, smart businessmen, in the words of AT&T's former chairman and CEO, Robert E. Allen, view a "diversity strategy" as a "competitive advantage." The market, which corrodes everything, can be a good way of corroding white male privilege.

Private sector support for affirmative action puts ideological conservatives in a bind. If they celebrate when the courts step in and strike down voluntary programs, they are betraying one of their basic tenets–the Republican distrust of government–by demanding that private citizens be prevented from doing what they've decided is best for them. In fact, there are no conservative arguments against the most effective and prevalent forms of affirmative action in America, those implemented by companies. One of the few writers on the right who recognize this is Richard Epstein, of the University of Chicago Law School. In *Forbidden Grounds: The Case against Employment Discrimination,* Epstein argues that private sector discrimination ought to be lawful and the Civil Rights Act of 1964 ought to be repealed; but he also looks with libertarian equanimity upon corporate efforts to diversify the workplace. He writes, "Any organization can opt for a little bit of affirmative action or a lot"–a formula that, in this diverse world, is likely to lead to more rather than less.

Thoroughgoing opponents of affirmative action have had to fall back on such traditionally liberal ideals as individualism, equal opportunity, meritocracy, and universality. The prevalence of these arguments, which the left sees as a defeat, is anything but. America has never been so united behind liberalism as it is now. That's because conservatives have only two choices: to become liberals if they are to reject affirmative action in the private sector, or to accept such affirmative action if they are to remain conservatives. So why haven't more conservatives endorsed affirmative action? One answer is that a surprising number of them have–or, at least, did. Even the Reagan administration, for all its professed opposition to affirmative action, adopted the practice of "race-norming"; that is, raising the scores of minorities on standardized tests to make them more comparable with the scores of whites. The right has long argued that the left, unable to get its out-of-touch ideas legislated, resorted to bureaucrats and judges to impose affirmative action on an unwilling society. But this isn't the whole story. John David Skrentny points out in *The Ironies of Affirmative Action: Politics, Culture, and Justice in America* that the "most radical civil rights employment measure in American history," the Philadelphia Plan—which imposed quotas to integrate that city's construction unions—was resurrected in 1969 by the Nixon administration. Republicans share the responsibility for a policy of counting and choosing by race, and their motive was perfectly cynical: to weaken the Democrats by driving a wedge between unions and minorities.

IV

A CONSERVATIVE CONVERSION TO the civil rights consensus would be cause for celebration, if it weren't that a surprising number of liberals, in their zeal for affirmative action, undermine the very consensus that conservatives want to join. The Civil Rights Act of 1964 was impeccably liberal in both the old and the new senses of that term. Like eighteenth-century liberalism, it gave preference to individuals as such rather than to the caste, stratum, or group to which they belonged. But, in accord with twentieth-century liberalism, it gave government the authority to impose public objectives on private economic transactions. Polemics in defense of affirmative action usually cut against both kinds of liberalism, either by assigning more importance to the group than to the person or by undermining the rationale for government intervention in the economy.

Affirmative action is by no means the first public policy in America to confer advantage on people as members of a particular group. Skrentny points to special benefits for veterans as an example of politically acceptable preferences. But, as Skrentny also notes, Franklin Delano Roosevelt, good liberal that he was, fought against veterans' benefits. "Able-bodied veterans should be accorded no treatment different from that accorded to other citizens who did not wear a uniform during the World War," Roosevelt stated in 1935. Public policy in America can give priority to groups, but never without discomfort.

Barbara Bergmann's *In Defense of Affirmative Action* provides an inadvertent illustration of what makes the rhetoric of group entitlements so troubling. Bergmann, in the spirit of concession, says that "when goals and timetables are implemented, some people are denied advantages they might otherwise have had because others are able to share in the advantages they previously monopolized." But the white person who gives up a job or a place in college so that a minority person will get it has not monopolized any advantage as an individual; the most that can be said is that members of the group he belongs to were given preference. Bergmann's language obscures what the debate is about. Everyone can agree that it's unfair for one individual to have a monopoly on goods. Disagreement enters when we consider whether it's fair to deny someone goods in the future because the group to which that person belongs was overindulged in the past.

To understand how supporters of affirmative action weaken the case for government intervention in private transactions—the other liberal principle embodied in the Civil Rights Act of 1964—it helps to see how the nature of the debate has changed since the seventies. In those days, affirmative action was held to be necessary to rectify the consequences of past discrimination. These days, the favored desideratum is diversity. Conservatives argue that the former rationale at least had the advantage of being temporary: when past wrongs were finally corrected, future affirmative action could wind down. They say that the diversity rationale allows no such cap—that if we take it seriously affirmative action will be with us forever, since institutions will never diversify on their own.

But since institutions are diversifying on their own, and most affirmative action programs, as Bergmann notes, are voluntary, the question is how successful they have been in promoting social and economic equity. Opponents, convinced that social engineering is dangerously utopian, believe that such programs must fail. "The dirty little secret is that affirmative action doesn't work," Bob Zelnick writes. You might think that supporters would rush to disagree with him. Some have, in particular, William G. Bowen and Derek Bok in *The Shape of the River: Long-Term Consequences of Considering Race in College and University Admissions.* Yet not all do. In the pro–affirmative action collection *Economic Perspectives on Affirmative Action* published by the Joint Center for Political and Economic Studies, we read that "the measurable benefits to individuals [are] quite small." The reason that supporters tend to agree with opponents here isn't far to seek: if most affirmative action is both voluntary and effective, we might not need as activist a government as liberals would like.

The agreement between right and left that affirmative action has failed is especially striking given that many of the economic studies that both sides draw upon actually show the opposite: that it worked, as long as governmental pressure for compliance was maintained. Yet even after that pressure was turned down, in the 1980s, American workplaces continued to diversify on their own. The most impressive data in the debate are those gathered by Barbara Bergmann, who lists the percentages of blacks and women in managerial positions at various companies. For African Americans, those shares are between 10 and 11 percent at AT&T, Southwestern Bell, Xerox, and General Motors, and around 15 percent at Federal Express, Potomac Electric, and McDonald's. All these corporations, in other words, have a percentage of black managers roughly equal to the proportion of blacks in the American population, or higher. Even when we recognize that *manager* is a loose term, which can include jobs far down in the hierarchy, the figures are significant, for these are national companies, which sell their products in national markets and have offices and outlets throughout the United States. Reviewing these numbers, you might conclude that affirmative action has been a great success. But Bergmann doggedly finds a way to call the record "bad," using for comparison the percentage of blacks "in the population in the areas where the companies have their facilities." For Bergmann, good news is no news. Defenders of affirmative action are ever on the lookout for criteria by which they can never proclaim victory.

Plainly, champions like Bergmann have just as much trouble with the love affair between business and diversity as foes like Eastland and Zelnick do. If the right doesn't want to admit that affirmative action has the blessing of the marketplace, romantic leftists, who want to believe that affirmative action is "progressive," find its embrace by big business equally mortifying. The notion that more social change can be brought about through actions in the suites than through actions in the streets is simply not within their understanding.

V

THERE MAY BE A WAY OUT of the impasse, but it won't come from clarifying our values or principles. That's a negative lesson we can take from *Not All Black and White: Affirmative Action, Race, and American Values* by Christopher Edley Jr., who coordinated the White House's 1995 review of affirmative action. For Edley, public policy has to recognize a basic social fact: "the 'birds of a feather' tendency to prefer people like oneself." Because such a tendency can work to deprive African Americans of opportunity, he argues, "we may need race-conscious decision making to lean against that tilt in the playing field that helps those who are familiar to us and hinders those who are different—even when there is no unlawful discrimination."

Edley wants more coherence—what he calls "a unified approach to myriad issues about race"—in the affirmative action debate, because such consistency is "an undervalued commodity" in our society. But coherence is the enemy of consensus. Anyone who knows exactly where society ought to go is unlikely to stop and tarry so that people with a different goal can be brought along. That may be why Edley, for all his understanding of the importance of narrowing affirmative action's ambitions, winds up recommending the retention of just about every one of its tenets. And it may also explain why Edley finds himself "sick to tears" when he reads the opinions of Justice Clarence Thomas: principled people tend to be exasperated with those who hold different principles.

By the end of his book, Edley is proposing to move the debate forward through means more religious than political. Let's stop arguing about rights and instead explore "'postliberal' efforts to emphasize communal values and goals," he urges, and he asks, "What secular experiences will have a transformative effect on people so that their racial thinking is redeemed–so that their values and sense of community, connections, and possibilities are transformed to make possible a different structure of race relations?" If there is a problem with elevating principle above prudence in the affirmative action debate it is this: what begins as a narrow effort to tailor a program to specific goals ends as a call for a new kind of person.

Although Edley winds up conceding very little to affirmative action's critics, there are others on the left who spend considerable time imagining a world without affirmative action. Michael Tomasky, a former *Village Voice* staffer who now writes for *New York*, is one such: in his book *Left for Dead: The Life, Death, and Possible Resurrection of Progressive Politics in America*, he calls affirmative action "an ambiguous enterprise, both practically and morally." Tomasky questions both rationales–reparations and diversity. On what ground, he wants to know, does past racism justify giving recent immigrants from Africa or Latin America preference over unemployed white workers? And–as Richard D. Kahlenberg points out in his immodestly titled *The Remedy: Class, Race, and Affirmative Action*–diversity as an end in itself can easily turn against the interests of African Americans, for whom affirmative action was originally designed. Should black Americans, who constitute 28 percent of the workforce of the government of Los Angeles County but only 10.5 percent of the county's population, be laid off so that more Latinos can be hired?

If conservative opponents of affirmative action have discovered an allegiance to a civil rights agenda they never supported, liberal supporters of affirmative action need to remember a commitment to justice they used to pride themselves on. So Kahlenberg concludes, anyway. Affirmative action, in his view, is a long detour from the class politics once espoused by both Robert Kennedy and Martin Luther King Jr. At best, its time is up: sufficient numbers of African Americans have been brought into the middle class to enable us to shift our attention back toward economic inequality, which would subsume concerns about racial inequality. At worst, affirmative action is a convenient way of ignoring injustice altogether, allowing Ivy League college presidents to feel that they have accomplished some important social goal by attracting tuition-paying suburbanites who happen to be black.

The arguments of leftists against affirmative action are generally cogent, but they are not without problems, too. "Attacking lack of access to capital and public education imbalances requires a program more radical than affirmative action, as does attacking the vast inequities and difficulties that millions of working people face," Tomasky writes. He, at least, recognizes that affirmative action is not "progressive." Let's not forget that it is the Fortune 500 companies, the historic enemy of the left, that so strongly support it. But maybe businessmen know something that the left has never learned: that taking quiet steps to deal with the smaller things can be preferable to flailing away noisily at the bigger ones. Affirmative action will never usher in socialism, or even an American version of social democracy. But it's already helping enlarge the black middle class, and that is no mean accomplishment.

The left is surprisingly like the right in failing to appreciate the prudential side of affirmative action; Kahlenberg, for example, is skeptical of arguments in favor of hiring minorities to serve minority constituencies, or to hold up as examples of minority accomplishment. Yet surely there are good, prudential reasons for wanting the racial composition of an urban police force to approximate the racial composition of the city, if only to make plainclothes assignments credible. Kahlenberg's book urges the left to turn away from a politics of symbolism in favor of a politics of substance. But that will be more costly than Kahlenberg acknowledges, for symbols matter. Affirmative action, by identifying race as a salient aspect of an individual with respect to eligibility for jobs and education, stood as a symbolic corrective to America's racist past. The Civil Rights Act of 1964 could not, in itself, achieve that objective, because, at least on its face, it made discrimination by blacks against whites no less illegal than discrimination by whites against blacks. Something like affirmative action was necessary to acknowledge the pain that so many white Americans had inflicted on so many black Americans. Moreover, by putting the power of the government behind the effort at racial redress, affirmative action proclaimed that this country would not be satisfied with mere words about equality: actions would have to follow. That's the context in which business has done its voluntary thing. The question often posed now is this: Has the time come for the law of the land to move beyond race?

One way to respond to that question is to warn against any definitive answer. It may be that convincing justifications for or against affirmative action simply do not exist. Keep it, and advocates of liberal and meritocratic principles will never stop drumming up anecdotes and incidents to support their position. Drop it, and believers in racial justice can claim, not without reason, that America reneged on its commitment to diversity just as the going got tough. If these books represent the best thinking on the subject, neither side has found a winning argument.

Look at what we do about affirmative action rather than what we say, however, and you can discern the outlines of a future consensus. Prudential affirmative action is hardly perfect. Without governmental enforcement, some private companies may indeed drop their enthusiasm for diversity and retreat to "birds of a feather" hiring policies. And university admissions committees guided only by a vague desire to diversify their student bodies may find themselves less diverse when classes begin. Moving from principle to prudence will surely disappoint those for whom principle is what life is all about. But prudential affirmative action will also disappoint those to whom racial preferences of any kind are anathema. What does it matter, they will argue, if someone deserving of a job is passed over because the company or the university, not the government, chose to pass over that person? They will have to be told that it does matter: we do not yet live in a color-blind world, and, while it makes sense for government to aspire to color blindness in order to underscore the importance of universality, companies and private universities ought to be free to take race into account for reasons of pluralism. Out of mutual disappointments a new approach to affirmative action may emerge. A compromise between the two sides will start when both accept a simple dictum: a policy can be a bad idea in theory and a good one in practice.

PART IV

Schools

•

The Jeremiah Racket

I

ORRIED, LIKE ANY CONCERNED father of children under thir-
teen, about the moral lives of today's kids, I responded positively
to the announcement that William Damon, the prominent educator
from Brown University, would be coming to our local high school to
help form a "youth charter." (Damon has since moved to Stanford.)
Damon's *Greater Expectations* (1995), in contrast to so many of the flaky
products of America's schools of education, was a serious book. Damon
argued that we are misled by the panaceas of self-esteem, and tone-deaf
to religion, and afraid to pass judgment, and so we do not demand
enough of children. I agreed with him. Suburban public education, as
my wife and I experience it, refuses to acknowledge that some kids are
too intelligent to be anything but offended by peer grading, too curious
to have their brightness treated the same way one treats the learning
disabled, and too good in their hearts to understand why their teachers
would be vengeful toward them because they were going to go much
further in the world than their teachers had.

But the all-day session over which he presided turned into quite a
surprise. It started off with Damon explaining that children cannot be
left in a moral vacuum. Then we broke out into smaller sessions. Ours
had not been going for more than five minutes before one of those designated to lead us launched into an attack on irresponsible parents. The
reason so many kids take drugs, I learned from her, was because their
parents are so preoccupied with their careers and so materialistic in
their desires. When I protested that most parents love their children

dearly and make sacrifices beyond imagination to treat them right, a number of parents agreed, at which point our facilitator was bereft of an agenda.

I may have headed off what Dana Mack calls *The Assault on Parenthood: How Our Culture Undermines the Family*. Still, I had to confess defeat when we all reassembled in the auditorium. It turned out that all the smaller sessions except mine had concluded that the blame for the low moral development of our children had to be assigned to their parents. Ministers bewailed their lack of faith. Women attacked men who teach aggressive behavior on the soccer fields of suburbia. Parents confessed their sins. The police chief asked them not to leave their kids alone for the weekend to party while they went on ski trips. Teachers pleaded with them for their cooperation. According to accounts in the local paper, the day was a great success. Enough, my wife and I concluded. We are going to try private schools.

If social trends can be proclaimed based on my personal experience, suburban public schools are about to face the same precipitous declines in enrollment suffered by urban ones. All around our community—which contains not only well-off professionals, but two world-class colleges—friends and neighbors, having moved there for the schools, find themselves shopping around for alternatives. These are people willing to undergo double taxation—property taxes for the public schools that they will not use and tuition for the private schools that they will use—because they feel the same combination of hostility and anti-intellectualism that we experienced that awful and enlightening day at the high school.

We chose to investigate only one private school, a small and academically challenging one in Boston. Sitting in on classes with our daughter, we were astonished by the dedication and the intellectual excitement of the faculty. The students seemed to be in love with the place. Aside from the fact that it cost more than we ever could afford, it was a dream come true. Then we went to the very last orientation meeting for new parents. One thing you must understand, the admissions director told us, is that your kids do not want you to stop by during the day if you happen to be in the neighborhood, for they quite rightly view the school as their own. The message conveyed was clear. Turn your kids over to us, and keep out. (We opted to keep our kid out instead and chose to move to another community where the public schools were better.)

II

BACK IN THE 1970S, a number of the country's best conservative intellectuals took up Lionel Trilling's idea about the "adversary culture" and turned it into the theory of the New Class. This theory holds that the revolutionary values of the 1960s, especially relativism, secularism, pacifism, and sexual liberation, won the war for the American mind. Countercultural veterans, no longer committed to the discipline and the delayed gratification associated with the Protestant ethic, led a long march through American institutions. Capitalists would not, as Lenin famously put it, sell the rope with which they would be hanged; they would sell instead the culture with which their values would be obliterated.

Dana Mack believes that educational professionals are in the vanguard of the New Class, and that they are waging a war against parents. Long influenced by ideas of reform that can be traced back to the Progressives and John Dewey, teachers, in Mack's view, have discovered in recent decades two things about their profession that are indispensable to furthering their political agenda. One is that they can use the children in their classes to "re-educate" their parents. Fill kids up with enough ideas about recycling, the dangers of alcohol, world peace, or multiculturalism, and, before you know it, they'll be lecturing their parents at the dinner table (assuming they eat dinner together).

Educators adhere to their own ideology, Mack argues, one which emphasizes choice (though they always coerce children into making the "right" ones) and equality (though they always prevent others from challenging the decisions that educational professionals make in its name). This ideology is the source of their power. When parents uphold an alternative vision of "moral dictates, rules, and authority," the kids too often choose the easy way out.

The other tactic educators have learned is the capture of government. "Here's to the only union that owns its own cabinet department," Mack quotes an official of the National Education Association as saying when President Carter signed the Cabinet post of Secretary of Education into existence. With the federal government involved, educational professionals could now "mandate" standards through regulations which would impose not only costs but also dubious pedagogical nostrums on every school board in the country. Special education, bilingualism, and instruction in sexual technique, according to Mack, have proliferated through educational bureaucracies owing to federal involvement. Worst of all is "outcomes based education," which Mack calls "a federally funded brainchild," designed to ensure that no one will be advanced to a new level of learning until every student in the class has mastered the material.

But Mack is just warming up with the educators. She has a larger jeremiad in mind. Therapists who discover examples of child abuse so deeply repressed that they never took place; best-selling authors who write about "toxic parenting"; secularists hostile to traditional religion; lawyers advocating children's rights; gay activists intent on transforming heterosexual fears of AIDS to respect for their sexual preferences; feminists who will not give up on the notion of women's equality in the labor force, no matter how significant the harm to children; judges who rip children away from loving adopted parents to give them to biological parents whom they do not know; cynical media executives eyeing fast bucks; even conservative welfare reformers who insist that poor mothers should work—all these villains, in Mack's view, are part of a fairly systematic campaign to undermine the confidence of parents.

Why systematic? Because, according to Mack, all those involved in the assault on parenting, whether employed by the schools or elsewhere, are bureaucrats with a vested interest in expanding the services that they offer. Their bad intentions are best conveyed by their efforts to do good things. One of her examples is a decision of the Meriden, Connecticut, school board in 1993 to reject the state's plans requiring schools to provide free or subsidized breakfasts to poor kids. Heartless middle-class cruelty toward the poor? Hardly, in Mack's account. The school board, she argues, was correct to reject the state's interference in its community. Poor and minority residents of Meriden had every reason to challenge the supposition that they were not feeding their children, Mack claims. Those pushing for the plan, by contrast, were not really interested in helping kids; their larger goal was "an agenda of expanding 'direct services' to children who may or may not need them." Get hold of their stomachs for breakfast, Mack implies, and you can get their minds at dinner. Parents have every right to object to such schemes, for "the notion that parents are incapable of raising children without the help and oversight of an army of social service professionals provided by the schools is rapidly gaining currency."

If social service providers want nothing more than to invade the American home and to abduct the children who live there, then parents, in Mack's account, are now fighting back to retain custody of their progeny. Having talked to a lot of them around the country, she has found resentment brewing everywhere against the educational establishment. Initiatives to assert and to protect parental rights have appeared on state ballots, and a Parental Rights and Responsibilities Act was introduced in Congress. Parents are learning about charter schools and voucher plans that enable them to have more control over what their children learn. Christian academies, dedicated to teaching the old-fashioned way, are sweeping the country. And, in the most dramatic move of all, more and more parents are educating their children at home.

This emerging resistance has created what Mack calls "two distinct political cultures in our nation." One, that of the professionals and social service providers, is "a culture of conformity, of homogenization, collectivization, peer orientation, and a dictatorial vision of political activism," while the other, to which the parents adhere, is "a culture that values individuality, pluralism, privatism, intergenerational interaction, and grassroots political activism." Since the stakes in this culture war are so great, parents who choose options such as home-schooling "are barely aware of the subversive implications of their choice." They might think they are merely deciding how best to convey knowledge to their kids. But in reality they are foot soldiers in a revolutionary cause.

III

MUCH OF WHAT PASSES for social commentary these days is marred by the number of writers who have a good idea they treat in a bad way. Mack's good idea is that some professionals—based on my experience, I am even willing to say most professionals—who deal with children think that they know more than the parents of the children with whom they deal. Very little of what Mack writes about is foreign to me. I pride myself on resisting conspiracy theories, but I have not been able to dismiss from my mind the notion that our kids are given a lot of meaningless yet time-consuming homework so that they will be unable to play Scrabble with their mother and father. Nor am I pleased when they come home spouting their knowledge of the latest drug paraphernalia helpfully provided by the local police through the DARE program. Our daughter has taken to chastising us for our wine drinking at dinner, and one of our sons has been known to transform himself into an ecoterrorist if I try to slip a soda can into the ordinary trash. There are lots of people out there in the world who see my kids as grist for their political mills.

Mack's bad idea—a very bad one—is to react to this situation with so partisan and so doctrinaire a screed for reaction that she winds up worse than the liberal professionals whom she attacks. Prevent the kids from ever falling into her clutches, I vowed to myself, as I digested her exaggerations, her mistakes, her double standards. I would trust the National Education Association, I would trust even the DARE program, over this kind of brazen politicization.

There are frequent distortions in Mack's book. Not especially important, but annoying nonetheless, is the way in which Mack places various academic authorities at the wrong universities or, in another case, gets the university itself wrong. (It was Columbia University, and not the New School for Social Research, which attracted the intellectuals of the Frankfurt School.) Mack is described by her publisher as a parent living in Connecticut and as "an Affiliate Scholar with the Institute for American Values" (on whose academic advisory committee I sat until I read this book and opted to resign). I have nothing against writers with little scholarly or journalistic experience entering the terrain of social criticism, but they ought to obey the elementary conventions of the craft.

More serious is Mack's "no enemies to the right" strategy to guide her through this complicated terrain. This is the first book I have read that treats *The Bell Curve* as a normal work of social science to be cited as if its findings were established matters of fact. Conservative writers are invariably "enlightening" (Rita Kramer) or speak "eloquently" (Michael Medved). They are never identified by their politics, but are instead labeled as "experts" or "investigative journalists"; and their opinions are presented to the reader as examples of disinterested conclusions or objective research.

It is not clear whom Mack is deceiving more, her readers or herself. From time to time, I did feel that Mack was trying to pull a fast one on her readers. At one point, for example, she calls Of the People, an Arlington, Virginia, group formed to support parental rights initiatives around the country, "nonpartisan." Since the group refuses to reveal the sources of its funding, its status as nonpartisan is hard to challenge. Mack then makes an effort to present the organization as consensus-seeking, but since the group takes one side, and one side only, in very sectarian fights, the effort is surely misleading.

Mack also spends time recounting the evolution of a sexual education controversy in Falmouth, a community on Cape Cod. In 1992 the school committee decided to make condoms available to all students from the seventh grade up. As Mack relates what happened next, a grassroots group developed to challenge the committee, focusing attention on a survey designed to gather information on the sexual activity of

Falmouth teens. Angry parents turned to Judith Reisman, the president of the Center for Media Education, who conducted an "evaluation" of the survey and found in it a "disregard for scientific standards." With Reisman's report and "three other professional evaluations" in hand, opponents of sex education managed to get the survey withdrawn at a public hearing.

Since the three professional evaluators are never named, it is impossible to judge their credentials. Reisman is a different story. In a footnote, Mack informs the reader that she was "the first scholar to challenge the Kinsey Institute research on child sexuality, is an expert on child pornography, has been a consultant for the Department of Health and Human Services and the Department of Education, and has done in-service training for the FBI Academy and the Center for Missing and Exploited Children in Washington, D.C." That version of Reisman's curriculum vitae barely hints at the fact that she is about as capable of conducting an impartial evaluation of a sex survey as Johnnie Cochran was capable of judging O. J. Simpson's guilt. Reisman is a perfect example of a single-issue inside-the-Beltway ideologue, a one-woman crusader against pornography whose concern with "scientific standards" pales compared to her conviction that pornography is always and everywhere harmful.

Yet the more I read, the clearer it became that Mack is not engaged in a disinformation campaign, for she deceives herself with far more regularity than she deceives her readers. Ideology is little more than self-deception on a grand scale, after all. Those who believe that anyone who has the right answers must have the correct analysis are living in a world in which illusions are never checked by reality. Conservative educational criticism, in particular, resembles a Ponzi scheme: each writer cites another conservative writer for proof of this point or that, with the result that a veritable library of books is assembled, all of them resting on the same nonfoundations. Take that juicy quote from an anonymous NEA official toasting the creation of the Department of Education. Mack's source for the quote is Charles Sykes's *Dumbing Down Our Kids.* Sykes's source for it is Gilbert Sewall's *Necessary Lessons.* Sewall does not give a precise source, but refers the reader to articles in the *American Spectator* and *Commentary*. And those articles never mention the alleged incident at all. Did someone actually say it? Maybe, maybe not. But even in the best case, no one can tell us who that someone was.

Mack's book is full of such ideological self-referentiality. I have yet to read a conservative account of sex education without seeing Roger Coulson's name prominently displayed. A former adherent of the human potential movement associated with Abraham Maslow and Carl Rogers, Coulson's criticisms of therapeutic educational techniques are always taken by conservatives as the last word, because he has been there and done that. Mack adduces him to support the proposition that "behavioral programs"–her term for psychological techniques that play down discipline and play up self-esteem–are associated with juvenile violence. And a fascinating correlation it would be, if Coulson (or anyone else) had established it. But Mack cites no scholarship on this point. The reason, surely, is that Coulson is not a scholar; he is just another voice in the right's circle of like-minded critics. The closest that Mack herself comes to a correlation coefficient is when she cites with approval the comment of a home-schooling mom who pointed out that the one thing gang members have in common is that they all went to school. Maybe they were all of women born, too.

Perhaps Mack came across Coulson's name in Beverly K. Eakman's *Educating for a New World Order,* for his crusade against the human potential movement is featured in that book. Eakman's underground best-seller posits the existence of a vast conspiracy run by the Educational Testing Service. The testers have a plan: taking advantage of the captive environments called schools, they are socializing America's youth through behavior modification, hypnosis, assertiveness training, and the use of subliminal messages into a "New World Order" dominated by third world countries hostile to American capitalism. This New World Order, Eakman writes, "is extreme, pure fascism, totalitarian–and very high tech." By contrast, she helpfully notes that "Adolph [*sic*] Hitler is sometimes referred to by the media as extreme right-wing," but never as a "conservative."

And even Eakman is accepted by Mack as an authority. Mack does point out that her book "is hardly an exemplary work of scholarship" and "at times it verges on incoherence." And yet, Mack writes, "she tells some compelling stories," which Mack then goes on to retell. That Mack would pay serious attention to a book that makes Pat Robertson seem level-headed comes as something of a surprise—but not after reading Mack on Robertson himself. In her view, Robertson's Christian Coalition is a "broad-based, middle-class movement claiming adherence by up to a third of the voting population." Its success, she opines, "seems obvious enough." Parents, you see, "look around at rising social chaos and the implementation of social policies with which they cannot identify and simply close ranks." Robertson has been called an anti-Semite by some. But whether this bothers Mack, who makes her Jewish faith a point of pride in her book, I have no way of knowing, for she chooses not to mention the controversy at all. She does manage to describe Betty Friedan's ideas (see "The Mystique of Betty Friedan," this vol.), in truly despicable fashion, as an "*Arbeit macht Frei* mentality."

Sometimes it proves difficult even for Mack to fit every item in her parental rights agenda into her conservative blinders. Thus, to her credit, she denounces conservative versions of welfare reform that insist on women entering the labor force, and she does not shy away, as some conservatives do, from attacking the capitalist media for their blithe disregard of childhood's integrity. Americans, moreover, are fascinated by scenes of children taken away from adoptive parents and returned to their biological parents, even ones who disowned them when they were born; but Mack does not come down, as one might expect, on the side of the biological parents. For her, and for me, the tragedy is to see children taken out of loving homes. But whereas for most people such examples would lead to the conclusion that issues involving parents and children are too emotionally and morally complicated to fit into any political agenda—one could support the biological parents, after all, as an example of an "assault on parenthood"—Mack merely acknowledges them before moving back to her crusade.

If there is anything new in Mack's book, it is not her tired criticism of educators and social service providers, but her reports from the field.

She talked to 250 parents around the country, Mack tells her readers, offering her book as "a petition on their behalf." The parents with whom she spoke, in her account, are seething with anger at the educational professionals, "mounting a strong and concerted movement to reclaim the powers they've lost."

Mack provides no explanation of how and why she chose her subjects, so it is impossible to know whether their views are representative, whether the anger that they manifest bespeaks the potential for a major populist campaign for parents' rights. Certainly conservatives are banking on such a campaign. Having failed to win much support for their views on the environment or government regulation of business, they sense in the hostility toward educators a possibility of a new majority.

But there is an empirical problem here. Every time parental rights has been on a state ballot, it has lost. Mack attributes such losses to the power of the education lobby. I have a different explanation. Like Mack, I have also talked to parents around the country about these issues. (My interviews formed the basis of my book *One Nation, After All*.) Like her, I detected strong undercurrents of dismay about childhood in America combined with a distinct sense that schools are failing. But I also heard something else. Middle-class Americans are suspicious of liberal educator professionals, not because they are liberal, but because they are political. Schools should be about schooling, they believe, not about teaching respect for native languages or the rights of animals. Reformers who use the schools to promote their own conceptions of equality or social justice are viewed as confusing the distinction between learning and indoctrination.

If I am right, such people would be equally as skeptical if the politics were conservative rather than liberal. The truth is that Dana Mack is just as much a member of the New Class as any radical educational theorist. For every liberal horror that Mack identifies, she proposes a conservative horror. Instead of getting God out of the schools, she would get God back in. Banal songs about global understanding would be replaced by "an appreciation of high art and authentic folk art." Liberals like the Internet because they think it is democratic; Mack likes it because she thinks it is populist. Even the term *parental rights,* which conservatives love so much, is an odd affectation, since it was liberals who first launched the rights revolution. (Mack is aware of this irony, but her awareness never brings her to reflection.) "The New Familism is becoming political," Mack gushes, unaware that, since Americans hate politics, that also means it is becoming unpopular.

American culture will survive the assault of *The Assault on Parenthood.* And, alas, that is a mixed blessing. For our schools are in terrible shape, and the major responsibility for their condition surely ought to be assigned to those educational professionals and social service providers whose fascination with dubious schemes is undoubtedly due to the fact that it is other people's children who bear the burden of their application. But they will easily escape the criticisms launched by Mack against them, just as they have escaped all conservative versions of educational reform. By playing the political card, Dana Mack plays right into their hands.

Subject Matter Matters

I

IMAGINE A SMALL GROUP of revolutionaries intent on taking over society. Certain that they know what is best for all, they insist that science undergirds their venture, and as a result they produce jargon incomprehensible to anyone but themselves. Cloaking their ideology in the rhetoric of democracy, they dismiss all opposition as elitist, even if they really believe that most people are incapable of thinking for themselves. They are remarkably successful in their takeover, if for no other reason than that their single-minded determination enables them to purge dissenters and to ignore critics. Once in charge, their work consists of one failure after another, but this in no way leads them toward introspection or apology. By century's end few take them seriously, but their control is so tenacious that no one can safely assume that they will ever be dislodged.

Such, in brief outline, is the plot of Diane Ravitch's *Left Back: A Century of Failed School Reforms,* an account of how educational progressives have taken over, and nearly destroyed, America's public schools. Expressed in such schematic fashion, her treatment seems a caricature of what is surely a more complicated affair. And yet, once one has digested the extraordinary material that she has assembled, it becomes clear that Ravitch does not exaggerate. *Left Back* is the most important book written in many decades about America's most important public institution.

II

FOR MANY LATE-NINETEENTH-CENTURY educators, it was axiomatic
that schooling ought to inculcate academic skills. Charles W. Eliot, the
president of Harvard, advocated that schools stress "the power to think,
reason, observe, and describe." William Torrey Harris, superintendent
of schools in St. Louis and then U.S. commissioner of education,
emphasized that the freedom to control one's life emerges out of the
discipline required to direct oneself toward that purpose. In 1892, the
National Education Association created the Committee of Ten, a blue-
ribbon panel that included Eliot and Harris. Its report, published in
1893, summarized the leading educational ideas of the period. It was a
reform document that sided with the teaching of new subjects, including the sciences. It frowned on memorization, but it insisted that
schools should train the minds of all the students who attended them,
even if only a few secondary school students would go on to college.
"Every subject which is taught at all in a secondary school should be
taught in the same way and to the same extent to every pupil so long as
he pursues it," the report urged, "no matter what the probable destination of the pupil may be, or at what point his education is to cease."

As Eliot and Harris were putting their pedagogical conceptions
down on paper, a movement began to develop committed to the idea,
expressed by John Dewey in 1897, that the school "must represent present life—life as real and vital to the child as that which he carries on in
the home, in the neighborhood, or on the playground." As Ravitch
recounts the beliefs of the reformers who began to cluster around
Dewey, not all of which Dewey himself endorsed, they amount to four
distinct efforts: a mental-testing movement designed to measure who
would benefit most from which type of instruction; a child-centered
movement that maintained that, in matters of education, the needs of
the child come first; a social efficiency movement whose premise was
that schools should serve social needs; and a social reconstruction
movement committed to using the schools to reform society's inequities. The ideas that linked these movements were not always compati-

ble, but what held them together, Ravitch argues, is that they all shared one fundamental commitment: distrustful of the life of the mind, they were determined to move the schools away from the Committee of Ten's insistence on high academic standards designed to be met by all students.

In this post–*Bell Curve* era, we sometimes forget that the movement for IQ testing emerged as a progressive force. Edward L. Thorndike, one of the founders of educational psychology, attacked the idea that training in one activity transfers over into another. If learning Latin has no demonstrable effect on how effective one will be as a worker, why not teach work skills directly? And as intelligence tests became more refined, they offered to school administrators a way to distinguish between those who would benefit most from an academic curriculum and those on whom academic training would essentially be wasted.

Why raise the expectations of students who lacked the qualities necessary to succeed? Would it not be better to give them the kind of training that would help them in the here and now? Justified on the grounds that classification by intelligence was in the best interests of all, educational testing would move schools far away from the ideals associated with men such as Eliot and Harris. "The decision to offer different educational programs, depending on children's IQ," Ravitch writes, "repudiated the fundamental concept of the American common school idea, which was to provide the same curriculum to all children in the first eight years of their schooling."

G. Stanley Hall, otherwise known as the man who invited Sigmund Freud to lecture in the United States, instigated the child-study movement in America, treating the formal academic curriculum as an interference with the natural curiosity of children. Similarly romantic views of children led John and Alice Dewey to create the Laboratory School at the University of Chicago in 1896 and formed the basis of the "project method" developed by William Heard Kilpatrick of Teachers College at Columbia University. (The project method essentially urged students to pursue activities that emerged out of their own curiosity.) Ravitch treats Dewey fairly, noting, for example that the Lab School did include a role for academic subjects and that, designed for relatively few students, it was not held up as a model for all. But she is much harsher on Kilpatrick, a man who responded to criticism from Robert Maynard Hutchins in 1937 by comparing him to Hitler: "When you have a professed absolute, then you have to have some authority to give it content, and there the dictator comes in."

An even more arrogant educator brought back to life by Ravitch is David Snedden. Commissioner of education in Massachusetts from 1909 until 1915, and later a professor at Columbia Teachers College, Snedden developed nothing less than a theory of social control. Society could no longer rely on autocratic means to win legitimacy, he argued; it needed instead the cooperation of its members. For this, schools could play an important function, not to undermine the social order but to change "the motives leading to submission to it." A leader of the social efficiency movement, Snedden disdained the teaching of actual subjects such as history and mathematics in favor of providing students with "ideals of right social action." Those who insisted that all students were capable of doing academic work he dismissed as "wrapped up in the cocoons of blind faiths, untested beliefs, hardened customs."

If the right theories about learning could remake the schools, why couldn't they also remake society? The ideas of educational reformers began to have their strongest impact in the 1930s, a time when the Great Depression encouraged radical proposals designed to overcome capitalism's inherent instability. George Counts, who would later become a passionate critic of Soviet communism, was one of many educators who went to the Soviet Union and came back intent on linking education with social reform. In 1932, Counts published *Dare the Schools Build a New Social Order?*, answering with a firm yes. Other educators agreed with Counts, and unlike him they never lost their faith in some kind of top-down planning. From such a perspective, schools that encouraged genius, let alone those that talked of children's inherent creativity, came to be viewed, in their anarchic individualism, as lamentable instruments of capitalistic values. Thus did school reformers become promoters of adjustment and conformity—which was one reason why, despite their leftist politics, even the most conservative districts found something to like in the reformers' ideas and approaches.

Not everyone agreed with these educational advocates. In 1923, Carl Brigham, a Princeton psychologist, published *A Study of American Intelligence*, which suggested that the Nordic races were intellectually superior to the Mediterranean; by 1930, Brigham, now at the College Board, was calling his earlier views "without foundation," since they did not take into account the fact that familiarity with English could influence IQ scores. (His story is told in greater detail in Nicholas Lemann's *The Big Test*.) William C. Bagley, although identified with the social efficiency movement, became a critic of figures such as David Snedden and expressed his skepticism toward the progressive attack on academic subject matter. Isaac Kandel, the first Jew to teach at Teachers College, offered a devastating critique of the movement's anti-intellectualism in his book *The Cult of Uncertainty* in 1943. "Education is not a commodity which can be handed over the counter as in a department store or a cafeteria, nor can the selection of its constituent elements be left wholly to the learner," he wrote. "Society has as much interest in the character of the education given in its schools as has the individual." In the topsy-turvy world of educational reform, these men, who wanted to offer everyone, including immigrants and African Americans, the opportunity to advance by their own efforts, came to be called reactionaries. (It did not help that one of them, Michael J. Demiashkevich, who wrote books arguing passionately for the reading of books, really was a reactionary.)

Despite the efforts of the critics, a new consensus about schools solidified in the 1940s. This consensus held that subject matter and the academic curriculum were outmoded; that the curriculum should never be prescribed by city or state officials but jointly planned by teachers and pupils; that it should be based on students' interests and needs, not on the logical organization of subjects; that experiences and activities were more valuable to students than reading and study; that schools should offer different programs to different groups of students, depending on whether they were preparing for work or college; that

students should be promoted every year, regardless of their performance; and that professional educators should think of themselves as
social engineers, empowered to decide what was best for students and
the rest of society.

III

AS CONVINCED AS EDUCATORS were by their goals and their methods,
the public never really accepted this consensus. The result, once the
shocks of the Depression and World War II came to an end, was a full-
scale revolt against the schools. During the 1950s, educational traditionalists began to attack their mediocrity. Schools failed to teach Johnny
how to read. Their poor performance made Sputnik possible. Schools of
education downplayed subject matter.

As Ravitch tells the story, educational reformers were at first taken
aback by all the criticism. But they quickly learned to meet any challenge through a two-pronged response that simultaneously denied that
their ideas were all that innovative and then took credit for the innovations they introduced. Nobody was more helpful to their cause than
James Conant, the former president of Harvard, whose book *The American High School Today,* which appeared in 1959, was (in Ravitch's
words) "the whitewash the educational establishment had been hoping
for."

One sees echoes of the 1950s in contemporary controversies over
schooling. Efforts to create national standards produced either complete failure (in the teaching of English), contentious controversy (in
the teaching of history), or excessive reliance on jargon (in the teaching
of math). Illustrative of all these contemporary debates is the argument
over the "whole language" approach to reading that became popular in
the 1980s and 1990s. The advocates of "whole language" insisted that
reading should be learned as naturally as speaking, making unneces-
sary any reliance on phonics, a traditional approach which teaches students to recognize the forty-four basic speech sounds formed by the
twenty-six letters of the alphabet. Children come already equipped,

they said, with richly inventive language skills that schools ought to cultivate, not to replace. Citing studies proving the value of this approach, Kenneth Goodman of the University of Arizona accused traditionalists of having a "flat-Earth view of the world" and of advancing the cause of "the Far Right." As in the 1950s, the education establishment was unwilling to concede any ground at all. As late as December 1999, the annual meeting of the National Council of Teachers of English formally opposed phonics instruction.

Ravitch, by contrast, is no scorched-earth traditionalist. She does not oppose the whole-language approach: in her view, students need both to learn phonics and to make efforts at reading comprehension. Indeed, Ravitch has kind words to say about progressive education when it is done right. If reformers can be faulted for neglecting academic rigor, she argues, traditionalists sometimes ignore the real needs of children. "At their best, both philosophies have made valuable and complementary contributions to American education," Ravitch writes. She especially admires Theodore Sizer, Deborah Meier, and Howard Gardner for bringing up to date "the strain of progressivism that championed students' joy in learning without denying the importance of academic disciplines."

School reformers, in Ravitch's view, made three big mistakes. Schools should not try to solve society's problems. They should avoid offering different curricula to different students. And they should avoid responding to the immediate instincts of their students. Once those mistakes are avoided, Ravitch continues, there are many ways to achieve the proper goal of cultivating qualities of mind, including efforts to recognize and to appreciate multiple intelligences as well as attempts to find lively, even relevant, ways to impart knowledge.

We tend to look for educational reformers on the left and for educational traditionalists on the right. Yet many of Ravitch's antagonists believed in the idea of inherent genetic inferiority, while Ravitch's commitment to academic education for all seems naturally compatible with racial, and even economic, equality. Now that educational reformers are in charge of American education, moreover, they are the true conservatives, committed to defending whatever exists against any change that would undermine their privileges. To the degree that education remains a hotly contested political issue, we will increasingly see odd alliances: hippies and conservative Christians in favor of home-schooling, African Americans and white Catholics in favor of vouchers, old-fashioned leftists and political conservatives in favor of standards, multiculturalists and advertisers in favor of "relevance."

In such a world, Ravitch's plea for a new emphasis on academic subject matter is anything but a right-wing manifesto. Political debates, moreover, involve matters of public policy, while educational doctrines involve fundamental philosophical ideas about human nature and human purpose. It ought not to be surprising that one of Ravitch's heroes, William T. Harris, was an American follower of Hegel, nor that G. Stanley Hall, whose romanticism was fueled by a reading of Rousseau's *Emile,* could write that "there is one thing in nature, and one alone . . . fit to inspire all true men and women with more awe and reverence than Kant's starry heavens, and that is the soul and the body of the healthy young child." When we argue over schools, we engage in a debate that has divided philosophers at least since the advent of modernity.

Are we in charge of our own fate? Is character there inside us, needing only to be brought to light? Or does character require formation, the presence of some external authority to guide our actions and help us understand who we really are? Ravitch herself clearly sides with the bildung tradition of Kant and Hegel against the naturalism of Rousseau and Dewey. "Whether or not individuals get a better job with a better education," she writes, "they will nonetheless find personal, lifelong value in their knowledge of history and literature, science and social science, art and mathematics." Autonomy is an essential value without which no person can be fully human; but to possess autonomy, a person must learn how to reason, how to interpret the lessons of the past, how to speak and write effectively, and how to appreciate great works of human creation.

Ravitch's political balance is not matched by a balanced treatment of the two sides to her story. One does not find many kind words offered in defense of zealous progressives, nor much sympathy for today's educational establishment. She quotes Alice Miel, a professor at Columbia Teachers College: "To change the curriculum of the school . . . means bringing about changes in people," which in turn implies "methods of arousing dissatisfaction," and Miel's words alone suggest the kind of pompous self-certainty that drives Ravitch to distraction. Those educators who insisted on training students for jobs, especially when, as in the case of African Americans, jobs were few, Ravitch denounces as practicing "social adjustment in its meanest sense." And more ideological versions of multiculturalism that insist on teaching students from non-European backgrounds the positive aspects of their culture represent, in her view, "an inverted form of racism."

Critics may respond to Ravitch by pointing out how public education, despite its many problems, still works. Surely there are many good public schools remaining in America, and one will always find good teachers who give of themselves so that others may learn. Yet *Left Back* is not an attack on public schools or on those who teach in them, nor even on the American Federation of Teachers, whose leaders share Ravitch's views on the need for higher standards. It is instead a no-holds-barred criticism of the educational-industrial complex, that huge industry of unreconstructed ed schools, academic researchers, school administrators, organizations like the National Education Association, textbook publishers, and public ideologues who insist that, for whatever reason, not all students need to be taught in rigorous academic fashion.

I am myself generally unsympathetic to one-sided treatments of issues, but Ravitch's side-taking is more than justified. The way in which American public schools came to advance the agenda of a self-interested, narrow-minded, politically biased, intellectually mediocre, and antidemocratic establishment is one of the great scandals of our time. If anything, considering the stakes involved in democratic education, Ravitch shows admirable restraint.

The costs of anti-intellectual education will in the first instance be borne by those who can least afford to pay them: poor and minority students whose parents cannot opt out of the public school system. But everyone will eventually wind up paying if a large number of Americans, whatever their race or social class, are not introduced to the life of the mind. By devaluing the academic aspects of schooling, educational reformers open the door to all forms of anti-intellectualism, including those identified with the right. All students will be harmed by those who insist that creationism is just as valid as Darwinism or that logic and abstraction are just Western ways of thinking. "A society that tolerates anti-intellectualism in its schools," Ravitch rightly observes, "can expect to have a dumbed-down culture that honors celebrity and sensation rather than knowledge and wisdom." Hollywood and the National Education Association seem quite well-suited for each other.

If a scandal comparable to the dumbing-down of American education had involved the extortion of billions of dollars in public finds, its perpetrators would find themselves in jail. But this scandal involves only minds; and for reasons that we have not fully grasped, Americans, for all their occasional expressions of anger at the schools, have not called to account those responsible for this great waste. Perhaps the explanation lies buried in Ravitch's book, where we learn that when schools insist on meeting the desires of their students, encourage a false sense of democratic participation, and reward immediate sensation and instinct, they produce a population content with anything that it receives, even with something as thoroughly failed as the American public school system.

It follows that if schools make demands on students, and hold them responsible for their actions, and push them, often against their will, in ways that run counter to their inclinations, they will form individuals capable of rebelling against illegitimate authority. We value democracy in our politics, and for this reason we think that we ought to value it in our schools. But just the opposite is the case: political freedom and educational discipline go hand in hand, as do educational freedom and political apathy. It is a great and urgent paradox; and to appreciate it our schools need to teach a greater respect for the complexities of the world than they now do.

PART V

Sex

•

The Mystique of Betty Friedan

I

WRITING SOCIAL CRITICISM is uncomfortably similar to selling life insurance. Your potential readers may not even want to think about your subject, and, to make things more difficult, you have to persuade them to sit still for disquieting information about it. If you can manage that, you then have to reassure them that you have the right answers. And it's a brutally competitive business. An awful lot of critics are out there making a pitch. Yet only a few break through and change the world.

One who did was Betty Friedan. *The Feminine Mystique*, first published in 1963, remains one of the most powerful works of popular nonfiction written in America. Not only did the book sell in the millions but it has long been credited with launching the contemporary feminist movement. How did Friedan do it? For one thing, she told a compelling personal story about her own career choices—one that resonated with the experiences of her readers. But Friedan also translated the ideas of academics—many of them European refugees from Nazism—into the language of popular culture. An outstanding student at Smith College, who for a time pursued a graduate degree in psychology at the University of California at Berkeley, Friedan introduced her readers to the nature-versus-nurture debate and functionalist sociology. Americans, for all their cynical anti-intellectualism, crave the authority of experts. And Friedan cited experts aplenty, as her copious and very academic footnotes attest. Freud came in for sustained criticism in her pages; Abraham Maslow came in for extended praise. Friedan also paid close attention to the writings of other scholars, including Margaret Mead, Alfred Kinsey, and Bruno Bettelheim.

And there's the rub. In the thirty-six years since *The Feminine Mystique* appeared, much has been written challenging the authority of the sources on which Friedan relied, raising the uncomfortable question of whether a book can arrive at the larger truths if the bricks on which it is built won't stand up to time.

II

To EXAMINE THE FOUNDATIONS of *The Feminine Mystique* one can begin with Margaret Mead. Friedan preferred the more anthropological Margaret Mead of *Coming of Age in Samoa* to the more Freudian author of *Male and Female.* In her anthropological fieldwork Mead had discovered, according to Friedan, a "vision of the infinite variety of sexual patterns and the enormous plasticity of human nature." This was "a truly revolutionary vision of women finally free to realize their full capabilities in a society which replaced arbitrary sexual definitions with a recognition of genuine individual gifts as they occur in either sex." But that is not the vision that America chose to see. Indeed, it is not even the vision that Margaret Mead ultimately chose to see: Friedan criticized Mead's later work, arguing that it, unlike her studies in the South Seas, owed far too much to Freud to offer anything pathbreaking to women. Mead, Friedan concluded, wound up strengthening, not challenging, the feminine mystique. To be sure, she led a wonderfully free and feminist life. More the shame, then, that "she cut down her own vision of women by glorifying the mysterious miracle of femininity."

When Alfred Kinsey first came to the attention of the reading public, in Friedan's account, he was wrongly cited for having demonstrated that uneducated women were more sexually satisfied than educated women—a finding that, if true, would have given plenty of ammunition to all those who believed that it was a mistake to educate women in the first place. But this finding, Friedan informed her readers, was not true. Once *Sexual Behavior in the Human Female* (1953) was finally published and we had access to the full 5,940 case histories of women in Kinsey's archives, we knew that education was no barrier to orgasm.

Despite her joy at discovering that Kinsey's research confirmed her sense that women were not being punished sexually for getting out of the house and getting an education, Friedan was bothered by his findings. For one thing, those women were having a lot of sex outside marriage, and Friedan, puritanical in these matters, felt that sex was a form of escapism for middle-class women who ought to be working rather than having affairs. Kinsey also reported that he found a seemingly large number of male homosexuals in America. Friedan was certain that "the homosexuality that is spreading like a murky smog over the American scene" was due to the "parasitical mother-love" of all those bored suburban women who were kept out of the workplace. The situation was, in her view, rather distasteful, because "homosexuals often lack the maturity to finish school and make sustained professional commitments." We could be sure this was true because Kinsey told us so. He had "found homosexuality most common among men who do not go beyond high school, and least common among college graduates."

Because suburban women were so frustrated and unhappy, Friedan dramatically compared them to the inmates of Nazi concentration camps. Here her authority was the distinguished psychologist Bruno Bettelheim, whose *The Informed Heart: Autonomy in a Mass Age* was published three years before *The Feminine Mystique*. Friedan was impressed with Bettelheim's emphasis not only on the physical brutality of the camps but also on the psychological manipulation by which they functioned. In the camps, as she described his findings, one lost all autonomy and came to identify with one's oppressors. Indeed, as Friedan wrote, it was "not the SS but the prisoners themselves" who "became their own worst enemy."

Although she called the chapter in which she discussed Bettelheim "Progressive Dehumanization: The Comfortable Concentration Camp," Friedan was clear that American women were not on their way to the gas chamber; Bettelheim, after all, had written about "a real concentration camp." And precisely because the incidents he described were real, they became "unforgettable"–none more so than the powerfully evoked case of a dancer who, when ordered by an SS officer to dance, got close enough to shoot him dead before being killed in turn. Still, Friedan could not give up the analogy. Like Bettelheim's fellow inmates in Dachau and Buchenwald, suburban women had "learned to 'adjust' to their biological role," had "become dependent, passive, childlike," had "given up their adult frame of reference to live at the lower human level of food and things." Maybe the world so chillingly brought to life by Bettelheim was not so different from suburbia after all.

III

AT A TIME WHEN commercial houses are reluctant to publish serious nonfiction, it is bracing to realize that a 1963 best-seller could have a chapter title like "The Sexual Solipsism of Sigmund Freud." (When I taught Friedan's book in one of my classes recently, none of the students in the room knew what *solipsism* meant.) In discussing serious ideas from the academic world, Friedan accomplished what her editors at the women's magazines to which she contributed never let her do, which was to assume that her readers had the intelligence to read and absorb scholarly authority. How ironic, then, that much of the impressive scholarship she amassed turned out to be seriously compromised.

Margaret Mead may have discovered in Samoa a form of sexuality that in its promiscuity and lack of guilt constituted an alternative to puritanical conventions, but the discovery had little to do with reality. One need not accept all the arguments of Mead's critic Derek Freeman to recognize that he has undermined the empirical claims of *Coming of Age in Samoa.* In *The Fateful Hoaxing of Margaret Mead: A Historical Analysis of Her Samoan Research* (1999), Freeman shows in detail how Mead's most important informant, a young product of a culture that placed great emphasis on female virginity before marriage, was so embarrassed by Mead's probing that she responded in typical Samoan fashion by jokingly telling Mead the opposite of the truth. Meanwhile, Mead, who had shirked her investigations into sexuality in order to write an ethnology of Samoa for the Bishop Museum, in Hawaii, accepted the hoax as true, not only because it confirmed her theory that sexuality is shaped by culture more than by nature but also because she could thereby cut short her research and set off to meet her husband in France.

If Mead was wrong, then so were all those who built their cases upon hers. For Friedan, the hoaxing of Margaret Mead was particularly unfortunate. It was precisely those of Mead's books that Friedan liked best that have not withstood later scrutiny.

Then there is the lamentable Alfred Kinsey. Thanks to his biographer, James H. Jones, Kinsey is now known as anything but a passionless scientist pursuing the truth wherever it led (see "The Professor of Desire," this vol.). On the contrary, Kinsey's academic interest in human sexuality was stimulated by his voyeurism and sexual adventurousness. Kinsey's private life is, however, the least of the problem. Far more significant is the fact that his research methods would be considered unscientific today. Even as Kinsey was collecting his data between the publication of *Sexual Behavior in the Human Male* (1948) and of *Sexual Behavior in the Human Female* (1953), Jones reveals, professional statisticians were finding significant problems with Kinsey's sampling methods; random sampling would have been not only cheaper but also more reliable. Kinsey's backers at the Rockefeller Foundation would not listen. They were so awed by the fact that Kinsey was going to challenge conventional American pieties about sex that they could not throw money at him fast enough.

Sexual Behavior in the Human Male and *Sexual Behavior in the Human Female* misrepresented the sexual habits and practices of Americans because Kinsey's interviewees were so unrepresentative. That is why Kinsey, who found many of his homosexual subjects in prisons and bars, could manage to characterize a group acknowledged for its strong influence in the arts and the universities as barely able to graduate from high school. Even at the time *Sexual Behavior in the Human Male* was published, many critics—among them the literary critic Lionel Trilling—smelled something wrong with its conclusions.

Friedan, a former graduate student in psychology who had taken courses with scholars known for their quantitative work, ought to have been suspicious as well, given her familiarity with research methodology. Her nonetheless easy acceptance of Kinsey's biased sampling makes one wonder about her own sampling. In the preface to her book she wrote that she was stimulated to undertake the project by a questionnaire she had administered to her Smith College classmates fifteen years after graduation, which revealed "a strange discrepancy between the reality of our lives as women and the image to which we were trying to conform." But Friedan had relied on the same survey to paint a far more positive picture of suburban life in at least one magazine article that preceded the publication of *The Feminine Mystique.* Her sense that the suburbs were populated by bored housewives turning themselves into sexual vampires seems about as realistic as Kinsey's portrayal of fairly frequent sexual interaction between people and animals. The invented sexuality of Mead's Samoa became in *The Feminine Mystique* the invented sexuality of suburban America. One may have been pictured as happy and the other as sad. Yet neither, for better or worse, actually existed.

Bruno Bettelheim also turned out to be a very complicated case. Like Kinsey, Bettelheim led a private life radically in contrast with his public image. In *The Creation of Dr. B: A Biography of Bruno Bettelheim* (1997), Richard Pollak discusses the many liberties Bettelheim took with the truth, from inventing academic credentials to qualify for his first teaching position to, allegedly, plagiarizing in his book on fairy tales. No misrepresentation was more serious than Bettelheim's self-portrayal as a patient, caring professional committed to overcoming the mental disorders or the deeply rooted psychological problems of the children he observed and treated at his Orthogenic School. In reality, as Pollak makes clear, Bettelheim was a petty tyrant whose insistence that parents were often to blame for their children's problems became an excuse for abusive behavior.

Bettelheim's authority as an expert in the psychology of extreme situations was derived from his accounts of his experiences at Dachau and Buchenwald. Were those accounts also fabricated? At the edges they certainly were. In his discussion of the camps, Bettelheim was less than forthright about the bribes his family and friends paid to help obtain his release, and about the fact that neither camp was a death camp. Of course, these are quibbles; there is no doubt that what he witnessed ranks among the most brutal episodes in history.

The interpretations Bettelheim offered of his experience are, however, open to question. In particular, Bettelheim's portrayal of his fellow inmates as childlike has been challenged, especially by those who insist—with considerable justice—that it was the Nazis, not the Jews, who were their worst enemies. As Pollak says, this criticism of Bettelheim was fueled by the publication of Terrence Des Pres's *The Survivor: An Anatomy of Life in the Death Camps* (1976). The victims of the Holocaust, Des Pres argued, were not characters in a play by Sigmund Freud; to use them as symbols in a psychodrama ignored the fact that they were desperate people trying to survive the day. And if it was true that we ought not to find in the presumed passivity of the victims larger symbolic lessons about the human condition, it followed that we ought not to read too much significance into acts of courage. Des Pres made much of the dancer discussed by Friedan. (As Pollak points out, the story actually originated with Eugen Kogon, and was retold by Bettelheim.) In Des Pres's account the dancer was more suicidal than heroic. To uphold her actions as an exception to a general pattern of passivity was to impugn all those sent to the camps for no reason other than their Jewishness.

Again, the conclusions of *The Feminine Mystique* come into question if facts and interpretations that Friedan took as true are later discovered to be false or mistaken. To make her case that women required freedom, Friedan felt it necessary to exaggerate the degree to which they lived in slavery. "They are in a trap," she wrote, "and to escape they must, like the dancer, finally exercise their human freedom, and recapture their sense of self." For Friedan, as for Bettelheim, people were apparently more interesting as symbols than as flesh-and-blood individuals struggling to live in the real world. There's nothing especially wrong with that; the world needs metaphors as well as facts. But a treatment of a serious social problem which relies on the authority of experts appears far less persuasive if the experts turn out to be telling just-so stories.

IV

THE POWER OF *The Feminine Mystique* rests on two kinds of authoritative sources: the findings of experts and Friedan's testimony about her personal experience. Some of the experts, we now believe, were unreliable to a considerable degree. In the past year two biographers of Betty Friedan, Judith Hennessee and Daniel Horowitz, appear to have shown that her treatment of her personal experiences was unreliable as well.

Friedan wrote in *The Feminine Mystique* of her decision to give up her fellowship at Berkeley, suggesting that she chose the love of a young man who was jealous of her success over an academic career with its presumed loneliness. "I never could explain, hardly knew myself," Friedan wrote, "why I gave up this career. I lived in the present, working on newspapers with no particular plan. I married, had children, lived according to the feminine mystique as a suburban housewife." By presenting herself this way, Friedan suggested that she was not some academic authority writing from afar about the conditions that made women unhappy. No, she suggested, she had been as passive as any of her readers: her authority to speak had nothing to do with her graduate work in psychology; it came instead from her decision to lead a life typical of suburban middle-class women of her generation.

Both Hennessee's *Betty Friedan: Her Life* and Horowitz's *Betty Friedan and the Making of the Feminine Mystique: The American Left, the Cold War, and Modern Feminism* demonstrate that everything Friedan offered in this account, though technically true, was also highly misleading. According to Hennessee, she had many boyfriends at Berkeley, one of whom, David Bohm, was a graduate student in physics working with Robert Oppenheimer. (Bohm, a member of the Communist party, was later indicted for invoking the Fifth Amendment before the House Un-American Activities Committee and soon thereafter left the United States.) But her relationship with Bohm, which was over rather quickly, had little to do with her decision to drop out of Berkeley. Horowitz suggests that Friedan's increasingly radical politics may have had something to do with it. In Friedan's year at Berkeley, 1942–43, America was involved in World War II, and the grand struggle between totalitarianism and democracy in Europe made the idyllic life of Berkeley seem unexciting by comparison. Furthermore, Friedan, an activist by inclination, became bored with the highly specialized scientific discipline that psychology had become.

Passive housewives do not usually first try their hands at popular-front journalism. Friedan did. From 1943 to 1946 she worked at the Federated Press, in New York—"the most sustained effort in American history," in Horowitz's words, "to develop a left-wing news service." From there she moved on to a six-year stint writing for UE News, the official publication of the United Electrical, Radio and Machine Workers of America, a left-wing union. Soon married to Carl Friedman (the couple agreed to drop the *m* in his name), Friedan moved out of Manhattan, first to Parkway Village, in Queens, and then to suburban Rockland County.

Neither of these was a typical suburb. The Queens neighborhood was a racially integrated area filled with UN employees, and when rents there were raised, Friedan, as the editor of the *Parkway Villager,* played a leading role in the rent strike that followed. The Friedan house in Grand View-on-Hudson was a large in-town Victorian not far from the houses of C. Wright Mills, Harvey Swados, Herbert Gutman, William J. Goode, Charles Frankel, and Roger Angell, all of whom Friedan got to know through her community activism. During this period she wrote articles for women's magazines, worked on a television documentary, and taught classes at New York University and the New School for Social Research.

Like the suburban housewives she wrote about, Friedan was

unhappy. Her marriage, according to her biographers, was unusually violent, although both stress that she gave as good as she got. But there all similarity with the passive victims of the comfortable concentration camp ends. In reality Friedan was the concentration-camp dancer, brave and resourceful. Had she portrayed herself as she really was, Friedan would have undermined the thesis of her book—if one woman could avoid the feminine mystique, then why couldn't others? Friedan clearly knew enough psychology to understand that in America only victims can speak for victims. The personal asides in *The Feminine Mystique* conform to the conventions of the genre of sin and redemption: I was once like you but now I have seen the light—and you can follow my example. It makes for great inspirational literature. But when combined with flawed academic expertise, the made-up life of Betty Friedan leaves contemporary readers uneasy about whether anything at all in her book can be trusted.

The obligations of a political activist can easily interfere with the obligations of a social critic. As an activist, one can believe that dramatic but not completely accurate depictions of the status of women are from a moral perspective no different from the strategies of those people who exaggerate the prevalence of breast cancer in order to scare women into seeing their doctors. Saving even a small number of lives justifies the latter. Helping more women to put a name to the problem that had no name justified the former.

Did Betty Friedan sacrifice the truth in order to advance her cause? In the short run the answer must be no, because *The Feminine Mystique* spoke truthfully enough to inspire many women both at the time and since. Yet in the longer run the faults of the book loom large. If the pursuit of a good cause is accompanied by too much bad testimony, the social critic will eventually lose the trust of the very readers she wants to influence.

The Professor of Desire

I

NOTHING IN THE BACKGROUND of Alfred C. Kinsey seemed likely to produce a man who would devote his life to the study of sex. He was born in 1894 and grew up in unbohemian Hoboken and South Orange, New Jersey, the son of a self-made shop teacher at the Stevens Institute of Technology. He was an Eagle Scout. A sickly boy, Kinsey worked diligently to please his repressive, dictatorial, sanctimonious, and ambitious father. That proved to be an impossible task. Turning his back on a career in engineering, Kinsey dropped out of Stevens to attend Bowdoin College. There he discovered that his impulse to collect things, when connected to his love of nature, made him a taxonomist–a biologist seeking to understand the world through patient observation rather than through experimentation or the newly emerging mathematics of population ecology. An accomplished, hardworking student, Kinsey took his doctorate at Harvard before assuming an assistant professorship at the then second-rate Indiana University.

Taxonomists, as James Jones patiently explains in *Alfred C. Kinsey: A Public/Private Life,* were divided into "lumpers" and "splitters." Lumpers, the dominant group, believed that there were relatively few species in nature, so that the task of the scientist became one of classifying individual organisms into preexisting categories. Kinsey strongly dissented from this Platonic essentialism. In his view, most attempts to designate distinct species owed more to the scientist's need to bring order to reality than to the diversity of life itself. Kinsey focused his research on gull wasps, tiny parasitic insects that leave growths on their hosts, most commonly oak trees. Splitter that he was, he reasoned that the more gull wasps he collected, the more new species he could identify. So collect he did—all over the country, then all over the world. Kinsey seemed very much the typical Midwestern academic. He married Clara Bracken McMillen, an Indiana University undergraduate whom he met during his job interview, and before long they owned a large house in town and produced four children. He published his research on gull wasps with Indiana University Press to a few generally positive reviews and wrote a textbook designed to make money.

Yet not all was well with his career. For one thing, he had committed himself to a very old-fashioned kind of science; Kinsey, said Robert Kroc, one of his younger colleagues (and the brother of Ray Kroc, the entrepreneur who created McDonald's), was the first scientist he ever met who studied evolution outside the laboratory. Moreover, Indiana University suffered under the reign of an old president more interested in settling scores than in advancing the prestige of his institution. And, perhaps to Kinsey's chagrin, no offers from elite institutions came his way. Still, Kinsey was keeping busy. His voracious work habits had led him to read whatever sex manuals he could find. "You know, there isn't much science here," he told Kroc. In 1937, the trustees of Indiana University appointed a new president named Herman Wells; and when students began to agitate for more relevant sex education, Kinsey volunteered and was asked to design a course on marriage.

Kinsey's expertise in biology colored the course from the start. He appeared to be teaching just the facts of nature; but he presented himself as a scientist, and so he was quite graphic in his depiction of sexual organs and sexual acts, and he claimed to be entirely nonjudgmental about human sexual practices. Ultimately the explicitness of the course aroused the opposition of many on campus, and by 1940 Kinsey was forced to withdraw from it. But by then the die was cast.

Kinsey had transformed himself into a sex researcher. He would never again teach a marriage course—indeed, within a few years he would not teach at all. Kinsey was rescued from his professional malaise by the Committee for Research in Problems of Sex, a standing committee of the National Research Council. The Rockefeller Foundation, which financed the NRC, had for years been seeking to shift the work of the CRPS in the direction of human sexuality. Kinsey appeared as a godsend to Robert Yerkes, the NRC's director, who now could appease Rockefeller with a serious scientist in command of extensive data concerning human sexual behavior.

For Kinsey had not just been teaching about sexuality. As part of his course on marriage, he had begun to administer a questionnaire to students asking them about their sexual experiences; and this was eventually transformed into a face-to-face interview. Flush with his success at eliciting information, Kinsey interviewed everyone he could find. He had even gone to Chicago and won the trust of its very suspicious homosexual community. By the time he approached Yerkes, Kinsey had obtained the sexual histories of more people than anyone else in history. His collection would soon include Yerkes himself. Inviting his funders to Bloomington, Kinsey told them that they could not appreciate his interviewing skills unless they agreed to provide their sexual histories. Remarkably, Yerkes and his two colleagues agreed.

Within six years the Rockefeller Foundation would be making huge grants to Kinsey to support his Institute for Sex Research. Wells, the university's president, was thrilled; but he was also wary, and so he encouraged the institute to establish itself as an independent corporation. It came into existence officially in 1947. Kinsey's relations with his backers were never smooth. Determined to reap the prestige of the Rockefeller name, Kinsey trumpeted his relationship with the foundation, alienating Yerkes and violating the gentlemanly code of discretion to which foundation trustees adhere. Ultimately the foundation, under pressure from conservatives in Congress, would drop Kinsey. But by then he had published his books, *Sexual Behavior in the Human Male* in 1948 and *Sexual Behavior in the Human Female* in 1953.

Kinsey brought out the results of his sex research with a medical publisher, and he laced his account with dense prose and technical terms, but everyone knew these books would be best-sellers, and their sales exceeded the wildest expectations. Clearly, large numbers of

Americans were ready to receive the news that nothing erotic ought to be alien to them. Now famous and rich, Kinsey no longer needed Rockefeller patronage. Yet he never raised much money after the Foundation withdrew its support; many interlocutors introduced Kinsey to rich potential donors, but he was a terrible fund-raiser, unable to close a deal by making the crucial "ask" for funds.

Kinsey died in 1956 a frustrated and angry man. He had failed to complete his lifework: volumes on topics including homosexuality, prostitution, Negro sex, and sex offenders were planned. And the critics had already begun to wield their knives. Such distinguished representatives of American letters as Margaret Mead, Geoffrey Gorer, Lionel Trilling, and Lawrence Kubie were critical of Kinsey's books. America had entered the golden age of the Eisenhower years. The country did not seem interested in replacing its religious and moral prohibitions on sex with Kinsey's naturalistic, anything-goes advice.

II

WITHIN FIFTEEN YEARS OF Kinsey's funeral, the Food and Drug Administration approved a birth control pill, *Penthouse* made its first appearance in England, Johns Hopkins became the first American medical school to perform sex change operations, San Francisco's Haight-Ashbury blossomed, *Human Sexual Response* by Masters and Johnson was published, topless waitresses became the rage, new movies such as "I Am Curious, Yellow" portrayed new levels of sexual explicitness, the Stonewallers rioted in Greenwich Village, and Kate Millett wrote *Sexual Politics.*

We now know from Jones's book that Kinsey anticipated the sexual revolution not only by what he wrote, but also by what he did. There was a private life behind the public figure–and, we are frequently told, a shocking one. A workaholic and a man of authoritarian temper, Kinsey employed a number of graduate students who were expected to share his passion for long workdays and to accompany him on field trips. An inveterate exhibitionist, he would frequently walk around naked in camp. His surviving letters reveal a scatological Kinsey, a man fascinated with burlesque shows, graphic descriptions of sexual acts, and juvenile sexual boasting. An atmosphere of homoeroticism pervaded these all-male field trips, Jones writes: "It is not hard to suspect that oral sex was going down under canvas tops." (Jones's language in that sentence is especially unfelicitous.) Jones is convinced that Kinsey had fallen in love with one of his students, Ralph Voris, and that he had designs on others as well. No wonder he wanted so much to study Chicago's gay community, for there "he could slip away and engage in furtive, anonymous sex with the crowd that patronized Chicago's 'tea rooms,' slang for the public urinals frequented by homosexuals interested in quick, impersonal, faceless sex."

Voris died young, but soon thereafter Kinsey found "the third and final love" of his life: Clyde Martin. According to Jones, Martin resisted, and suggested sex with Kinsey's forty-two-year-old wife (and first love) Clara. The world's most famous sex researcher quickly agreed. Martin would be only the first of her many extramarital lovers, most of them taken with Kinsey's permission–if not his active encouragement. Kinsey's Institute for Sex Research was rapidly turning into a free-sex zone. Martin, who was hired as an interviewer and would later be listed as one of the authors of *Sexual Behavior in the Human Male,* watched helplessly as his wife began an affair with Paul Gebhard, another member of Kinsey's staff. And the third chief interviewer, Wardell Pomeroy, was the most promiscuous of them all, "a kind of equal opportunity Don Juan" who would sleep with as many people of either sex as he could.

For all his kinkiness, however, Kinsey was not Pomeroy. Indeed, Kinsey appears to have had very few lovers, male or female. Kinsey got his pleasure indirectly: "Watching others have sex satisfied both the scientist and the voyeur in Kinsey," Jones writes. Take those interviews. It is not hard to conclude that Kinsey's desire to interview everyone he could find was his version of Leporello's catalog aria: he was excited by the conquests in other people's sex lives. But Kinsey was not just a metaphorical voyeur. In 1949 Kinsey hired a photographer for his staff, and his job was to film the members of Kinsey's circle having sex with each other and masturbating for the camera.

The newly hired photographer, William Dellenback, later told Jones about Kinsey's deeply ingrained masochism. In front of the camera, Kinsey would take an object such as a swizzle stick, place it into the urethra of his penis, tie up his scrotum with a rope, and then pull on the rope as he pushed the object in deeper. Masochism, Jones informs his readers, is like a drug addiction; once the masochist gets accustomed to a certain level of pain, more intense techniques have to be found. That explains why Kinsey once circumcised himself without anesthesia—or why, on another occasion, he tied the usual knot around his scrotum but then threw the other end of the rope over a pipe, took it with his hand, jumped off a chair, and hung there in the air as the pressure increased.

If Kinsey's private sexual habits were extreme, so were some of his public views. A man on a mission, Kinsey would bring to sex the same concern for efficiency and technique that Frederick Winslow Taylor, another student at the Stevens Institute of Technology, brought to industrial production. Like all revolutionaries, Kinsey was reluctant to find enemies among those who shared any part of his agenda. Sympathetic to prisoners arrested for sex crimes, he would ultimately come to believe that even pedophiles were unfairly persecuted. Incest, including child abuse, Kinsey seemed to suggest, was much ado about nothing; so long as children did not make a big deal of their experiences, no real harm, he believed, could come to them. Kinsey, Jones concludes, "saw civilization as the enemy of sex." In his life and his work, Kinsey was, according to Jones, "the architect of a new sensibility about a part of life that everyone experiences and no one escapes."

III

JAMES H. JONES'S BOOK, a quarter century in the making, is a fascinating account of a fantastic American. Jones, the author of a previous book on the Tuskegee experiment, is a historian with a knack for writing books about the past that are bound to be discussed in the present. He is not a great stylist, but he manages to hold his reader's attention as he moves exhaustively through a proliferation of increasingly peculiar detail. Yet what held my attention most has little to do with the sensational side of Kinsey's sex life. Jones's discussion of such matters as the controversies around Kinsey's methodology and the politics of foundation support are far more interesting than his accounts of how Kinsey wrestled with his own libido.

Erotic arousal, Kinsey and his coauthors wrote regretfully in *Sexual Behavior in the Human Male*, "could be subject to precise instrumental measurement if objectivity among scientists and public respect for scientific research allowed such laboratory investigation." Since it did not, Kinsey had to settle for accounts that people themselves provided about their sexual lives. Kinsey took great pains to convince his readers that interviews could be an effective substitute for laboratory observations. In a general sense, he was right: selected carefully and interviewed correctly, we can learn much from people about human sexual behavior.

But Kinsey was careless in his selection. What, for example, constitutes an orgasm? Ever the splitter, Kinsey rejected the uniform descriptions of orgasm that he found in marriage manuals in favor of a six-point orgasm scale, ranging from primarily genital reactions (22 percent frequency) to "extreme tension with violent convulsion" in which "the legs often become rigid, with muscles knotted and toes pointed . . . breath held or gasping, eyes staring hard and tightly closed . . . whole body or parts of it spasmodically twitching, sometimes synchronously with throbs or violent jerking of the penis" (16 percent). His source for this simultaneously clinical and pornographic description was "adult observers for 196 preadolescent boys"–pedophiles, one presumes, observing very closely indeed.

Moving from definition to classification, Kinsey and his colleagues described the frequency of orgasm among men by age, social class, occupation, and religion. (Orthodox Jews, he found, were the least sexually active people in America.) Again, Kinsey was instinctively attracted to the unrepresentative, such as men who were unusually sexually active. "Our large sample," the authors wrote, "shows that, far from being rare, individuals with frequencies of 7 or more sex acts per week constitute a considerable segment (7.6 percent) of any population." Was it reality or fantasy that led Kinsey to pen this sentence: "Where the occupation allows the male spouse to return home at noon, contacts may occur at that hour of the day, and, consequently, there is a regular outlet of fourteen to twenty-one times per week"? And so it went. Between 92 percent and 97 percent of American males masturbate. "The number of college-bred males who have some premarital intercourse is high enough to surprise many persons." Use of prostitutes was common, if unevenly distributed by social class. Thirty-seven percent of men experienced orgasm through homosexual contact at least once in their lives. Finally, there was sex with animals, "the only chapter in the book," wrote Lionel Trilling, "which hints that sex may be touched with tenderness." But even here Kinsey was precise: "The accumulative incidence figures for animal intercourse go to about 14 percent for the farm boys who do not go beyond grade school, to about 20 percent for the group which goes into high school but not beyond, and to 26 percent for the males who will ultimately go to college."

Kinsey informed his readers that he had collected 5,300 sexual histories, "forty times as much material as was included in the best of previous studies." This may have impressed the general reader, but no scientist could be taken in by Kinsey's boasting. Utterly eclectic in his methods, Kinsey interviewed wildly disproportionate numbers of college students, prisoners, people willing to be interviewed, and people preoccupied with sex. He could have multiplied his interviews by a hundred and still have come away with a group of Americans whose sexual conduct would have been abnormal. By the late 1940s, statisticians had discovered that scientific sampling was far more effective in representing a given population than exhaustive but futile efforts to interview everyone. Yet Kinsey refused to engage in proper sampling techniques, making it impossible for him to make even near-accurate generalizations about the distribution of sexual behaviors among the American population.

Kinsey's approach to sex was as scientific as *Peyton Place*. And since his methods were so poor, Kinsey and his coauthors left their readers with the impression that there was far more sex taking place in America, and far more exotic sex, than corresponded to the real-life experiences of those readers. The message was that people should listen to Kinsey rather than to their conscience, their God, or their superego. It was quite explicit in Kinsey's text: a wide variety of sexual activities "may seem to fall into categories that are as far apart as right and wrong, licit and illicit, normal and abnormal, acceptable and unacceptable in our social organization. In actuality, they all prove to originate in the relatively simple mechanisms which provide for erotic response when there are sufficient physical or psychic stimuli." Properly instructed by Kinsey's improper data, they would be free to engage in premarital sex, pursue extramarital affairs, act out their homoerotic fantasies, and jettison whatever inhibitions prevented them from claiming their share of the Gross National Orgasm.

In theory, peer review should have stopped Kinsey from embarrassing his discipline, his university, and himself. Yet the Rockefeller Foundation continued to pour money into his coffers. Periodic appraisals of his work commissioned by the Foundation never raised the issue of sampling, or did so only to back off. Responding to the concern of Kinsey's editor that the statistics be "bullet proof" against attack, Alan Gregg of the Rockefeller Foundation assured him that Kinsey's methods had been thoroughly reviewed by experts; he also agreed to write a preface endorsing Kinsey's investigations as "sincere, objective, and determined." Kinsey even survived, for a time, a review of his data commissioned by the American Statistical Association that was carried out by three of the most high-powered statisticians in America.

The most far-reaching scandal narrated by Jones has nothing to do with masochism and everything to do with the irresponsibility of scientists and foundation officers. Perhaps they admired Kinsey's message. More likely, they were unwilling to admit a mistake. Whatever the reason, they abused every canon of proper scientific procedure to support research that, for all its volume, was as shallow as it was sensational. In endorsing Kinsey, his backers were endorsing the idea that sexual repression was a bad thing–a proposition for which scientific evidence is, to say the least, lacking.

As it turns out, a group of contemporary scientists has developed the accurate samples that Kinsey never did. *The Social Organization of Sexuality,* by Edward O. Laumann, John H. Gagnon, Robert T. Michael, and Stuart Michaels, appeared in 1994; and while it is not the last word on American sexual habits, it is a far more reliable guide than *Sexual Behavior in the Human Male.* Anticipating the kind of reception that Kinsey received, the authors wrote a technical version of their book for a university press and, with the help of a journalist, a popular version designed for the best-seller lists. Bestsellerdom never came to pass. And the reason was quickly obvious. When social scientists tell the real truth about sex, they are telling people–whose own experiences, after all, constitute the story–what they already know.

In the realm of sex, Laumann and his colleagues found, Americans are boringly conventional. Homosexuality is roughly as common as most people think it is: 2.8 percent of men think of themselves as gay, 1.4 percent of women. Adultery is quite uncommon: 90 percent of married women and 75 percent of men report monogamy. Very few Americans are attracted to, or interested in, passive anal intercourse, having sex with a stranger, violent sex, or group sex. Sexual athletes–highly promiscuous people with many sexual partners in the course of a year–are very rare. These data are obviously not without flaws. People will often overreport or underreport their sexual experiences, depending on who they are and who they are talking to. Still, the data do seem to show that, for most people most of the time, sex is just one experience among many: pleasurable, valued, important, but central neither to their identity nor to their mental health.

The lesson of the Laumann book is clear. If sex researchers are scrupulous and fair, determined to capture reality as it is, then they will generally find nothing very dramatic to report. If they are attracted, however, to the study of sexuality to make a point, then they will distort reality, as Kinsey did, in the service of some larger cause. Sexuality is now a booming academic subject. Many of those engaged in it have points that they wish to make. They want to show that our common categories—homosexual/heterosexual, male/female, normal/abnormal—are arbitrary conventions. Or they want to take the side of the sexually stigmatized. But the most common point is that sex itself is a good thing, which means that restraints on sex are bad.

Whether or not any of these points need to be made is not my concern here. What is true, however, is that the very act of making them distorts the study of sex, for it rules out of order or dismisses out of hand people who willingly accept sexual repression, who think it is right to pass judgment on those who cannot control their sexuality, who are convinced that human beings were given the gift of sexuality primarily to make children, who believe that some kinds of sexual behavior are joyous and others are sick.

IV

AMONG THOSE ACADEMIC WRITERS who have a point that they wish to make is James H. Jones, who, when all is said and done, treats Kinsey as a hero because he was willing to attack sexual repression. To be sure, Jones writes, Kinsey was a man consumed by demons: "somewhere along the lines, he veered off the path of normal development." Attracted to men, but forced to lead a conventional life, Kinsey was drawn to the study of human sexuality in order to find in science answers to his personal sexual confusion. Yet Jones is enthralled. Comparing his subject at one point to Martin Luther and John Calvin, Jones writes that "if Kinsey's views were amoral, they also reflected a strong dose of common sense." As odd as Kinsey's sexual habits may have been, "his problems, albeit in exaggerated form, were the nation's problems." Kinsey's "great achievement was to take his pain and suffering and use it to transform himself into an instrument of social reform, a secular evangelist who proclaimed a new sensibility about human sexuality."

Since he has a point that he so ardently wishes to make, Jones runs the risk of distorting Kinsey in roughly the same way that Kinsey distorted American sexual behavior. The parallels between Jones and

Kinsey are striking. Like Kinsey, Jones has written a book exhaustive–even obsessive–in its detail. Kinsey was one of the first 77 Eagle Scouts in America. The labels he used to classify his gull wasps were three-eighths of an inch by five-eighths. Between 1919 and 1937, he wrote 3,193 pages. His fully developed interview schedule contained a maximum of 521 items. Kinsey completed exactly 7,985 sexual histories. And so on. Jones is a splitter, not a lumper: he classifies Kinsey's output with the same passion for variety and detail with which Kinsey classified gull wasps. "Kinsey thrived on meticulous tasks," Jones writes. So does his biographer.

Precision is a virtue. But in this case it is something else as well. Jones stresses that Kinsey was an expert manipulator of public opinion, a man so taken by his image that he tried to manipulate the reviewers of his books and the stories written about him in the press. "Everything about the book," Jones writes of *Sexual Behavior in the Human Male,* "was designed to impress the reader with the richness of Kinsey's empirical data." In portraying numbers with such exactitude, Jones, too, is engaged in image management. If Kinsey was determined not to leave any stones unturned in his campaign to convince Americans that his approach to sex was scientific, Jones will leave nothing to chance to convince his readers that Kinsey is worthy of epic treatment.

Yet the strongest correspondence between Kinsey and Jones is that both are voyeurs. Jones is as fascinated by Kinsey's sex life as Kinsey was by the sex lives of his 7,895 people. Indeed, Jones's book can be understood as an effort to record Kinsey's sexual history. If, as Jones stresses, Kinsey used his ability to obtain sexual histories in order to exercise power over those he interviewed, Jones will seek even more power by putting the power-hungry Kinsey in his place.

One of the most sensitive methodological issues with which Kinsey had to deal was whether the histories that he obtained were accurate. To ensure their truth, Kinsey went to great lengths. He preferred an interview to a questionnaire, which required him to commit to memory all the questions that he would ask. To assure confidentiality, all transcriptions were carried out in a complex code that only very few people ever learned. No one can ever know whether Kinsey's meticulous methods produced accurate accounts. But we do know one case where the truth of a sexual history can be questioned: James Jones's.

It is important to make distinctions here. The source for Jones's treatment of Kinsey's masochism is the filmmaker who recorded his adventures. If these films are to be believed—and I see no reason why they should not be believed—then Kinsey was a very strange guy. But was he a homosexual? If he was, what kind of homosexual was he? With whom did he have sex? Was he a participant or an observer in those Chicago "tea rooms"? One of the consequences of Kinsey's work is that America is now more open in its discussion of sex. But it was not open while Kinsey lived; and therefore Jones has a choice: he can admit that there are things he will never know about Kinsey's sex life, or he can engage in conjecture. Invariably, he does the latter.

"Despite the injunctions of his religion, despite the vigilance of parents, teachers, and police, and despite the warnings of social hygienists who shaped the sex education programs of his beloved YMCA and Boy Scouts," Jones writes of his subject as a young man, "Kinsey masturbated." And Kinsey, unlike other boys, was moved to extreme self-condemnation when he masturbated. If there is a source for these conclusions, it is the conversations that Kinsey had later in life with Paul Gebhard. But those conversations, at least according to Jones's references, dealt with problems of sexual repression of youth in general rather than with Kinsey's personal behavior. Indeed, the only examples of camp-inspired masturbation cited by Jones deal with people other than Kinsey who attended summer camp in the 1950s, not, as Kinsey did, in 1912 and 1913.

"Falling in love with another man is a defining moment in the life of any homosexual," Jones writes. "Until it happens, many men can deceive themselves about their true sexual identity." For Jones, Kinsey's "defining moment" was his relationship with Ralph Voris. Given the times, it would be unlikely that any incontrovertible proof of a sexual relationship between Kinsey and Voris exists. And none does. Kinsey kept a picture of Voris on his desk. He also wrote intimate letters to him, although mostly the intimate details were about his marital sex life. If those letters are amorous, the passion seems to go one way, with Kinsey constantly trying to keep the relationship close, even over Voris's resistance. Two individuals told Jones of a sexual relationship between the men, one of whom added that he too had slept with Kinsey; but their testimony is ambiguous, for one says simply that Kinsey "was in love with Voris from day one," which does not necessarily imply sex, and the other only thinks that he knows when a homosexual relationship between the men began, which means he is guessing. And in any case both did not want their names used and are cited as "anonymous." Thus their testimony cannot be checked.

Other sources are cited by name. One of them called attention to Kinsey's exhibitionism. Another described a night when Kinsey was in a foul mood because he and his students slept in a hotel. "Griped and sulked about everything," he wrote in his diary, "I guess because he couldn't sleep in his damn, prick nibbling tent." This observer, Jones comments, usually meant what he said, so that we should take "prick nibbling" as a literal description of what went on. Kinsey sent erotic books to this man as well. All of them dealt with heterosexual sex, but this was "entirely in keeping with Kinsey's approach," Jones writes.

Does all this add up to definitive proof that Kinsey was, as Jones insists, "homosexual"? Hardly. For one thing, Kinsey was a married man with four children, all of which suggests that, if he was attracted to men, he was also bisexual. And Kinsey may have been satisfied by prattle, rather than by actual contact. By insisting that the category "homosexual" applies to Kinsey, Jones uses a term whose meaning has been shaped in the 1980s and 1990s to describe conduct that took place more than half a century earlier. A historian more sensitive to evidence and to the texture of the times should have more respect for ambiguity.

About the camping trips, at least, there is evidence of homosexual attraction, however inconclusive. When Jones writes about Kinsey's research in Chicago, however, he steps over a line into irresponsibility. He informs his readers that Kinsey sought sexual release in the underground gay scene, even though he cites no sources. And when he does cite a source–a letter that Kinsey wrote to Voris–he notes that Kinsey avoided any mention of any sexual adventures. Bereft of data, Jones turns surreal: "Although it is highly unlikely that he abandoned himself to those outings very often, Kinsey must have relished the arrangement." Absent any data, Jones cannot know anything. And so he should not say anything.

One's first impulse is to charge Jones with sensationalism so as to sell books. But the odd way in which Kinsey's life and Jones's scholarship intertwine suggests another explanation. For Jones, Kinsey was engaged in an effort to overturn a "Victorian" sexual code. Yet Jones fails to appreciate what Steven Marcus has called the "other Victorians," such as the author of *My Secret Life*, who, like Kinsey, recorded sexual adventures of all kinds. Since Kinsey did have a secret life, he was as much a Victorian as he was a rebel against Victorianism. And since Jones is so determined to uncover Kinsey's secret life, he, too, is more Victorian than he realizes.

There are many ways to be obsessed with sex. One is to suppress it. The other is to find it everywhere–and if it is found to be homosexual or in any way "deviant," so much the better. All of which suggests that Kinsey's contribution to America's sexual revolution is more ambiguous than it appears. The usual way in which these things are treated–certainly the matter is treated this way in Jones's book–is to suggest that different historical periods are characterized by different degrees of sexual openness. As society swings from repression to liberation, not only are people freer to express their sexuality, but individuals with sexual tastes outside the mainstream experience less pain and suffering.

But there is another way to read the events since Kinsey's day. It is to suggest that Americans have always been consistently conventional in their private sexual behavior and consistently fascinated by public accounts of other people's sexuality. Obviously there have been times when American sexual manners changed: the Pill clearly transformed the rules of sexual engagement, though even in this case the 1990s are witnessing a return to more conventional sexual patterns. From this perspective, what we call a sexual "revolution" is not so much a change in actual behavior as a shift in cultural emphasis, in public conscious-ness about sexuality.

And even such a shift does not involve a swing from a time when sex is at the center of public consciousness to a time when it is at the periphery. In America, sex is never at the periphery. Sometimes the American fascination with sex tends to result in prohibition and cen-sorship, while at other times it produces exhibitionism and curiosity. Sex can be a force for procreation and joy, and it can be a force for chaos and irresponsibility. Americans make their peace with both sides of sex by varying their public representation of it while changing their private practice of it as rarely as technology will allow.

Alfred C. Kinsey—the Midwesterner, the family man, the product of a proper Christian upbringing, the scientist—grew up in an atmosphere of sexual repression and led a revolution for sexual openness. But how much really changed? Father and son were linked in ways that neither could appreciate, for neither was capable of accepting sex as just a part of life: no more, no less. It is in this sense (and it is absent from Jones's book) that Kinsey was a representative American. Once we had Anthony Comstock and Maria Monk. Now we have Jesse Helms and Karen Finley. It is a cliché to say that the censors and the exhibitionists need each other; but it is also true that they understand each other. The censors hear about public accounts of sexuality and believe that people are actually doing such things in their bedrooms. And the exhibitionists listen to the censors and believe that people will, if the censors get their way, stop doing whatever they are doing in the privacy of their bed-rooms. Neither seems all that much concerned with what actually hap-pens behind the closed doors. For what goes on there is more interest-ing to the parties involved than it is to all those trying so desperately to listen in. And that is why it is fitting that those doors stay closed.

Up from Scientism

I

YOU MIGHT THINK THAT a book filled with correlation coefficients, careful attention to problems of selection bias, detailed consideration of counterfactual cases, and ingenious ways to present data would be a model of scientific method. Its author certainly thinks so. "Methods from the behavioral sciences," Frank Sulloway confidently writes in *Born to Rebel: Birth Order, Family Dynamics, and Creative Lives,* "can be gainfully employed to test historical hypotheses that have previously been accepted on faith." One of his book's many aims is to advance the notion that rigorous quantitative methods yield more truth into human affairs than "those interpretative fads that pass for progress within the humanities."

But if you did think all those things, you would be wrong. Sulloway's book fails the most important test of science. It is not tables and hypotheses that make an inquiry scientific, it is attitude. Humility, tentativeness, a willingness to be open to explanations more parsimonious than one's own: those are the characteristics which have distinguished the rise of scientific method. Sulloway, by contrast, is immodest, bombastic, ambitious, combative, defensive. The audacity and the inventiveness of Sulloway, and others who advance a neo-Darwinistic synthesis in the explanation of human behavior, cannot be doubted. But when applied to human beings, about whose behavior so much is unknown, we must never call it science. A great deal of contemporary neo-Darwinism is, instead, an example of the very interpretative faddishness that, according to Sulloway, characterizes those more willing than he to accept things on faith.

Sulloway's idea is that birth order explains a great deal of why some people rebel and other people conform. Why was it, he asks, that when Charles Darwin published his revolutionary work on evolution, some scientists embraced its principles enthusiastically while others denounced it as wrongheaded? Clearly, different individuals respond differently to innovation, not only in science but in politics: the reception of women's suffrage, or of abolitionism, by and large contemporary with Darwin, was also divided between some who embraced change and others who joined the forces of the status quo.

As he pondered this phenomenon, Sulloway noticed that people within the same family often separated into one or the other camp. And if so, then the two most influential theories which seek to explain social change have to be discarded, or at least significantly modified. One is Marxism, the other is Freudianism. Since just about all members of the same family are also members of the same social class, class position alone cannot determine an individual's consciousness. And "offspring are not trying to kill one parent in order to take sole possession of the other. Childhood is about maximizing parental investment, not reducing it by half."

The best theory to explain the receptivity to Darwin's ideas, Sulloway argues, was offered by Darwin himself. Siblings compete for parental attention. The more there are, the harder it is for any one to get it. In this highly competitive game, some will have a natural advantage: they will have been born first. Having grabbed parental attention when they held a monopoly, firstborns tend to do everything in their power to keep their privileged place after later children are born. And later-borns, desperately searching for a strategy to break open a closed cartel, must become extremely inventive to find their way into their parents' hearts. Darwinian theory tells us that in the vigorous competition of the nonhuman world, species adapt and survive or they stay the same and die out. Siblings in the human world have to adapt, too. They do so by finding a niche and cultivating it. Since firstborns already occupy their own niches, later-borns, if they are to be noticed, have to find unoccupied niches. If they do so successfully, they will be rewarded with parental investment.

Individual temperament is thus shaped by birth order. It stands to reason that firstborns will be conservative, since already existing niches most benefit them. For later-borns, by contrast, the alternative is innovation or obscurity. No wonder that Voltaire, a younger brother, became a leading figure of the Enlightenment, while Armand, his firstborn brother, became a religious fanatic. But how common is this pattern? To find out, Sulloway studied twenty-eight scientific debates, ranging from the Copernican revolution to quantum mechanics. Consulting with scientific experts, he compiled a lengthy list of all the scientists who took public stands on each debate, determined their order of birth, and uncovered dramatic results: later-borns were twice as likely to support scientific innovations as firstborns. Translated into the terms of statistics, Sulloway points out that the odds of this happening by chance are a billion to one. Unsatisfied even with that impressive demonstration, Sulloway then divides his twenty-eight controversies by their degree of radicalism and discovers even more significant results.

What about innovations outside of science? Sulloway anticipates the question, and he analyzes historical controversies in much the same way. Birth order tells us why Henry VIII's wives responded differently to their husband, why the Terror after the French Revolution was particularly bloody, why some people opposed slavery more readily than others, why Che Guevara and Carlos the Jackal became terrorists, why some justices of the Supreme Court are more likely to write dissenting opinions than others. It is not only radicalism, moreover, that is determined by birth order. Political style is similarly determined. Firstborns are more likely to be moralistic and militant, middle children to be compromisers, and later-borns to be mushy idealists. Sulloway finds that birth order is the single best predictor of why some theologians were attracted to the Protestant Reformation; only one other predictor, age, came anywhere near sharing its explanatory power.

Emboldened by the strength of the correlations that he uncovers,

Sulloway proposes nothing less than that "birth order provides a potential Rosetta stone for deciphering some of the basic principles that govern family niches." His subject may seem small, but Sulloway's objective is large. If it is true that the influence of birth order on scientific discovery is, in his choice of word, "indisputable," we are on the path to appreciating not the contingency in human behavior, but the consistency. Sulloway believes that he has resolved debates that have characterized the study of human beings since Machiavelli and Hobbes. There really is such a thing as human nature, and birth order determines it.

II

TO SURVIVE SCRUTINY, SULLOWAY's claims have to pass two tests. His correlations have to stand up; and if they do stand up, his theory about the childhood competition for niches must be shown to be the best explanation of why they do. On both counts, Sulloway's confidence is unwarranted.

Sulloway fully understands why it is important to demonstrate statistical relationships between birth order and receptivity to innovation. Anecdotes will get you nowhere. For every interesting case like Voltaire's, there are others which upset or deny the importance of birth order, including Voltaire's protector Frederick the Great who, like most monarchs, was a firstborn. It may be true that later-borns disproportionately supported the Protestant Reformation, but it was led by two firstborns named Martin Luther and Philipp Melanchthon. Isaac Newton was a firstborn, as was Johannes Kepler. Since birth order cannot explain every case, statistical generalization is the proper way to appreciate patterns and tendencies.

But statistical generalization is not quite the neutral, value-free procedure that Sulloway thinks it is. It involves making judgments. Even the simplest question—who was born first?—is not as straightforward as it seems. If society consigns women to second-class status, should we count as a firstborn the first male child, since females would be unlikely to be taken as serious participants in the competition for parental affection? If longevity is not a fact of life, should we consider as firstborn someone actually born second, but whose older brother died when that child was two, or ten, or twenty? What about stepfamilies? Orphans?

Sulloway, the reader quickly learns, does not use biological birth order in his correlations. He prefers "functional" birth order. This means that one of Darwin's severest critics, Louis Agassiz, confirms the statistical generalization because he was "firstborn" and a scientific conservative, even though he actually was the fifth child of his parents. Whether it is justifiable to classify him this way—Agassiz's older siblings all died in infancy—is not the point. The point is that functional birth order is a construct. Unlike biological birth order, functional birth order depends on subjective decisions made by the investigator many times over. So let us be clear that Sulloway never actually shows that birth order as the casual reader might understand it correlates with receptivity to innovation. In fact, as Sulloway notes rather astoundingly in one of his appendixes, "controlled for functional birth order, biological birth order is not a significant predictor of radicalism." In this not unimportant way, the whole project amounts to nothing.

Subjectivity enters into the definition of birth order in a second way as well. For some of the participants in the scientific and political controversies that Sulloway analyzes, no information exists about birth order. Rather than accept missing information as a fact of historical life, Sulloway instead adopts a statistical model designed to tell us what the "probable" birth order of an individual was, given all the other things that we know about the person. Using the example of an eighty-year-old who supports Darwin but whose birth order is unknown, Sulloway reasons that the odds that such a person was a later-born would be over 100 to 1. Hold on. Birth order was supposed to explain response to innovation. By using response to innovation to guess birth order, Sulloway breaks down the barrier between his dependent variable and his independent variable.

Sulloway is careful to note that in such a case he would not include his birth-order guess in his correlations; but in his chapters dealing with politics, especially those on the Reformation and the French Revolution, he does use a statistical technique designed to supply missing information. "Usually the missing data involve predictors such as parent-offspring conflict, temperament, and age gaps between siblings, which are particularly difficult to document for everyone in the sample," Sulloway writes. Technically speaking, then, Sulloway shows that (functional) birth order does not so much predict an individual's temperament as it does the probability that an individual would have a particular temperament if only we knew more about him.

If it is anything but straightforward to classify a "simple" variable such as birth order, imagine the subjectivity involved in deciding who is a radical innovator and who is a conservative obstructionist. Consider two cases. Ernst Haeckel was a nineteenth-century biologist whose flirtations with racial supremacy endeared him to those Nazis, including his biographer Heinz Brucher, who championed experiments in human breeding. (The story has been recently told in gory detail by Ute Deichmann in *Biologists under Hitler.*) Margaret Mead was a feminist anthropologist who set out to disabuse Americans of what she took to be their puritanical and oppressive ideas about sexuality. I need hardly tell you that Sulloway classifies the first as an innovator, indeed an extreme one, and the second as a conservative, thereby confirming his theory. (Haeckel was a lastborn, Mead was a firstborn.)

Why? As reactionary as his politics were, Haeckel was a scientific pioneer and an enthusiast of Darwin; we owe the term *ecology* and the expression *ontology recapitulates phylogeny* to him. And as radical as her politics were, Mead was not a particularly original thinker; she applied and popularized the ideas of her mentor Franz Boas, and she distorted her fieldwork to conform to her politics (see "The Mystique of Betty Friedan," this vol.). The fact that someone can be radical in politics and conservative in science shows how arbitrary such classifications can be, and therefore how untrustworthy are the correlations based upon them. It also suggests that people may have more than one temperament. And if they do, all single classifications are partial ones.

Faced with classification problems of this magnitude, one begins to understand why humility in interpretation is the appropriate mood for scientific analysis. To guard against the possibility that correlations, even when significant, measure the ways we classify reality rather than reality itself, the scientist should properly emphasize the limits, rather than the significance, of his findings. To some degree, Sulloway does make such admissions; his technical skills are outstanding, and he sprinkles his analysis with qualifications. But when it comes to the most important question of all–exactly how significant is a particular correlation?–Sulloway commits an egregious sin.

The odds that mere chance could have produced these patterns, he often tells the reader, are a million or a billion to one. If this were true of the odds that firstborns would be as likely to be innovators as last-borns, such probabilities would indeed be impressive. But that is not what Sulloway measures, at least most of the time. Although he does account for spacing between siblings, and from time to time he examines middle-borns, especially in his appendixes, it is later-borns, not lastborns, who attract the bulk of his attention. Since every large family will have only one firstborn and many later-borns, the significance of the correlation coefficients is substantially reduced by that fact alone. Thus, when we are told that 96 percent of those in Sulloway's sample of Reformation figures who were executed for their religious convictions were later-born (twenty-three out of twenty-four), our astonishment at the high percentage is reduced the moment we realize that, at a time when very large families were the rule, such a result could well be due to chance. This is an obvious point, one unlikely to survive even the most cursory review, which makes it all the more odd that Sulloway did not present his findings in a way more likely to downplay its significance than to exaggerate it.

Still, it may be the case that, even had he engaged in the proper discounts, Sulloway nonetheless would have uncovered statistically significant patterns. Common sense tells us that later-born children experience the world differently than their older siblings. (Certainly my third- and lastborn does.) Let us concede, therefore, that an important discovery has been announced in this book: social scientists, as a result of Sulloway's exhaustive statistical investigations, will now have to give the question of birth order its proper due.

Many scholars would have stopped there; establishing the importance of birth order is, after all, a major accomplishment, worth the decades of effort that Sulloway put into it. But Sulloway is anything but content to say that something we once tended to neglect is far greater than we imagined. He wants to close his case beyond a shadow of doubt. To do so, he turns to Darwin. And it is in his application of Darwinian theory that Sulloway leaves science behind for the realm of imagination and conjecture.

The attraction of applying Darwinian ideas to human behavior–once called sociobiology, now evolutionary psychology–is its potential universalism. Biological theories, unlike social ones, are presumed to be true at all times and in all places. Sulloway shares this vision. The causes of rebellion, he writes, "reside within every family. This story is about all of us." Had he possessed more of a scientific temperament, Sulloway would have asked himself, before jumping to such a breathtaking conclusion, whether something other than evolution might have explained the correlations that he found. I have already alluded to one candidate: his correlations can be explained by the very techniques that have been used to gather them.

Aware of the problems of selection bias, Sulloway went to great lengths to neutralize it by relying on the judgment of scientists and historians before classifying his historical figures as radical or conservative. Yet significant sources of potential selection bias remain ignored by him. One of those sources lies in his definition of his problem. For the whole notion that such a thing as birth order exists is dependent on ordered family patterns. And this is a thoroughly ahistorical assumption. Social historians have convincingly demonstrated the wide variety of forms that families can take in different societies and at different times. Neither eleventh-century families in England nor nineteenth-century families in Africa resembled the families of Charles Darwin and Emma Wedgwood. Sulloway's emphasis on family dynamics assumes a stable family structure within which those dynamics play themselves out. To confirm a theory that is presumably universal, Sulloway carries around a model of the family so culture-laden that he never recognizes it as such.

Then there is the fact that Sulloway tests his hypotheses in only two areas, science and politics. By concentrating on them, he leaves open the possibility that it may be something in the nature of science and politics, and not something in the nature of birth order, which explains the relationships that he finds. Literary and musical innovation, after all, could be governed by dynamics completely different from scientific and political ones. The last two James children were named Garth Wilkinson and Robertson, not Henry, William, or Alice, and none of Johann Sebastian Bach's sons was an especially innovative composer. We know that creativity in different fields requires different talents, which is why mathematicians and physicists make their breakthroughs early on while artists are more likely to do their best work when they are old. If different areas of human endeavor are differently influenced by age, it stands to reason that they may also be influenced differently by birth order.

All this only begins to limn the problems of selection bias in *Born to Rebel*. From time to time, Sulloway invokes the scientific principle of control groups, testing out his ideas on a group quite different from the one under study, so as to see whether the same statistical patterns in one are found in the other. In looking at the way gender and race interact with birth order, for example, he compares reformers with a distinct group of conservatives. Yet all members of both groups have one thing in common: they were famous enough for biographical information on them to exist, and this is a clear example of selectivity, since it excludes (I am guessing here) around 99.5 percent of everyone who lived during the time of the controversies that Sulloway recounts. Surely people who become famous enough to have biographies written about them are more driven than those who do not; and the internal dynamics in driven families may be very different from those in families that simply disappear into history.

It should now be clear that one bias in selectivity can interact with another, multiplying the difficulties of making universalist claims. Those about whom biographies are written are likely to be Western and products of a specific family type. They are also likely to be dead, biasing against the possibility that in our times–when families are much smaller, women work, and merit is more widely recognized–an entirely new set of statistical correlations would be found. When one considers how long human beings have been on this planet, and how many different ways they have organized their social lives, the concept of birth order, let alone its relationship to other variables, appears so much the product of one particular time and place that the "all" and "every" to whom its principles presumably apply are a very select, and selective, group indeed.

Even giving Sulloway the most generous benefit of the doubt, then, he has discovered only this: in two particular fields of human endeavor, in one part of the world, and over one broad but still limited period of time, firstborns are different by some impressive but by no means constant magnitude than those born after them. The question is not whether Darwinian theory can explain all of human behavior, but whether it can explain the much more limited slice of life that Sulloway has cut off to analyze.

Again, a scientific temperament would ask: Is there a more parsimonious explanation for what I have found than my instinct to apply Darwinian ideas? An obvious one suggests itself, yet it is never considered by Sulloway. The great majority of Sulloway's examples occurred in the middle decades of the nineteenth century, a period of tumultuous social change. Sulloway invites us to consider the Grimke sisters, prominent abolitionists from South Carolina. Sarah, a sixth-born, became active in the antislavery movement, while her younger sister Angelina, the fourteenth and lastborn in the family, became even more radical in her commitments. Later-borns, we are also told, were overrepresented among radical suffragists, thus offering still more confirmation of the importance of birth order.

But revolutionary times have their own logic. In such times, later-borns will be more radical for no other reason than that they were born later. I was twenty-six in 1968 and considered myself quite radical, but it was obvious to me that those born just a few years later than myself were even more radical. In radical periods, timing is everything: the assassinations of Kennedy and King affected people differently depending on their age. Much the same was true of abolitionism and women's suffrage, movements that grew more radical year by year. The very intensity of revolutionary periods is what might explain the tendency of younger siblings to be more radical; it is their youth, not their sibling status, that counts. This could actually be tested: the appropriate control group would be a cohort of abolitionists the same age as Angelina Grimke who were not lastborns. Sulloway offers no such test.

Rather than searching for a more concise explanation of his findings, Sulloway does the opposite: he overexplains what he finds. Confronted with a deviant case, he does everything in his power to explain it away rather than to explain it. Yes, Martin Luther was a firstborn, but he was a German and a member of the lower clergy, either of which might explain his radicalism. When birth order does not explain temperament, Sulloway argues, something else does. By using multivariate statistical techniques, we can add predictor to predictor, ultimately explaining why deviant cases exist. And so we can; but each time Sulloway adds an additional variable to birth order, he is obligated to note that, in doing so, he is vitiating his own neo-Darwinism. He never does that, either.

Instead he shifts the argument to a debate over the appropriateness of statistical methods in the study of history. And he gets that debate wrong. Offended by a reviewer's comments rejecting a National Science Foundation proposal that he submitted, Sulloway writes as if historians were hostile to the use of statistical techniques. Statistically speaking, he is wrong: some are, some aren't. And just about everyone I know has received a stupid or ill-informed review of a well-wrought proposal or article at some point in his or her career. Few of them would leap from that experience to a generalization about the state of knowledge.

Sulloway writes more like an advocate seeking to nail down a case than a scientist interested in explaining an observation. He differs little, in this regard, from neo-Darwinians such as Richard Dawkins or Daniel Dennett, who defend Darwin in ingenious ways not dissimilar from those used for generations to defend Marx. Ideological thinking is ideological thinking, whether it is socialism or sociobiology; and a future observer of our contemporary intellectual scene will no doubt wonder why intelligent and eloquent writers devoted books to proving how Darwin must be right under any and all circumstances. *Born to Rebel* is a fine example of this tendency to conflate science and ideology, and it deserves to be read primarily as a work of rhetoric–and powerful rhetoric. No number of correlation coefficients can disguise that.

III

WHAT, THEN, ARE WE to make of Sulloway's efforts to persuade us that Darwinian theory explains why birth order is so important? Is family life really "an evolutionary arms race"? Do we occupy niches in a competitive struggle for parental investment? Even to ask such questions is to recognize the sheer amount of speculation involved in inquiries of this sort. Without having found a gene for sibling rivalry comparable to a gene for Parkinson's disease, we are unlikely ever to establish cause and effect in family matters in quite the way that they exist in natural matters. (Or even in natural matters: the controversies over evolutionary theory analyzed by Sulloway continue to this day.)

Thankfully, science does put certain matters to rest. There is no longer a debate over the fact that variation among the species is due to natural selection governed by the ways in which one genetic material reproduces itself from one generation to the next. But it is also in the nature of science to raise new questions for every question that is resolved. For this reason, it is proper for scientists, when confronted with the limits of our present understanding, to speculate about what we still have not yet nailed down. Evolutionary theory is good at explaining how complexity develops, but it has not yet convincingly demonstrated how complexity originated. It may someday be proved that out of the primeval muck a self-replicating molecule arose, but even Richard Dawkins, among the most orthodox of neo-Darwinians, acknowledged recently in *Climbing Mount Improbable* that "nobody knows how it happened," that "there are arguments to the contrary," that we "speculate" when we talk about the origins of life.

The persistence and the development of human arrangements, like the origins of life, constitute a subject about which we can only speculate. At a time when we barely understand how genes cause disease, sociobiologists, when they make the huge explanatory leap from non-human species yesterday to human beings today, are speculating wildly, positing the existence of "memes" as a mechanism of cultural transmission, suggesting that human minds can shorten the time needed for evolutionary adaptations to take place, or reasoning backward from the fact that a particular transformation happened to an argument about why it had to have happened. There is no harm in such speculation, but it must not pretend that it is anything other than speculation. At this stage in its development, sociobiology offers occasionally interesting illuminations about how human practices came to be, close to no illuminations about the ways specific societies or individuals behave, and no illuminations at all about how ethical and moral issues ought to be resolved. The notion that such an underdeveloped science could settle the kinds of questions that Sulloway poses is preposterous.

Why has Sulloway's book gotten so much attention? Allow me to speculate. Human beings, or some of them, place a great deal of value on certainty. About themselves, at least, they would prefer not to live without some kind of intellectual closure. And reducing human beings to their animal nature conveys the message that we have discovered a rock-ribbed truth about them: their actions can be understood, their choices analyzed, their tastes explained. This search for certainty transcends political ideology: Friedrich Engels was just as attracted to the Darwinist writings of Ernst Haeckel in the nineteenth century as the Nazis were in the twentieth century. Critics of sociobiology who identify the biologizing of politics with conservative ideologies are wrong. Any ideology with a master plan will want the cloak of science to direct people to their proper slots. It does not take much to imagine left-wing versions of *The Bell Curve:* one researcher might find men genetically programmed to abuse women, another researcher might discover innate propensities among blacks for more holistic cognitive styles.

Sulloway's book has no politics, or none that I can discern. This makes it more powerful than *The Bell Curve* as an illustration of how pseudoscientific scientism can be. Race and equality are issues we care about; and if someone comes along and says he can prove racial inferiority, we will be properly skeptical and challenge his findings. Birth order, as fascinating as it may be, is not a matter of public policy, and it is not held up as a mirror into the nation's soul. Important enough to be interesting and frivolous enough to provoke nervous laughter, birth order is the ideal way to sneak scientism past us. Those of us reluctant to hear that our race determines our intelligence may be willing to hear that our birth order determines our temperament. But we will still have surrendered to a false and awful notion: that who we are can be pinned down and explained by what is least human about us, by a fixed drive put into place at the moment of our birth from which it is futile to try to escape.

Sulloway's book is important for its unwitting demonstration that the biologizing of human beings is not only bad humanism, but also bad science. For science is not a method in search of a subject. It is an attempt to understand a subject by using the methods appropriate to it. Just as you do not use a microscope to study huge objects in distant places, you do not use fixed principles to study a species whose major feature is its ability to seize control of a great part of its own development. This is not at all to say that social science is impossible, or that correlation coefficients tell us nothing, or that human behavior cannot be predicted, or that quantitative methods have no place in the study of history. Quite the contrary. The best work done by social scientists tends to be strongly empirical, disconfirming what we thought to be true by marshaling impressive statistical evidence to the contrary. But it refuses to claim, as a matter of philosophical and methodological principle, what *Born to Rebel* claims, which is that its findings are "indisputable" and that, by the by, it has found the secret of history.

He never says so explicitly, but the message that Sulloway conveys throughout his book is that he, like Darwin, is a scientific rebel, willing to follow ideas wherever they lead, unlike those who, owing to conservatism and a failure of nerve, resist innovation and the sheer power of scientific truth. But he classifies himself as poorly as he classifies others. For he has written a deeply reactionary book, not in its politics, but in its deafness to nuance and its intolerance for ambiguity. *Born to Rebel* has more in common with nineteenth-century taxonomy than with late-twentieth-century efforts to understand human beings as they really are. It is an advance on phrenology, but not by much.

PART VI

Consumption

•

Undialectical Materialism

I

"AT THE END OF the twentieth century," writes Gary Cross in *An All-Consuming Century: Why Commercialism Won in Modern America,* "never had Americans taken critiques of consumer culture less seriously, though that culture may never have needed criticism more." There is much to be said for both halves of his proposition. If Americans have long preferred roast beef to socialism, they have also been partial to Christianity, virgin forests, small-town fellowship, and family solidarity—all of which place limits on the reach of the market. There have been resources aplenty in the American tradition, even as late as the twentieth century, to sustain a criticism of consumption. As Cross reminds us, Prohibition called upon those resources, which was one reason why business interests, including those that had little to do with the manufacture and the distribution of alcohol, worried about the implications of regulating drink. Hard as it is now to imagine, credit was once considered a sign of shame in America, and department stores were reluctant to extend it to their customers. As conservative a man as Herbert Hoover was disturbed about excessive advertising on radio: "If a speech by the President," he remarked in 1924, "is to be as the meat in a sandwich of two patent medicine advertisements, there will be no radio left." By the 1950s, Americans were buying unprecedented numbers of small houses and large cars, but they were also buying books by such social critics as Vance Packard, Rachel Carson, and John Kenneth Galbraith that warned against their proclivity to consume.

It takes a historian to provide an appreciation of how far Americans have wandered from the days when consumerism was slightly suspect, and Gary Cross is superbly up to the task. His short but punchy book argues that the arrival of trophy homes, SUVs, lotteries, and IPOs represents the triumph of an "ism." In a way that needlessly downplays the real differences between democracy and totalitarianism, Cross argues that the ultimate winner in the ideological wars of the twentieth century was consumerism. Still, if a way of life is defined as a set of organizing principles that constitute the meaning of the good life, and establish obligations between both strangers and friends, and provide the meaning of right and wrong, then consumerism has vanquished all its religious and political competitors, not least because of the indifference to belief that it inculcates. Liberal democracy still defines America, but liberty is coming more and more to mean that everything is, and ought to be, for sale; and democracy is being turned into the notion that whatever people want the most must be the best for them.

One would think that a revolution of such magnitude would at least give rise to sustained commentary and criticism, yet until recently very little had appeared. Cross offers an explanation of why. Neither the left nor the right could hold power in America unless it tailored its political views to accommodate a deeply held passion on the part of Americans to accumulate material possessions. Bowdlerized Keynesianism allowed liberals to downplay their redistributive inclinations in favor of the attractive proposition that government, to avoid a return to the Great Depression, had a duty to spend. It was not long before the need for public consumption was expanded to include private spending. Spurred on by the proposition that a rising tide lifts all boats, John F. Kennedy sent Galbraith off to India and turned his attention to winning business confidence. Liberals remained tied to obtaining improvements for labor and to new social policies, but these would be financed out of the tax revenues brought about through economic growth. Without consumerism, there would have been no postwar liberalism.

So attracted was the left to consumerism that even the rebellion against liberalism led by the counterculture of the 1960s eventually succumbed to its allures. For all of Charles Reich's talk of a new level of consciousness, adherents to the counterculture, Cross writes, "became rebels through consumption." If anything, hippies and druggies "improved on the consumerism of the 1950s rather than really challenging it." The consequence of their search for new experience was the opening of new markets. Manufacturers and advertisers heard their pleas for personal authenticity and responded by tailoring goods to meet them. When the psychedelic impulse had played itself out, the urge to satisfy the self was all that remained.

And conservatism became as dependent on mass consumerism as liberalism. Robert Taft's dour Republicanism, suspicious of cosmopolitanism and devoted to budget-balancing propriety, could never survive the movement of its Midwestern base to Phoenix and Los Angeles. Quick to step in and meet the need for a new form of conservatism was a curious mixture of evangelical Protestantism and regulation-free capitalism, the one denouncing the forces of uncontrolled hedonism launched by the other. Had Ronald Reagan moved to satisfy the former, America might well have experienced a religious revival whose impact would have included the reminder that wealth alone does not open the gates of heaven; but Reagan, like Kennedy before him, wanted himself and his party to be liked, and it is always more popular to satisfy desires than to limit them.

Turning his administration over to such all-but-forgotten enthusiasts for the market as Anne Gorsuch, Mark Fowler, and James Miller—who in turn deregulated the environment, the airwaves, and federal trade policy—Reagan took consumerism to new heights. Cross is rightly astonished that a movement calling itself conservative would be so willing to invade the home, the churches, and the schools—all of which once taught a culture of restraint. By the time Reaganism finished working its way through American society, such quaint notions as uninterrupted family meals, commerce-free Sundays, unspoiled places, and unindebted self-reliance had almost completely disappeared.

Consumption, the essence of the profane, has become sacred. It is not that putative critics bow down mute before it, for such critics can still be heard. But on what ground can they stand? The socialism that was once the alternative to the capitalist market had no chance of surviving once those who lived under its strictures caught a glimpse of what the market could do. Conservative Christianity was fueled by its hostility to modernity, presumably including modern capitalism, but it never allowed that hostility to stand in the way of its fund-raising prowess. Americans would rather be unsafe at any speed than safe at speeds they cannot choose. Attack the American love affair with goods, and you attack the American way of life.

Still, it is only a matter of time before Americans begin to develop second thoughts about the direction their society has taken over the past twenty years or so. The question of whether those Americans will be prepared to listen to a new round of complaints about consumerism is quite open. Should the critics make their case in the attenuated manner of Galbraith–barely concealing their disdain for those who prefer to shop at Wal-Mart than to watch public television–they will, in this age of triumphant consumerism, be as immediately obsolete as the Corvair. The tradition of skepticism toward the market brought to life by Gary Cross can only be revived if it finds a language as innovative as the capitalism that it seeks to condemn.

II

FUELING THE RECENT AMERICAN love affair with the market has been the spectacular rise in the one dealing in stocks. Since stocks represent ownership in companies, and since companies usually own valuable assets, we naturally think that to own stock is to own something real. People seem to believe that those dollar amounts listed on their retirement and investment accounts are a form of consumption like any other, for whether you buy a car or stock in a car company, you have purchased something that enables you to enjoy the good life.

But what if the value in the stock market does not reflect any equivalent valuation in the real world? Robert J. Shiller, a Yale economist, offers a plausible scenario that this is the case in *Irrational Exuberance.*

In the last decade of the twentieth century, stocks rose in value far out of proportion to the economic growth registered in the economy. In an effort to explain why, Shiller points to the convergence of a wide range of noneconomic factors, all of which worked to push prices up. The Internet not only offered the prospect of a radically new industry, it also changed the way Americans thought about stocks in general. Baby boomers reached a stage in their career wherein they needed outlets for their incomes after they finished paying the college expenses of their children. The Japanese threat withered away. Capitalism recaptured the moral high ground from socialism. Discount brokers urged people to make their own financial decisions. Gambling lost its association with sin.

All of these developments possessed self-fulfilling qualities. "As prices continue to rise," Shiller writes, "the level of exuberance is enhanced by the price rise itself." As a result, Americans began to lose touch with the fact that trading in any commodity, particularly stocks, is a risky business. Suppose the market goes down 3 percent on any given day, Shiller asked a group of wealthy Americans: what would happen the very next day? In 1989, 35 percent of them said it would increase; in 1999, 56 percent of those polled thought an increase likely. Exaggerated investor confidence creates what Shiller calls a "naturally occurring Ponzi scheme."

Unlike the shenanigans associated with confidence men, natural Ponzi schemes require no criminal mastermind. All it takes for a speculative bubble to expand is a willingness on the part of large numbers of people to believe that the price they pay for a stock now, no matter how seemingly high, is actually low compared to what it will be in the near future. Since there is no real foundation for this belief, Shiller identifies it as "irrational." At some point, the mutual delusion that fuels naturally occurring Ponzi schemes loses its credibility, and when that happens, again without any criminal intent, stocks will rapidly fall in price, inevitably harming the most gullible. (Surely Shiller ought to win whatever prize is offered to books that are, simply put, right; the collapse of the stock market following the publication of *Irrational Exu-*

berance is, irrational as it may be, as much vindication as any author could want.)

To understand the irrational exuberance behind the stock market, one has to turn from economics to psychology. Human beings need to anchor their beliefs in something, Shiller argues. When we lay out money for a car, we justify our decision in terms of the amount of time and trouble that the possession of the car saves us, as well as the remaining book value of the car should we need to trade it in for cash. Since prices have lost touch with any underlying economic valuation, the anchors justifying high stock prices, unlike those involved in high car prices, are sunk in turbulent waters. We say that the high price that we just paid for a stock is fine because similar stocks also have high prices. Or we take confidence from bits and pieces of folk wisdom: diversification protects you against ups and downs; markets are by definition efficient; price does not matter because, like the millionaire next door, one should hold on to the stock for many years. The theories or the explanations offered to explain high stock prices are really just rationalizations, and none more so than the chimera that, with the emergence of the Internet, America has somehow created a new economy. But it is not the new economy that explains the rise in stock prices; it is the rise in stock prices that tempts us to believe that we have a new economy. About this, Shiller is depressingly convincing.

In turning to psychology, Shiller recognizes that, however irrational the exuberance of the stock market may be, its appeal, even to those who once resisted the lures of what is little more than speculative gambling, transcends the cut-and-dried logic of utilitarian calculation. If there is a problem with Shiller's analysis, it is that the psychologists on whom he tends to rely remain within an economic paradigm (broadly defined). The phenomenon of overconfidence provides an example. As experimental psychologists study overconfidence, they find that a belief that the market will continue to go up, while not rational in economic terms, may be rational in psychological terms: people may conclude that if they like a stock, others will like it, too, and they thus gain a certain amount of security by joining the herd.

Following these psychologists, Shiller calls this "magical thinking."

But true magical thinking has little to do with rationality in either the economic or the psychological sense. Shiller might have pondered a bit more the role that dreams and fantasies play in offering people a sense that, if they do not join in a speculative frenzy, they will miss out on a near-ecstatic experience enjoyed by others. "The market is high," Shiller concludes, "because of the combined effect of indifferent thinking by millions of people, very few of whom feel the need to perform careful research on the long-term investment value of the aggregate stock market, and who are motivated substantially by their own emotions, random attentions, and perceptions of conventional wisdom." He is right, but he does not draw out the full implications of how broad-based is the desire to fulfill one's fantasies through the market.

So long as trading in stocks was undertaken by relatively few people for the benefit of relatively few people, limits existed on how far crowd psychology could push stock prices up. Yet the historic American love affair with consumption could not stop with consumer goods; once Americans got used to the idea of buying things, it was only a matter of time before they started to buy ownership in the companies that made them. Rising stock prices have made more Americans wealthier than ever before. At the same time they implicate more Americans than ever before in the risks of market exuberance. Crowd psychology matters more because the crowd has gotten so much bigger.

That the benefits of stock ownership are no longer reserved to the privileged few but have trickled down to the middle class is surely cause for celebration. How ironic, then, that the very economic security tantalizingly held out by this development requires a psychological security in the stock market that neither history nor economics can justify. The next crash to come will be the first crash after the democratization of the market. When it comes, we will have a hard time blaming it all on the machinations of elites, though some will try. But it will be impossible to avoid the conclusion that the pain we will suffer after the disaster happens will have a direct link with the pleasure that we sought before it happened. What the market giveth, economically and psychologically, the market is quite capable of taking away.

It must be a sign of increasing discomfort with markets in general that Shiller is not the only Yale professor turning to psychology to shed light on the irrational aspects of consumption. Robert E. Lane wants to know why rapid economic growth has not brought along an increase in human happiness. Put two lines on a chart, one measuring GNP between 1940 and 1990 and the other plotting the percentage of people who respond "very" to the question of how happy they are, and you will observe that the two lines move in exact opposite directions. Markets are supposed to satisfy human desires. But if we take seriously "subjective well-being"–people's own account of their satisfaction with life– they seem to do the exact opposite.

To explain this paradox, Lane has written *The Loss of Happiness in Market Democracies,* a book rich in data that explores why capitalism and liberal democracy, both of which justify themselves on the grounds that they produce the greatest happiness for the greatest number, leave so many dissatisfactions in their wake. Like Shiller, Lane finds economic theories wanting, because their reasoning tends to be circular: people with more money can satisfy more preferences, and since the satisfaction of a preference counts as happiness, it follows that the more money people have, the happier they are. The problem is that the more money we have, the more likely we are to compare ourselves to those who have even more. Moreover, there is a diminishing marginal utility associated with materialism; the more goods that we can buy, the less the satisfaction of each good that we do buy. Something in the very dynamics of the way markets work, Lane believes, prevents them from delivering on the satisfaction that they promise.

By encouraging people to put a monetary value on everything, markets, in Lane's account, undermine the ties of solidarity associated with friendship and family–ties that, if they are to endure through thick and thin, must be noneconomic in nature. Hence survey data show that companionship tends to suffer as income levels tend to rise. The market provides cognitive overload, giving us more choices than we need; and the loss of companionship results in emotional underload, taking away even the most minimal satisfactions for sociability we crave. The evidence, Lane concludes, is "ambiguous," but it leans toward the conclusion that "markets themselves are an inherent cause of social isolation."

Liberal democracy, like capitalism, is premised on the pursuit of happiness, and it too, Lane believes, has not delivered on its promises. Although he insists that he is not a nostalgist longing for worlds we have lost, Lane's data leave the reader with the strong impression that something equivalent to Shiller's naturally operating Ponzi scheme influences the politics of liberal democracy. We are all encouraged to believe that prosperity in economics and individualism in politics ought to make us happier, and we presume that everyone else around us must be happier; and this makes us more vulnerable to the melancholy and the dismay that will occur when we all wake up to discover that we really have been quite dissatisfied all along. Such a cycle of confidence followed by disillusion may well explain the periodic outbursts of populist anger throughout America these days. How can a society whose wealth has risen so dramatically be so vulnerable to political demagogues who insist that Armageddon is nigh?

Lane's book is at one and the same time scrupulously careful and wildly ambitious. He does not want to make a generalization unless he can find empirical support for it, and since empirical data rarely all point in the same way, he is bound by his responsibilities as a social scientist to avoid overinterpretation. Yet Lane's general thesis is as ambitious as they come—on a par, in sheer audacity, with the grand old speculation about gemeinschaft and gesellschaft. For if it is true that wealth breeds unhappiness, we face nothing less than the prospect of rethinking just about everything that we have been taught about economics and politics.

Fortunately for those of a less ambitious bent, Lane finally does not prove his claims. The increase in unhappiness that he seeks to explain is something of a nonevent. As Lane himself concedes, the overwhelming majority of Americans consider themselves quite happy. From 1972 to 1994, moreover, the decline in those who consider themselves "very happy" was roughly 5 percent: significant enough, but hardly earth-shattering. One could imagine any number of explanations for this modest drop-off. It could be that women and African Americans, having gained greater degrees of equality during this period, began to view remaining inequalities as more unfair. It could be that in an increasingly exhibitionistic and therapeutic culture, unhappiness that once would have been stifled is now expressible. There is, in short, the possibility that subjective unhappiness, in modest amounts, is produced by the very success of capitalism and liberal democracy. Give people voice, and they will kvetch.

The modest rise in unhappiness during these years is also an American phenomenon: in Europe, the percentage of those who were satisfied with their lives increased by 4 percent between 1981 and 1990, almost as large a percentage as the American decrease. If he had been more faithful to what his data showed, Lane would have avoided any explanations dealing with such abstractions as "the market," "democracy," or "modernity"–since Europeans enjoy, or do not enjoy, all three–and would have concentrated instead on specific aspects of the American experience. Yet Lane, who seems to have read everything on the subject that he could find, mentions, but surprisingly fails to focus on, the phenomenon of "American exceptionalism." Anyone as attuned to psychological explanations as Lane should recognize that psychology's insights are not universal truths of the human condition. They are cultural products of a particular time and a particular place. Keeping up with the Joneses means comparing yourself to the actual people nearby, not to the abstract others far away.

Even if we reduce the problem of unhappiness in what Lane grandiloquently calls "market democracies" to the problem of a slight increase in unhappiness in one particular country, we are still left with an awkward question: are those who tell survey researchers of their greater unhappiness willing to do something about it? There is nothing preventing people, should they conclude that their lives would be richer with more friends and fewer goods, to stop buying the one and to start acquiring the other. Yet people rarely do so. The literature reviewed by Lane suggests that, when faced with a conflict between money and happiness, people would rather have the money. The truth, as Lane himself puts it, is that "many people . . . derive genuine satisfaction from their standards of living, their income, and their material possessions or wealth."

Given this popular support for materialism, Lane asks whether people are "the best judges of their own well-being." His answer, once all the qualifications are discounted, is that they are not. For all his reliance on social science data, Lane has aspirations toward social criticism; but in that role he is, alas, unpersuasive, for he cannot avoid the trap that has bedeviled critics of consumerism since Marx. Certain that a more richly authentic world is possible, he finds himself unable to accept the world in which people actually live.

III

THE ECONOMIST AND SOCIOLOGIST Juliet Schor has written two books that give new meaning to the concept of a joyless economy. In *The Overworked American* (1991), she argued that Americans were stretched to the limit because they spent too much time trying to make money. In *The Overspent American* (1998), she enhanced the misery index by claiming that we were also too obsessed with spending the money we obsess about making. The source of our victimization is what she calls "upscale emulation": the reference groups against whom we compare ourselves are increasingly out of reach. It is no longer the neighbor down the street whose life-style sets the standard, but the world-class athlete or the Hollywood celebrity featured in glossy magazines and on television.

Schor offers an article-length treatment of her criticism of consumption in *Do Americans Shop Too Much?* which is preceded by an introduction from Ralph Nader and followed by commentary from a disparate group of critics. The question mark in the title is superfluous. When it comes to consumption, Schor has emerged as our leading public scold. Her indictment of consumer culture may have its roots in Marxism, but, as Craig J. Thompson points out in his contribution to the book, it bears more resemblance to the Puritan fear that worldly goods are incompatible with the piety that makes for an authentic soul.

Distracted by the prospect of buying the good life through the products offered to us, Schor writes, we make more money only to spend more money. The poor among us are seduced by easily available credit at usurious rates. Middle-class Americans, wanting to send their children to the best schools, work long hours and then have to spend enormous amounts on commodities and services necessitated by their absence from home. We no longer save; and because we do not save, we worry all the time. Fearful to protect what we have, we support tax cuts and conservative policies that leave us without public goods such as day care or a national health insurance system, which might relieve some of the pressure. In *The Other America,* Michael Harrington argued that the presence of poverty constituted an indictment of the American way of life. Juliet Schor comes to the same conclusion about the presence of wealth.

Schor has little patience for any psychological explanations of the attractions of consumerism. "Americans did not suddenly become greedy," she writes. Instead, "structural changes" in the economy and the political system constrained the available choices. Trapped by rising inequality and by what Schor calls "heightened penalties for failing in the labor market," Americans adopted consumerism defensively. Buying things, she strongly suggests, is not what people really want to do; but if you build highways and not bike paths, people will drive cars and not ride bikes. The notion that people might actually appreciate laborsaving devices, or that they might actually enjoy attractive frivolities, is foreign to Schor's pinched sensibility.

Schor thus brings back to life the tradition of social criticism associated with Galbraith—and in so doing, she also brings back to life Galbraith's disdain for the tastes of most of those who live in America. Convinced that people's perceptions of their own needs are false, Schor advocates a politics of consumption, a movement that would organize Americans toward the goal of spending less on their own goods and more on the goods they share in common. "Why not stand for consumption that is democratic, egalitarian, and available to all?" Schor writes. "How about making 'access,' rather than exclusivity, cool, by exposing the industries such as fashion, home decor, or tourism, which are pushing the upscaling of desire?"

Asked what the goal of the labor movement should be, Samuel Gompers once replied: "More." If that program eventually failed to make America labor-friendly, it is hard to imagine that "less" will have better results. Schor seems aware of the difficulties. She confesses that for many years she shared the left's commitment to the principle that the way to redistribute wealth was to get more of it in the hands of those who have less of it. And if Schor is right that one of the causes of "upscale emulation" is the fact that women entered the workplace, where they were exposed to wider horizons than could be found in the neighborhood, then a politics of consumption is as much an attack on the women's movement as on the labor movement. No wonder that Schor's critics in *Do Americans Shop Too Much?* are so skeptical of a politics of consumption. It would deprive people of whatever empowerment consumer goods offer, and it would also strip from them the few gains that their modern political movements have won for them.

Schor's examinations of the way Americans work and buy do have one advantage over earlier attacks on consumption. Unlike the counterculture of the 1960s, and indeed unlike the labor movement, they do not blend the bashing of capitalism with a furtive longing for pleasure, for the enjoyment of all that capitalism has to offer. Honest to the point of pain, Schor's anticapitalism is the genuine thing: if we are to be true to our principles, we ought to tie ourselves to the mast of resistance no matter how seductive the allure. The trouble is that Schor's honesty exposes the flaws in her program. Consumerism's critics from the left have sought two major goals. One is the political goal of equality: consumerism is unjust because when goods are plentiful, some get more of them than others. The other is the aesthetic goal of simplicity: consumption is bad because it distorts people's needs and spoils their environment. Both goals are important to seek. When they are combined, as they are in Schor's books, any equality that we might achieve becomes unattractive, enabling those hostile to equality to offer pleasure as their alternative.

Why not, then, just enjoy the cornucopia? It is not an unreasonable question, and it has been asked, with joyful exuberance, by James

Twitchell in a series of books, most recently in *Lead Us into Temptation*. Not for Twitchell any dour complaints about materialism. If anything, he argues, we are not materialistic enough. "We currently live in a culture in which almost anyone can have almost anything"; and, if Twitchell had his way, those modifying "almosts" will soon be gone. "Okay, okay," Twitchell addresses Juliet Schor and like-minded critics by name, "money can't buy happiness, but with it you stand a better chance than with penury." Twitchell finds most academics, unduly influenced by the perverse high-culture tastes of the Frankfurt School, contemptuously patronizing of the people with whom they share their country. He writes not to reveal to people the true nature of their presumably false needs, but to warn them against the killjoys that are secretly jealous of the fact that so many Americans seem to be enjoying themselves without reading Proust and listening to Beethoven's late quartets.

Once freed from the necessity of lecturing people for their bad taste, Twitchell treats the things that people buy–and the places in which they buy them–as cultural artifacts replete with meaning for how they lead their lives. Advertising, for example, is not just about pushing unwanted goods into the hands of distracted consumers. Magical thinking–in the sense of a belief in miracles–is, in Twitchell's view, at the heart of advertising, as it is of religion, which suggests to him that it is through advertising that Americans experience classic tales of sin and redemption. The media in which advertising appears offer not so much programming as object lessons in "how branded objects are dovetailed together to form a coherent pattern of selfhood."

As Andy Warhol and Roy Lichtenstein recognized, packaging is art and art is packaging. When people go to the supermarket, they are in effect museum-hopping, passing before one representation of their world to another. Collecting consumer goods is no different, in Twitchell's account, than the way Renaissance dynasties collected art: they searched for brand names, and so do we. When we drape our houses in furniture and our bodies in clothing, we demonstrate to the world not our conformity with the taste of others, but the distinctly individualized presentations of the self chosen by us to serve our purposes.

Capitalism has a way of undermining the arguments made on its behalf, and no sooner did Twitchell begin to publish his encomia to the cultural meaning of shopping than along came the Internet. Once the kinks are worked out–for the technologically advanced, they already have been worked out–the Web will allow people to buy things in truly a no-frills fashion, which means not only at the cheapest price, but also without such superfluous phenomena as salesmen, trips to the mall, and the off chance of running into people they know. What will it be: the market as social spectacle or the market as ruthless efficiency?

"Don't bet on it," Twitchell advises those who, under the spell of the Internet, would presume to sell goods without the cultural meanings that go with them. If Twitchell is right, the good news is that, in choosing the best display over the best price, we will sacrifice a bit economically to enjoy the benefits of the grand carnival. It is a sign of how far we have traveled down the road to commercial culture that we somehow want Twitchell to be right. The true nightmare of contemporary capitalism is not that it is a system that deluges us with goods, but that it is a system that reduces the purchase of those goods to heartless calculation.

Critics of consumerism do not want Twitchell to be right; they share with capitalism's apologists the sense that the only value that commodities possess is monetary. If we begin to admit that consumption has its pleasures, they fear, we will quickly find ourselves arguing that, since America has taken consumption to new heights, all must indeed be for the best in this best of all possible worlds. Twitchell offers no resistance against such a conclusion. "To some degree," he concludes, "the triumph of consumerism is the triumph of the popular will. You may not like what is manufactured, advertised, packaged, branded, and broadcast, but it is far closer to what most people want most of the time than at any other period of modern history."

With these words, Twitchell becomes as sterile in his satisfaction with consumer culture as the critics are with their discontents. If our only choices are to celebrate consumption for what Twitchell calls its "liberating role" or to condemn it for its illusion of freedom, then America's long debate over consumerism will have come to an end. But surely there must be more to the story than this. Critics of consumer culture have to accept with Twitchell that "there are no false needs"–or at least not very many of them–before going on to attack capitalism for its distortions. A little more of Twitchell's joie de vivre is required, not only to make the reading more interesting, but also to make the analysis more credible.

IV

IF A MORE VIBRANT criticism of consumerism is ever to be forthcoming, Thomas Frank is the most likely to provide it. Although he was trained as an academic, Frank showed at least some of capitalism's entrepreneurial spirit when he founded a new magazine, *The Baffler*, that quickly developed an underground reputation as spunkier than the more predictable leftist criticism of the market associated with weekly opinion magazines. His new book, *One Market under God*, is far and away the best of the recent spate of books critical of consumerism.

Frank argues that, with respect to capitalism, very little has changed, but with respect to the ideology through which capitalism justifies itself to the world, everything has changed. Wherever and whenever it appears, capitalism wants the same things: high profits, weak labor unions, extended markets, and a world safe for making money. No talk of a "new economy" will change any of that. All that is new in the new economy is some dazzling technology that may or (more realistically) may not deliver on its promises. "What the term describes," Frank writes in *Communist Manifesto*-like style, "is not some novel state of human affairs but the final accomplishment of the longstanding agenda of the nation's richest classes."

The rest, and best, of Frank's book is not about how the economy works, but about how it sells itself as a cultural product. Since capitalism benefits the rich and impoverishes (at least relatively) the poor, it has always had something of a public relations problem in modern liberal democracies. If captains of industry and their political allies spoke honestly about their plans, which invariably benefit themselves at the expense of everyone else, they would not get many votes. And so they seek ways of selling the benefits of a system that works to their advantage. They used to do this, following Adam Smith, by arguing that capitalism was the only economic system capable of promoting human freedom. The problem with this approach was its "tough luck" attitude toward those who lacked the material goods to enjoy their freedom. Read Hayek, Friedman, or early George Gilder, and you do not come away with anything at all ennobling. Capitalism's wonders were technological, materialistic, utilitarian; they did not speak to any deep human craving for the good society.

All this has changed in the past two decades, Frank argues, and no one is more emblematic of the change than Gilder. The frankly elitist theorist of *Wealth and Poverty* has emerged as the guru of a new class war. For those who have not been following Gilder's success on the lecture circuit, this war is not between rich and poor, it is between the once rich and the future rich. Old-style capitalism, the kind that we associated with monopolistic manufacturing firms that employ large numbers of manual workers who belong to unions, is the enemy. New technology companies, with their entrepreneurial instincts, long working hours, egalitarian life-styles, and hip irreverence, are the good guys.

His eyes fixed on the future, Gilder, in Frank's account, was among the first right-wing conservatives to give up on the culture war. In ways that echo David Brooks's *Bobos in Paradise* (see "The Greening of Conservatism," this vol.), Frank recognizes that, for Gilder's dream of a new economy to come into being, alliances would have to be made with alumni of the counterculture, not with the stuck-in-the-past dinosaurs of the Christian right. The energy necessary to create new technology companies came from some of society's least respectable segments, "immigrants and outcasts, street toughs and science wonks, nerds and boffins, the bearded and the beer-bellied, the tacky and uptight, and sometimes weird, the born again and born yesterday, with Adam's apples bobbing, psyches throbbing, and acne galore," in Gilder's irreplaceable words.

By finding a new bourgeoisie among the Lumpenproletariat, Gilder stumbled on the secret of how capitalism could make itself popular in a democratic society. Once upon a time, capitalists were elitist, and protest movements were populist. Why not reverse the imagery, and call the new business ventures populist and the resistance from labor unions–and leftists like Juliet Schor–elitist? It was, as Frank tells the story, a brilliant stroke. But it also got a great lucky break. When the stock market began to rise, fueled by these same high technology companies celebrated by Gilder, the idea of market populism caught fire. Don't listen to stuffy brokers who barely know your name, discount brokerage firms advertised. Trust your own instincts. Become your own Wall Street manager. Day trade. The stock market became the people's market. Far more than Robert Shiller, Thomas Frank recognizes the power of fantasy that propelled the market to new heights. For the first time in human history, the average person could not only hope to obtain a fortune, he could also manage it through his own insight and pluck.

It was not long before market populism turned against capitalism itself, or at least against that form of capitalism that insisted on obedience, conformity, and corporate loyalty. Management gurus came forward to proclaim the irrelevance of management. Magazines such as *Fast Company* attacked the stuffiness of the conventional corporation more radically than leftist social critics, promoting a version of free-agent mobility in which the individual and his own needs came first. In perhaps the greatest public relations success story of the era, corporate downsizing, which threw untold numbers of Americans out of work, was hailed as a great advance in human potential, making it possible for those same Americans to find their inner selves.

American capitalism, in a word, went postmodern. Just when English professors began to wonder whether they had taken Derrida too far, advertising companies began to run ads attacking advertising. You do not want brand loyalty for the same reason that you do not want corporate loyalty. New Age advertising industries presented themselves to sell the idea that, in a populistic democracy ruled by consumer choice, potential customers need to be empowered. As it turns out, postmodern marketing was also developed by a French intellectual, the advertising executive Jean-Marie Dru, who urged companies, in the spirit of 1968, to identify their products with movements for social and ecological justice.

One of the most suggestive sections of Frank's book describes a meeting of Dru-inspired advertising activists—that is the only appropriate description—enthusiastic about the revolutionary transformation that they were effecting in public consciousness. Comparing the advertisers to the leftist meetings that he regularly attends, Frank cannot help but note the differences. Words such as *revolution* came up in the former, but not in the latter. "A generalized spirit of exhaustion tended to hover over the proceedings," he writes of the leftists. They have seen the future, and it is not them.

Frank tells his story well, and this is important; the first step in effective social criticism is being interesting. Yet Frank's sparkling prose and satirical bent is not accompanied by a corresponding breakthrough in political understanding. Indeed, his entire analysis of market populism presupposes that the appeal of markets to ordinary people cannot be compared to the real populism of angry farmers and militant workers back at the end of the nineteenth century. Since market populism is not true, it must be false—and before long, we find ourselves back on familiar leftist grounds. People are somehow deluded when they believe that a more dynamic economy gives them more choices.

Frank's analysis is carried out at the level of what elites think. His book focuses on management gurus and corporate planners, not on the people on behalf of whom Frank is presumably writing. And this is its biggest flaw. Market populism may drive the apologists for what Frank calls "extreme capitalism," but it does not drive the actual economy. It is true that large numbers of Americans, distrustful of authority, would rather make investment decisions on their own than pay the once hefty fees of rather lazy investment brokers. And they will react with disdain, as well they should, against companies that conspire with each other to keep prices high. Still, Americans have not come to accept, as Gilder would have them do, that a new stage in the evolution of humanity has been ushered in with the development of the microchip. They merely do not want to be left out of the good deals that they see all around them.

V

CONSUMPTION IS ONE OF those categories of human experience that demands Aristotelian moderation. Ban it, and the result will be a society impoverished by a paucity of the symbolic imagination–or, even worse, one that drives the symbolic underground, distorting its creative capacities into the illicit and the uncontrollable. The ascetic impulse is rarely a healthy impulse. If we want, as Robert E. Lane is right to insist that we ought to want, a society that establishes a priority for human happiness, we are better off trying to emulate a Catholic appreciation for finery than a Puritan preference for frugality.

Yet no society can allow its members to pursue their taste for goods to the point of excess, or look on with indifference as some are allowed to satisfy their indulgences while others are not, and consider itself either a decent society or a just society. The desire to own a home of one's own is so powerful that a society would be foolish to crush it in the name of what Michael Walzer has called "simple equality," but there is no particular reason why a society need respond to someone's quest for a sixteen-bathroom mansion in the Hamptons with an ocean view. Excess consumption distorts the human imagination as thoroughly as enforced poverty.

By encouraging some to believe that there can never be legitimate limits on their wants, immoderate consumption encourages illusions of omnipotence. In asking others to accept less so that some can acquire more, it perpetuates resentment and it sustains badges of inferiority. By rewarding luck–and beyond a certain point, excess wealth is always a consequence of luck–it undermines bourgeois respect for hard work and the benefits of personal integrity. Ultimately, excess consumption destroys the very richness of the imagination that consumption can provide, for it reduces all sacred objects to a price, and blurs any lines between inherent value and perceived value, and places the creative capacity of the human race into the hands of those with the means to restrict access to them.

It does not take a seer to recognize that Americans will eventually look back on these times as a period of excess. The evidence will consist not just in the trophy homes of Microsoft millionaires, or the Hummers sitting in parking spaces that cost more than apartments. Tackiness is nothing new. The corrosive effects of compulsive consumption will be found, rather, in the selling-off of collective assets: state-run lotteries that give government sanction to a relaxation of a long-established heritage against gambling; efforts by universities to transform intellectual curiosity into marketable products; decisions by public television stations to raise money with the efforts of self-help gurus; the opening up of public parks and natural resources to corporate naming opportunities and marketing ventures; and the placing of corporate products and logos into the performances and the displays of both popular culture and elite culture.

Those are the excesses that provide the critics of consumption an opening to make their case. Yet that case is unlikely to be persuasive if it comes from leftists who, frustrated by the power of the market to shape people's fantasies and to respond to their desires, adopt an equally unrelenting opposition to the way that the good life has come to be defined by most Americans. Nor will it come from conservatives so wedded to the companies that finance their political campaigns that they cannot place effective limits on corporate rapaciousness, which is finally the least conservative force in American society. It will have to come instead from those who are capable of reassuring Americans that there is nothing wrong with their instinct to want goods capable of improving and ornamenting their lives, yet who also can respond to their sense that, in offering those goods, capitalism cannot be allowed to trample on their privacy, or to treat them with contempt, or to stand between them and their God, or to destroy their families, or to violate their sense of justice.

If it takes revolutionary rhetoric to advertise and to sell goods, then the next round of the criticism of consumption, if it is to be truly radical, will paradoxically have to speak in the language of tradition. Americans saw glimpses of a revolution in the 1960s and turned away from them. The same will no doubt prove true of the revolution that is now being promoted by the prophets of globalization and scorched-earth competition. An aggressively dynamic capitalism that emerges from the nothing-to-lose freaks and misfits celebrated by George Gilder is bound to upset those trying to live according to the dictates of 1950s conventional morality. To the knowing sophisticates of SoHo and Silicon Valley, their commitments to corporate loyalty will be naive, and their adherence to family values will be obsolete, and their belief in God will limit their opportunities for a quick killing; but it is people such as them, whose instincts for moderation stand in sharp contrast to Yuppie consumers' and their demographic heirs', who offer the best chance of standing in the way of capitalism's latest juggernaut.

Buying Alone

I

WHETHER RESPONDING TO WORLD events or proposing domestic policy initiatives, the Bush administration seems to be guided by one simple imperative: buy. The way to demonstrate our resolve against jihad, the president asserted with considerable conviction after September 11, was to shop; and not even the administration's war in Iraq provoked the president to consider the possibility that in the name of national security Americans ought to consume less energy. At home, the Bush administration's response to what is increasingly perceived as its own recession is, similarly, to put as much money into the hands of consumers as possible. In fact, the more money people or corporations have with which to consume, the more money the Bush administration wants to give them.

The administration's emphasis on buying is in part a carefully considered strategy. Republicans discovered during the Reagan years that tax cuts constitute a preemptive strike against future public policy. Preemption, indeed. Why wait to kill a program until it has popular support and powerful interest groups behind it, when you can abort it–so to speak–before it even comes into being? Although polls consistently show that Americans are willing to support tax increases if they finance credible services, voters (or so legislators of both parties agree) cannot resist the promise of more disposable income. When the Framers talked about the power of the purse, little did they know that the most powerful purses would prove not to be the ones in the government's hands.

Still, the administration's emphasis on spending teaches us that not all talk of consumption is willful. The terrorist attack against us was so completely unexpected that we must assume that the president, when he urged us to consume, was not reading from Karl Rove's playbook. Instead Bush spoke in a language so ingrained in the American consciousness as to seem perfectly natural. Consumption is the first thing that came to mind when he required a definition of the American way of life because consumption has become the American way of life. Our freedoms are enviable and ought to make us inordinately proud, yet it was not the Bill of Rights to which the president called our attention– which is understandable, given his administration's contempt for some of its provisions–but the right to buy and to sell what we choose. It made intuitive sense to us that a man as devoted to unfreedom as Osama bin Laden would choose to ally himself with the poorest country in the world. Over there, they wear veils because they cannot buy skirts. Here, we can speak our minds and we can satisfy our desires anytime, as long as we have the cash.

Lizabeth Cohen's refreshingly bold and ambitious *A Consumers' Republic: The Politics of Mass Consumption in Postwar America* is an effort to explain how the republic for which we stand came to be shaped by our economy's insatiable demand for demand. Cohen breaks sharply with an often frustrating tendency in contemporary historiography. For the past two or three decades, historians have been studiously thinking small. Persuaded that real life is often more complicated than sweeping generalizations about "modernity" or "progress," they brought to life the factories in which people worked, and the families in which they were raised and raised others, and the communities in which they lived. As important as social history has been, however, it has also been mind-numbingly narrow in its evocation of detail and in its reluctance to consider the larger meanings of its findings. But Cohen thinks big. Although she pays homage to social history by focusing on one place, the northern New Jersey suburbs in which she grew up, she has also taken on a large subject–in important ways, the largest of all subjects in its ubiquity and in its power to influence the kinds of lives that Americans lead. One hopes that her book will stimulate her colleagues to take similar risks, even the risk of emulating historians of previous generations whose efforts at intellectual synthesis and grand narrative are treated now with contempt by postmodern pygmies.

While Cohen breaks with one academic convention, however, she adheres faithfully to another. For her, storytelling must have didactic purposes, and her purposes are all conventionally left-wing. She wants to bring into the picture the experiences of women and African Americans, often doing so in ways that seem more dutiful than enlightening. And she makes no bones about who, in her opinion, are the good people (New Deal regulators, World War II price controllers, Betty Furness, Jesse Jackson, and numerous grassroots folks who opposed suburban malls and racist companies) and who are the bad people (corporate executives, sprawl developers, market researchers, and nearly all Republicans). Cohen is entitled to her views, of course; but the truth is that consumption is an activity difficult to weave into a progressive understanding of how the world is supposed to work. There is no necessary linkage between buying things, no matter what is purchased or how, and the struggle to create a more equal or more democratic society. Indeed, trying to organize people around consumption frequently results in a petty-bourgeois approach to politics that is sharply at odds with a progressive agenda.

Cohen's history is impeccable; her almost superhuman investigations into obscure sources and archives bring many rewards, and she writes well enough to sustain a reader's attention throughout a very long book. Yet the very thoroughness of her narrative serves to undermine the conclusions that she wants her reader to draw from it. *A Consumers' Republic* is best read as an account of how consumption came to play such a pronounced role in American public life, not as a guide to what we ought to do about it.

II

COHEN BEGINS HER BOOK with the New Deal, appropriately enough, since the Great Depression, at least in the view of Keynesians, was the consequence of insufficient demand. The Roosevelt administration was intent on spending more, but it was divided, Cohen argues, over the proper means by which to do so. One method, more explicitly Keynesian, relied on what she calls "the purchaser consumer," the American whose spending would lead us out of economic despondency. Among Roosevelt's famous "Four Freedoms" was freedom from want, represented in the equally famous Norman Rockwell magazine cover, which, Cohen writes, can best be viewed "as a celebration of the plenitude that American families reaped through their participation in a mass consumer economy." Against this rather limited notion of the obligation to spend, Cohen much prefers what she calls the ideal of the "citizen consumer," which "sought consumer representation in government and new legislation and regulation to protect consumers better in the marketplace." The 1930s, in her account, are notable for the number of grassroots consumer movements, often led by women or African Americans, that tried to mobilize purchasing power for political ends such as equality and solidarity.

The ideal of the citizen consumer received considerable energy from the need to mobilize domestic support during World War II. Wartime, in Cohen's view, came as close to realizing the proper model of consumer conduct as America would ever experience. Cohen cites the patriotic "Consumer Pledge Song" that one American in 1942 set to the tune of "The Battle Hymn of the Republic." Its chorus proclaimed:

> *I will be a wise consumer,*
> *Gladly do so with humor,*
> *That's the way to win the sooner*
> *To Peace and Victory.*

The Office of Price Administration, Cohen is eager to point out, was run by enlightened policymakers such as Chester Bowles, who listened carefully to the consumer advocates, many of them women, whom Cohen so admires. Price controls, in her view, made everyone a bit more equal, contributing to the sense of fairness required for effective wartime solidarity. So laudatory was the consumer ideal developed during World War II that Cohen views it as a model for the postwar economy. "Essential to the success of this conception," she observes, "was the extension of price and rent controls beyond victory into peacetime, so as to prevent the spiraling effects of inflation that had proved so damaging after World War I and to protect the progress toward economic equality made during wartime."

The country, needless to say, did not follow such advice. In 1947, Walt Disney's Scrooge McDuck made his first appearance in American popular culture, underscoring William F. Whyte's comment that "thrift is now un-American." The force of consumption had been unleashed, and its power could not be curtailed. "Wherever one looked in the aftermath of war," Cohen writes, "one found a vision of postwar America where the general good would best be served not by frugality or even moderation, but by individuals pursuing personal wants in a flourishing mass consumption marketplace."

To demonstrate the hold of consumption on postwar Americans, Cohen chooses to focus on what, for most Americans, was their single biggest good: their house. Twenty-five percent of all American homes in 1960 were built during the 1950s. (Cohen has a special talent for finding telling bits of evidence to support her story.) The homes themselves, the appliances with which they were stocked, and the cars necessary to reach them together gave birth to what Cohen calls "the Consumers' Republic," which she defines as a society bent on achieving "the socially progressive end of economic equality without requiring politically progressive means of redistributing existing wealth." Mass consumption settled the dispute between competing conceptions of the good citizen that had fought each other during the Great Depression and World War II.

The tale of America's preoccupation with consumption in the postwar years has been told many times, including by contemporaries such as Vance Packard and David Riesman. Cohen's objective is to link that tale with a political one. Consumption, she argues, shaped not only our bodies but also our body politic; it influenced our public life as much as it responded to our private wants. We, not the Russians, had created the first classless society, our politicians of the 1950s declared. Businessmen could proclaim themselves true stewards of our society, responsible for the goods we all came to enjoy. In Cohen's consumers' republic, credit cards replaced the voting booth as the proper means of registering opinion. Although critics such as John Kenneth Galbraith warned that we were engaged in mass deception by seeking satisfaction through consumption, we paid little heed, so certain were we that we had discovered "an elaborate, integrated ideal of economic abundance and democratic political freedom, both equitably distributed, that became almost a national civic religion from the late 1940s into the 1970s."

The birth of the consumers' republic, in Cohen's account, also shaped our understandings of gender, class, and race, transforming more compelling ideals about responsible consumption revealed by depression and war into passive ones that left the status quo in place. Women may have been active in the New Deal and in wartime experiences with price controls, but in the postwar years they not only retreated from the ideal of the citizen consumer, they even lost their hold on purchasing power. Seen through the lens of gender, legislation such as the GI Bill or consumer practices such as credit cards seem like efforts to reimpose patriarchy. Since most GIs were men, men benefited disproportionately from legislation designed to reward them. Not only that, but women, as the head of New Jersey's Advisory Commission on Women Veterans put it many years later, "don't categorize themselves as veterans." Men also received special advantages in the private market. Mortgages and credit cards were issued in their names. As late as the 1970s, Cohen reports, women whose incomes were listed on mortgage applications were asked by the Veterans Administration to submit letters certifying that they were sterile or—where is the religious right when we need it?—committed to birth control or willing to undergo an abortion. We all know that after the war Rosie the Riveter was sent home. Cohen shows that the means of transportation upon which she relied was the gravy train that made America so prosperous.

With so much of her focus on housing, Cohen has no trouble demonstrating the ways in which consumption reinforced racial inequality, for the segregation of home purchasing and home financing that continues up to the present is one of America's greatest shames. In 1953, the largest town in America with no black residents was Levittown on Long Island; by 1960, it had only fifty-seven blacks, and by 1980, that number actually went down to forty-five. When Cohen shifts her attention to New Jersey, the most suburban state in the country, the record is even more sorrowful. It took three major decisions of the New Jersey Supreme Court and an act of the legislature before the residents of Mount Laurel, a rapidly expanding suburb about twenty miles from Philadelphia, would accept mixed housing in their community.

New Jersey is also the state that pioneered the development of suburban malls, with a prime example in Paramus, seven miles from the George Washington Bridge, which in 1957 was the largest mall in America. (Cohen provides a picture of herself and her sister in 1956 as properly dressed little girls in front of their Paramus home, perhaps on their way out to shop.) The mall did not so much replace the city as re-create it in controlled circumstances located at some remove from where people actually lived. Offering everything the consumer could possibly want–except, as one reporter cited by Cohen commented, a funeral parlor–the mall not only sold goods but also established a new model by which democracy would be organized.

Speech, Cohen goes to some length to show, would be less free in the mall than it was in the town square, because under these new arrangements the First Amendment came into direct conflict with property rights and, at least in some places, was considerably restricted. (New Jersey was actually one of the states in which speech in malls was protected.) Along similar lines, malls undermined equality, in Cohen's view, because they were quickly segregated by gender; wives spent their time there spending what their husbands made in the city. Intent on offering low prices, shops in the malls wanted to hold down labor costs, which undercut the ability of unions to organize their employees. "Overall, an important shift from one kind of social order to another took place between 1950 and 1980 with major consequences for Americans," Cohen writes, and the mall was responsible for that shift.

To get people into malls, it is important to stimulate their wants, which leads Cohen into the dark realms of marketing and consumer research. One theme dominates her discussion of these subjects. In theory, consumption, whether we like it or not, ought to unify us, because we all become consumers of roughly similar goods. In reality, marketing specialists discovered in the postwar years that the best way to sell goods is to segment the audience that is buying them. A handful of beer makers replaced many local and independent ones, but in order to mimic the diversity that they abolished they proceeded to market a variety of beers with different names appealing to different kinds of beer drinkers. The same happened with cars, breakfast cereals, laundry detergents, and even newspapers and television stations. "Much the way suburban residential communities and shopping centers, originally conceived to be widely accessible new postwar spaces, became increasingly stratified by class and race as they targeted distinct populations," Cohen concludes, "so too as the postwar era progressed did the mass market itself fracture into numerous constituent parts." Once again, consumption determined politics. We shopped alone before we bowled alone. Segmented into our zip codes, is it any wonder that our politics became so contentious and our unity around a common conception of the good so impossible?

One ray of hope broke the depressing downward spiral away from the enlightened consumer: the Kennedy years. Seemingly out of nowhere, books began to appear showing us how unsafe were our cars and how unattractive were our homes. As difficult to believe as it may seem in the age of George W. Bush, legislators rushed to regulate industries, establishing standards to reverse environmental degradation and to ban unsafe products. This was the time when we worried about inflammable pajamas and began to give up our Liebestod with tobacco. Celebrating this "third wave" of consumer activism, Cohen nonetheless concludes that it made no real dent in the creation of the consumers' republic. Protection and regulation were not accompanied by incorporation; consumers never achieved "a permanent voice in government through a separate department of the consumer or other such agency within the executive branch." Without secure footing, it all eventually came to naught. Jimmy Carter scolded us for our "worship [of] self-indulgence and consumption," and we responded by electing General Electric's Ronald Reagan in his place.

Cohen, like America, runs out of energy during the Carter years. She devotes just a few pages to the Reagan, Bush, Clinton, and Bush II administrations. Still, she does not shy away from big themes. Briefly surveying the consumer landscape of the present, Cohen sees ever more depressing consequences of the historical events that she has recounted. Catalog buying and Web-based commerce threaten to undo the malls with even more privatized forms of shopping. Public spaces such as libraries attract patrons by opening branches of Starbucks. Housing developments put up gates. "A history that extends into our own lifetimes, that continues to shape our daily lives, is hard to bring to a conclusion," Cohen remarks. Indeed it is, for we are in the middle of a period in which modes of consumption are changing before our eyes—difficult enough terrain for economists to capture with their models, let alone historians with their archives.

III

ON HER LARGEST POINT, Lizabeth Cohen is right: the way we buy does influence to a considerable degree the way we come together as citizens. Considering how much time we spend shopping or inhaling messages urging us to shop, how could our politics resist modeling itself on economics? Both the ways in which Americans elect their politicians and the means by which those politicians fashion programs and policies bear an eerie resemblance to the segmented markets, the focus group techniques, the short-attention-span messages, and the consumer-driven product development Cohen chronicles. It is a long way from *The Federalist Papers* to The O'Reilly Factor.

The problem that Cohen faces is that consumption has proved so powerful as to render pathetic—if not obsolete—the alternatives that she hopes our history offers. This problem revealed itself right at the birth of the consumers' republic. In the years after World War II, the United States debated whether and for how long price controls would be maintained before quickly deciding to abolish them. Cohen says that there was nothing inevitable about the outcome. But her discussion shows the exact opposite. It is hard to imagine why anyone would allow the supply and the demand for houses and cars to be regulated by blue-nose patricians such as Vassar College's Caroline Ware, who urged "keeping down with the Joneses" as if that were a good thing. Citing statistics seeming to prove that Americans liked the World War II–era wage and price controls and wanted to keep them, Cohen underestimates the everyday longing for unrestrained spending unleashed by the war's necessary restraints. "The defeat of price control was a slap in the face to the tens of thousands of women who mobilized for its extension." Yes, and it brought cheers from millions more who could now begin to buy what they wanted.

"Rent control was the sole survivor of the massive wartime price-control machinery," Cohen writes, failing to appreciate how devastating that comment is to her larger political argument. Rent control in places such as Manhattan served few, if any, progressive ends. The primary beneficiaries of rent control were not the poor who needed housing but the middle-class people who already had it. To find an apartment during the era of rent control, you needed to have connections, and to be willing to pay exorbitant "key" fees, and to know how black markets operate, and to have been lucky in your choice of parents. Imagine, then, if controls on other valued goods had somehow been allowed to remain in place during the years after World War II. Manufacturers of cars and houses would have let the quality of their products deteriorate (even more than they did) in order to capture profits not allowed by higher prices. Instead of paying more for the goods that they purchased, consumers would have paid exorbitant prices to have them repaired or serviced (assuming that those prices were not also controlled). Mostly, though, price controls in general would have frozen into place advantages that well-off people already had, harming the poor more than anyone else. The enthusiasts for price controls during World War II were the kind of people who lived in Greenwich and sent their children to Ivy League colleges. Cohen never stops to reflect that for all their talk of responsible consumption, they may well have been trying, like privileged people throughout history, to protect their position.

Race is another subject that fits uneasily into Cohen's political agenda. She does fill an important gap in our understanding of recent race relations by reminding us how much of it–from the sit-ins at Woolworths to the urban riots of the 1960s and 1970s–was focused on goods. The dream of racial equality came to life by insisting on an equal right to buy things, just as it started its descent into marginalization by violently protesting the inability to do so. But none of this meant that African Americans could serve as a vanguard for a consumer movement that would inevitably serve the needs of middle-class buyers. The affluent society scorned by Galbraith was, for them, a dream to be realized.

This, after all, would seem to be the real meaning of the riots that shook so many American cities, including Newark, on which Cohen, true to her New Jersey roots, concentrates. One of Cohen's most effective visuals is a set of two pictures of a Newark resident named Foy Miller taken in the same spot, one in 1967 and the other thirty years later. In the former, she is being asked for identification by a National Guardsman against a backdrop of scarred but nonetheless visible buildings. In the latter, she stands before empty lots, a downtown denuded of activity. Yet what point, precisely, is being made here? Cohen includes her discussion of what she calls the Newark "rebellion" in the same chapter that deals with the consumer activism of the 1960s, as if black attacks on Jewish shopkeepers were the African American equivalent of Nader's Raiders. But to see the 1960s riots as a protest against consumption downplays the extent to which, in their own self-destructive way, they were about obtaining goods by any means necessary.

In one of her ingenious asides, Cohen contrasts two Newark-born writers, Philip Roth and Amiri Baraka. Yet what the writers actually had to say undermines her more didactic treatment of these issues. Cohen tries to link the Newark riots to the larger picture of consumption by showing that urban devastation sent more whites to the suburbs and the malls, but *Goodbye, Columbus* was published in 1959, and by then the Patimkins had already moved out to Short Hills. And Baraka, whose angry screeds Cohen takes as progressive, illustrates how little the New Jersey riots had to do with politics of any kind. "Families worked together, carrying sofas and TVs collectively down the street. All the shit they saw on television that they had been hypnotized into wanting they finally had a chance to cop," Baraka observed. He seems more aware than Cohen of the desperation of many African Americans to join the consumers' republic, not to tear it down.

Cohen faces her greatest difficulties trying to reconcile her politics with her history when she discusses the tendency of marketing strategists to segment consumers into ever more refined categories. Back in the 1930s and 1940s, when Cohen's story begins, progressive consumer advocates would have had no problem denouncing such tactics. Those were the days of the Popular Front, and leftists, including those in or close to the Communist party, outdid themselves in appealing to unity and solidarity. But in the intervening years many progressives have found themselves sympathetic to identity politics. No longer can one appeal to solidarity, either because (in the manner of Stanley Fish) there is no such thing or because solidarity is a distraction from a person's "real" interest as a woman, or a homosexual, or an African American. If she is to cast herself with her heroes from times past, Cohen should denounce market segmentation without hesitation. But if she is to identify with identity politics, she needs to tread more carefully. Is not affirmative action a way of segmenting a market—and in the case of a college education, a market for one of life's most valuable goods?

Realizing that she finds herself on "fragile ground," Cohen waffles. She cautions that "one must beware of promoting false or naïve notions of a universal 'common good' and unified 'public' and thereby denying the more diverse and complicated multi-cultural America that has greeted the twenty-first century," but then she goes on to add that "not all divisions among Americans are sacrosanct." The best that Cohen can do here is to call for a "concerted effort" to find a way to express our diversity while committing ourselves to a common purpose. Compared to that, the Popular Front politics of the consumer activists of the 1930s, as naive as they may have been, were at least consistent. Cohen wants us to "assume collective responsibility for each other," but if the cost of doing that is to insist that our multicultural proclivities have to give way to our common identity, that price, for her, is too high.

IV

THERE IS AN OBVIOUS REASON why leftists hope to be able to organize people through their consumption: just about everyone is a consumer. Displaced farmers, angry workers, racially oppressed minorities: none of these groups has the sheer numbers represented by consumers. Desperate to find historical agents whose discontents would usher in a new era, consumer advocates from the New Deal to the 1960s chose, rather opportunistically, to organize people around their most ubiquitous contacts with capitalism. But in so doing they ran the risk of strengthening the capitalist order that they hoped to alter or to supplant. This is a dilemma that Cohen never squarely faces, but face it she must, for the weakness of consumption as a means of pursuing progressive politics certainly complicates her story. Cohen tends to treat the history of postwar consumption in America as one long retreat from the idealists who urged us to shop more responsibly in the 1930s and the 1940s. In significant ways, however, those reformers triumphed, even if the venue of their victory became the conservative wing of the Republican party. "Consumer benefit is the bottom line," said Christopher deMuth of the American Enterprise Institute when he was executive director of the Vice President's Task Force on Regulatory Relief in the Reagan administration. If all of us shop but only some of us vote, politicians seeking broad public support will appeal to the one thing we all have in common just as opportunistically as New Deal progressives.

This is not a conclusion that Cohen wishes to reach. To avoid it, she argues that in the years since Jimmy Carter "the Consumers' Republic transmogrified into the Commercialization of the Republic." All of our recent presidents, but conservative Republicans in particular, by deregulating government and promoting greater inequality, gave up on the promise of abundance for all in favor of benefits that "increasingly became reserved for those who paid for them." Cohen then goes on to contrast the ideology of conservative America–"what's best for me is what's best for America"–with what she calls the message of the consumers' republic at its most idealistic: "the interests of individual purchasers as citizens and of the nation were one and the same." But her own book demonstrates with exceptional force that the idealism was only for show. In reality, the denizens of the consumers' republic were instructed to buy as much as they could to satisfy their individual needs. Consumption is like that. It is always about buying. Those who think that they can urge people to buy less or more responsibly delude themselves.

The real lesson of Cohen's book is that if you want to redistribute income or to promote equality, you should try to redistribute income and promote equality. And if you try to make your agenda more popular by appealing to consumers, you will only make people more avid consumers. It was not just perversity that led Ralph Nader, a hero of Lizabeth Cohen's youth, to work so hard on behalf of the Republican party. He must have realized on some level–and if he did not, then consumers certainly did–that if small cars are unsafe at any speed, one ought to buy SUVs instead. And for that ignoble end, conservative Republicans are the ones to have in office.

The Greening of Conservatism

I

WE SPEND FAR MORE time interpreting the 1960s than we spent experiencing the decade. It is mostly conservatives who, unable to leave those years behind, invoke every theory at their disposal to account for why they happened. No sooner had demonstrations broken out at Berkeley in 1964 and at Columbia in 1968 than Freud was trotted out to explain why each generation rebels against its parents. Reflecting the socialist roots of so much neoconservative thought, Marx was cited to make sense of the ways in which radicals had become a "new class," poised to seize power from the bourgeoisie and to put it into the hands of therapeutic professionals. And in the most inventive twist of all, Allan Bloom found in the sixties the triumph of right-wing German philosophy, recognizing how soon Sartre would be forgotten and Heidegger would be revered.

In the past year, a new generation of conservatives, too young to have experienced those tumultuous years themselves, have begun to propose explanations of their own. In *How We Got Here*, David Frum argued that much of the personal liberation that we associate with the sixties actually took place in the 1970s, so that what at first glance appears to be a brief interlude in American life hints at more long-lasting cultural transformations. Mark Lilla has suggested that the "left" movements of the sixties and the "right" movements of the eighties were "one and indivisible," with the consequence that young people "see no contradiction in holding down day jobs in the unfettered global marketplace—the Reaganite dream, the left nightmare—and spending weekends immersed in a moral and cultural universe shaped by the Sixties." And now David Brooks develops and expands a similar explanation of how the radical chickens of the sixties came home to roost in the upper-class pretensions of the 1990s in *Bobos in Paradise: The New Upper Class and How They Got There.*

Brooks plays down his credentials as a theorist–"Max Weber has nothing to worry about from me"–but his curiosity did lead him, with the assistance of Irving Kristol, to one of the truly unappreciated classics of contemporary sociology: César Graña's *Bohemian versus Bourgeois,* which appeared in 1964. Graña wrote that the novelists and the intellectuals of nineteenth-century France, whatever their ostensible politics, united in condemning bourgeois life and in romanticizing bohemian life. Picture the first encounter between Allen Ginsberg and Norman Podhoretz as undergraduates at Columbia and you have some sense of how long Graña's antagonists have fought each other. In that fine pre-sixties moment, the future author of *Howl* and the future author of *Making It* define the two contrasting styles of American life: one rejects materialism in celebration of spiritual wholeness and personal pleasure, or one sublimates the impulses in pursuit of power and financial reward.

Nowadays, according to Brooks, we would look back on this meeting and wonder why a choice was necessary. Dot-com millionaires and workaholic lawyers have surely made it financially, yet their life-style choices are tinged with bohemian affectation. They rip out the ornate Victorian furnishings in their homes to expose brick and wood. Their consumption, however munificent, is inconspicuous. In their presentation of self, they give off the impression of disdaining wealth, as if, to be true to themselves, they would rather be off on some spiritual retreat. "The hedonism of Woodstock mythology," Brooks writes, "has been domesticated and now serves as a management tool for the Fortune 500." Daniel Bell was wrong, he suggests, to describe capitalism as torn between its ascetic drive to accumulate and its hedonistic urge to consume. Bourgeois values and bohemian values adjust to each other so easily that a new term–*Bobo*–is required to capture the full flavor of upper-class life in America.

In Brooks's account, the rebellious sixties turn out to have been, of all things, a ticket to upward mobility. The way to join the Establishment was first to attack it. The demonstrators who congregated at Berkeley's Sproul Plaza went on to create Chez Panisse, the upscale restaurant of the 1980s and 1990s, and behind every Chez Panisse there exists an entire infantry of fresh vegetable markets, boutique wineries, espresso bars, and kitchen appliance outlets. One of the latter, Williams-Sonoma, offers sausages whose origin can be traced back to the curing techniques pioneered by Native Americans. "This is not some Upton Sinclair jungle," Brooks writes, "but a noble lineage of craftsman sausage makers, and we members of the educated elite are willing to pay $29.50 for 24 little links in order to tap into this heritage."

"Comic sociology" is how Brooks describes his methodology, but this is comedy–and sociology–of a particular sort. Brooks writes that he is, overall, a defender of Bobo culture, which is not quite true. Despite his frequent inclusion of himself as a member of the species that he is analyzing, he is anything but an enthusiast for the tendency of Bobos to resolve all contradictions in favor of some higher cosmic consciousness. Yet in style, if not always in substance, *Bobos in Paradise* is an ideal Bobo book. It is, for one thing, a book, and in that sense it aspires to a certain seriousness; but it is also a short book whose humor continuously undercuts its own importance, as if Brooks himself were a bit too bohemian to want to leave behind a monument to bourgeois culture along the lines of, say, *The Cultural Contradictions of Capitalism.* Bobos are too detached from emotions such as rage to take much of anything too seriously, and so is Brooks. The satire here is pointed and witty, but it is never nasty. His book will sell only if Bobos buy it, and Bobos are likely to buy it because they will recognize its author as one of their own.

Brooks's sociology is similarly casual. If his roving eye discovers something that strikes him as an interesting commentary on our times–wedding announcements in the *New York Times,* travel brochures urging visits to faraway places, corporate mission statements–he will immediately incorporate it into his story. The method does not always work. Brooks has a chapter on how to become a public intellectual, for example, in which he offers guidance for developing the right Rolodex and learning the snappiest sound bites. Not only does this chapter fail to fit the thesis of his book, it is also heavy-handed and flat. But when Brooks's method works, it works marvelously. It is indeed worth pondering why a Boston-based consulting firm gives job applicants a "Lego/Play-Doh" test or why British Airways has an official corporate jester. Brooks's chapter describing the ways cutting-edge companies go out of their way to pretend that they have little or nothing to do with making money is as devastating a commentary on the modern corporation as anything in C. Wright Mills or William H. Whyte.

As corporations become more bohemian, bohemians become more bourgeois. Yesterday's radicals, Brooks points out, are today's defenders of the need for moral order. It is not just a matter of feminists condemning pornography or Hillary Clinton praising the kinds of villages that were once vilified by Sherwood Anderson and Sinclair Lewis. Before the sixties, Brooks writes, the symbol of bourgeois philistinism was the bowling alley; but now the bowling alley has become the symbol of civic renewal. Boboism is a matter of give-and-take. Established institutions no longer sure of their purpose meet former rebels no longer sure of their radicalism halfway. The most regularly cited lines used to describe the sixties were Yeats's in "The Second Coming." Bobo culture is precisely what you get when the center cannot hold, but anarchy, contrary to Yeats, is not yet loosed upon the world.

As both comedy and sociology, *Bobos in Paradise* succeeds nicely. A terrifically entertaining read, it is fundamentally correct in its premise: bourgeois and bohemian may have been antagonistic to each other in nineteenth-century France, but they work perfectly well together in twenty-first-century America. If Brooks's thesis has a flaw, it is that it is offered too modestly. For it is not only the wealthy who aspire both to material comforts and quests for higher meaning. These days the stores that sell to exurbanites have branch outlets all over America. Personal trainers–indeed, personal gurus–can be hired by middle managers and secretaries. Evangelical congregations attractive to the lower middle class can be just as therapeutically spiritual as upper-class Unitarians. Boboism is not a slice of American life. It is American life.

II

DAVID BROOKS IS THE PRODUCT of a conservative intellectual subculture. That such a subculture even exists is one sign of the degree to which the sixties changed America. Children of privilege–some of whose fathers literally planned the war in Vietnam or managed the companies that dominated the alleged American empire–turned radically, sometimes violently, to the left. But no such transformation took place on the right. Those neoconservatives who found themselves in opposition to everything for which the 1960s stood also had children, literally and figuratively. (One of the literal ones, William Kristol, runs the *Weekly Standard,* at which David Brooks is a senior editor.) Those children grew up in a world in which the left had become the establishment. For them, the right was the only credible counterculture.

Not all radicals of the sixties became comfortably bourgeois, of course; but nearly all of them came to suffer from intellectual complacency. As the New Left became the defender of the university that it once wanted to tear down, it lost the critical spirit that had once produced energetic social criticism. The long march through the institutions turned out to be a vertical march up the institutional hierarchy, eventually producing a First Couple capable of speaking sixties talk while persuading Wall Street of their reliability.

But it was not just political moderation that overtook the left. The tone of its writers took on a weighted pomposity, as if the left were the natural ruling class of the society, the rightful place that it had been denied by the clever tactics of the right. Once there were radical books– *The Sociological Imagination, Growing Up Absurd, One Flew Over the*

Cuckoo's Nest–that enlightened and enraged. Now there is only pious sermonizing, bureaucratic obfuscation, and old-folks resignation. One cannot find a single interesting radical nonfiction writer in America under (or over) fifty. The brightest young star produced by the American left, Jedidiah Purdy, wrote a book attacking the very quality that brings *Bobos in Paradise* to life: irony.

No wonder, then, that popular social criticism has been taken over by people who (I presume) vote Republican. If there were no social criticism coming from the right these days, America would have almost no social criticism. Social criticism is provoked when people take themselves too seriously, and nobody these days takes themselves more seriously than leftists who believe that Americans who like the free market and dislike affirmative action are incapable of thinking for themselves, and have somehow been duped by the nefarious forces of the right. The left is no longer the instigator of social criticism; it has instead become its target.

III

STILL, THERE IS SOMETHING odd about conservative social criticism. To understand why, consider how Brooks's book differs not from what the left produces now, but from what the right produced just a few years back. There is, first of all, Brooks's humor. Humor is not a quality that springs to mind when one thinks of a conservative outlook on the world; one does not read Gertrude Himmelfarb or Midge Decter for the jokes. Like contemporary leftists, neoconservatives became too sanctimonious, too convinced that only they stood between civilization and barbarism; and there continue to be conservatives who write in this dour, self-important manner. Even when conservatives have been funny, most notably P. J. O'Rourke, there has lurked behind their words a bitter aftertaste.

The big news out of the conservative camp is therefore the arrival on the scene of writers such as David Brooks and David Frum who are simply (but smartly) funny. One wonders what their ideological elders, so preoccupied with saving Western civilization, make of such insouciant sensibilities. Are they writers slouching, however gingerly, toward the Gomorrah of irony and relaxation?

They may well be. Brooks's book suggests that one cannot be both funny and conservative for too long. For humor is not the only characteristic of Brooks's writing that distinguishes him from the neoconservatives of the previous generation. Brooks also has mixed feelings about wealth—and about the corporations whose aim is to maximize it.

Irving Kristol's version of conservatism had little to say about the rich. To be sure, Kristol argued that capitalism had a bad reputation among intellectuals, and he urged capitalists to defend themselves more vigorously against the frequent attacks launched against them. But if every intellectual has to have a favorite class or two, for Kristol it was the respectable poor and the lower middle. Those are the people, Kristol wrote in one essay after another, who truly believe in such bourgeois virtues as faith, country, and family. To defend and to protect them, he railed against the new elites ensconced in the media, government, and the clergy who dismissed such virtues as obsolete. It was a brilliant tour de force, but it did suffer a fatal flaw. As many critics have shown, capitalist priorities did more to break up families and to undermine loyalty to country than any feminist tract or government regulation. Their silence about the corporate rich became the shame of the neoconservatives.

But Brooks has no trouble criticizing corporations, if for no other reason than that he sees no difference between them and the "new class" which, at least according to Kristol, despised capitalism. The theory of the new class, one of neoconservatism's most interesting ideas, is totally demolished by Brooks. Kristol, and others like him, took the radical writers of the 1960s—Norman O. Brown, Herbert Marcuse, and Charles Reich—too literally. Whatever the writers of such tracts meant to say about the evils of corporate America and the pleasures of subversion, readers came away persuaded of the need for greater personal freedom on the one hand and for more caring and sensitive environments on the other—qualities that corporations, always on the lookout for fresh talent and new markets, were perfectly willing to provide.

The corporate elite proved itself to be indifferent to self-defense and completely uninterested in bourgeois virtue. Lenin had it only half right: capitalists are not only willing to sell the rope with which they will be hung, they will also build the platform, pay for the executioner, and create a fund to clean up the mess. Fortunately for them, the likely hangmen are more interested in the price of the rope than in actually using it, as if they could come up with a business plan that would enable them to transform the hemp into something with potential medical uses.

American capitalism has so little in common with conservatism that Brooks feels no need to rush to its defense. For Brooks and many of his colleagues at the *Weekly Standard,* conservative virtues are more likely to be found among military patriots than among global profiteers. These are writers who recognize, as many neoconservatives did not, that conservative virtues predate the rise of the bourgeoisie. Their sources are the heroic epics of ancient Greece and Rome, not the everyday practicality of Benjamin Franklin and Andrew Carnegie. Brooks was a strong supporter of John McCain in the Republican primaries for the same reason that the Roosevelts were so long associated with the navy. If we are to be inoculated against Bobo culture, it will have to come from war or the moral equivalent of it. Honor, courage, and loyalty are not tested through initial public offerings or sustained by clever accounting techniques. Bobos may succeed in business without really trying, but you do not see them lining up for ROTC.

The military may well prove more resistant to bohemian life-styles than the corporation, though one suspects that at least some of what Charles Reich called Consciousness III—especially gender and racial sensitivity—has left its mark there. Still, Brooks longs for the kind of politics that America once had when it was more prepared to contemplate the possibility of war. (Brooks, needless to say, became a strong supporter of the American war against Iraq.) "The people of the left and right who long for radical and heroic politics are driven absolutely batty by Bobo politics," he writes.

Implicit in that sentence is an idea that is worthy of being unpacked. America's two parties are not liberals and conservatives. There is instead a party of resignation and a party of ambition. The former includes Clinton and Gore moderates as well as Republicans so tied to the lobbies that enrich their campaign coffers that they are incapable of articulating any new policies at all. The latter includes both those who think that America needs a new way of financing health care and redistributing income as well as those who think that America ought to intervene in other countries to promote global stability. Brooks longs for a version of conservative ambition; but he seems to recognize that this leaves him with a temperament closer to liberal activism than to conservative complacency. Brooks has little in common with Ralph Nader, but they both have mixed feelings about Boboism.

Once the idea of the new class is thrown out, the concept of the culture war cannot be far behind. It was axiomatic to an earlier generation of neoconservative writers that America, as Gertrude Himmelfarb has recently written, has two cultures: a more religious and patriotic lower-middle-class culture and a more relativistic and skeptical elite culture. But Boboism represents a peace treaty in the culture war. Occasionally a neoconservative writer will acknowledge that the culture war is over, but only because the secular humanists won. As Brooks describes the terms of the treaty, however, it seems that conservatives may have won after all. "It is more of a temperament than a creed," Brooks writes of Bobo spirituality. "Bobo moralists are not heroic, but they are responsible. They prefer the familiar to the unknown, the concrete to the abstract, the modest to the ardent, civility and moderation to conflict and turmoil."

It could be that I appreciate Brooks's description because it relies heavily on my own research; but what I find most striking about his characterization of the American mood is that it supports the thesis that we have one culture, not two. Brooks resonates with the unapocalyptic conservatism of Michael Oakeshott rather than the Sturm und Drang conservatism of Himmelfarb (who entitled one of her books *Looking into the Abyss*). Once again Brooks does not draw out the full implications of what he is saying. I take him to mean that the culture warriors of the right had better tone down their rhetoric because they simply do not understand the America that they presume to be defending.

Brooks has his worries about Bobo culture. Its spiritual life, for all its moderation, is "tepid and undemanding." Under its reign, we may well "become a nation that enjoys the comforts of private life and local life but has lost any sense of national union and any sense of a unique historical mission." Unlike the best and the brightest of the early sixties, the meritocrats among the Bobos are "only dimly aware of themselves as an elite and unaware yet of their capacities."

Brooks is right to emphasize the ways in which Bobos have saved us not only from the extremes of the sixties, but also from the extremes of the eighties. Compared to People's Park–that slice of liberated Berkeley territory that became the home of drug addicts and street people–there is something to be said on behalf of Chez Panisse. And compared to the firebrands of the Reagan revolution, there is something to be said for Ben and Jerry's style of capitalism. If the worst thing that we can say of a generation is that it craves higher-powered ovens to roast its organic quail, our society must be in pretty good shape.

That ought not make it immune from criticism, of course. But the best social criticism is likely to share a Boboesque sensibility: puzzled rather than ponderous, aloof and not partisan, and capable of winking at its own foibles. Conservatives, if they are to avoid complete marginalization, need a writer like Brooks. Chances are they will not be able to keep him.

PART VII

Left and Right

•

The Snake

A s . . . THE TWENTIETH CENTURY draws to a close," write Michael Hardt and Antonio Negri in *Empire*, "capitalism is miraculously healthy, its accumulation more robust than ever." For these writers, though not for most consumers and citizens, capitalism's capacity to survive, and even to flourish, poses a grave problem. "How can we reconcile this fact," they ask, "with the careful analyses of numerous Marxist authors at the beginning of the century who pointed to the imperialist conflicts as symptoms of an impending ecological disaster running up against the limits of nature?" Everything that is flawed about this deeply flawed book is contained in the way the authors ask, and then try to answer, this question.

The most obvious of these flaws is the premise that there is anything to reconcile in the first place. Analysts committed to falsifiable ways of developing theories about the world, when faced with a gap between what was expected to happen and what actually happened, would likely reason along these lines: Marx predicted frequent crises in the capitalist mode of production that would eventually lead to socialism, but in reality capitalism succeeded and socialism failed, and so something must be wrong with Marxism. But the argumentation in this book cares as little for logic as it does for empirical reality.

For Hardt and Negri, Marxism is simply a given. This does not mean that it is sacrosanct: on the contrary, much of this book is devoted to moving beyond just about everything that Marx had to say about modern capitalism. Yet all these exertions are made in the name of

Marxism, including the choice of language and metaphor, the reliance on ponderous theory, and the weakness for the issuance of manifestos. Whereas Marx separated these tasks, producing an all-time best-seller as well as long volumes of historical and economic analysis, Hardt and Negri throw it all together in one meandering, wordy, and incoherent book—a book that, as the authors themselves suggest, need not be read from start to finish but can be hopscotched through if the reader prefers. (I chose to read it the old-fashioned way.)

Even if one does believe that Marx is worth consulting about the trajectory of capitalism, the notion that Marxism was concerned with an impending ecological catastrophe is the second mortal flaw in the question that Hardt and Negri pose. Marx himself was a celebrant of industry over agriculture, a determined modernist quite happy to see "the idiocy of rural life" destroyed once and for all. And the twentieth-century writers who extended Marxist theory to the relationship between capitalist societies and their colonies—Lenin and Luxemburg are the two most prominent intellectuals in this regard, and the two most discussed by Hardt and Negri—were similarly oblivious to any limits that nature might impose on man's capacity to expand. Lenin, having shed so few tears over the killing of one of nature's more interesting creatures (I mean us), was hardly likely to weep at the demise of the snail darter. It is equally difficult to imagine Luxemburg—urban, cosmopolitan, Jewish—as a lover of the Polish landscape. Ecology, far from being a term identified with the left, was actually coined by Ernst Haeckel, a German writer with distinctly fascist sympathies (see "Up from Scientism," this vol.). Thus one has to read Hardt and Negri's question many times over, so flat-out wrong are its assertions and its assumptions, in order to judge whether they can possibly be serious.

As irrelevant as ecology was to Marxism, it is very relevant to today's political activists—or militants, as these writers prefer to call them. Unlike Marx, who developed a theory and then looked for a class that might embody its realization, Hardt and Negri begin with angry and disaffected people and then try to raise a theory that might explain, or explain away, their frustration. Some (but not all) of those concerned

with the condition of the environment are indeed furious, and sometimes their fury takes radical, even violent, forms. And so Hardt and
Negri make a dangerously opportunistic move: they simply reinterpret
the tradition out of which they write to accommodate the new radicalism, as if Marxism can be moved this way or that way depending upon
who happens to be protesting what on any particular day.

Hardt and Negri provide a brief catalog of the protests that they find
most thrilling. Some of the events on their list–Tiananmen Square, the
intifada, Chiapas–are either fresh in memory or still taking place, while
others–the Los Angeles race riots in 1992 and the strikes in France in
1995 and in South Korea in 1996–are already a little hazy. The authors
quickly acknowledge that those protests were brief, inspired few imitations, and were not focused on a common enemy. Still, "we ought to be
able to recognize that although all of these struggles focused on their
own local and immediate circumstances, they all nonetheless posed
problems of supranational relevance, problems that are proper to the
new figure of imperial capitalist regulation."

The same recognition, presumably, would apply to such protest
movements as the 1999 Seattle demonstrations against the World Trade
Organization or the 2001 Genoa protests against the G-8 meeting. (Hardt
and Negri wrote an op-ed in the *New York Times* in support of the
Genoa protests.) For whether the participants in any of these events
realize it or not, Hardt and Negri instruct, they are all engaged in the
same activity, which is "a refusal of the post-Fordist regime of social
control."

Fordism! The term was coined by the Italian Marxist thinker Antonio Gramsci to characterize a society in which the assembly line no
longer organizes just the factory but spreads to society as a whole. It is
a radical term of art for industrial settings. But Mexican peasants, Chinese students, and Palestinian nationalists neither live nor work in
highly organized industrial societies, a fact that deserves to be regarded
as a problem for anyone who would interpret the Mexican, Chinese,
and Palestinian movements as evidence of a rebellion against capitalism. But Hardt and Negri hasten to reassure us that there is no problem

at all, because capitalism itself is no longer Fordist, and this opens up new possibilities for opposition.

Under Fordist modes of production, they explain, protest spreads horizontally: workers in one country would go on strike, hopefully stimulating workers in other countries to do likewise, and the eventual result (assuming the theory works, which of course it does not) would be a general strike across all nation-states that would paralyze capitalism and render it powerless. In post-Fordist conditions, by contrast, protests "are forced to leap vertically and touch immediately on the global level." Marx developed the metaphor of the mole to portray the ways in which movements of workers would bore through tunnels hidden from sight, only to emerge from time to time to make themselves seen and heard. The appropriate metaphor for the conditions in which protest movements now find themselves, in Hardt and Negri's view, is the snake. Slithering around at the edges of the new global order, these movements "are immediately subversive in themselves and do not wait on any sort of external aid or extension to guarantee their effectiveness." They are capable instead of coiling themselves up to "strike directly at the highest articulations of the imperial order."

The authors of *Empire* see no reason to exclude explicit reactionaries, including religious fundamentalists, from the catalog of post-Fordist movements that they admire. Fundamentalists, they write, are often portrayed as antimodernist, but this is Western propaganda. "It is more accurate and more useful . . . to understand the various fundamentalisms not as the re-creation of a pre-modern world, but rather as a powerful refusal of the contemporary historical passage in course." Neglecting to mention the Taliban's treatment of women, Hardt and Negri go out of their way to reassure readers of the genuinely subversive nature of the Islamic version of fundamentalism. These movements are motivated not by nostalgic attempts to reconstruct the past, but by "original thought." They are anti-Western, which means that they are anticapitalist. Properly understood, they are postmodern rather than premodern, since they engage in a refusal of Western hegemony, with the proviso that fundamentalism speaks to the losers in the globalization project and postmodernism to the winners. Hardt and Negri even leave the impression that, if they had to choose between the postmodernists in Western universities and the fundamentalists in Iran, they would prefer the latter: "The losers in the process of globalization might indeed be the ones who give us the strongest indication of the transformation in process."

We cannot know, of course, whether Hardt and Negri, in the light of the September 11 atrocities at the World Trade Center and the Pentagon, will want to change their minds about the progressive potential of Islamic fundamentalism. But their book gives no grounds on which such attacks can be condemned. For if being against the West is the sine qua non of good and effective protest, well, no one could accuse the murderers in New York and Washington of not being against Western hegemony. And if it is true, as Hardt and Negri blithely claim, that efforts to find legitimate reasons for intervening in world affairs are only a smokescreen for the exercise of hegemonic power, then the way is cleared for each and every illegitimate act of global intervention, since in the postmodern world of this book no justifiable distinctions between good and evil acts can ever be made.

Never saying so explicitly, the authors of this book, in identifying their hopes with such disparate movements of protest whatever their targets or their political coloration, are throwing over the most central proposition of Marxism: class consciousness. Workers no longer need to be aware of themselves as workers in order to bring down capitalism. They need not develop a revolutionary strategy, for under contemporary conditions "it may no longer be useful to insist on the old distinction between strategy and tactics." They do not even need to be workers. All that is required is that they set themselves up against power, whatever and wherever power happens to be.

Never mind that movements that do so can stand for wildly different objectives—an open society here, a closed society there; or that they are also, as Hardt and Negri point out, often unable or unwilling to communicate with each other. Indeed, as Hardt and Negri do not point out, they might, if they had the chance, prefer to kill one another. But this lack of communication and mutual appreciation "is in fact a strength rather than a weakness." Traditional Marxism aimed to find the weakest link in the capitalist system and to exploit it. But there are no more weak links. Capital has become so pervasive that it exposes itself nowhere, but this means that it is really exposed everywhere. Protest movements simply cannot be peripheral: since there is no center, there is no periphery. Everything that dissents—even "piercings, tattoos, punk fashion and its various imitations"—foreshadows the stirrings that are necessary to challenge the new forms that capitalism is taking.

II

MOST OF *EMPIRE* IS an exercise in nominalism, in the attempt to name, rather than to describe, to analyze, or even to condemn, the new order that its authors see emerging. Although it is presumably devoted to outlining the contours of a new mode of production, the book contains no data, offers no effort to demonstrate who owns what or holds power over whom, and provides no indicators of any of the deplorable conditions that it discusses. As if once again to distinguish itself from Marx, *Empire*, like the left Hegelians whom Marx once attacked, moves entirely at the level of ideas. Unlike the left Hegelians, however, Hardt and Negri handle ideas incompetently.

This would-be revolutionary book starts, of all places, with the ideas of Hans Kelsen, before jumping over to John Rawls and Niklas Luhmann. Each new chapter seems to suggest that Hardt and Negri, having cleared their throats, are about to turn to the world around them—but then, out of nowhere, there arrives a discussion of Augustine, Machiavelli, or Polybius. It is impossible to know which of the two authors was primarily responsible for which portions of the book, but the reader comes away with the impression that one of them—Negri—has spent so much time in prison reading and taking notes that he is determined to cram into the book everything that he has uncovered, pertinent or not.

The point of this exercise in intellectual name-dropping is to argue that imperialism has been replaced by something called "Empire." Although global in its ambitions, imperialism was dependent on the nation-state, for each imperial power attempted to organize the globe on behalf of the national corporations that it represented. In that sense, imperialism was associated with Fordism. Organized horizontally, moreover, imperialism divided the world into blocs, each controlled by a central power that looked with suspicion on–and from time to time engaged in war with–rival imperial powers. That form of capitalist organization, however much it may have concentrated the mind of Lenin, is on its way out, and Hardt and Negri bid it good riddance. Just as Marx celebrated capitalism's victory over feudalism, they exhort radicals today to take heart in the fact that imperialism is being replaced by Empire.

Empire itself emerges with postmodernity. (In its initial formulation, *postmodern* was an adjective modifying a noun such as a condition, a novel, a building, or a city; but as Hardt and Negri use the term, it is transformed into an actual thing that presumably began at a particular point in time and exists in a particular place, though neither the time nor the place is ever specified by them.) Unlike imperialism, Empire has no center and is not controlled by anyone. As the authors characteristically put it: "Empire exhausts historical time, suspends history, and summons the past and future within its own ethical order." Empire is–this is where Luhmann comes in–autopoietic, that is, it runs by itself. "The imperial machine lives by producing a context of equilibria and/or reducing complexities, pretending to put forward a project of universal citizenship and toward this end intensifying the effectiveness of its intervention over every element of the communicative relationship, all the while dissolving identity and history in a completely postmodern fashion."

Under conditions of Empire, everything is in flux and up for grabs. It no longer follows, as it did under imperialism, that economic factors determine all other aspects of life. Capitalism, especially in its Fordist forms, aimed to impose order on otherwise anarchic processes, but it was content to transform the surplus labor of workers into capital, and so it managed to stop short of exercising full control over the individual's mind and body. Post-Fordism went further: by extending the factory to social life as a whole, it also extended power's reach into schools, prisons, and asylums. People living under Empire require even more control than those forms found in early versions of post-Fordism, for the essentially post-Fordist disciplinary institutions analyzed by Michel Foucault "did not succeed in consuming them completely in the rhythm of productive practices and productive socialization; it did not reach the point of permeating entirely the consciousness and bodies of individuals, the point of treating and organizing them in the totality of their activities." In the stage in which we find ourselves now–let us call it post-post-Fordism–society is "subsumed within a power that reaches down to the ganglia of the social structure and its processes of development and reacts like a single body. Power is thus expressed as a control that extends throughout the depths of the consciousness and bodies of the population–and at the same time across the entirety of social relations."

Hardt and Negri call this process of total control "biopower," which they define as "a form of power that regulates social life from its interior, following it, interpreting it, absorbing it, and rearticulating it." By transforming Marx's economic determinism into a form of biological determinism, Hardt and Negri manage to remove every last shred of humanism in Marxism. For all his insistence that his criticism of capitalism was motivated by considerations of science rather than by considerations of morality, Marx never fully abandoned the anthropocentric character of the romantic movements out of which he emerged. He was, for one thing, persuaded that human beings possessed an irreducible nature; inspired by Prometheus, Marx took it for granted that they came equipped with a drive to create. It was precisely this productive capacity–this determination on the part of human beings to create value–that drove capitalists to try to expropriate from workers their human essence, their "species being."

But Hardt and Negri will have none of this talk of human nature, or use value, or labor power. Capital will exploit wherever and whatever it can. With biopower in command, our bodies are no longer irreducibly ours. Our bodies have instead turned against themselves; they are the very instruments by which we are controlled by forces external to us. We therefore have to "recognize our posthuman bodies and minds" and see ourselves "for the simians and cyborgs we are" before we can begin to unleash whatever creative powers we may have left over.

But all is not lost for us simians and cyborgs. Unlike the writers of the Frankfurt School, who also emphasized the authoritarian character of contemporary capitalism, writers such as Gilles Deleuze and Felix Guattari, who are the true intellectual heroes of *Empire,* recognize that efforts at total control create contradictions of their own. Here, in prose that insults language, is how Hardt and Negri summarize what they have understood: "The analysis of real subsumption, when this is understood as investing not only the economic or only the cultural dimension of society but rather the social bios itself, and when it is attentive to the modalities of disciplinarity and/or control, disrupts the linear and totalitarian figure of capitalist development." What this means is that under Empire there emerges a "paradox of power" in which all elements of social life are unified, but the very act of unification "reveals a new context, a new milieu of maximum plurality and uncontainable singularization—a milieu of the event." Even when Empire seems to rule everywhere and over everything, there are opportunities for resistance, if only those opportunities can be grasped and seen.

Although Empire is not controlled by anyone, it does require coordination, and therefore it also requires communication. Communication is to Hardt and Negri what production was to Marx: the central activity of society without which nothing else is possible. And, like production, communication requires workers, or immaterial labor, as the authors call those people who do not produce goods but instead deliver services. It thus follows that "the central role previously occupied by the labor power of mass factory workers in the production of surplus value is today increasingly filled by intellectual, immaterial, and communicative labor power." So professors have a purpose after all: they can "develop a new political theory of value that can pose the problem of this new capitalist accumulation of value at the center of the mechanism of exploitation (and thus, perhaps, at the center of potential revolt)." All those demonstrators out there who fail to communicate with each other require someone to communicate for them, and who better to do the communication than those who make the production of words central to their existence?

III

EMPIRE IS BEST UNDERSTOOD as an attempt, using Marxist jargon, to bring back to life the political urge that Marx spent much of his energy opposing: anarchism, and particularly the more destructive form of anarchism associated with writers such as Bakunin. "You are just a bunch of anarchists, the new Plato on the block will yell at us," Hardt and Negri declare, before responding that they cannot be anarchists because they speak "from the standpoint of a materiality constituted in the networks of productive cooperation, in other words, from the perspective of a humanity that is constructed productively, that is constituted through the 'common name' of freedom." I have no Platonic aspirations, but it does strike me that the account the authors provide of their enterprise is wrong on every count. *Empire* rejects materiality in favor of immaterial labor, production in favor of communication, humanity in favor of cyborgs, freedom in favor of hybridity.

The anarchist flavor of *Empire* is conveyed most strikingly by its romanticization of violence. Although by now everyone knows that there are terrorists in this world, there are no terrorists in Hardt and Negri's book. There are only people who are called terrorists, "a crude conception and terminological reduction that is rooted in a police mentality." Terms such as "ethnic terrorists" and "drug mafias" appear within quotation marks, as if no serious revolutionary could believe that there were such things. "Totalitarianism" is another pure construct, simply an invention of cold war ideology, that has been used to "denounce the destruction of the democratic sphere." Certainly the term has little to do with actual life in the Soviet Union, which Hardt and Negri describe as "a society criss-crossed by extremely strong instances of creativity and freedom."

Negri, when not in prison, has been a political philosopher, and he is the author of numerous books, manifestos, and theses on subjects ranging from Spinoza's metaphysics to the nature of insurgency under contemporary capitalism. In nearly all this work, as in *Empire,* he invariably associates violence with states in the exercise of their power, never with opposition groups and their tactics. For the latter, any action, no matter how insurrectionary, is justified. For the former, any action, no matter how peaceful, is terrorism in disguise.

From this warped perspective, all states are equally bad and all movements of opposition are equally good. Only the working of such a myopia can help the reader to understand why the authors of *Empire* are incapable of mustering any rigorous historical or moral consciousness of Nazism and its policy of Jewish extermination. In their view Nazism is capitalism, and that is the end of the story. Nazi Germany, Hardt and Negri write, far from a unique excursion into human evil, "is the ideal type of the transformation of modern sovereignty into national sovereignty and of its articulation into capitalist form."

Since Nazism is merely normal capitalism–this point of view was once associated with the Frankfurt School, and it survives almost nowhere outside the pages of this book–there is no reason to single out the Nazis or their sympathizers for crimes against humanity. Astonishingly, Hardt and Negri are worse than neutral in their discussion of the Nazi period: they actually heap praise on the ordinary Germans who supported the regime. The obedience of these citizens is called "exemplary" in this book. The authors also celebrate "their military and civil valor in the service of the nation," before moving on to identify the victims whom they valorously helped to send to Buchenwald as "communists, homosexuals, Gypsies, and others," the latter, presumably, being the Jews (whom Hardt and Negri reserve for Auschwitz).

I am not making this up. Lest anyone consider these apologetics for Nazism a misreading of my own—how can good leftists, after all, engage in a downplaying of the Holocaust?—Hardt and Negri twice acknowledge that they are completely fed up with the whole question of totalitarianism. It is certainly much less interesting to them than the depredations of Empire. The phenomenon of totalitarianism, they write, has already been described "with great fanfare" by "many (in fact too many) authors"; and then they announce, in the one sustained passage in their book devoted to Hitler and his regime, that, despite their efforts to write a book aiming to discuss everything, they plan to "leave this story to other scholars and to the disgrace of history."

It is one thing to put quotation marks around a word such as "terrorist" and to be so morally obtuse to the most violent regimes of the twentieth century. It is another thing entirely for Antonio Negri to do so. For the question of whether Negri was himself a violence-prone terrorist is still open. In April 1979, Negri, who was then a professor at the University of Padua, was arrested and charged with armed insurrection. He was not convicted on the most serious charges, which amounted to the accusation that, as the leader of the Red Brigades, he was responsible for the assassination of Christian Democratic politician Aldo Moro; but he was found guilty of lesser charges and sentenced to preventive detention. (Among other things, the judge in the case quoted from a letter written by Negri in which he said that "without weapons, the mass struggle doesn't exist.")

Determined not to go to jail, Negri won a seat in parliament, which gave him immunity; but the Italian Chamber of Deputies stripped him of it, and he fled to France in 1983. In 1997, he voluntarily returned to Italy and was incarcerated. He took this action, he said, in order to clarify the situation of other New Leftists who were in exile. He is still a prisoner, a feature of his biography that is prominently displayed by Harvard University Press on the back of *Empire*. So as not to detract from the dramatic flair of their author, the publishers neglect to mention that Negri is released during the day to live in his apartment in Rome with his girlfriend, spending only his nights in jail.

As is the case with so much of the violence associated with the New Left, it is difficult to know exactly what Negri did. We do know that Italy, like Germany, experienced considerable political violence in the 1960s and 1970s, and that many radical groups, distrustful of the cautious conservatism of the Community party, created ultraleftist sects such as Autonomia Operaia that either engaged directly in criminal acts or sought to justify them as a necessary stage in the destruction of capitalism. Negri, who was closely associated with these splinter groups as a member and a theorist, has had many opportunities since then to revisit his past and to reflect on whether the violence of the times was wrong. He has chosen not to do so. Instead he has argued that violence is built into all the institutions and all the practices of capitalism, as if to conclude that because society itself is so violent, one can hardly be surprised that its opponents tend in that direction as well. *Empire* is merely the latest of a series of books in which a completely unrepentant Negri defends himself. No wonder that efforts to win his full release from prison—efforts that will surely escalate now that Negri has received the imprimatur of America's most prestigious academic press—have failed.

With the memory of three thousand dead bodies destroyed beyond recognition by deadly terrorist attacks still so fresh, readers in America these days do not need to be reminded of the ugliness that violence brings in its wake. Yet Hardt and Negri evidently need such a reminder. Their book, as it comes to a close, contains an apologia for violence past and present that, in the light of recent events, ought to send a chill down every reader's spine. Those singled out for special praise in *Empire* include the Industrial Workers of the World, or Wobblies, an oft-romanticized anarchosyndicalist group that Hardt and Negri manage to describe as "radical republican." IWW militants, they write, offer a prototype of resistance to Empire. "The Wobbly constructed associations among working people from below, through continuous agitation, and while organizing them gave rise to utopian thought and revolutionary knowledge." A similar movement today would take the form of what Hardt and Negri call a "postmodern posse." They are attracted to this term because posse is Latin for "having power," but it does not escape their notice that the term is also identified with the posse comitatus of Hollywood Westerns. (They neglect to mention that this is also the name of choice of some of America's most violently inclined right-wing sects.)

The Marxist historian E. J. Hobsbawm once wrote a book called *Primitive Rebels,* about seemingly medieval gangs of Robin Hood–like bandits, such as the Neapolitan Camorra or the Tuscan Lazzarettists, that persisted into the nineteenth and twentieth centuries in Italy and Spain. Sometimes anarchistic, sometimes fascistic, these millenarian movements appealed not to the urban workers of capitalism, but to the displaced Lumpenproletariat. When Hardt and Negri celebrate rap groups or window-smashing anarchists, it is these bandits, who have always been viewed with great suspicion by Marxists, that they see.

To such movements of resistance, Hardt and Negri offer praise but no advice. Never has a revolutionary manifesto been so devoid of actual content as the one contained in this book. The real militant against Empire, Hardt and Negri insist, is not one "who acts on the basis of duty and discipline, who pretends that his or her actions are deducted from an ideal plan." (The Jesuits are, somewhat bizarrely, offered as an example of such discipline, but any Marxist would read this as a rejection of a Leninist revolutionary vanguard.) No, to be a militant you must turn the biopower directed against you inside out, by exploring "the productive cooperation of mass intellectuality and affective networks, the productivity of postmodern biopolitics." Hobsbawm wrote of the chiliastic bandits of the nineteenth century that, whatever their other differences, they shared "a fundamental vagueness about the actual way in which the new society will be brought about," and no better description of anarchism in its postmodern form has yet been written.

The anarchism advocated in *Empire* does have one rather idiosyncratic feature: it is informed by Christianity. Hardt and Negri find in Christendom a precursor for Empire—not that odd a comparison if we live in a world in which chronological time no longer means anything, but an odd comparison certainly if particular historical periods are built on the events that preceded them. Once Christendom is introduced as a topic, it becomes immediately clear that the great theorist of *Empire* is not Marx, it is Augustine. *Empire* is a postmodern twist on *The City of God*. "In Empire," Hardt and Negri write, echoing Augustine's denunciation of Rome, "corruption is everywhere," reflected in "the supreme government of Empire and its vassal administrations, the most refined and the most rotten administrative police forces, the lobbies of the ruling classes, the mafias of rising social groups, the churches and sects, the perpetuators and persecutors of scandal, the great financial conglomerates, and everyday economic transactions." Although Hardt and Negri would never use such language, they are clearly persuaded that life under Empire is suffused with sin.

And redemption will come from the multitude, who despite their oppression under empire–or Empire–remain pure in heart. In them, one can see the emergence of the new city that will put us at one with the world. Unlike Augustine's, of course, their city cannot be the divine one, since "the multitude today . . . resides on the imperial surfaces where there is no God the Father and no transcendence." Instead, they will create "the earthly city of the multitude," which the authors esoterically define as "the absolute constitution of labor and cooperation." About the practical question of how this can be done, Hardt and Negri have nothing significant to say. "The only response that we can give to these questions is that the action of the multitude becomes political primarily when it begins to confront directly and with an adequate consciousness the central repressive operations of Empire." This, too, is a Christian conception of revolution. We cannot know how we will be saved; we must recognize that if only we have faith, a way will be found.

Empire ends not with a paean to Marx or Lenin, but with a prayer for Francis of Assisi: "To denounce the poverty of the multitude he adopted that common condition and discovered there the ontological power of a new society. The communist militant does the same, identifying in the common condition of the multitude its enormous wealth. Francis . . . posed a joyous life, including all of being and nature, the animals, sister moon, brother sun, the birds of the field, the poor and exploited humans, together against the will and power of corruption."

Pierce your ears, paint your face, run angry through the streets, and you too can be a saint. It is not clear whether you will ever actually stop companies from merging or bankers from providing loans, but the glimpse that you will be vouchsafed of the heavenly city that is available to us on Earth, so long as you are sufficiently militant, is reward enough. If you do all this, you will find yourself in "a revolution that no power will control—because biopower and communism, cooperation and revolution remain together, in love, simplicity, and also innocence. This is the irrepressible lightness and joy of being communist."

IV

THERE IS NO IDEA in *Empire* that has not been expressed before. In a rare moment of lucidity, Michael Hardt correctly told Emily Eakin of the *New York Times* that "Toni and I don't think of this as a very original book. We're putting together a variety of things that others have said." Still, *Empire* has become something of a publishing sensation. The *Times* has pronounced that it has "buzz," the most enviable epithet of all. It has sold out in bookstores around the country; it is being translated into at least ten languages; and it has been featured in gushing media accounts, including Eakin's uninformed account in the *Times.* (For the *Times*'s reporter on "Arts and Ideas," testimony from tired Marxists such as Stanley Aronowitz or Fredric Jameson is taken as proof that *Empire* may be the next big thing among other equally washed-out Marxists.)

Still, there is no denying the book's relevance. The fate of *Empire* and the fate of globalized protests against globalization have become intertwined, as if the one has become dependent on the other. Every revolution needs its obscure, well-thumbed, and probably unread paperback, and now the anarchists and the new caravan of protesters have one to call their own. This is a terrible shame. After two decades in which the left has been reduced to defending such reactionary policies as classification by race and the suppression of free speech, the question of global inequality has finally emerged, and with it emerged an opportunity for the left to regain its sanity.

One need not defend socialism, whatever that means these days, in order to recognize that there is something profoundly wrong about the staggeringly huge gaps in wealth that exist between the world's richest regions and its poorest regions. Any movement that directed itself against the arrogant and aloof policies of the world's richest countries, and that did so by appealing to commonly agreed-upon conceptions of justice, would be in a position to achieve some real good in the world. From the appalling costs of anti-AIDS medicines in Africa to the efforts by the International Monetary Fund to impose stringent requirements on countries that are barely able to feed their own people, there are more than enough good and burning issues that could not only enable the left to gain the moral high ground, but could also win the hearts of moderate and even conservative people who have little at stake in defending the policies of increasingly rapacious global corporations.

But such a sensible and decent left will not emerge if *Empire*–a lazy person's guide to revolution–has its way. The authors of this book, having taken no steps to learn anything about what globalization actually is and what its continuation would actually mean, cannot inspire their readers to do likewise. Rather than developing a tutorial attitude toward protest, bringing to younger militants the knowledge of history and the wisdom of experience, they glorify know-nothingism and turn obsequious before fascists. Instead of reminding protesters that politics is a demanding business, they romanticize the self-indulgence of punks and freaks. Faced with the difficulties of constructing a theoretical account of how an ever-changing capitalism has changed once again, they paper over their contradictions with jargon and borrow promiscuously from every academic fashion. There is indeed corruption in the contemporary world–and none more noteworthy in this context than the intellectual corruption that can enable a book as shabby as this one to be taken seriously by anyone.

Empire is to social and political criticism what pornography is to literature. It flirts with revolution as if one society can be replaced by another as easily as one body can be substituted for another. It gives academic readers the thrill of engaging with the ideas of the New Left's most insurrectionary days, all the while pretending that the author of these ideas is an "independent researcher and writer," as Harvard's book jacket calls Negri, while secretly hoping–imagine the glamour in radical academic circles that this would give him!–that he really was guilty of the acts for which he was imprisoned. For angry militants who have never read Bakunin but who understand in their gut that every destructive urge is a creative one, *Empire* offers the support of professors who are supposed to know what they are talking about; and if one is too busy running through the streets to grasp the full implications of what Homi K. Bhabha says about binary divisions, or to reflect on Althusser's reading of *The Prince*, one can at least come away rinsed in the appropriate critique. *Empire* is a thoroughly nonserious book on a most serious topic, an outrageously irresponsible tour through questions of power and violence–questions that, as we cannot help but remember as we mourn our dead in Manhattan and Washington, demand the greatest responsibility on the part of both writers and readers.

The New Left got a lot of things wrong, but it got one thing right: institutions that wield tremendous authority over the lives of ordinary people cannot be trusted with unlimited power, for, in the absence of checks and constraints on their activities, they will do whatever they can to maximize their advantage. As the New Left turned violent and sought support from the fringes, it lost that significant insight, eventually decomposing into sectarian paranoia or academic obscurantism. The most remarkable accomplishment of *Empire* is to combine both of those degenerations into a frightfully unstable mixture. There is bad news in this, and worse news. The bad news is that antiglobalization protesters, should they find anything of value in this book, will lead their very promising movement into the same dead ends as the New Left. The worse news is that, to reverse Marx's famous dictum, this will happen the second time as tragedy rather than as farce.

The Revolution That Never Was

I

IN 1948, RICHARD WEAVER published *Ideas Have Consequences,* a book that would become, according to Frank Meyer, "the *fons et origo* of the contemporary American conservative movement." Weaver explored the consequences of one particular idea: that there were no transcendental truths lying beyond the capacity of man to make sense out of the world. Scientific and philosophical rationalism led to the denial of original sin, Weaver argued, and so man was cut off from eternals and forced to live with nothingness. Ideas, then, could be very pernicious things; but the title of Weaver's book–chosen, incidentally, by his publisher–left the opposite impression. For if bad ideas had consequences, so presumably did good ideas. Conservatives had never quite lived down Mill's description of them as "the stupid party"–especially in America, whose best conservative minds, Henry James and T. S. Eliot, preferred to live abroad. Weaver's manifesto was read to suggest that American conservatives must develop ideas of their own.

Yet another conclusion, equally pertinent to the fate of conservatism in contemporary America, could be drawn from Weaver's title. If ideas have consequences, so does the absence of ideas. Nothing is more important to an understanding of contemporary conservatism, I think, than this stark but little noticed fact: despite decades of trying, and a golden opportunity handed to them by liberal failure, conservatives in America have been unable to come up with any sustained and significant ideas capable of giving substance to their complaints against the contemporary world. I say ideas, not slogans.

This should have been the golden age of conservatism. Liberals–understood in the New Deal, Keynesian sense of the term–had quite a run for their money; but time runs out on even the most consensual of philosophies, and by the 1980s the twin triumphs of Reaganism and Thatcherism appeared to herald a revolution in thought and in policy. No longer would conservatism be a "remnant," attractive only to "superfluous" men. (The words are Albert J. Nock's.) Barely containing their triumphalism, conservative intellectuals bypassed universities to create think tanks that spewed out books, articles, and position papers at dizzying rates. No activity of the modern state–from its economic interventions to its drug policy–was left uncriticized.

And so liberals became the tired party, tied down by their constituents to unimaginative tinkerings at the margins. To their astonishment, 1968ers discovered that younger intellectuals were more likely to be attracted to the right than to be impressed by war stories about Mayor Daley or Bull Connor. The term *social critic*, once reserved for the cantankerous C. Wright Mills, now seemed to apply to the cantankerous Allan Bloom. An ideology that had been attractive primarily to Southern racists, Midwestern isolationists, aristocratic European émigrés, and devout Catholics all of a sudden dominated the dinner parties of Georgetown and Manhattan.

Out of such ferment, two things should have happened. One is that someone should have written a serious, original, philosophically fundamental book that would do for conservatism what John Rawls had done for liberalism: systematize its principles, or, if that were considered uncongenial to the conservative point of view, explore in analytical depth its relevance for contemporary conundrums. The other is that, at least in part based on such a book, governments should have introduced programs that not only marked a sharp break with liberal ideas (there were plenty of those), but also demonstrated that conservative policies could work on their own terms. Neither happened.

Consider the case of the United States. Disenchanted with liberalism, Americans voted for Ronald Reagan and then continued to love him because he never took the conservatism that he preached all that seriously. They elected Bill Clinton and then decided to keep a check on him by supporting Republicans for the House and the Senate. Conservatives responded to the latter opportunity first by trying to shut down the government and then, when that proved to be a disaster, by trying to shut down the government again. Americans took one look at the conservative members of the House of Representatives who managed the Senate trial of Bill Clinton and reached an unequivocal conclusion: if conservatism means a powerful state pushing its nose into private affairs, judging the morality of others while acting immorally itself, trampling on tradition, scorning bipartisanship, trying systematically to overturn the results of two elections, and all along insisting that the voice of the people ought to be ignored, then they did not very much like conservatism. And when a conservative finally did assume the presidency in 2001, he did so without winning a majority of the popular vote and hitched his domestic program to a tax cut justified by appeals to Keynesianism and the pro-growth agenda of John F. Kennedy.

Surely the governmental failure of conservatism is one of the consequences of the failure of its ideologists to produce lasting ideas. The financial resources poured into the think tanks were enormous, but all the furious publication notwithstanding, conservatives seemed congenitally unable to write significant books. Irving Kristol's magnum opus was a collection of articles. Roger Scruton, the leading conservative intellectual in Britain, turned to the defense of foxhunting and joined with leftist romantics to denounce the corrosive effects of cities. James Q. Wilson and Mary Ann Glendon wrote thoughtful and persuasive books on bureaucracies and rights, and Wilson dealt with larger themes in *The Moral Sense,* but they still seemed to deal with the parts rather than the whole of a conservative mentality. Charles Murray, an especially well-financed conservative policy wonk, found himself unable to compete with social scientists on their technical terrain; *Losing Ground* and *The Bell Curve* exposed him as little more than a mean-spirited soul spouting quasi-academic language. The most interesting writers that Peter Steinfels listed in *The Neo-Conservatives* in 1979– Daniel Patrick Moynihan, Daniel Bell, Nathan Glazer, Seymour Martin

Lipset–turned out to be either liberals or people with serious reservations about the conservative campaign against affirmative action.

Instead of moving forward, conservatism actually moved backward in the 1990s. Before Barry Goldwater, as George Nash recounts in *The Conservative Intellectual Movement in America,* conservatives were bitterly divided among libertarians, antimajoritarians, and anticommunists. Frank Meyer's contribution to the movement was to push for "fusionism," a way of uniting conservatives around key principles while avoiding the issues that drove Friedrich von Hayek–whose faith in free markets allowed little place for right-wing hostility toward progress–to write essays such as "Why I Am Not a Conservative." Such unity, always precarious, is now in complete disarray. The anticommunist wing of conservatism has had no role to play since 1989. The gap between libertarians and Christian conservatives in the Republican party is as wide, and as unstable, as the gap that once existed between Southern Bourbons and African Americans in the Democratic party. If there are any antimajoritarian aristocrats still thumbing their noses at the masses, they are irrelevant to a movement that now thinks of itself as populist. These days, conservatives can bear to be in the same room with each other so long as they never talk about ideas.

Some day the history of this great intellectual failure will be written. It will likely emphasize the paradox of success: conservatives got too much money, and too many votes, too soon. It may have been wise for conservative thinkers to avoid the universities–where no idea is ever too arcane–but think tanks proved to have problems of their own: worried about pleasing their funders, unable to resist the lure of talk shows and press conferences, and exacerbating ideology rather than sharpening it, conservative think tanks destroyed any possibility of serious intellectual work. And convinced that their ideas were winning support from the voters, conservatives saw no need to lead rather than to follow public opinion–until the Clinton imbroglio, when their invocation of Burkean theories of representation proved insincere.

But as important as such explanations may be, they do not go far enough. For the conservative failure may not be a matter of this decision or that. There is another possibility to be considered, which is that conservatism itself is an impossible idea, at least for the twentieth century. Twenty years of conservative excitement seemed to give the lie to the theory of Louis Hartz that no conservatism was possible in the United States; but the conservative failure in this decade suggests that Hartz may have been right all along.

II

IF CONSERVATISM IS ABOUT anything, it is about balance. Poised somewhere between the radical's desire to move forward and the reactionary's insistence that backward is the only way to go, the conservative emphasizes proportion in all things. The trick is to get the mixture right: a sufficient amount of passion cut with just enough reason; a willingness to accept change in order that things be kept essentially the same; an appreciation of the particular without a total rejection of the universal; a reverence for tradition and faith set off against a defense of the market and its insistence on individual freedom. Yet balance is precisely what contemporary conservatives seem to lack.

This deformity may be due to their inheritance. Two great Europeans have disproportionately shaped contemporary American conservatism, Michael Oakeshott and Leo Strauss. Almost nothing that one said could be balanced with anything that the other said. Even more important, neither could find balance in his own work. Oakeshott was a proponent of Little Conservatism—a disposition, he called it, as if all that being conservative required was the right psychology. Strauss taught a Big Conservatism; his ideas were rarely expressed in the revolutionary style of the manifesto, but anyone who took him seriously understood that the achievement of his ideals would require a radical reconstruction of the contemporary world. Yet there was one point on which the ideas of these two thinkers converged. If Little Conservatism left the world pretty much in place because it was resigned to defeat, Big Conservatism also left the world in place because its ambitions were utterly unrealizable.

Little Conservatism is temperamentally unsuited to risk or, in Oakeshott's terms, to the "dangerous and the difficult." One sees in Oakeshott's writings a hostility toward planning, a weariness with proclamation, a distrust of experts, and, above all else, a suspicion not only of grand schemes to change the world but also of grand ideas designed to understand the world. Oakeshott is to conservatism what Isaiah Berlin is to liberalism: an essayist rather than a systematizer, a conversationalist more than a sermonizer, a writer who, while not immodest about displaying his learning, also takes pains to make himself clear.

Human beings are not by nature conservative, Oakeshott believed. Fascinated by the new and the unknown, they are too quick to throw caution to the winds in the hope that they can find something better tomorrow than what surrounds them today. If it is to resist such trends, conservatism cannot seek its own goals too quickly or too ambitiously. "What makes a conservative disposition in politics intelligible," Oakeshott wrote, as if to Strauss, "is nothing to do with natural law or a providential order, nothing to do with morals or religion; it is the observation of our current manner of living combined with the belief . . . that governing is a specific and limited activity."

Resigned as he was to offering instructions in how to live properly, Oakeshott was not a theorist of a conservative road to power. If anything, he seemed to have anticipated the idea that conservatives might want to gain control of government in order to reform human nature—and warned against it. Conservatives do not win the battle for ideas by insisting on one right way to live and then trying to harness the force of the state to ensure that people live the way that conservatives believe they should live. Quite the contrary. Much like contemporary liberals from Habermas to Rorty, Oakeshott admired the conversation—"the greatest but also the most hardly sustained of all the accomplishments of mankind," he called it—as a model for political education. "In a conversation the participants are not engaged in an inquiry or a debate; there is no 'truth' to be discovered, no proposition to be proved, no conclusion sought." This is a drawing-room conservatism, a high-table complacency, lacking the passions and the convictions that can stir masses to repudiate the decadent liberalism around them.

Strauss could hardly be said to have wanted to stir masses. If anything, Strauss clung to then-very-fashionable ideas about mass society that saw ordinary people as little more than "unintelligent, uninformed, deceitful, and irrational." But Strauss's Big Conservatism could not be further in sensibility or in ambition from Oakeshott's Little Conservatism. Many of Strauss's students insist that their mentor was not a conservative at all, that Strauss was, properly understood, a liberal—even, in his own way, a democrat. Strauss himself once said that the friend of liberal democracy should not be a flatterer of liberal democrats.

But these are unpersuasive definitions. If you are prepared to believe that liberalism is another word for "human excellence or being honorable and decent," and that liberalism existed in pre-Socratic Athens, and that one of the greatest liberals of all time was Lucretius, then, yes, Strauss was a liberal. But if you believe that liberalism is a political philosophy committed in one way or another to the proposition that individuals ought to have the autonomy to determine for themselves the appropriate morality to guide their lives, then Strauss must be understood as one of liberalism's most implacable critics.

Genuine autonomy could never be realized in a modern democracy, according to Strauss. In order to lead good lives, people needed a standard of excellence that could only be provided by a cultivated elite. The ancients had such standards, and, if properly read, their texts could offer guidance to those able to read between the lines to divine the truths that they contained. And while such capable readers do exist—Strauss left no doubt that he was one of them—modern people, attracted to the superficial and the vulgar, will surely be unwilling to heed them.

Like Oakeshott, Strauss had no interest in developing a plan to shape the world in the image of his ideas, though he did produce a number of disciples who pursued careers in the political world. Yet Strauss possessed a temperament far removed from Oakeshottian caution. His was the voice of didactic instruction: a one-way conversation, if a conversation at all. His goal was Truth—the one unambiguous standard for judging political action. Reading between his lines, one can detect hints of a mentality not altogether dissimilar from Lenin's theory of a vanguard party. Those blessed with the correct ideas just might come to serve as modern princes capable of leading their society, unbeknownst to its members, to greater excellence. No wonder that, for so many, reading Strauss was an exhilarating experience. Here, in its cryptic way, was a chance to save the world.

American conservatism is torn between Oakeshott and Strauss, or torn between its psychology and its politics. If it lives by its principles of gradualism and moderation, it is prevented from offering a program bold enough to grasp history and bring it to a stop. If it seeks boldness in vision, it loses all connection with the sort of conservative temper that might prove attractive to ordinary people upset with the disruptions that modern capitalism has produced in their lives. The legacy of Oakeshott and Strauss is not a rich body of ideas upon which contemporary conservatism can build a philosophical and political worldview. What they have bequeathed to conservatism is a spectacular contradiction—a reminder of the impossibility of conservatism in the modern age.

III

NO WONDER, THEN, THAT so many contemporary conservatives spend so much of their time attacking liberalism. Nobody has undertaken that task with more energy and zeal than the British philosopher John Gray, whose *Post-Liberalism,* in its shift from defending Thatcher to defending the Greens, remains consistent in its distaste for the liberalism that lies in between, Gray's admiration for Isaiah Berlin notwithstanding. A recent American version of this familiar genre comes from the philosopher John Kekes.

As Kekes acknowledges in *Against Liberalism,* there is no one easily identifiable thing that he can oppose; there have been many liberal writers, some of whose ideas are distinct from others. Still, Kekes believes that liberalism does promote certain fundamental values, and that the most fundamental of them is autonomy, which "requires the kind of control that involves an unforced choice among alternatives that the agent has reasonably evaluated in the light of sufficient understanding of the significance of choosing one among the available alternatives."

The problem, for Kekes, is that evil exists in the world. If we allow individuals to be autonomous, then they may use their unfettered powers to do evil things. Under such conditions, liberals face an impossible dilemma: if they insist on autonomy, they enhance the amount of cruelty in the world, but if they demand the diminishment of cruelty first, they undermine their commitment to autonomy. Much of liberal thought, says Kekes, is devoted to unsuccessful attempts to avoid this dilemma. When liberals argue backward from the fact of evil to the view that anyone who commits such an act could not have been "really" autonomous, for no autonomous person would choose an evil course, they are attaching preconditions to agency which, whether they admit it or not, reduce the agent's autonomy to establish his own conditions, and in this way they are compromising themselves philosophically.

And other values prominently identified with liberalism face similar internal inconsistencies, in Kekes's account. Liberals believe that a person cannot be autonomous if his conditions of life are so unequal with respect to others that he is unable to develop his capacities for autonomy. Yet programs designed to help him achieve such equality, because they require takings from others, will reduce autonomy elsewhere. Worse, a commitment to equality means taking resources away from those whose lives manifest important virtues such as self-control and giving them to those whose lives, for better or worse, have been marked by vice. Hence liberalism, despite its self-proclaimed affinity with justice, is really unjust, since it is incapable of honoring the real meaning of justice: arrangements which allow individuals to get what they deserve. Finally, Kekes argues that liberals are correct to insist on the importance of pluralism, but that their single-minded pursuit of the goal of autonomy, which is viewed as trumping any and all other considerations, gives liberalism an excessively monist character.

Kekes believes that if one can simply point out the logical inconsistencies of liberalism, then its unworkability will become apparent. But political philosophies are not developed to meet tests of scrutiny developed by academic philosophers. Any comprehensive set of ideas whose purpose is to guide individuals and societies to do the right thing could, of course, strive for consistent principles; and if it achieved perfect consistency, it might, depending on one's taste, be attractive as a moral philosophy. But it would be useless as a political philosophy. The realm of politics is a realm of inconsistencies—between values, goals, strategies, persons, groups, states. If there were only one way to attain justice, liberty, or equality—or if those terms referred to the same good called by different names—then there would be no clash of people trying to achieve those ends, and therefore no need for all those institutions—parties, leaders, representative bodies, interest groups, and campaigns—that exist to adjudicate between competing ends.

This does not mean that we ought to celebrate political philosophies for their incoherence. But surely it is a primary fact for any philosophy of politics that human beings are complicated creatures who often desire mutually exclusive ends. For this reason, political philosophies developed to guide the actions of human beings need to be concerned with the actual consequences, and the peculiarities of human psychology, and the variations of time and place, and the likelihood of unanticipated consequences. Conservatism, at its most attractive, welcomes contingency over consistency. That is what makes it so odd for Kekes, in the name of conservatism, to criticize liberalism because its worldview leads to dilemmas that in turn demand political choices. To charge liberalism with incoherence in this sense is really to acknowledge its strength.

Still, there are some very unattractive varieties of contemporary liberalism, and Kekes has properly identified them. One winces, for example, to read Ronald Dworkin on abortion and euthanasia. He begins in good liberal fashion by appealing to moderation and reason, and he concludes by defining his principles in a way that works to the advantage only of those who support his version of what liberalism requires. His liberalism is a rigged liberalism. Yet the problem with such versions of liberalism is that they strive for precisely what Kekes demands of a political philosophy: a relentless commitment to principle. It may be true, as Kekes points out, that they fail to achieve that commitment; but what makes such versions of liberalism illiberal is that they try in the first place. Liberalism remains essentially an unfinished project. Its tenacity would be impossible without a certain protean quality that is bound to frustrate its critics. Against such a target, Kekes's bullets cannot even wound.

Paul Edward Gottfried, like John Gray and John Kekes, is a conservative who cannot help but include liberalism in the title of his book. *After Liberalism: Mass Democracy in the Managerial State* begins, as do so many of these kinds of books, by acknowledging that the philosophy to which it is opposed takes many forms: once identified with individual freedom against the designs of the state, liberalism has become a defense of statism. Whatever form they take, however, all contemporary versions of liberalism, or so Gottfried wishes to show, are committed to a particular version of the good, and they are not averse to forcing people's adherence to that version when they are otherwise inclined. Sometimes this element of coercion is hidden; Rawls, according to Gottfried, never discusses power and shies away from any realistic consideration of what form the difference principle should take in practice because "liberals do not want to be seen as imposing their will upon others." At other times, liberals are quite content to reveal their debts to statists such as Hegel, for they have been the most explicit advocates for the emergence of an administrative class determined to ensure obedience to its vision.

In recent years public administration has lost much of its luster, as it became identified with cumbersome public planning and governmental inefficiency. But other forms of liberal statism survive, as Gottfried reminds us. Liberals, for one thing, are strongly committed to a form of therapeutic politics. In theory, therapeutic ideals are pluralistic in the sense that, unlike forms of religious absolutism, they insist on a relativistic stance toward competing conceptions of the good. But in an age in which the state has gained the power that the church has lost,

pluralism is a sham, for it will inevitably side only with those conceptions of the good that have the power of the state behind them—and
those will be liberal conceptions.

Since the managerial state and the ideology of pluralism have
been "the defining features of contemporary Western life," liberalism
is, as Gramsci would have put it, hegemonic. It is true, Gottfried
acknowledges, that people want what the liberal state provides; they
have not exactly demanded a full rollback of the welfare state. Yet Gottfried has no doubts that the price of liberalism's hegemony is huge.
For we have been taught, by thinkers from Cicero to Carl Schmitt, that
the subject of politics is the majesty of power. It should reward the vir-
tuous and punish the wicked. Its vast powers should be used sparingly
but purposively to "shape and reshape people's lives." The liberal
state, with its vast reach of powers, certainly shapes people's lives, but
without the majesty, and without sufficient checks. Hiding its coercive
capacities behind a language of caring, liberalism (this is Gottfried
speaking) is both adrift and power-hungry, an unstable combination
bound to carry out fantastic damage before its powers can be brought
under control.

In their own way, Kekes and Gottfried are fighting the war between
Little Conservatism and Big Conservatism that was begun by
Oakeshott and Strauss. Gottfried writes in the apocalyptic tones of Big
Conservatism. He makes no attempt to apply the tools of analytic philosophy to an examination of liberalism's incoherence, as if modern
philosophy were a part of the problem with which liberalism is
inevitably linked. Gottfried harkens back to an even older version of
American conservatism than Straussianism, to an older tone (it is
Richard Weaver's tone) of hopeless rage against the modern world. It is
almost refreshing to read a writer so reactionary that he is willing to
defend the authors of *The Bell Curve,* to explain away the anti-Semitism
of Jean-Marie Le Pen, to describe the racist Southern League as a "pop-
ulist-regionalist movement," and to characterize writers such as Jean
Bethke Elshtain, Elizabeth Fox-Genovese, and myself as socialist.

Gottfried is so far outside the mainstream of conventional thinking that his book, for all its quirks, is actually quite interesting. He is correct to see Mill's *On Liberty* as a transitional document in the transformation of liberalism into an administrative force, for that short book does, alas, elucidate a "vision of a new clerisy crafting and directing a democratic order." Similarly, Gottfried quite rightly sees a tension in the writings of John Dewey between his proclaimed commitment to pluralism and his admiration for administrative planning. (It is not a contradiction that can be resolved by such Deweyan deceptions as faith in science.)

Unlike many American conservatives, moreover, Gottfried is multilingual, and he brings to the attention of his readers obscure European writers who are as offbeat as he is. Still, there is no way that Gottfried can overcome the fact that his book feasts off the liberalism it denounces. Citing the work of Stephen Holmes, Gottfried points out that liberalism survives by attacking its enemies. Yet Holmes's tone is the exception among liberals, whereas Gottfried's is the rule among conservatives. Finding fault with liberalism continues to substitute for the conservative understanding of the modern world that never seems to issue from the pens of conservative writers.

IV

RECOGNIZING THAT SOMETHING MUST be said about what conservatism is, John Kekes published *A Case for Conservatism* as a follow-up to *Against Liberalism*. As the reader might suppose from his philosophical criticism of liberal principles, Kekes believes, unlike Oakeshott, that it is possible to offer a systematic treatment of what it means to be a conservative. Yet Kekes's conservatism remains Little Conservatism, for in his effort to show that one can "articulate the basic beliefs of conservatism, show that they are true, and defend them against criticism," he robs conservatism of high historical and intellectual drama.

Liberals argue that rights, justice, and equality come first, while other conditions—prosperity, security, or order—come later, if at all. But conservatives, according to Kekes, believe in the value of all these goods. They do not establish one or two of them as always "trumping" the others. Instead they resolve conflicts among the values temporarily, based not on principle but on what works in specific circumstances to maximize all of them. This makes conservatives reflective rather than traditional. They cannot merely defend what exists, or what used to exist; they must show that certain sets of arrangements actually do work to permit as many people as possible to lead good lives. Kekes's conservatism is decidedly Humean. It does not set itself up in opposition to the Enlightenment. It understands itself as offering a more realistic way of achieving Enlightenment goals than theories of utopian perfectibility.

In theory, Kekes continues, conservatism is open to many ways that good lives can be realized, but it is prepared to rule out-of-bounds possibilities that would make leading good lives impossible. Hence conservatism is a philosophy of limits. There will be certain freedoms that people will claim which, for conservatism to be possible, will have to be denied. Lest we assume that conservatism stands for repression, however, we first must recognize that what is permissible and what is not permissible exists on three levels. There are certain things that are universally true–for example, that murder or slavery so violate human dignity that they cannot be allowed. Other things are permissible or not, depending on societal considerations: what is not tolerated in some places–say, homosexuality–may be tolerated in other places. Finally, there is an individual level of morality. Each person, by participating with others around him, will or will not find a match between the forbidden and his own conceptions of good character. Since conservatism recognizes these three levels, Kekes argues, it is more committed to pluralism than is liberalism. "Conservatives can readily acknowledge that some particular beliefs hold on one level and go on to deny without inconsistency that it holds on another level." The philosophical incoherence that he denounces in liberalism magically becomes flexibility when it appears in conservatism.

As he would be the first to acknowledge, Kekes's version of conservatism is not one that all conservatives would share. If one considers the problem historically, indeed, very few would have shared this version, for conservatism developed as a defense of those social classes, customs, and ideals that were left in the dust by the rapid development of capitalism—and, eventually, the democracy that followed in its wake. "I think that wise and good men ought to rule those who are foolish and bad," wrote James Fitzjames Stephen in 1874. Those Strauss-like sentiments, it seems to me, constitute true conservatism, and Paul Gottfried, who quotes this sentence longingly, is a conservative because he admires them.

Thinkers who preferred some kind of natural aristocracy to modern democracy could be more readily found in Europe, where there was an aristocracy, than in the United States. In his useful anthology *Conservatism: An Anthology of Social and Political Thought from David Hume to the Present*, Jerry Z. Muller provides a well thought-out selection of classical texts, from the obvious choices of Hume, de Maistre, and Burke (though not Coleridge) to the more obscure. Among the latter was Justus Möser (1720–94), who, in arguing against a well-meaning Habsburg ordinance giving illegitimate children the same rights as legitimate ones, sounds eerily contemporary when he writes that "in some states more has been done for whores and their children in recent decades than for wives in the last millennium."

Muller does include some Americans in his book—James Madison, Rufus Choate, Irving Kristol—and he could have chosen others: Irving Babbitt or the Southern Agrarians. But in defending the notion that one can properly speak of an American conservatism, Muller also acknowledges the central fact that what American conservatism tries to conserve are the fruits of a constitutional system won through revolution. For this reason, the reader comes away from his anthology convinced that conservatism, if it means anything distinctive at all, means the defense of an order that never really took hold in the United States.

This impression is reinforced by Muller's introductory attempt to offer a definition of conservatism. Rooted more in sociology than in moral philosophy, Muller defines the essence of conservatism as "historical utilitarianism." The very survival of an institution is a reason for believing that it must serve some purpose which ought to be defended. Familiarity, as Muller puts it, breeds comfort, not contempt. Such a definition would seem to make little room for Hayek, for the market is a relatively young institution. Still, Muller points out, it evolves in a Darwinian sense as the most efficient mechanism for what it does, and in that sense it represents a form of historical utilitarianism. Once we understand the premium that conservatives place on historical survival, we can also understand why conservatives are skeptical of human reason. "If there you wish to conserve all, consecrate all": de Maistre's dictum has its own power. Institutions that have survived historically are likely to be revered only if we do not ask how they came into being and whether they still work.

Muller argues that conservatism is not necessarily an anti-Enlightenment phenomenon. There were, as he puts it, many Enlightenments, some more hospitable to conservatism than others. But his inclusion of de Maistre and thinkers like him also makes clear the degree to which conservatism finds unacceptable one particularly powerful form taken by modernity: the notion that popular majorities using their own mental powers can choose for themselves the political and social arrangements under which they will live. To assemble the best conservative writers, as Muller has done, is to raise the awkward question of whether elites in Western history have done enough to justify deference to their once-unquestioned privileges. Voters who have observed those elites lead the twentieth century into one disaster after another are not apt to vote for platforms that ask them to accept their own intellectual inferiority.

Since conservatism began as a protest against modern capitalistic democracy, it faces dilemmas as unresolvable as liberalism's dilemmas. The conservative dilemma, in Kekesian terms, is this. For conservatives to believe in any transcendental values against which actual societies ought to be judged, they have to assert the priority of first principles. But the first principles that conservatives have historically asserted—God's will, natural right, rule of the aristocracy, racial supremacy—all render them irrelevant to societies in which popular rule is viewed as a preciously guarded asset. Conservatism can be faithful to its historical roots, it can be intellectually elegant and bursting with philosophical integrity—and completely irrelevant to the actual societies that exist in the world today. Or it can be a significant force in the modern world, but only by becoming opportunistic, unwilling to assert its true agenda, and eventually transforming itself into the very liberalism it claims to detest.

Kekes's *A Case for Conservatism* is a valuable book because it demonstrates how far one self-described conservative is willing to go in the latter direction. Consider Kekes's treatment of the question of what moral beliefs and practices a society ought to permit. At his universal level, no problem exists, since a society seeking to make good lives possible would make illegal those practices that violate human respect and dignity at all times and in all places. But once we move from the universal level to the societal, the issue becomes dicier. At that level, Kekes argues, the limits of what is permissible and what is not permissible ought to be guided by the moral traditions of the particular society in question, for those traditions have become a "second nature" deeply embedded in the consciousness of those who live in that society. Yet the traditions of some societies at some times have included barbaric, immoral practices.

May a conservative criticize the traditions of his society if those traditions violate human dignity? Kekes answers in the affirmative. He is not one of those who believe that if you like Sicily, you must like the Mafia. One can—though Kekes does not say how—separate out the bad from the good without damaging the tradition. And even good moral traditions, when they are "unresponsive to technological, demographic, or other changes in the non-moral circumstances of life," can be criticized, and so can traditions that "may be too inflexible to incorporate changes suggested by contact with other traditions." In contrast to those conservatives who insist on the need to reinforce virtue, Kekes would not have society abolish practices associated with "racists, anti-Semites, creationists, paedophiles, pornographers, and so forth." The proper conservative attitude toward those "who live according to their beliefs without violating any required conventions" is to tolerate them without extending them any respect.

Kekes's Little Conservatism is so paltry that it is unwilling to assert any first principles at all upon which conservative morality can be grounded. And this reluctance extends not just to social traditions. Kekes is not a fideist; his conservatism is based on reason, not faith. One finds in *A Case for Conservatism* no defense of aristocracy as a way of life better able to inculcate conservative values than a society organized by the market. Indeed, Kekes does not even offer as a primary justification for conservatism the most liberal of possible justifications: meritocracy. All that is left is the sense that justice consists in rewarding people for working hard and obeying the rules, a principle that, according to Kekes, is violated by the redistributive policies of the modern welfare state. Thus a book that wants to uncover the "basic beliefs" of conservatism and to prove that they are "true" offers instead a menu designed to avoid the indigestible in favor of bland tastes unlikely to offend anyone except the most doctrinaire liberals.

The problem in all this is not that conservatism is philosophically incoherent, that it is forced to choose between its principles and programs that violate its principles. Ambiguity gives political philosophies, whether liberal or conservative, their character. No, the problem is that the dilemmas that structure conservative choices–especially among those writers, including contemporary Straussians, who have a bit more conservative spine than Kekes–are illusory. It is difficult to choose between liberty and equality, individual freedom and respect for law, oneness and diversity. Modern society forces upon its citizens one situation after another in which their basic beliefs are in conflict. But all these very real choices are between one liberal value and another. Americans are not asked to choose between a theocracy and a state committed to the separation of church and state; between legalizing slavery and abolishing it; between restricting the vote to property-holders and expanding it to all adults.

Both Gottfried and Kekes praise conservatism for its realism. It has, they claim, an essentially pessimistic outlook on the world. Yet the idea that conservatism is identified with a tragic view of life, and that liberalism is given to Candide-like optimism, is long gone. Since the tragic choices that modern people have to make are between competing liberal goods, it is liberalism which wrestles with the actual realities of politics in the modern world.

Kekes is careful to say that he did not write his book to influence conservative politics in the world around him, and Gottfried barely seems to care whether his version of conservatism could ever be made electorally appealing. Yet both books help us understand why conservatism never emerged as a true governing philosophy in the late twentieth century. Conservatism is a choice between two conceptions of the good, one of which can never be chosen. It is not merely that we cannot go back to a system of Greek virtue or aristocratic privilege; we cannot even discharge a president who committed adultery. With no anchor on one side, conservatism lacks, as liberalism did in its nineteenth-century utopian visions, a sense of responsibility, a Weberian understanding of the ways in which power can obtain some objectives only by foreclosing others.

Kekes demonstrates the irresponsibility of having no real choices to make by redefining conservatism so that it is most things for most people. Gottfried, by contrast, offers a vision of conservatism so austere as to be of almost no interest to any people. Both responses betray an unease with the actual business of governance, and it may well be this that makes conservatism in modern form unappealing to large numbers of voters. They want to elect politicians who are cognizant of the realities of power. All too often conservatives, the first in the Western political tradition to write openly and honestly about power, fail to convince them that they can be responsible in the exercise of it. Fifty years after Oakeshott and Strauss, conservatism remains unable to decide what it really is about.

V

THE BEST ARGUMENT FOR conservatism with which I am familiar comes from Virginia Postrel, the editor of *Reason* magazine. One should not assume that because Postrel's magazine is libertarian in origin, and because libertarians are sometimes thought of as being on the right, she writes in defense of conservatism. *The Future and Its Enemies: The Growing Conflict over Creativity, Enterprise, and Progress* is a no-holds-barred attack on all forms of conservatism. But at a time when at least some conservatives have more in common with liberals than they are prepared to admit, it takes a true opponent of conservatism to reveal its potential strengths; and one cannot find a temperament more opposed to stasis than Postrel's.

Postrel divides up the way we think and act in the world into two categories. There is stasis and there is dynamism. Stasists seek to keep the world as it is; or, if they adhere to a reactionary version, to take the world back to some place it was. They come in all political colorations. Pat Buchanan, the *Weekly Standard,* Leon Kass, William Bennett, Ross Perot, and John Gray, all of whom are or were on the right end of the spectrum, are stasists. So are Benjamin Barber, Daniel Bell, Jeremy Rifkin, Al Gore, Christopher Lasch, the *Nation,* and Kirkpatrick Sale, all of whom are usually classified, in one way or another, as being on the left. Their urges, Postrel asserts, are uniformly repressive. It matters less what they want to ban or to limit–foreign competition, Wal-Mart, Big Macs, rock music, shopping malls, skimobiles, pornography, genetic engineering, hedonism, or immigrants–than their certainty that they know the one best way to bring order to a chaotic world.

Dynamists are less well known, says Postrel, because most of them are doers rather than thinkers. They are the people who develop the Web, understand how species evolve, restructure companies, subvert government regulations, flout racial and ethnic categories, play beach volleyball, and invent new technologies. Opponents of inflexible systems are unlikely to write treatises, but their understanding of how the world actually works can be seen in the writings of Esther Dyson, Hernando de Soto, Tom Peters, and Jonathan Rauch. Dynamists, says Postrel, are "the party of life." Celebrating systems that have no closed ends, they recognize that rules must be kept as simple as possible because nobody can predict unanticipated consequences. They are not against order, but they are against design. Systems will find their own ways to reduce complexity, and we are better off allowing them to do so than imposing artificial restraints. A dynamic world is not built top-down based on expertise. It is created bottom-up based on local knowledge. There is no one best way. There is only trial and error.

Postrel's dynamist manifesto is, appropriately, a lively, engaging, and thought-provoking book. She is surely correct that temperamental factors such as the fear of change transcend the political categories of left and right. She is also correct to note that we seem to be going through something of an intellectual revolution: in biology, ecology, economics, computer science, and demography, scholars and theorists are voguishly emphasizing unplanned dynamic change.

Still, translating all this ferment into an appealing political outlook is no easy task. Postrel fails at it. For there is no compelling evidence that the way systems evolve in nature or in technology holds any lessons at all for understanding how societies grow or people develop. And to the degree that we know anything about the goods that people value, we know that temperaments not only vary between people, they vary within people. Nearly everyone wants closure about some things some of the time, which is why they are unlikely to give their assent to a vision of the world that asks them to take risks all the time in everything that they do.

For a book designed to influence how people ought to live, there is relatively little in Postrel's book about how people actually do live. To be sure, Postrel cites Jane Jacobs and Joel Garreau on cities, but these are thinkers for whom cities are not just interesting places but also metaphors for the human condition. And that is the problem with Postrel's many examples of dynamism from the worlds of technology, nature, and migration: they are all metaphors. It is interesting to know that popular music and slang evolve because practitioners refuse to follow strict rules and prefer to apply their own creativity and initiative to the materials available to them. But does this mean that we should pay no attention to time-honored conventions as we worship God, raise children, choose friends, search for moral principles, or decide what to read? Life as it actually is lived–by real people, in communities, bound through generations, searching for identity–bears little if any relationship to the ways in which species evolve or weather systems develop. Chaos theory is fine for numbers. As a principle for how humans ought to live, it is extremely unimpressive.

Indeed, it may be that people crave stability and predictability in some parts of their lives because other aspects of their lives have become unstable and unpredictable. Compared to the security sought by the generation that experienced world war and depression, younger Americans are certainly more open to innovation and circumstance. But they also hedge their bets. People may vote for Republicans in Congress to stimulate the economy, but then they also elect Democratic presidents to protect Social Security. They will invest in high-growth stocks, but they will also put something in government bonds. They may be open to sexual adventure, but they usually calm down and form lasting relationships. They still buy insurance and take out thirty-year mortgages when interest rates fall.

Postrel cites the economic historian Joel Mokyr's warning that periods of technological dynamism rarely last a long time: "Sooner or later the forces of conservatism, the 'if-it-ain't-broke-don't-fix-it,' the 'if-God-had-wanted-us-to-fly-He-would-have-given-us-wings,' and the 'not-invented-here-so-it-can't-possibly-work' people take over and manage through a variety of legal and institutional channels to slow down and if possible stop technological creativity altogether." Postrel calls this a "pessimistic" vision. I call it a realistic one. Human beings are temperamentally complex. They need consolidation as much as innovation. If they followed Postrel's advice, the time for consolidation would never come.

Conservatism—understood more as the Oakeshottian temperament than as the Straussian dramaturgy—enables us to consolidate the risks that are taken when we are younger. The young and the childless are rarely conservative, but they are often libertarians. Libertarianism is a political philosophy for Peter Pans, an outlook on the world premised on never growing up. It will never become a major political force because most of us do grow up. In Postrel's world, the future is the enemy of the stasists. This may be true for society as a whole; but for individuals, the future is the enemy of the dynamists. It is because we think we might have a future that we become reluctant to be risk-takers in the present.

And that is why the failure of conservative thinkers and conservative activists to develop a meaningful political philosophy is such a wasted opportunity. Any political philosophy in tune with the rhythm of life will appeal to Oakeshott's conservative temperament, whether it calls itself conservative or not. Conservatism, in this construction, has a natural advantage over its rivals. To the degree that liberalism leans toward libertarianism—as it does in Mill's *On Liberty*—it cuts artificially against the life cycle; for the emphasis that Mill places on eccentricity and genius seems less attractive the more people look backward to the life that they have actually lived. We need conservatism because life is so rich that we become desperate to protect it against uncertainty.

All of this, I think, helps to explain why neoconservatism became popular when it did. It was a movement of consolidation, the correction of a liberal course. The 1960s, after all, were truly a destabilizing period, in which institutions and traditions of all kinds were asked to justify themselves—and many could not. Since they represented a cultural revolution, the decades of the 1960s and 1970s demanded a stabilizing reaction, and this is what the neoconservatives were the first to understand and to offer. One need not agree with everything that they said to acknowledge one's debt to the neoconservatives for helping to stop certain destructive social trends in their tracks.

Yet our debt to the neoconservatives is really our debt to liberalism. For if conservatism is an impossible ideal, then the best that conservatives can do is to force liberalism, when it goes awry, back in the right direction. The neoconservative movement of the 1980s is one more confirmation of Louis Hartz's insistence on the ubiquity of American liberalism. Having performed a historical service to the liberal order of the United States, neoconservatism retreated from the stage, the latest in a long line of modern conservative defeats. All these bitter attacks on liberalism only make one realize just how embedded in the American way of life liberalism truly is. We really have progressed, and we have no reason to regret it.

Idiot Time

I

A S LORD BRYCE NOTED in 1888 in *The American Commonwealth,* the American way of choosing presidents rarely produces politicians of quality. Subsequent events vindicated his point: in the half century after his book appeared, Americans elected to the presidency such undistinguished men as William McKinley, William Howard Taft, Warren G. Harding, Calvin Coolidge, and Herbert Hoover. An era that included two wars, the assumption of an empire, a stock market crash, and the beginning of our greatest economic crisis was also marked by as mediocre a political leadership as we have had in our history.

Two features stand out in this roll call of incompetence: the presidents with the lowest reputations over the past hundred or so years were all Republicans, and they were all guided by the conviction that their job was to side with the powerful in any potential conflict with the poor. Our current president is a Republican whose policies favor the rich. His political guru, Karl Rove, is a great admirer of William McKinley and his strategist Mark Hanna. Will this administration, therefore, take its place among the worst presidencies of modern times? In his recent book *Public Intellectuals* (see "The Fame Game," this vol.), Richard Posner mocks anyone who makes predictions about such matters. Forgive me, then, for making this one: George W. Bush, despite his military success in Iraq, will be lucky if his presidency ever rises to the level of Taft's or Harding's.

A strong case can be made that the Bush administration is the most pro-business presidency that the United States has ever endured. In

1952, Charles Wilson, President Eisenhower's secretary of defense, opined that the good of the country and the good of General Motors could be entwined. Often ridiculed, his statement is, in comparison with the policies of the present administration, a model of statecraft. General Motors, after all, was unionized, so what was good for it was also good for huge numbers of American working-class families. And automobiles, its major product, offered to the upwardly mobile Americans of the period a dramatic opportunity—in that age before the politics of smog—to improve their living conditions.

The companies that the Bush administration confuses with the public interest, by contrast, stand out for their rapaciousness in a generally vicious business climate. Enron, to which the president was unusually close, not only destroyed the retirement prospects of its own workers, it also schemed to cause deliberate discomfort to California's energy users—a no-holds-barred approach to doing business that foreshadowed the hideously ugly efforts of this administration to issue frequent and confusing warnings of potential terror attacks when confronted with perfectly appropriate questions about its preparedness for the big attack that took place on its watch. And Halliburton, which now faces an SEC inquiry into its accounting practices during the time that the firm was run by Vice President Dick Cheney, is one of many companies that would presumably benefit from the administration's energy policy, discussions of which it has gone to some length to keep out of the public's hands (there also awaits business for this firm in the reconstruction of Iraq). The business of the Bush administration is not just business, but sleazy business. America's worst firms picked America's most complaisant politicians (and vice versa) because they knew that they could work with each other.

Even when terrorists gave George W. Bush his great moment of leadership, he retreated, when the active fighting in Afghanistan and Iraq stopped, to a policy of appeasing the already powerful. Although America was vulnerable to attack in part because of the way certain large private companies routinely carried out their business, not once has this president challenged any established industry. The administration committed itself to drilling for oil in Alaska during the campaign, and nothing in the subsequent violence in the Middle East has caused it to rethink alternatives such as energy conservation. It has not used its considerable powers of persuasion–"jawboning," as it was called when presidents knew that business leaders could be sons of bitches–to force airlines into compliance with the security improvements mandated by Congress. On trade policy and farm policy, the administration caved so quickly to the demands of lobbyists that it managed to evoke nostalgia for Bill Clinton (whose free-trade positions cost him votes with labor unions and captains of dying industries). Presidents such as Bush, who jog softly and carry no stick at all, signal to every entrenched interest that nothing will stand in the way of an inclination to have government always on the side of those who already possess influence and power.

But when historians make their judgments about Bush, it will not be the similarities between Teapot Dome and Enron that strike them, nor will it be a tax cut so biased in favor of the rich that it makes a mockery of fairness and so huge in size that it will cripple the ability of this administration, or any other administration, to bring security to innocent civilians against whom war has been declared by as evil an enemy as the American people have ever faced, let alone to bring financial security in old age and decent health care coverage. The true shame of the Bush years lies not in debates over levels of taxation or specifics of regulatory policy: there are, and there should be, differences of opinion over those kinds of questions. Nor is the fact that Bush is pursuing a pro-business and conservative agenda the reason to judge him harshly: Americans have never pushed their leaders to equalize incomes, nor have they revolted in anger when, in the name of economic growth, those leaders pursue programs that benefit some at the expense of others. With Bush, questions of method and timing are more significant than questions of policy.

Whatever one thinks of Bush's mediocre Republican predecessors, they received a mandate from the voters to pursue their programs of unabashed support for business. They promised pretty much what they delivered: a return to "normalcy," as Harding–like Bush, a linguistically challenged man–so memorably put it. Their policies evoke an era before focus groups and media consultants, when politicians had no problem proclaiming their true allegiances.

But Bush never received a mandate for his policies, and not just because he was handed the presidency by the Supreme Court, which was acting with barely concealed partisan fervor against its own well-established legal doctrine. Even had Bush won fair and square, he would have done so by distorting beyond recognition the true beneficiaries of his programs dealing with taxation, government regulation, the environment, and energy. During the 2000 election, Bush's advisers discovered something that no one before had ever quite known: there are simply no limits to how much you can lie in American politics and get away with it. And it is the transposition of that approach to politics into policy that constitutes the disgrace of the Bush method. A tax cut radically biased toward the rich is not nearly so damaging as a tax cut passed while one side to a much-needed debate responds to criticism by simply making up figures.

There exists a kind of slack in democratic politics. Most people are too preoccupied with their own affairs and not sufficiently interested in wonkish matters to call politicians to account when they lie. Politicians know about this slack; they pay people to study it closely, and they are frequently tempted to take advantage of it. They may, of course, be deterred from doing so. For one thing, they might conclude–how naive this seems now!–that not every opportunity to win should be exercised, because politics requires long-term cooperation among politicians with different views of the public good. Or they might make a strategic calculation that winning one battle through such methods might cause them to lose subsequent battles, and perhaps more important ones, down the road. Or they might conclude that too much distortion would give their political opponents an advantage to attack them.

None of these constraints mattered to the Bush administration. It somehow knew that Democrats would be too craven to challenge them effectively. It had no interest in the long-term effects of its slash-and-burn political methods. It treated the informal rules of the political game as territory for suckers. As a result, it got its tax cut. And the poison that it has introduced into the body politic will remain long after some other administration is forced to deal with the tax cut's rampant irresponsibility.

And then there is the disgrace of timing. As Kevin Phillips points out in *Wealth and Democracy: A Political History of the American Rich,* not all conservative presidents have been bad ones. Washington, Lincoln, and Theodore Roosevelt stand in a completely different class from Taft, McKinley, and Hoover. Phillips has devoted his career to explaining a fundamental American paradox: we have a pro-business economy and a populist political culture. Since we admire business, we frequently elect politicians whose policies favor the rich; but since we want to ensure that fairness is honored, we reserve our greatest admiration for those who "made their own names fighting elites." It is not that Lincoln and Roosevelt were predisposed to take on the powerful. They governed in times of crisis and, responding to the situations in which they found themselves, they did what they had to do, even if what they had to do put them into confrontation with some of the most powerful forces of their era.

Our crisis is certainly not of the magnitude of the Civil War or the Great Depression; but this country, especially after September 11, has serious issues on its hands. Ambivalent in their approach to economics and politics, Americans continue to appreciate capitalism, which is why they are willing to give Bush's proposals a hearing, although without any great enthusiasm. But at the same time they know that fairness matters, and that there is more to membership in the American nation than getting and spending. The Bush administration hears only the first language of business as usual; it is tone-deaf to the second, deeper, and ultimately more important language of purpose. Its response to a people who have suffered one political scandal after another, only to find themselves suddenly defined as the enemy by large numbers of people throughout the world, is to refuse, as if on principle, any calls for greatness or sacrifice, any efforts to mobilize the forces of government on behalf of national objectives, any visions of who we are as a free people, any attempts to broaden and to define the meaning of citizenship.

Whatever one thinks of President Bush's war against Saddam Hussein, the president demonstrated what leadership can do; especially compared to his predecessor, who never seemed to have grasped the powers available to him as president, Bush developed his agenda, pushed it to the point of execution against all opposition, and saw his goal reached with relatively little sacrifice of American life. How odd, then, that when it comes to domestic policy, Bush does not lead because he does not believe in leadership, a concept that he would no doubt dismiss as a devious effort on the part of liberal elites to deter him from his predetermined goals of cutting taxes and redistributing income to the wealthy. But it is precisely because Americans are not demanding leadership that we need it so desperately. Instead of a president who can speak to the best in all of us, we have a president willing to listen only to some of us.

In its time so far in office, the Bush administration has not merely obliterated the memory of Republicans such as Lincoln and Roosevelt. It has also distanced itself from Eisenhower's warning about a military-industrial complex, from Nixon's attempts to steal the left's thunder by adopting programs such as wage and price controls, and even from Reagan's willingness to back off from right-wing nostrums that had little public support. The Bush administration knows that the tradition of Republican stewardship of the nation came to an inglorious end with the watered-down version represented by the current president's father, and it has no plans to resurrect it. Noblesse oblige is dead; ignobility is to be praised; obligation is to be shunned; and, as the president's foreign policy in Iraq suggests, allies are to be dissed. We know that Bush is not the hardest-working of modern presidents—and yet he seems to have made all those fund-raising phone calls, and given all those GOP speeches, and appeared at all those county fairs and professional conventions, not out of some deep sense of duty to the nation, but to reward those who so generously rewarded a man so unfit for office as himself. His mediocrity concerning domestic policy is not a by-product of his mistakes. It is his very intention. He has seen what historical greatness would cost him and his supporters, and he has chosen another path.

II

KEVIN PHILLIPS'S *WEALTH AND DEMOCRACY* can be read as an explanation of how we arrived at such a state. Since we have a free-market economy and a populist political culture, we do not in America have a politics of class. The poor do not, as socialists of one stripe or another hoped they would, vote for candidates who offer to redistribute income to their benefit. Yet neither do we have a politics of plutocracy: the rich, or at least their children, can often be found expressing solidarity with society's most disadvantaged. Instead we have uneasy swings between periods of excess, such as the Gilded Age and the 1920s, and periods of reform, such as the 1930s and the 1960s. Phillips leaves little doubt where we are now: "The last two decades of the twentieth century . . . echoed the zeniths of corruption and excess . . . when the rich in the United States slipped their usual political constraints, and this trend continued into the new century."

Although Phillips's book begins and ends with the present, its intellectual reach is far greater. Phillips wishes to rewrite such progressive and populist classics as Charles and Mary Beard's *Economic Interpretation of the Constitution of the United States* (1935), Gustavus Myers's *History of the Great American Fortunes* (1936), and Ferdinand Lundberg's *America's Sixty Families* (1937). In tables that spell out who the richest Americans were at various points in our history and how they made their fortunes, Phillips adds little to what those books have already told us; but he is right to try to bring them up to date. What has been seriously missing from our national conversation about money and political influence in recent years is a tone of principled anger.

For since 1980, America's already unequal distribution of income and wealth, in Phillips's account, has become outrageously more unequal. The top 1 percent of Americans held 9.3 percent of America's income in 1981, according to one of Phillips's tables, compared with 15.8

percent in 1997. Levels of wealth concentration now approach what they were just before the stock market crash of 1929. And the rich in America do better than the rich anywhere else; the top fifth of Americans make 11 times more than the bottom fifth, compared to ratios of 4.3 in Japan, 7.1 in Canada and France, and 9.6 in the United Kingdom.

No doubt some of the advantages enjoyed by the rich are due to their entrepreneurial foresight. But Phillips, a critic of the free market, emphasizes the degree to which public policy contributes, often arbitrarily, to the gap between the rich and everyone else. In his view, the tax cuts of the Reagan years rank among the four most significant transformations in wealth distribution in American history, along with the Hamiltonian financial reforms of 1789–92, the effects of the Civil War, and the New Deal. The poor, unlike the rich, did not benefit from Reagan's tax cut; any gains achieved by lower rates were eaten up by higher payments for Social Security. Squeezed between declining real income and fewer benefits, the worst-off Americans found themselves working longer hours or borrowing more extensively to keep up. Even though the country's gross domestic product went up, its index of social health declined, as child poverty and youth homicide increased while health care coverage deteriorated.

Phillips is not always a reliable guide on these issues. Like all advocates of a cause, he cites data that support his point of view, but when he is presented with contrary indications he simply shifts the grounds of his argument. Unemployment rates were far higher in Europe during the last decades of the twentieth century than they were in America; but instead of congratulating the American economy for putting people to work, Phillips instead attacks the quality of the jobs that were produced. And when he points out that for middle-class Americans the costs of health clubs and private schools increased because the rich could pay more for them, he verges on caricature: most middle-class Americans were too busy enjoying their newfound access to such goods to pay too much attention to the price. Phillips should be read as a social critic, not as an economic historian. Righteous anger is his forte, not nuanced analysis.

Yet he does concentrate our attention. The rich did get richer in the last two decades of the twentieth century, and to a considerable degree their gains came at the expense of everyone else. In times past, such periods of excess gave rise to opposition in forms ranging from utopian novels to political realignments. Yet neither political party during this period felt called upon to respond. At a time when the right was concerned with abortion and homosexuality and the left pushed affirmative action and multiculturalism, the single most important moral issue facing the country—the right of every individual to be treated by government with equal dignity and respect—went all but undiscussed. As a result, a once-vibrant populist tradition degenerated into the vile Pat Buchanan and the narcissistic Ralph Nader.

Even more intellectually ambitious than his retelling of American economic history is Phillips's extended comparison between sixteenth-century Spain, the golden age of the Netherlands in the seventeenth century, and the British industrial expansion of the nineteenth century. In each case, he points out, new elites arose to accumulate, with the help of government, fantastic wealth. New technologies, from Leeuwenhoek's microscopes to Watt's steam engine, furthered exploration and advance. (Spain somewhat mysteriously drops out of Phillips's story.) Flushed with their success, the elites overextended themselves, falling victim to what Phillips calls "the hubris, even self-deception, that attends leading world economic power status." Decadence set in, as sober and industrious values were replaced by those of luxury and snobbery. Ultimately war followed peace, and defeat followed victory. The great years of Holland and Britain are now to be found in museums, as the actual economies of those societies fell back to normal.

Analogies between different countries in different eras can be offered as suggestive or they can be offered as determinative. Phillips leans toward the latter. It is not the intricacies of Dutch religious wars or British activities in India that interest him so much as the lessons that these historical events might hold for the United States now. Like other empires at other times, America's recent economic growth was fueled by a new technology and received considerable support from government. We, too, overextended ourselves, especially in Vietnam. Money corrupted our culture just as it did theirs. And our future looks grim, he believes, for democracy will be in trouble if we do nothing to curb the influence of wealth.

Although Phillips is quite vague in his calls for reform–he speaks at one point of "a more democratic approach to taxation, money, and banking"–he does not offer them with much enthusiasm. He seems to believe in some kind of economic nationalism, but he also notes "its poor prospects for long-term success." With such perfunctory proposals, Phillips leaves us feeling that we too may find ourselves best represented in a museum, so that some future economic power may ponder the mistakes that we made.

Over the course of thirty years, Phillips has written two wonderful books. *The Emerging Republican Majority* (1969), still a favorite among conservatives, outlined the ways in which the Republican party could overcome the liabilities of its elitist reputation by appealing to Northern working-class ethnics and displaced Southern whites. *The Cousins' Wars* (1999), one of the most insightful books written about American society in the last fifty years, brilliantly analyzed the common religious and ethnic divisions that underlay the English and American Civil Wars, as well as the American Revolutionary War. *Wealth and Democracy* is not in their class. It lacks the powerful realism of the former, substituting in its place a free-floating anger that never attaches itself to a program for correcting the abuses it documents. And it does not achieve the startling originality of the latter, for it is badly organized, sloppily written, and loosely argued. One of the best informed and most sober political commentators in America has unfortunately produced something of a rant. And we are all the worse for it, because *Wealth and Democracy*, its lack of focus and its forced analogies notwithstanding, is exercised by a matter of great importance.

Phillips argues that wealth and democracy are ultimately incompatible. The pursuit of the former requires an oligarchy, while the realization of the latter demands greater equality. Republicans can best handle this situation–Phillips rarely offers advice to Democrats–when they temper their natural affiliations with the rich and the powerful by adopting populistic language, and even populistic policy. Richard Nixon did that, in part by following Phillips's advice in *The Emerging Republican Majority*. George W. Bush, except for his appeals to conservative religious voters, has not shown much interest in populism (nor, it should be added, in Kevin Phillips, whose views have shifted in the direction of *Mother Jones*). So what options are open to him?

One way to resolve the inherent conflict between wealth and democracy would be to suspend democracy in the interests of wealth. At times Phillips darkly hints at such a prospect. "As the twenty-first century gets under way," he concludes, "the imbalance of wealth and democracy in the United States is unsustainable, at least by traditional yardsticks. Market theology and unelected leadership have displaced politics and elections. Either democracy must be renewed, with politics brought back to life, or wealth is likely to cement a new and less democratic regime–plutocracy by some other name." This is surely too extreme; the last I looked, elections were still in place. Democracy is strong enough to survive the ascendancy of George W. Bush and Dick Cheney.

If we take Phillips's insistence on the tension between wealth and democracy as a starting point rather than a tragic denouement, we can begin to appreciate why contempt has become so defining a feature of the Bush administration, whether it takes the form of the president mocking a journalist for his knowledge of French, or the secretary of defense responding to critics with sarcastic disdain, or the vice president simply refusing legitimate and legal requests for information, or the attorney general treating the Constitution as an impediment. An administration with no mandate pursuing with grim determination policies with no public support–and yet which must nonetheless operate within a system that has a free press, an investigative legislature, and an independent, if compromised, judiciary–has little choice but arrogance. It could decide, of course, that cooperation with other branches of government is actually a good thing for democracy and that the best policies are those pursued through informed public

debate, but then it could hardly hope to reward the rich and the powerful. And so it does the opposite, shifting as much of the country's wealth
as it can to those who need it least, while launching invective and attri-
butions of bad motives to anyone who opposes its goals. Democracy
and wealth do push in opposite directions, and for all its many flaws,
Democracy and Wealth helps us understand why.

III

SOMETHING ABOUT THE SUBJECTS of wealth and power seems to bring
out the worst in people. The more populistic he becomes, the more
ominous Kevin Phillips sounds; and it is a shame to see him fall into the
company of people like Ross Perot, Patrick Cadell, and Ralph Nader.
But for Michael Moore there is not much room to fall. Films such as
Roger and Me and books such as *Downsize This!* marked him as ego-
centric and frivolous from the start. Still, he has tried his best to stoop
even lower with *Stupid White Men . . . and Other Sorry Excuses for the
State of the Nation!* A more irresponsible book on a more important
topic would be impossible to write.

Phillips only raises the prospect of an unelected leadership, but for
Moore, the coup, as he calls it, has already taken place. Al Gore, he says,
is the actual president of the United States, because "he received 539,898
more votes than George W. Bush." (At least John Ashcroft knows what
is in the Constitution that he routinely ignores; Moore seems not to
know that the document calls for a victory in the electoral college.) But
instead of Gore, the coup brought to power the "Bush junta," which is
composed mainly of millionaires. One of them is Dick Cheney. "When
nominated for the vice presidency," Moore writes, "Cheney hemmed
and hawed about divesting himself of his Halliburton stock. I guess he
knew that the good times were coming." It is beneath Moore, of course,
to point out that Cheney did in fact divest himself of the stock–or that
Halliburton, which was selling for roughly $40 per share in the fall of
2000, is now worth less than $20. (If Cheney knew anything, evidently,
it was that the bad times were coming.)

Moore, to put it mildly, does not write to inform. Attitude is all. But if you are writing a book critical of a president who has a problem with the truth, it does not require all that much intelligence to figure out the importance of being truthful yourself. Moore could not care less. He describes how he decided one day to watch *The McLaughlin Group*, where he found the conservative pundit Fred Barnes complaining that kids no longer knew about the *Iliad* and the *Odyssey*. So Moore decided to call Barnes and to ask him whether he knew what they were. "Well, they're . . . uh . . . you know . . . uh . . . OK, fine, you got me," he quotes Barnes as responding. "I don't know what they're about. Happy now?"

I don't know Barnes, but the story struck me as implausible, and so I e-mailed him about it. "It never happened," he wrote back. "One, I've never talked to Michael Moore. Two, I have read the *Iliad* and the *Odyssey*. I didn't read them until I got to college, but I did read them. So I know exactly what they're about. Besides that, I've seen movie versions of them." Choose whom you wish to believe, but I am disinclined to believe someone who tells me, as Moore does, that 200,000 Americans may be suffering from mad cow disease, that the United States practices apartheid, that first-year airline pilots for commuter airlines live below the poverty level, and that the Confederacy won the Civil War.

Thirty or so years ago–*Roe v. Wade*, decided in 1973, is a good benchmark–conservatives concluded that they were unrepresented in liberal America. They decided to organize themselves politically to reverse the course of their country. Whether one agrees with them or not, one cannot fault them for lacking determination and seriousness of purpose. They did the research, mobilized the voters, tracked the votes of the politicians, and raised the money necessary to achieve their objective. They never did overturn that Supreme Court decision, although they are responsible for weakening it. But owing to their efforts the whole complexion of America shifted rightward, and now we have a president who pays careful attention to everything they have to say.

The contrast with Michael Moore could not be greater. Instead of analyzing an issue, he personalizes his opponents, even charging

Prescott Bush with ties to the Nazis (which he admits that he cannot prove) or asking his grandson the president whether he is an alcoholic and how this may be affecting his job performance. Rather than searching for a credible cause, Moore resorts to some of the most outlandish appeals to gender and racial identity politics that I have ever seen, as in this: "Women? They deserve none of the blame. They continued to bring life into this world; we continued to destroy it whenever we could." If this book is what passes for a political manifesto, then Tom Paine is truly dead. Moore peppers his book with factoids, weird memos, open letters, bizarre lists, LOTS OF SENTENCES IN CAPITAL LETTERS, and name-dropping accounts of how he happens to know some members of the Bush family personally. It is meant to be satire, I suppose; but the only person skewered is Moore, who proves himself to be the only stupid white man around. Anyone bent on redistributing income in favor of the rich could not get a luckier break than having a critic like Michael Moore.

One would think that a person who believes that George W. Bush stole the presidency from its rightful occupant Al Gore would at least prefer to see Al Gore in the office. But Moore is too "radical" for that, of course; he informs his readers that he did not vote for Gore, and he regularly engages in Nader-like rhetoric about how both parties are indistinguishable when it comes to issues such as arsenic in the drinking water. He even seems to relish the idea of a second term for Bush, for he concludes his book with a message to the Democrats: "So yes, WE denied you the White House. WE tossed you out of Washington. And WE will do it again." (As if to show that he cannot be consistent even on this obnoxious point, however, Moore tells us how he tried to persuade Floridians from voting for Nader so as to help defeat Bush.) Moore is astoundingly out of touch with the reality that he claims to care so much about. He is Chomsky for children. He does real damage to the cause that he thinks he is advancing. As is also true of Ralph Nader, the American right is much in his debt.

Theodore Roosevelt followed William McKinley, Woodrow Wilson came after William Howard Taft, and Franklin Delano Roosevelt took

over from Herbert Hoover. One thing mediocre presidents seem to do is
to prepare the ground for better presidents, and in some cases great
ones. When it comes to who will succeed George W. Bush, I make no
predictions. But there is reason to think that four or eight years of
Republican largesse to big business, accompanied by such extreme
efforts to keep its generosity from public scrutiny, will prepare the
American public to appreciate why government is necessary and why
its policies must, above all else, be fair.

The next chapter in the way our politics treats the rich and the poor
is unlikely to take the forms that it has taken in the past. If Kevin
Phillips's book is any indication, populism has run out of gas. No credible coalition can be built on the basis of nationalistic anger in this age
of global capitalism, leaving populists sputtering with impotent rage.
And if Michael Moore speaks for what passes for the American left–he
must be speaking for someone, as his book is a best-seller–no help can
be expected from that quarter either. But this should be taken as a sign
of hope rather than a sign of despair. It opens the political territory for
a challenge from a Roosevelt-style Republican such as John McCain. It
also suggests to Democrats that they will need to address directly, and
with considerable passion, the warping of priorities that occurs when
government shifts so decisively in favor of the rich.

Neither task will be easy. For McCain, it would mean, as it did for
Theodore Roosevelt, a break with his own party–not exactly the easiest
path to the presidency. For Democrats, it means finding a way to capi-
talize on the gains that Clinton's centrism bequeathed to the party while
breaking with his all-too-frequent subservience to big business, a trick
that no potential Democratic candidate for the 2004 nomination has yet
pulled off. But there is every reason to believe that there exists a hunger
for leadership in America even though not much leadership is in evidence. Finding ways to do what seems difficult if not impossible is a
crucial aspect of leadership. Any Republican or Democrat capable of
overcoming those odds would, if elected, be in a good position to repair
the damage done by the election of 2000 and its aftermath.

Conclusion

.

The Fame Game

A NY METHOD FOR RANKING the top one hundred public intellectuals in America cannot be all bad if it includes my name among
them. Opening Richard A. Posner's *Public Intellectuals: A Study of
Decline* to the chart that most of his readers will immediately consult, I
find myself barely making it at number ninety-eight, one step ahead of
Lani Guinier (and one step behind William Butler Yeats). But alas, any
sense of accomplishment that I might feel is immediately undercut by
two of the decisions that Posner made in conducting his study of public
intellectuals. One is methodological. The other is substantive.

The criterion for inclusion on Posner's list is media recognition. He
relied on the Lexis/Nexis database to count the number of times
between 1995 and 2000 that the names of intellectuals appeared in
major newspapers, stories, and transcripts. But to obtain his list of one
hundred, he first had to assemble an even larger list from which to
choose; and to get that list (which includes five hundred forty-six
names), although he consulted an earlier work on the subject and
refers to Web hits and media mentions as proxies, he essentially made
it up. As Posner correctly states, there is no census of public intellectuals that defines the whole group from which one can sample. What he
should have said explicitly is that, because no such census exists, any
list that is generated will be highly subjective.

To downplay the problem of subjectivity, Posner informs the
reader that individual names will be included or excluded based on the
categories to which they belong. Hence John Rawls is not on his list

because, although his work is widely discussed outside the academy—indeed, he receives more media mentions than Thomas Nagel, Martha C. Nussbaum, or Richard Rorty—he is primarily a scholar. But so, without question, are Nagel and the others; the only difference between them and Rawls is that, in addition to their considerable scholarship, they sometimes write an op-ed piece or a book review. Categories, in other words, can be as subjective as the items that they contain. To exclude Rawls but not the others is to judge public intellectuals by their motives in presenting their work, not by their work itself; but surely it makes more sense to call a public intellectual one whose views have seriously influenced the public, which Rawls has done to an admirable degree.

And so it goes with all of Posner's seemingly firm categories. He excludes politicians who write books, such as Richard Nixon, but he includes policymakers who write books, such as Nixon's secretary of state. (Kissinger ranks first in media mentions.) Journalists such as Maureen Dowd are left out, although her colleague Paul Krugman, because he is also an academic economist, is kept in; but Nicholas Lemann, Nat Hentoff, John B. Judis, E. J. Dionne, Thomas L. Friedman, Janet Malcolm, and Lewis H. Lapham are all journalists who do not hold academic appointments, and Posner includes them as well. Foreigners are included because their work appears in America (which means that most of them are primarily British, Australian, or Canadian), but while such Continental thinkers as Pierre Bourdieu and Jürgen Habermas are on the list, Adam Michnik, Hans Magnus Enzensberger, and Tzvetan Todorov are not. It is OK to be dead and still be included, as the presence of Yeats suggests, but you can also qualify if you were born in the past forty or so years, as were—I am presuming—David Brooks and Ann Coulter. Posner says that he did not want to include novelists such as Hemingway, but why then does his list mention Toni Morrison and Aldous Huxley, let alone poets such as Allen Ginsberg or Adrienne Rich?

"I acknowledge the arbitrariness of many of my decisions on whom to classify as a public intellectual," Posner writes. But his decisions are not merely arbitrary; they are nonsensical. Five hundred forty-six is a large number of people—so large that Posner's first cut at the problem reaches down fairly far into the fame game. In this, at least, his decision was sound, for if a smaller list is to be drawn from a larger one, then the larger one should be as inclusive as possible, erring on the side of generosity rather than strictness. Surely that explains why Posner includes among his five hundred forty-six such not especially well-known figures as Jonathan Turley, Stephen B. Presser, Nancy Sherman, Henry Manne, and Carol Iannone.

At the same time, Posner's large list manages to pass over a number of thinkers whose work literally free-associates with the term *public intellectual,* including Fouad Ajami, Paul Berman, Robert Brustein, Ian Buruma, Frederick Crews, Robert Dallek, Andrew Delbanco, John Patrick Diggins, Michael Eric Dyson, Gerald Early, Elizabeth Fox-Genovese, Jerome Groopman, Hendrik Hertzberg, Robert Hughes, Michael Ignatieff, Kathleen Hall Jamieson, Tony Judt, Wendy Kaminer, Robert Kuttner, Jonathan Lear, Jackson Lears, Sherwin B. Nuland, Kevin Phillips, Marge Piercy, Robert Pinsky, Katha Pollitt, David Remnick, David Rieff, Philip Rieff, Edward Rothstein, Alan Ryan, Juliet Schor, Simon Schama, Jim Sleeper, Peter Steinfels, Margaret Talbot, Sam Tanenhaus, Terry Teachout, Deborah Tannen, James Traub, Geoffrey Wheatcroft, C. K. Williams, Ellen Willis, James Wood, and Fareed Zakaria. Posner knows that he has a problem here; he informs the reader that he later expanded his list from five hundred forty-six to six hundred seven "by adding names that occurred to or were suggested to me" after he assembled the tables he presents in this book—a clear indication, if any were needed, of how inapplicable his statistical methods are to a subject as slippery as this one.

Posner himself is often mystified by the results his methodology produced. He points out that among those in the five hundred forty-six who did not make the top one hundred are Daniel Bell, Allan Bloom, Wayne Booth, Ronald Dworkin, Gertrude Himmelfarb, Robert Putnam, and David Riesman, as well as Nussbaum and Rorty. (Considering how influential many of these thinkers have been to me, you can see how my own sense of accomplishment begins to fade.) But rather than put the blame squarely on his methodology, he attributes this odd outcome to "the undiscriminating, short-memory-span character" of the market for public intellectuals—an odd interpretation considering that George Bernard Shaw, H. G. Wells, Timothy Leary, and C. S. Lewis not only make his short list of public intellectuals but appear among the top thirty-one. The more appropriate reason Posner's results are so often counterintuitive is because he simply forgot some people, while including others because their field or their political views were close to his own—and because some public intellectuals influence the culture due more to the quality of their work, which is admittedly harder to measure, than to the quantity, which measures all too easily.

Since no list can ever be as good as the larger list from which it is derived, not much ought to be made of Posner's findings. Posner himself says that his list should be "used with the greatest caution," but then he adds that caution should be exercised in making generalizations about the distribution of intellectuals across fields or races. When it comes to the more important question of making generalizations about intellectuals as a whole compared to other groups as a whole, Posner in fact generalizes with wild abandon, rarely stopping to consider the extent to which the basis for his generalizations lacks solidity.

And it is the generalizations made by Posner—the substantive conclusions he wants to reach—that constitute the other reason why I am not very happy to find myself among his top one hundred. For Posner is determined to show that being a public intellectual is no big deal, especially when compared with academic recognition. Each of the five hundred forty-six intellectuals on his list is checked for media citations, Web citations, and scholarly citations. Since public intellectuals who are also academics—there are fifty of them among the top one hundred—have high visibility and usually write well, their work ought to be cited by other scholars. But Posner informs us, after running the appropriate statistical tests, that there is no positive correlation between public visibility and scholarly reputation. And even when some public intellectuals, such as Stephen Jay Gould, are cited by other scholars, they are often cited outside their academic fields. Although the negative correlation between public recognition and academic recognition that he found was not statistically significant, Posner nonetheless concludes that public intellectual work makes little contribution to, and may even detract from, serious academic work.

The "decline" in Posner's subtitle therefore refers to a decline in quality. Posner reaches for as unflattering words as he can find to describe what public intellectuals do: "A proclivity for taking extreme positions, a taste for universals and abstraction, a desire for moral purity, a lack of worldliness, and intellectual arrogance work together to induce in many academic public intellectuals selective empathy, a selective sense of justice, an insensitivity to context, a lack of perspective, a denigration of predecessors as lacking moral insight, an impatience with prudence and sobriety, a lack of realism, and excessive self-confidence." This has all been said before, of course. There exists a long history of diatribes against intellectuals, best represented by Julien Benda's *The Treason of the Intellectuals,* published in 1928. But never before has it been said with correlation coefficients.

II

THERE IS A PROBLEM that requires some explanation here. One individual not on Posner's list is the former Nixon administration official Martin Anderson. True to his libertarian sympathies, Anderson in 1992 published a book called *Imposters in the Temple,* which blamed the inferior quality of academic work on the fact that, protected by tenure and adept at the guild system by which they decide who should join their ranks, professors are immune to the force of the market and, facing no razor of competition, have no incentive to sharpen their ideas. Posner, widely known as a legal scholar who has urged judges to rely more on economic reason to make legal decisions, should be firmly in Anderson's camp. But he is not; and this suggests that Posner is caught between the two objects of his love: the market and the academy. Faced with having to make a choice between them, he opts for the academy, thereby joining a long list of writers who find that they simply cannot abide the results that markets produce.

Posner makes much of the fact that public intellectuals exist in the world of markets, exchanging their ideas for money or (more often) fame. At the same time Posner also finds that the market for public intellectuals is a distorted one: it "operates without any rules or norms, legal or customary . . . and, unlike some other information markets, with little in the way of gatekeeping consumer intermediaries," sounding to all the world as if he were defending such gatekeepers as those nefarious consumer-products litigators routinely denounced by conservatives. Moreover, the publications that feature the writings of public intellectuals "do little screening for quality," Posner writes, thereby presupposing, against all economic reasoning, that markets are devices to make goods well rather than to make them cheap. Posner manages to chastise commercial publishers for emphasizing the "marketability" of their books, assuming, rather in the spirit of Jonathan Franzen's recent anxieties about the "brow" of his own writing, that popularity is an indication of intellectual and artistic corruption. He even looks with dismay on the fact that university presses are increasingly interested in publishing books that people might actually read. This determined advocate for law and economics has as much snobbish disdain for the commercial aspects of New Grub Street as anyone among the most left-leaning subscribers to public television.

Actually, Posner goes even further than the Upper West Side crowd in his hostility to laissez-faire. The public intellectual market, in his view, performs "badly" compared with other markets. What the market for public intellectuals lacks, Posner tells us, is "credence goods." For a market to work properly, people need some reassurance that the goods they buy will be of quality. Posner doubts whether the public intellectual market can provide such reassurance, for "there are no enforceable warranties or other legal sanctions for failing to deliver the promised quality, no effective consumer intermediaries, few reputational sanctions, and, for academics at any rate, no sunk costs–they can abandon the public intellectual market and have a safe landing as full-time academics."

Ever the tinkerer, Posner comes up with a plan to make the market for public intellectuals work better–which is to say, to make it work the way he thinks that a market ought to work. Posner would have universities require faculty to post their writings on the university Web page. Each year the Web pages' content would be downloaded and sent to libraries around the country. This way, he thinks, anything a public intellectual writes would be out there, available for public inspection. Posner fudges his proposal considerably, waffling back and forth from requiring it to suggesting that it be adopted voluntarily, which is actually a major issue if one believes, as Posner used to believe, that government regulation is often cumbersome and counterproductive.

But the idea behind Posner's proposal is clear enough. "Academics who abuse the privileges that the modern academic career confers, by writing or speaking irresponsibly in the public arena," he writes, "should be hauled before the bar of academic and public opinion." Along similar lines, Posner would regulate what public intellectuals do in ways that are analogues to the ideas of those advocating campaign finance reform; he would have intellectuals disclose all their income from their marketplace activities "in order to enable the public to monitor their honesty and application and their compliance with the rules against financial conflicts of interest." When it comes to a market like the one in which he himself operates, Richard Posner turns out to be a progressive reformer willing to use the powers of government to get the results that he wants.

The oddest aspect of this diatribe is that the market for public intellectuals actually works fairly well as it is. To ensure themselves outlets and readers, public intellectuals, who are not quite entertainers in the way that Posner sometimes imagines them to be, have little but their credibility to sell. Let public intellectuals destroy their credibility by taking the extreme and insupportable positions of the sort that Posner believes they inevitably take to gain market share, and the result will be—as Noam Chomsky has discovered by now—that they will be shunned by mainstream publications and confined to the margins of the debate. Contrary to everything that Posner says, the market, as Martin Anderson originally argued, improves the quality of public ideas. And it is not the money that acts as an incentive, though money helps. It is rather the notion that readers are not fools; and so if you want to reach a large number of them, you had better know what you are talking about, and be prepared to defend your ideas against letters to the editor and argumentative e-mails.

Need a sociologist remind an economist, moreover, that tinkering with the way markets work can have unanticipated consequences? One of Posner's proposals would encourage a norm designed to prevent magazines from publishing book reviews by individuals criticized in the book under review, or to require such reviewers to identify the potential conflict of interest. There are a number of problems with this recommendation. Posner seems to assume that readers lack the intelligence to find out for themselves whether the reviewer might be biased. He also believes that it is relatively easy to determine what criticism is. (Posner makes a number of references to me in his book, some of them supportive, some of them critical, so I am not sure whether, under his proposal, I would be required to disclose what I just disclosed.) But the most serious objection to his proposal is that, if followed scrupulously, it would quash the exchange of ideas, leading writers to avoid criticizing anyone who might be a potential reviewer and leading reviewers to avoid books that they have a natural interest in discussing. It is hard to imagine any reform that would take a relatively well-functioning market and subject it to the predictable dead hand of the planner more completely than the one that Posner suggests.

III

RICHARD POSNER'S DISDAIN FOR the market in ideas makes sense only against his love of academic standards. Like Marjorie Garber, whose work Posner never cites, and who is also left off his list of five hundred forty-six, Posner contrasts the professionalization of the academy with the amateurism of the public intellectual–and much prefers the former. One reason public intellectuals are in decline is that academic specialization is in the ascendancy. As he puts it, "Philosophy, economics, sociology, psychology, anthropology, and history are all fields that, like literary criticism, or for that matter, astronomy, were once far less technical and specialized, thus far more open to intelligent contributions from amateurs, than they have become." For this reason, we can no longer have many figures such as George Orwell because each of the many areas in which he worked–literary criticism, ethnography, political science–is now dominated by experts. Public intellectuals, Posner writes, trade scope in return for power; academics, by implication, renounce power in order to gain depth.

Although he distances himself somewhat from arguments in favor of pure specialization, Posner frequently contrasts scholars with intellectuals in ways that are invidious to the latter. "High up on the norm hierarchy of the scientific community," he writes, "are accuracy, open-mindedness, disinterest, and logicality," all of which leading public intellectuals "flout." Public intellectuals could be found on all sides of the Florida electoral debacle of 2000, but Posner singles out those who were shocked by what they witnessed, only to condemn their "emotionality," which stood "in particularly striking contrast to the official image of the academic."

Scholars, who pride themselves on their mastery of method, tend to look down on public intellectuals as people who just cannot make it in the more rarefied world of academic scholarship, and Posner sympathizes with them. "Other things being equal," he writes, "we would expect the ablest scholars to be the least drawn to the career of a public intellectual." Posner goes on to say that other things are not equal, but he circles back again to his main point. Some famous scholars do become public intellectuals, but generally at the end of their careers, when they no longer have the capacity for sustained work.

The purpose of these frequent contrasts is to underscore what Posner thinks his correlation coefficients reveal: the quality of the acade-

mic market is superior to the quality of the market for public intellectuals. But what kind of market is the academic market? To make an effective comparison between the market for scholars and the market for
public intellectuals, Posner ought to say something about the supply
and demand of the former; but he never subjects the academy to the
scrutiny that he imposes upon public intellectuals. Of course the academy is not, strictly speaking, his subject in this book; he is writing about
public intellectuals. But it is Posner who introduces the comparison in
the first place, so it would not have been that difficult for him to draw
up a list of scholars who disdain writing for the general public–people,
in short, like John Rawls–and find some method for comparing the
quality of their work with the quality of those who believe that academics–who are paid, one way or another, by the public–have an obligation to give the public something in return.

Were these two markets directly compared, I have no idea which
one would come out looking better. But it is still preferable to make the
comparison than simply to assume, as Posner does, that one must have
higher standards than the other. Grounds for thinking that the hypoth-
esis ought to be tested are furnished by the many examples of hiring
decisions made by universities that suggest the possibility of market
failure. In *Making Harvard Modern,* Morton and Phyllis Keller recount
how members of the department of history at that university, persuaded that no one out there was quite as good as themselves, passed
over C. Vann Woodward and Richard Hofstadter for appointments and
settled instead on Frank Friedel. And members of Harvard's department of political science horse-traded appointments, blending conservatives and liberals, or devotees of one approach and followers of
another approach, in order to achieve consensus.

A similar pattern continues until the present day. Harvard recently
hired Homi K. Bhabha away from Posner's beloved University of
Chicago. (Bhabha is on Posner's larger list, though not on his smaller
one.) Whatever one thinks of Bhabha's scholarship–his prose is the
very model of academic jargon so frequently ridiculed by public intellectuals–it is difficult to believe that Harvard simply wanted to hire the

best possible person that it could find to raise the quality of its English department. Whenever elite universities make hiring or tenure decisions, quality is the public criterion—but faddishness, contacts, race, ethnicity, ideology, and envy are the unspoken but nonetheless decisive criteria.

There is no reason to conclude, without examining any evidence, that the standards by which strictly scholarly work is judged are higher than those by which the work of public intellectuals is judged. Commercial publishers decide whether to accept a manuscript based on a guess about how many consumers might buy it. Academic presses, at least in theory, accept a manuscript because it has been given positive reviews by at least two scholars in the author's field. Can we really be sure that the latter procedure produces better quality? In many fields, the number of specialists is so small that reviewers have been known to praise a manuscript because they like the author, or want to curry favor, or expect a similarly positive review in return. (This is not the case with Posner's book, which was published by a university press: someone I know was one of the anonymous reviewers, and he is not only a scholar of considerable impartiality and discerning judgment, he is also an exemplary public intellectual, although he can be found on none of Posner's lists.) As with university presses, so with many journals, where, if anything, the range of available experts is even smaller. To be sure, prospects for commercial success may not produce better results, but it is also the case that books published by trade houses, like articles published in magazines of opinion, get much better editing and much tougher reviews than many an academic production.

Since the market for scholarship has its own flaws, Posner's comparisons between it and the market for public intellectuals quickly begin to crumble. Posner rightly points out, often with considerable relish, that there are academics with tenure who have all but given up scholarship for the sake of public recognition. But he does not emphasize that there are a surprising number of nonacademic public intellectuals who make contributions to academic scholarship, including Ian Buruma, Garry Wills, and Jack Miles. When all is said and done, Posner's book is more about celebrity than about accomplishment, and the interesting question of whether there is any relationship between them is not a question that he ever considers.

Posner is both an academic (he is a federal judge who retains an affiliation at the University of Chicago) and a public intellectual (he ranks himself seventieth among the one hundred leading public intellectuals, between John Kenneth Galbraith and Ralph Ellison, but, unlike many other public intellectuals on his list, he also ranks high on the list of scholarly citations, although that may be because law professors cite each other so copiously). So how should his own work about public intellectuals be judged?

By his own criteria—accuracy, open-mindedness, those kinds of attributes—Posner is not a very scholarly social scientist. One of the first rules of the scientific temperament involves an alertness to one's own possible fallibility, hardly a characteristic of Posner's approach. Quite the contrary. He rushes into print with problematic data, and he brooks no doubt about the proper conclusion to be drawn from his data. And so on the crucial point of whether the market for public intellectuals "is performing badly compared to other markets in symbolic goods, particularly the academic market," he tells his readers that "the theory and the statistics buttress the anecdotes; the trio of proofs is convincing." No serious social scientist would be so quick to reach such a judgment—and to announce it with so few qualifications, as if, because the evidence cannot speak for itself, the person who presents the evidence must speak on its behalf. Scientific modesty compels the conclusion that the anecdotes are scattered, the theory impoverished, and the data absurd.

Since Posner writes more like a public intellectual than like a scholar, does his own contribution to the genre support or contradict his assertions about the decline in quality of this way of dealing with ideas? The answer that immediately springs to mind is that Posner confirms his own thesis. It is not just the slapdash quality of his methodology or the breathtaking scope of his unproven generalizations that offend notions of quality. Rather than sustaining an argument from beginning to end, his book is sloppily put together, cutting and pasting from essays written for other occasions whether or not they are directly relevant to the topic at hand. The editing is often terrible, allowing the same thoughts to be repeated from one page to the next.

Posner has a voracious intellectual curiosity and a discipline for work rivaled by almost nobody in the United States. He is clearly capable of writing books that would meet anyone's standards for thoroughness. Instead he hastens his books into print as quickly as he hastens his data to conclusions, and their quality inevitably suffers. If this book is representative of what public intellectuals do, I can well understand his reservations about them. Still, I am reluctant to conclude that Posner is so anxious to prove his point about the low quality of public intellectual work that he wrote a book designed to confirm it. I have no way of knowing what his motivations are for writing, but I would seriously doubt that he presents his ideas for either money or fame. I would prefer to believe that Posner writes books because he is consumed with ideas and wants to persuade others of their validity. Whether he is good or bad in his efforts has nothing to do with the market in which he operates. It has everything to do with the quality of his mind and the care with which he presents his arguments. If the latter were up to the standards of the former, Posner's book would have made a valuable contribution to American letters. Instead he leaves his readers frustrated as much by his unexamined convictions as by his data-cloaked glibness.

The Calling of the Public Intellectual

I

IN 1987, RUSSELL JACOBY'S book *The Last Intellectuals: American Culture in the Age of Academe* created a stir by suggesting that the absorption of public intellectuals into the university in the 1950s and 1960s had produced a generation more preoccupied with methodological correctness and academic careerism than with the kind of fearless criticism once associated with nonacademic intellectuals like Edmund Wilson, Mary McCarthy, and Dwight Macdonald. The full implications of that thesis are still being debated: Witness two much-publicized forums on the fate of public intellectuals—one sponsored by Basic Books, the other by *Lingua Franca* and New York University—in the winter of 2000–2001.

I spoke at one of the forums, the latter, and what struck me was that we tend to approach the issue in the wrong way. It is not whether intellectuals work inside or outside the academy that is important, but whether—in either sphere—they have the courage to find their own voice.

There were reasons to both like and dislike the public intellectuals who clustered in New York after World War II: They were brilliant stylists throbbing with intellectual energy, but they also led irresponsible lives and made questionable political judgments. But love them or leave them—they certainly loved and left each other—what made the whole thing tick was the tension between their conservative views on culture and their radical views on politics. Politically, they all had qualms about capitalism—even Irving Kristol gave it only two cheers.

But instead of just urging political reforms that would spread the benefits of capitalism more equitably, they considered other options, led by their culturally conservative views: Hannah Arendt advocated returning to the Greek polis for ideas about participatory democracy, while the University of Chicago's Committee on Social Thought called for the study of great books.

Because their views on culture clashed with their views on politics, the New York intellectuals were forced to make their judgments one by one, especially when, as happens so often, it was impossible to tell where culture left off and politics began. That is why their views could be so unpredictable. Dwight Macdonald, something of a mandarin in his cultural views, was radicalized by the Vietnam War and marched on the Pentagon. Daniel Patrick Moynihan did not, as a senator, endorse all the positions he had supported as an intellectual, and not for reasons of political cowardice.

One found the same unpredictable attitude toward the institution with which Jacoby was concerned: the university. The New York intellectuals never wrote about academic life with the apology for professionalism of a Marjorie Garber; nor did they denounce it in the scathing words of a Roger Kimball. When the university was under attack by student radicals at Berkeley and Columbia, the New York intellectuals rushed to its defense. When the university became a home for postmodernism and affirmative action, they found much they disliked. In both cases, they saw the university in nuanced terms, as sandwiched between its links to the high culture of the past and the democratic pressures of the contemporary world.

How the New York intellectuals understood their world was also shaped by their anti-Stalinism; if you considered yourself on the left but were a fervent enemy of communism, you had to explain yourself frequently, and at some length. It was that constant need to draw distinctions—yes, I support socialism, one can still hear Irving Howe saying, but no, I do not support Cuba—that helped give the New York intellectuals a predisposition to judge events one by one. Such a stance is harder to find today, if only because outside of Cuba, socialism barely exists. The global triumph of capitalism is good for people who want to share the joys of consumption, but not for nurturing the questions of intellectuals, who thrive on opposition to what everyone else takes for granted.

II

THE UNITED STATES THESE DAYS has more than its share of opinion magazines, think tanks, advocacy journalists, and television commentators. But most of the time, those who are conservative in their cultural views are also conservative in their politics—and vice versa. On the right, a distrust of democracy informs commentary on both culture and elections, skeptical of a country capable of electing Bill Clinton and of considering Robert Mapplethorpe a serious artist. On the left, populism in politics and culture flows seamlessly together in opposition to those in power in either arena.

The trouble with such elitism and populism is that both are reflexive: You want either to strengthen or to weaken authority. Yet neither in politics nor in culture does such a reflexive response work. Since so much of high culture was once low culture, including such staples of authoritative taste as Italian opera, critical cultural judgments cannot be made by reviewing the popularity of any particular cultural event, or its source of funds.

Much the same is true of politics. At the very moment conservatives discovered that America had a moral majority, Americans refused to force Bill Clinton out of office. Yet when conservatives say that Americans have no morality at all, those same people voted George W. Bush into office. Democracy is like that. If you start with the assumption that everything the people do is wrong, you will be wrong about half the time—just about the same as if you begin with the proposition that the people are always right.

I doubt whether a new generation of think tanks or magazines will arise to support intellectuals who wish to think for themselves. The record of conservative foundations in this regard is not very encouraging, for while Washington is alive with the sound of ideas, they are mostly predictable ones meant to provide energy for one side in the policy debates with which that city is usually preoccupied. Our best hope for independent intellectuals instead may prove to be, as was not the case when Russell Jacoby wrote his book, the university. Because not all academic departments are convinced that publication in journals counts for more than the writing of books—or that books published in small numbers by university presses are inevitably more serious than those published in large numbers by commercial outfits—there remains some hope that tenure and other academic benefits could help support a culture of ideas in the United States and not just the life-styles of professors. If it happens, however, it is likely to occur outside the ideologically charged atmosphere of Washington.

Will American universities, ever faddish, discover a taste for independent-minded intellectuals? There are, as I suggested in the introduction to this volume, hopeful signs that they will. But whether they work inside or outside the academy, they will have to have the confidence to find their own voice.

III

INTELLECTUALS SPEAK WITH AUTHORITY, but what gives them the authority to speak? No one designated me an intellectual. I took on the role myself, found some people willing to publish me, and presumably drew some others willing to read me. If I have any authority, I developed it in the course of what I do. I am not saying that, on the matters of the day on which I have weighed in, I have always been right (although, rereading those essays in the preparation for this volume, I confess to believing that I was right more than I was wrong). But I have tried to convey that, when you get an opinion from me, it is my own. My authority for being an intellectual comes only from me, and to be true to that authority, I have to be true to myself.

I became an intellectual the day I decided that no one was looking over my shoulder as I sat down to write. Before that moment, I consid-

ered myself part of a political movement. My causes in the 1960s were
the causes of the left: racial justice, opposition to capitalism, protest
against the Vietnam War. Good causes all, but adherence to their
demands was deadly. When I wrote opinion articles, I understood my
role to be providing moral support to those on the side of all that was
presumed good and true. Now, when I look back on my writings from
that period, I do not see the fearless critic of the United States that I
thought I was at the time. Instead, I see someone simplifying the
world's complexity to fit the formula for understanding the world
developed by the left.

A few of the sixties radicals in my circle, like David Horowitz, chas-
tened by the violence and hypocrisy of the movements they once supported, shifted their political views quite drastically to the right. I reaf-
firmed my status as an intellectual when, having second thoughts of my
own about the left, I opted not to join them. Reading those born-again
conservatives, I feel as if I am reading ideology, stretched this way or
that to fit whatever topic is under discussion. Their efforts today to
prove how good things are under American capitalism strike me as
remarkably similar to their efforts, yesterday, to emphasize how bad
they were. I get the feeling that pleasing a movement explains much of
what they write.

Because the role of public intellectual resembles so much what
Max Weber called a vocation—you have to have a calling for it, and it
has to come from within—all institutions, not just magazines and think
tanks but universities as well, are capable of putting pressure on intellectuals that can undermine their authority to speak: the need to obtain
tenure and satisfy colleagues, the need to boost circulation, the need to
win the support of politicians. Resisting those pressures requires an
odd combination of self-confidence and humility, the former required
to have something valuable to say, the latter necessary to steer clear of
dogmatism.

There can be no guidebook on how to become an intellectual in
public. There can be only the desire to make sense out of the world one
issue at a time.

Books Discussed

"Alien Nation"

Will Kymlicka. *Politics in the Vernacular: Nationalism, Multiculturalism, and Citizenship*. New York: Oxford University Press, 2001.

Joseph H. Carens. *Culture, Citizenship, and Community: A Contextual Exploration of Justice as Evenhandedness*. New York: Oxford University Press, 2000.

Bhikhu Parekh. *Rethinking Multiculturalism: Cultural Diversity and Political Theory*. Cambridge: Harvard University Press, 2000.

Brian Barry. *Culture and Equality: An Egalitarian Critique of Multiculturalism*. Cambridge: Harvard University Press, 2001.

Walter Berns. *Making Patriots*. Chicago: University of Chicago Press, 2001.

"Strangled by Roots"

Gary Gerstle. *American Crucible: Race and Nation in the Twentieth Century*. Princeton: Princeton University Press, 2001.

"Anti-American Studies"

Donald E. Pease and Robyn Wiegman, eds. *The Futures of American Studies*. Durham: Duke University Press, 2002.

John Carlos Rowe. *The New American Studies*. Minneapolis: University of Minnesota Press, 2002.

David W. Noble. *Death of a Nation: American Culture and the End of Exceptionalism*. Minneapolis: University of Minnesota Press, 2002.

"The Return of Evil"
Richard J. Bernstein. *Radical Evil: A Philosophical Investigation.* Cambridge, UK: Polity Press, 2002.

Charles T. Mathewes. *Evil and the Augustinian Tradition.* New York: Cambridge University Press, 2001.

Susan Neiman. *Evil in Modern Thought: An Alternative History of Philosophy.* Princeton: Princeton University Press, 2002.

James Waller. *Becoming Evil: How Ordinary People Commit Genocide and Mass Killing.* New York: Oxford University Press, 2002.

"The Hermeneutic Hole"
Vincent Crapanzano. *Serving the Word: Literalism in America from the Pulpit to the Bench.* New York: New Press, 2000.

"White Magic in America"
Stephen R. Covey. *The Seven Habits of Highly Effective Families: Building a Beautiful Family Culture in a Turbulent World.* New York: Golden Books, 1997.

"Faith and Diversity in American Religion"
Diana L. Eck. *A New Religious America: How a "Christian Country" Has Now Become the World's Most Religiously Diverse Nation.* San Francisco: Harper, 2001.

Conrad Cherry, Betty A. DeBerg, and Amanda Porterfield. *Religion on Campus.* Chapel Hill: University of North Carolina Press, 2001.

Robert G. Fuller. *Spiritual, but Not Religious: Understanding Unchurched America.* New York: Oxford University Press, 2002.

Amanda Porterfield. *The Transformation of American Religion: The Story of a Late-Twentieth-Century Awakening.* New York: Oxford University Press, 2001.

"Higher Learning"
George Marsden. *The Soul of the American University: From Protestant Establishment to Established Non-Belief.* New York: Oxford University Press, 1994.

Philip Gleason. *Contending with Modernity: Catholic Higher Education in the Twentieth Century.* New York: Oxford University Press, 1995.

Mark Schwehn. *Exiles from Eden: Religion and the Academic Vocation in America.* New York: Oxford University Press, 1993.

Warren Nord. *Religion and American Education: Rethinking a National Dilemma.* Chapel Hill: University of North Carolina Press, 1995.

"Climbing the Mountain"
Taylor Branch. *Pillar of Fire: America in the King Years, 1963–65.* New York: Simon and Schuster, 1998.

"The Facts and the Feelings"
Stephan Thernstrom and Abigail Thernstrom. *America in Black and White: One Nation, Indivisible.* New York: Simon and Schuster, 1997.

David K. Shipler. *A Country of Strangers: Blacks and Whites in America.* New York: Alfred A. Knopf, 1997.

"Margaret Mead Goes to Harlem"
Katherine S. Newman. *No Shame in My Game: The Working Poor in the Inner City.* New York: Knopf and The Russell Sage Foundation, 1999.

"Affirmative Action, Inc."
Paul Craig Roberts. *The New Color Line: How Quotas and Privileges Destroy Democracy.* Washington, D.C.: Regnery, 1995.

Terry Eastland. *Ending Affirmative Action: The Case for Colorblind Justice.* New York: Basic Books, 1996.

Bob Zelnick. *Backfire: A Reporter's Look at Affirmative Action.* Washington, D.C.: Regnery, 1996.

Richard Epstein. *Forbidden Grounds: The Case Against Employment Discrimination.* Cambridge: Harvard University Press, 1992.

John David Skrentny. *The Ironies of Affirmative Action: Politics, Culture, and Justice in America.* Chicago: University of Chicago Press, 1996.

Barbara Bergmann. *In Defense of Affirmative Action*. New York: Basic Books, 1996.

Margaret Simms, ed. *Economic Perspectives on Affirmative Action*. Washington, D.C.: Joint Center for Political and Economic Studies, 1995.

Christopher Edley Jr. *Not All Black and White: Affirmative Action, Race, and American Values*. New York: Hill and Wang, 1996.

Richard D. Kahlenberg. *The Remedy: Class, Race, and Affirmative Action*. New York: Basic Books, 1996.

Michael Tomasky. *Left for Dead: The Life, Death, and Possible Resurrection of Progressive Politics in America*. New York: Free Press, 1996.

"The Jeremiah Racket"
Dana Mack. *The Assault on Parenthood: How Our Culture Undermines the Family*. New York: Simon and Schuster, 1997.

"Subject Matter Matters"
Diane Ravitch. *Left Back: A Century of Failed School Reforms*. New York: Simon and Schuster, 2000.

"The Mystique of Betty Friedan"
Betty Friedan. *The Feminine Mystique*. New York: Norton, 1963.

"The Professor of Desire"
James H. Jones. *Alfred C. Kinsey: A Public/Private Life*. New York: Norton, 1997.

"Up from Scientism"
Frank Sulloway. *Born to Rebel: Birth Order, Family Dynamics, and Creative Lives*. New York: Pantheon, 1996.

"Undialectical Materialism"
Gary Cross. *An All-Consuming Century: Why Commercialism Won in Modern America*. New York: Columbia University Press, 2000.

Robert J. Shiller. *Irrational Exuberance*. Princeton: Princeton University Press, 2000.

Robert E. Lane. *The Loss of Happiness in Market Democracies.* New Haven: Yale University Press, 2000.

Juliet Schor. *Do Americans Shop Too Much?* Boston: Beacon Press, 2000.

James Twitchell. *Lead Us Into Temptation: The Triumph of American Materialism.* New York: Columbia University Press, 1999.

Thomas Frank. *One Market Under God: Extreme Capitalism, Market Populism, and the End of Economic Democracy.* New York: Doubleday, 2000.

"BUYING ALONE"
Lizabeth Cohen. *A Consumers' Republic: The Politics of Mass Consumption in Postwar America.* New York: Knopf, 2003.

"THE GREENING OF CONSERVATISM"
David Brooks. *Bobos in Paradise: The New Upper Class and How They Got There.* New York: Simon and Schuster, 2000.

"THE SNAKE"
Michael Hardt and Antonio Negri. *Empire.* Cambridge: Harvard University Press, 2000.

"THE REVOLUTION THAT NEVER WAS"
John Kekes. *Against Liberalism.* Ithaca: Cornell University Press, 1997.

John Kekes. *A Case for Conservatism.* Ithaca: Cornell University Press, 1998.

Paul Edward Gottfried. *After Liberalism: Mass Democracy in the Managerial State.* Princeton: Princeton University Press, 1999.

Jerry Z. Muller, ed. *Conservatism: An Anthology of Social and Political Thought from David Hume to the Present.* Princeton: Princeton University Press, 1997.

Virginia Postrel. *The Future and Its Enemies: The Growing Conflict Over Creativity, Enterprise, and Progress.* New York: Free Press, 1998.

"Idiot Time"

Kevin P. Phillips. *Wealth and Democracy: A Political History of the American Rich.* New York: Broadway Books, 2002.

Michael Moore. *Stupid White Men . . . And Other Sorry Excuses for the State of the Nation!* New York: ReganBooks, 2001.

"The Fame Game"

Richard A. Posner. *Public Intellectuals: A Study of Decline.* Cambridge: Harvard University Press, 2001.

"The Calling of the Public Intellectual"

Russell Jacoby. *The Last Intellectuals: American Culture in the Age of Academe.* New York: Basic Books, 1987.